T0316650

A HISTORY OF SOUTH AUSTRALIA

A History of South Australia investigates South Australia's history from before the arrival of the first European maritime explorers to the present day, and examines its distinctive origins as a 'free' settlement.

In this compelling and nuanced history, Paul Sendziuk and Robert Foster consider the imprint of people on the land – and vice versa – and offer fresh insights into relations between Indigenous people and the European colonisers. They chart South Australia's economic, political and social development, including the advance and retreat of an interventionist government, the establishment of the state's distinctive socio-political formations, and its relationship to the rest of Australia and the world.

The first comprehensive, single-volume history of the state to be published in over fifty years, *A History of South Australia* is an essential and engaging contribution to our understanding of South Australia's past.

Paul Sendziuk is an Associate Professor in the Department of History at the University of Adelaide. He has expertise in the histories of 20th century Australia, immigration, disease and public health. He is the author of *Learning to Trust: Australian Responses to AIDS*, and, with Robert Foster, the co-editor of *Turning Points: Chapters in South Australian History* and *Foundational Fictions in South Australian History*.

Robert Foster is an Associate Professor in the Department of History at the University of Adelaide. He has published extensively in the field of South Australia's Indigenous history, and is co-author of *Out of the Silence: The History and Memory of South Australia's Frontier Wars*, and *Fragile Settlements: Aboriginal Peoples, Law, and Resistance in South-West Australia and Prairie Canada*.

Also published by Cambridge University Press

Geoffrey Blainey, *A History of Victoria*
Raymond Evans, *A History of Queensland*
Beverley Kingston, *A History of New South Wales*
Henry Reynolds, *A History of Tasmania*
Nicholas Brown, *A History of Canberra*

A History of South Australia

PAUL SENDZIUK AND ROBERT FOSTER

CAMBRIDGE
UNIVERSITY PRESS

University Printing House, Cambridge CB2 8BS, United Kingdom

One Liberty Plaza, 20th Floor, New York, NY 10006, USA

477 Williamstown Road, Port Melbourne, VIC 3207, Australia

314-321, 3rd Floor, Plot 3, Splendor Forum, Jasola District Centre, New Delhi - 110025, India

79 Anson Road, #06-04/06, Singapore 079906

Cambridge University Press is part of the University of Cambridge.

It furthers the University's mission by disseminating knowledge in the pursuit of education, learning and research at the highest international levels of excellence.

www.cambridge.org
Information on this title: www.cambridge.org/9781107623651

First published 2018 (version 2, February 2019)

Cover designed by Anne-Marie Reeves
Typeset by Integra Software Services Pvt. Ltd

A catalogue record for this book is available from the National Library of Australia

ISBN 978-1-107-62365-1 Paperback

Aboriginal and Torres Strait Islander readers are respectfully advised that images of deceased persons appear in this book and may cause distress.

CONTENTS

FIGURES

PREFACE

This book considers the history of a place and its people that begins in a time before European settlement and ends, in part, with prophecy about the future. The scope of the book is thus vast, but the space between its covers relatively narrow. Four principal themes provide the narrative structure for this story: the imprint of people on the land and vice versa, the relationship between settler South Australians and the land's Indigenous people, the advance and retreat of an interventionist State, and South Australia's distinctive socio-political formations. Not all of these themes share equal prominence; the passage of time sees some themes grow in significance, and others recede. It has occasionally been necessary to discuss significant events, eminent people and important places in less detail than they warrant, and neglect others entirely, in order to tell a coherent, broadly chronological story in a single volume. Political and economic issues are foregrounded in our account, as they tend to be in narrative-driven histories of states and nations. This is justified by the fact that there are no broad-scale economic histories of South Australia, and the piecemeal approach to discussing political and governance matters that has been taken in the existing historical literature. We give some attention to the everyday activities and social lives of South Australians, but a 'people's history' of the state remains to be written. Our selection of topics has been largely guided by the questions that our students often ask, and it is for them, and those curious to understand the society in which they now live or plan to visit, that this book is primarily written.

Land, as an occupiable space and an exploitable resource, is the bedrock of settler communities, so the book endeavours to chart the changing nature of the relationship between people and land. The distinctive nature of South Australia's climate and environment has always played a crucial role in shaping the communities that have occupied it, be they the Indigenous communities as hunters and gatherers, or the settler community driven primarily by farming, herding and mining. The irony of this part of the story is that the very nature of Indigenous land use crafted an environment tailor-made for the farming and herding practices of the settlers. However, what began as a blessing—good, easily appropriable land—became a curse, as the limits, and limitations, of those lands were reached.

The relationship between settlers and Aboriginal people is fundamental to this story. It has to be: Aboriginal people owned and occupied the country being claimed, making their dispossession a prerequisite for the successful establishment of the settler community. When Douglas Pike wrote his classic history of South Australia's foundations, the story of relations between Indigenous people and settlers hardly rated a mention.[1] That this was the case is not surprising. Pike was writing in the 1950s, when a policy of assimilation still anticipated the absorption of Indigenous people into the body of the nation. Today, ideals of reconciliation and recognition shape public discourse. Yet, this aspect of the history is not just retrospectively important, it is foundational. South Australia was settled at a time when the rights and welfare of Indigenous people were a fiercely debated topic within the empire, and the way South Australia has dealt with this relationship has always been prominent in public discussions.

Catastrophic periods of drought and the collapse of agricultural and pastoral commodity prices in the 19th century, and again in the late 1920s and 1930s, turned attention away from the land and towards industrial development and urbanisation. The State, especially during the premiership of Tom Playford, played a particularly interventionist role in this process and through ingenious means transformed South Australia's economic base and demographic profile. This provided the basis for a prolonged period of economic prosperity and near full employment, which in turn facilitated the social reforms pioneered by Don Dunstan's governments in the late 1960s and 1970s. But reliance on foreign investment and the uneven mix of industries that were established during this period meant that the manufacturing sector was vulnerable to shifts in the international economy, and thus sowed the seeds of the demise of blue-collar jobs and working-class communities at the end of the 20th century. State intervention in the economy was again apparent in the 1980s, when the government used the State Bank and publicly funded sporting events and real estate development to generate economic growth. The State Bank's collapse at the start of the 1990s, which saddled taxpayers with $3 billion of debt, dampened this entrepreneurial spirit.

South Australia's social and political origins set it apart from the other Australian colonies; it was a free settlement established without the deliberate importation of convict labour, and it was planned by profit-driven entrepreneurs who were informed by liberal ideas. These foundational principles favoured the emergence of a privileged colonial elite, whose wealth and influence derived mainly from farming and mining, but it also promoted more liberal attitudes toward social and political rights. These distinctive origins, many have suggested, produced a 'sense of difference' and enabled a degree of social and political innovation that sometimes set the colony/state apart from its continental neighbours. In the political realm alone, the evidence for South Australia's distinctiveness is certainly compelling. The establishment of representative government in the 1850s, consisting of a House of Assembly elected by universal male suffrage and a (more restrictive) Legislative Council, was achieved under a Constitution that was the most liberal in Australia. South Australia was the first state to have an elected town council, to accept Aboriginal evidence in court, to use the secret ballot and to grant women (including Aboriginal women) the right to vote for, and stand as, parliamentary candidates. South Australia was also among the first governments to separate Church and State, legalise trade unions, introduce industrial reforms and elect labour members to parliament. In addition, in the 1960s and 1970s, it introduced the first anti-discrimination, land rights, heritage conservation and marital rape legislation, and pioneered abortion and homosexual law reform.

Yet in many respects the extent of this social and political innovation, and South Australia's distinctive trajectory, has been exaggerated, even more so in popular memory. Two examples might suffice to illustrate this point. First, South Australia's founders and early residents may have rejected the use of transported convict labour, but they participated in the transportation system by sending the colony's own convicted felons to New South Wales and Van Diemen's Land, and they were helpless to prevent large numbers of escaped and former convicts crossing the border and settling in South Australia.[2] Second, South Australian parliamentarians may have been the first in Australia to grant women the vote—some 14 years before their Victorian counterparts, and more than a quarter of a century before English and most American women gained the franchise—but they did so reluctantly, and some only pushed for the inclusion of the provision allowing women to stand for parliament in the enabling legislation because they hoped it would lead to the Bill's demise. As it was, South Australia was the last state to elect a female candidate to parliament, more than half a century after women first gained the right to stand. So while it is true that South Australians have forged a distinctive path, this was not always for the reasons that one may expect, nor with the consequences that have been commonly assumed.

Histories of states and nations tend to take 'distinctiveness' as their analytical frame, often seeking to explain the history of a place and its people by reference to their distinctive origins. There are elements of this approach in most histories of South Australia, most notably those written by Douglas Pike and Derek Whitelock.[3] We are certainly alive to the distinctive aspects of the state's sociopolitical innovations, and draw attention to them where appropriate. However, we are reminded that histories aimed primarily at illuminating the distinctiveness of a particular society run the risk of simplifying the histories of others in order to sharpen the boundaries and diminish the commonalities.[4] Moreover, as historian John Hirst writes of South Australia: 'there are distinctions which are not so distinct and distinctions which origins don't explain or fully explain'.[5] The explanatory power of South Australia's origins undoubtedly erodes over time, especially with the coming of Federation and the mass mobilisation of people and production during times of war, and due to the growing influence of American popular culture, secularisation and the state's entanglement in a global system of economic, cultural and human exchange.

South Australia is now one of the world's most prosperous and comfortable societies in which to live, although this is not the case for all, nor guaranteed to remain. The local economy is undergoing what is euphemistically called 'structural change', which means something very different for those who are losing jobs in 'old' industries and those gaining them in emerging ones. South Australian pastoralists, farmers, winemakers and growers continue to produce an array of quality products for local consumption and export, but their yields, like all things, are threatened by climate change and environmental degradation. Technological advancement continues unabated and is contributing to greater productivity and efficiency, but it has had unpredictable and sometimes detrimental social and environmental consequences. Improvements have been achieved in the health and education of Indigenous residents, but they still fare worse than non-Indigenous South Australians according to many social and economic indicators. Clearly challenges remain, and it is hoped that this book, which suggests how South Australia arrived at these points and the lessons that might be learnt along the way, will inform the search for solutions.

Paul Sendziuk and Robert Foster
Adelaide, September 2017

ACKNOWLEDGEMENTS

This book was a collaboration in more senses than one. It is a product of many minds and imaginations, of scholars who have gone before us and upon whose shoulders we stand, and our colleagues and friends who stand with us and have supported our labour. Our intellectual debts will be clearly apparent from our endnotes and to readers who are familiar with the many interesting books and articles that have been written about South Australia.

We appreciate the assistance rendered by staff at the Barr Smith Library at The University of Adelaide (especially the irrepressible Margaret Hosking), the State Library of South Australia, State Records of South Australia, the Art Gallery of South Australia, and the History Trust of South Australia and the museums that it oversees. We are additionally grateful for their permission to reproduce some of the fascinating photographs and paintings in their collections.

Our undergraduate and postgraduate students continue to inspire us, and it is their questions that stimulated many of the inquiries that frame this book. We particularly thank former students Clare Parker, Steven Anderson, Sandy Horne, Claire Moffatt, Lawrence Ben, Walter Marsh, and Eden Blazejak for their research assistance and able fact checking.

We are indebted to Mark Peel, who recommended us for this project, and the capable staff at Cambridge University Press who commissioned the volume and guided it to print.

And we thank each other, for filling the gaps, for holding the fort and for not giving up. Anyone who has ridden a tandem bike will know that steering can be problematic, agility and responsiveness an issue, and the person on the back sometimes forgets to peddle. Co-authoring a book can be just like that, but not in this case. We began writing this book six years ago, and the friendship has lasted, though we might now wish to see less of each other.

Rob would particularly like to thank Alice for her love and support, and especially her patience in listening to yet another quite interesting fact about South Australian history. Paul reserves his most heartfelt admiration and gratitude for his wife, Katrina, whom he lured away from Melbourne with promises of a house by the beach and weekends spent camping in the country – one out of two ain't bad. This book has been part of her life, too, for many years, and is more than she deserved to bear, but she remained an enthusiastic supporter throughout. It is dedicated to Paul's two beautiful boys, Theo and Jarvis, who were born as it was being written and who ensured that he barely had time to finish it. He trusts they come to love this place as much as their Mum and Dad do.

Chapter 1

An Imaginary Dominion, 1802–35

In July 1840, Charles Sturt informed the South Australian colonists that the 'aboriginal people of the Province' exercised 'distinct, defined and absolute rights of propriety and hereditary possession', and had done so 'from time immemorial' – proverbially, 'beyond the reach of memory'.[1] In this statement, Sturt, the Assistant Commissioner of Crown Lands, was publicly articulating Governor Gawler's views on the nature of Aboriginal land ownership. While it is not certain how long Aboriginal people have lived on the continent, the archaeological record suggests at least 65,000 years.[2] The prevailing view is that they migrated to the continent by 'island-hopping' from Asia into north-western Australia at a time when climate change had significantly reduced ocean water levels. The historical migration of people into the continent is believed to have occurred in a number of distinct waves, which were partly responsible for shaping the variations in Aboriginal society, culture and even physical appearance that the settlers observed when they arrived and started to spread through the land.[3] These early Aboriginal migrations ceased when ocean levels rose again and separated Australia from Asia.

The continent that these first Australians occupied was an ancient one. As Tim Flannery has so evocatively described, by virtue of continental drift, it was sheltered from much of the tectonic disruptions and glaciation that were generating and regenerating landscapes in other parts of the world. As a consequence, many of its mountain ranges are weathered relics, its water courses comparatively few and shallow and often intermittent, and its soils typically thin and deficient in many nutrients. Added to this, the El Niño Southern Oscillation underpins a climate that is reliable only in its unpredictability.[4] The state of South Australia occupies almost 1 million square kilometres, about one-eighth of the continent, stretching from the Southern Ocean to Central Australia. Proverbially, 'the driest state in the driest continent', the capital averages 528 millimetres of rainfall a year, but 80% of the state receives less than half of that. This is a fact crucial in shaping both Aboriginal and European occupation of the land.[5]

Conservative estimates put the Aboriginal population of South Australia at the time of European contact at 15,000, with the lowest population densities in the arid north and the highest in the temperate south.[6] Sturt, while travelling through the lower reaches of the River Murray in late January 1830, expressed his surprise at the population he encountered, noting that it was greater 'than we had any reason to expect'.[7] Judging by the 'size and number of the huts' and 'the great breadth of the foot-paths' he concluded that this was a 'very populous district', adding 'we seldom communicated with fewer than 200 daily'.[8] An epidemic, probably smallpox, spread down the River Murray from the east at about the same time as Sturt's expedition.[9] The Aboriginal population that South Australian settlers encountered just seven years later was very likely considerably reduced, and perhaps traumatised, by the recent epidemic. Other introduced diseases to which Aboriginal people had no immunity (such as tuberculosis, measles, chickenpox and influenza) would continue to devastate the population as settlement spread.[10]

Across these regions were about 48 tribal groups, occupying distinct territories whose boundaries were well-known and respected by their neighbours. Travelling into another people's 'country' necessitated diplomatic protocols, and trespass was an offence punishable by death. Within their territories, Aboriginal people lived, on a day-to-day basis, in bands often consisting of several extended family groups that may typically have numbered between 25 and 50 people, but sizes could easily change depending on the sort of activities people were engaged in and the time of the year. These bands, as archaeologist Josephine Flood explains, were 'residence groups', whereas '"clans" were "country groups" with a common identity often based on a claimed descent from a single Ancestral Being'.[11] Tribes, the largest unit of social organisation in Aboriginal Australia, were made up of a number of clans sharing spiritual links to their country and a common language.[12] Aboriginal people were nomadic, moving from place to place in their country to take advantage of seasonal resources. However, the extent of that nomadism varied considerably: in the Western Desert, where water was a primary concern, people may have ranged over hundreds of kilometres, but in more resource-rich areas both the degree of movement and the range was much smaller. The members of a tribe would rarely have come together as a whole except for important social and ceremonial gatherings, and the number of people in a tribe varied considerably, depending on the productivity of their land. The Kaurna people of the Adelaide Plains, for instance, reportedly numbered about 700 people at the time of European contact, while the Ngarrindjeri of the Lower Lakes and Coorong, a sort of federation in which the constituent tribes were called *Lakinyeris*, numbered in excess of 3000 people.[13]

Governor Gawler, besides acknowledging Aboriginal land ownership, also commented on the use of the land. Aboriginal people, he observed, 'hunt game upon, catch fish in and eat the food of their own districts just as much as the English gentleman kills the deer and sheep upon, or fishes in, his private park'.[14] While this fairly describes the nature of Aboriginal land ownership and use, it misses a deeper point: Aboriginal people were not just hunters and gatherers; they were also active land managers. It has long been understood that Aboriginal people practised 'firestick farming', which involved the strategic burning of land. Fire used in this way cleared the dense under-storey of forests, making travel and hunting easier, and promoted the regrowth of vegetation, which maintained animal numbers and plant diversity.[15] Bill Gammage has recently argued that these land management practices were even more precisely calculated than has hitherto been acknowledged.[16] The skilful use of fire, he argues, was used to create 'a template, a deliberate and long-term distribution of plants to locate an animal species, making it predictable for day-to-day harvest'.[17] Such complex land management demanded 'intricate knowledge of plants and fire,

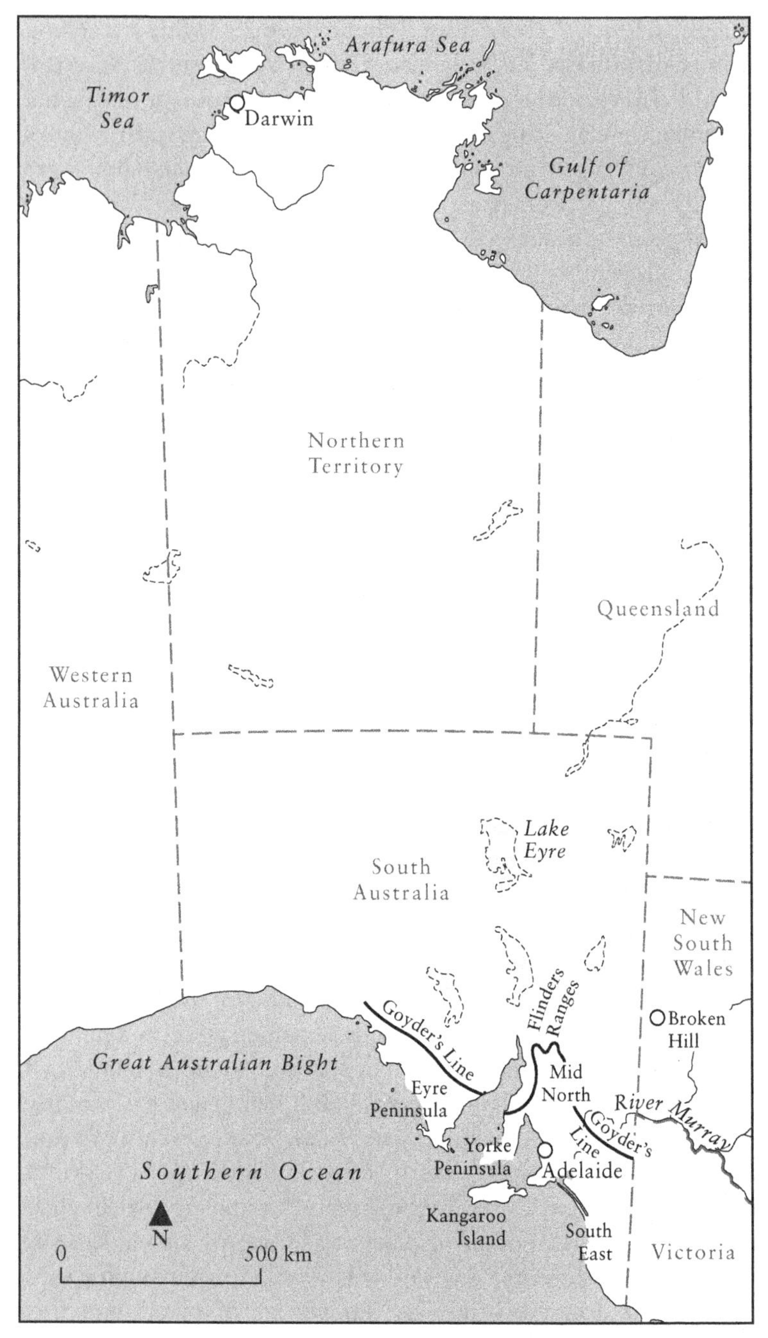

Figure 1.1: Map of South Australia and the Northern Territory

visionary planning, and persistence greater than anything modern Australia has imagined, or achieved'.[18]

While people did hunt and gather alone or in small groups, economic activities were often carried out cooperatively. In hunting larger animals, such as kangaroo, one technique was for people to fan out and drive animals into disguised pits, where they became trapped and could easily be killed. In the open country of the Flinders Ranges they constructed brushwood fences angled in a V shape: people would work together to drive the animals towards the narrow end where hunters would be waiting to spear them.[19] Comparable cooperative techniques were used to catch fish in rivers and coastal waters, with people forming a line to drive the fish into nets. A range of technologies and techniques were also used to make food-gathering easier. In coastal areas, weirs of stone and wood were constructed to trap fish on the receding tide.[20] In riverine areas and in the slow-moving waters of wetlands in the lower South East, elongated basketry fish-traps or net bags were used to capture fish as they washed through the narrow openings of dams that had been constructed.[21] Explorer Edward Eyre, who spent time as a Sub-Protector of Aborigines on a remote reach of the River Murray in the 1840s, witnessed this type of fishing and was amazed at how many fish were collected, and how easily.[22]

Plant foods were a staple of the diet and it was usually the responsibility of women, with the help of children, to gather them. A range of roots and tubers were gathered and eaten, and seeds, such as nardoo, could be ground into flour and baked into cakes. In coastal regions during the summer months, fruits, such as native cherries or apples, were a welcome addition to the diet. Among the Dieri in the north-west, it is estimated that women contributed 70% of the group's food.[23]

Aboriginal material culture varied considerably from region to region. In the arid north, where water was often scarce and bands needed to be highly mobile, people carried few possessions. In the temperate south, where water was abundant and where there was a rich variety of animal and plant foods, the toolkit was much more extensive. There were a range of spears available for hunting animals and fish, and a variety of digging implements, clubs and boomerangs for food gathering as well as fighting.[24] Nets were used not just for fishing, but for catching birds. Hunters would stretch a net between trees and use boomerangs to frighten flocks, causing them to become entangled in them.[25] The people of the lower Murray, Lakes and Coorong had a very rich basketry culture. Baskets woven from sedges were used for a variety of purposes; they were woven into mats that were used as a type of flooring, woven into baskets to carry possessions, and used to make fish traps.[26]

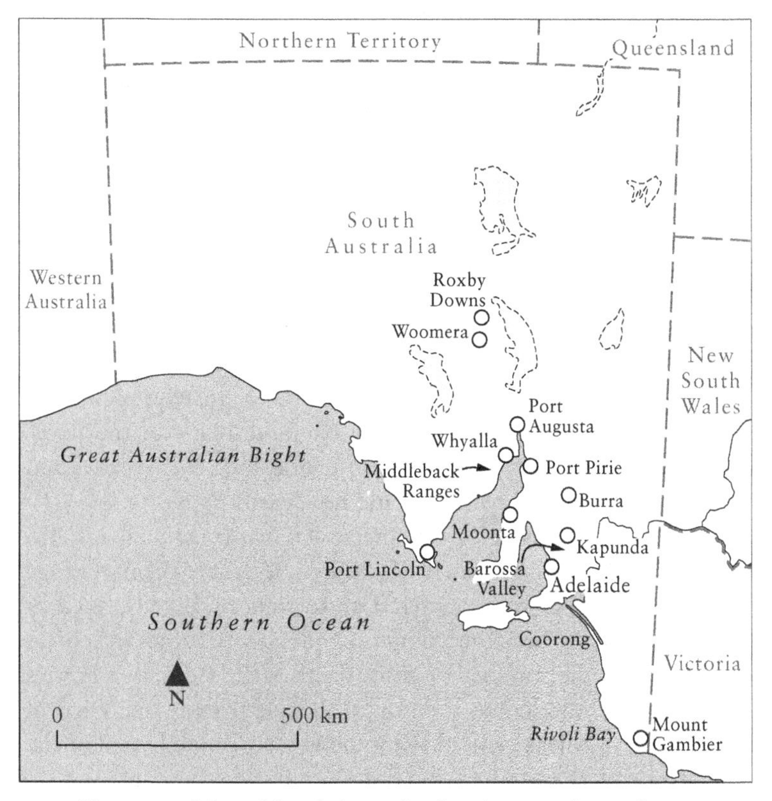

Figure 1.2: Map of South Australia showing prominent places

Trading networks crisscrossed the country, enabling rarer objects to circulate. Greenstone axes made in western Victoria were traded with people to the east. Baler shells from northern Australia, prized for their ornamental qualities and used in ceremonies, were traded south and are known to have been used by Aboriginal people on the west coast of South Australia.[27] Ochre was a highly valued commodity used for ceremonial body decoration. While ochre was obtained from a range of sites, the ochre from Parachilna in the lower Flinders Ranges was especially sought after. Aboriginal people from the Lake Eyre Basin, and further into Queensland, would travel for months to obtain supplies.[28] It was not only objects that circulated on these networks, but ideas too. Songs and ceremonies devised in one area – and thought to be particularly pleasing, propitious or powerful – might be learnt by other groups and passed on.[29] It was through these networks that many Aboriginal people would have first learnt about the white invaders, handled their objects and heard words in their language. By the early years of the 20th century a ceremony called the *Mulunga*, which originated in the Barkly Tablelands of Queensland in the early 1890s and enacted conflict with European settlers, had been transmitted south and was being performed by a number of Aboriginal communities in South Australia.[30]

Central to Aboriginal people's culture are religious traditions that tie them to each other and to their land. All tribal groups have their 'Dreamings'; traditions that tell of their ancestral origins, and link them to each other and to their country. For the Arrernte of Central Australia, the Dreaming is known by the term *Altyjerre*; for Western Desert people, such as the Pitjantjatjara, it is *Tjurkurpa*; while for the Yaraldi people of the lower Murray, it is the term *Kulhal*. The term also carries with it connotations of the 'Law' referring to that 'body of religious and cultural knowledge that is used to inform and direct Aboriginal society'.[31] As such, the Dreaming is the foundation of customary law in Aboriginal society. It also refers to a time past when spiritual ancestors created the world. For the Ngarrindjeri of the Lower Lakes and Coorong, one of the ancestral heroes was Nurrunderi, who fashioned the physical world in which they lived and gave them the laws that governed their lives. As he travelled across this formative landscape he carved out the River Murray, creating the plants and animals. At the end of his life, he is said to have travelled to Kangaroo Island from where he passed on to the sky-world.[32] For Ngarrindjeri people, Kangaroo Island is regarded as the land of the dead.[33]

In late March 1802, Matthew Flinders, while charting the coast of southern Australia aboard the *Investigator*, went ashore on

Kangaroo Island. He was puzzled to find no people there, and no evidence of human occupation. The fact was seemingly confirmed by the tameness of the island's kangaroos that were so unafraid of humans that they allowed members of his party to walk up to them and kill them on the spot. The archaeological record suggests that humans last lived on the island some 4000 years ago.[34] On 8 April 1802, while Flinders was in the waters between Kangaroo Island and the southern mainland, he was surprised by the appearance of another vessel, the French explorer Nicolas Baudin's *Le Geographe*. Flinders had been sailing from the west, while Baudin sailed from the east, both men charting the coast of a region that had hitherto been unknown to Europeans. As far as he knew, France and England were still at war, so Flinders went aboard Baudin's *Le Geographe* under the protection of a flag of truce. It was an amicable meeting in which both men exchanged stories and compared charts.[35] Up until this time, the relationship between the 'New Holland' of the continent's west and the New South Wales of the east was unresolved: were they part of the same landmass or were they separated by sea? It was now clear that they were charting a single continent.[36] After this meeting at Encounter Bay, Flinders continued his circumnavigation of the continent, while Baudin sailed on to Sydney.

Sydney at this time was a penal settlement under the governorship of Philip Gidley King with a population of just 7,000 people. Baudin's appearance gave rise to fears about French interest in the region and it encouraged the governor to establish a new convict settlement on the Derwent River in Van Diemen's Land the following year.[37] In coming decades, new settlements were established north and south of Botany Bay, but it was not until 1824 that a new penal settlement was established at Moreton Bay. In 1826, renewed fears of French ambitions led to the establishment of a military outpost at King George's Sound in the continent's south-west.[38]

With the exception of some tentative movements across the Blue Mountains, the interior was still largely unexplored. At this time the population of New South Wales was nearing 40,000, while that of Van Diemen's Land had grown to about 17,000. Australian settlement was still pre-eminently convict-based, but, as the profitability of sheep grazing was becoming increasingly evident and the prospect of free settlement was growing more attractive, interest in the nature of the continent's interior encouraged exploration. In the west, Charles Stirling was exploring the Swan River District, where a small military outpost had been established, with the view of establishing a free settlement there. Stirling pitched his proposal to the Colonial Office, assuring them that the colony would be self-supporting with grants of land awarded to settlers in proportion to the amount of capital they brought with them. The Colonial Office gave its approval and by June 1828 the first settlers were arriving at the newly proclaimed colony of Western Australia.[39]

As Governor Stirling was laying the foundations of his new settlement, Charles Sturt, with the backing of Governor Darling, began exploring the inland river systems of New South Wales. In 1829, he followed the Murrumbidgee to its junction with a hitherto unknown river, which he named the Murray, and in 1830 he traced it to its outlet to the sea at Lake Alexandrina. This was a place, he wrote, 'to which the colonist might venture with every prospect of success'.[40] News of Sturt's discoveries were a godsend to a small group of entrepreneurs in London who were making schemes to establish a colony, but had yet to identify a location for it.

In 1828, a London solicitor, Robert Gouger, was toying with the idea of emigration and was attracted to the novel settlement on the Swan River. A friend suggested that before he commit himself to the move, he should seek the advice of Edward Wakefield, a political economist and theorist of colonisation. Wakefield at that moment was serving time in Newgate Prison for eloping with an under-age heiress.[41] His term in prison gave him the opportunity to develop his ideas about emigration. In his discussions with Gouger in January 1829, he expressed his doubts about the Swan River venture, principally on the grounds that free grants of land would encourage a dispersal of settlement, stalling the progress of the colony. What was needed was 'concentration', and the sale of land at a fixed price, the proceeds of which could be used to pay for the emigration of selected settlers. With Wakefield in prison, it was Gouger who acted as publicist for this new system of colonisation. It was first outlined in a *Sketch of a proposal for colonising Australasia*, published in June 1829. In August, it was further elaborated in *A letter from Sydney*, purportedly written by a colonist in New South Wales, but actually penned by Wakefield while still in prison.

The proposal attracted favourable comment. The next task was to attract influential supporters.[42]

Emigration had emerged as a hot political topic of the day. The first phase of the industrial revolution had seen the population of major British cities soar, with the attendant problems of pauperism taxing the minds of politicians. The subsidised emigration of paupers was proposed as one solution. The most notable proponent of this type of emigration scheme was Wilmot Horton. As undersecretary in the Colonial Office, he had secured parliamentary grants in 1823 and again in 1825 to pay for the free passage of Irish poor to Upper Canada.[43] Horton was one of the people Gouger tried to win over when he established the National Colonisation Society in February 1830. The principles of concentration and land sales were linked to a philanthropic agenda of pauper emigration, but Horton was unimpressed and the embryonic society failed to secure support.[44] The prospects of the society revived when news of Sturt's discovery of the River Murray became common knowledge. As early as December 1830, the scheme was now regularly being pitched as a proposal to form a colony at Gulf St Vincent. With new supporters, the National Colonisation Society put a detailed proposal to the Colonial Office in May 1831. It incorporated the principles of using land sales to support emigration, the judicious selection of emigrants and the early establishment of a legislative assembly. The proposal received some support, but it was suggested that it be further developed. A revised plan for a chartered company went to the Colonial Office in August, but concerns about the financial support for the project stifled progress.[45]

The venture was re-conceived as the South Australian Land Company and by late 1831 new proposals were drawn up and efforts were made to enlist influential and wealthy supporters. The plans continued to stress the principles of concentration and migration, but also proposed an extraordinary degree of political independence: the company wanted the right to raise its own militia, control taxation, trade freely and achieve early self-government.[46] The scheme proposed that the Crown would have the right to appoint the governor but all other officials would be nominated by the company, which would make the 'rules and regulations' for the colony until the population reached 50,000, at which point an elected assembly would be established.[47] James Stephen, assistant under-secretary in the Colonial Office at the time, offered a withering response; he questioned the wisdom of transferring a territory, larger than the kingdoms of Spain and Portugal combined, to a private company, and asked what the Crown would receive in return for this generous act. The plan, he noted, preferred foreign settlers to British paupers, and it took from the Crown many of its ordinary prerogatives. As to the proposal for early self-government, the Crown, he wrote, had no intention to 'settle a republic'. The project, he concluded, was 'wild and impracticable'.[48] With this response, negotiations with the Colonial Office broke down and were not revived until early 1833. The Colonisation Society responded to Stephen's criticisms regarding the governance of the colony and many of the offending clauses in the charter were removed in the hope of satisfying him, but still nothing came of it.[49]

It was Robert Gouger's persistence and energy, and his faith in the principle of linking land sales to the support of assisted emigration, that maintained the momentum.[50] In October 1833, Wakefield's most detailed exposition of what was now termed 'systematic colonisation' was set out in the book *England and America*.[51] Gouger continued to garner support for the project through the establishment of the South Australia Association. The first meeting of the Association, which now included men of influence, many of whom were members of parliament, was held at Adelphi House in December 1833. In January 1834, Edward Stanley, the secretary of state for the colonies, met a deputation of the committee and, while not opposed to the colonising scheme itself, continued to express Colonial Office concerns regarding the proposed system of government. 'By the present plan', Gouger reported him to say, 'the Colony would be a republic, and as the officers were appointed by the trustees, the colony would be entirely independent of the mother country'.[52] A new draft of the charter was prepared which now replaced the term 'trustee' with 'commissioner' to emphasise that they were 'servants of the supreme government'.[53] With it apparent that Stanley would not accept 'the proposal of a chartered company nor allow a commission' to exercise 'legislative power', the Association backed down on these issues, as long as the core principles pertaining to land sales and emigration were accepted. The

Association changed tack, the idea of a charter was dispensed with and the principles were now set out in a Bill, which was submitted to the Colonial Office in mid-April. The colony was now being referred to as a 'province', a term that had no legal significance, but which served to distinguish the settlement from the existing convict colonies of Australia.[54]

The draft received Stanley's general approval, but there were still specific issues that he wanted clarified. Where, he asked, would the colony be situated? In light of Sturt's published account of his explorations in southern Australia and his personal representations to the government, the proposed South Australian site seemed perfectly feasible. They were able to assuage the Colonial Secretary's concerns that sufficient capital could be raised to underwrite the establishment of the colony. Stanley was also concerned about the price of land, suggesting that it be no higher than 10 shillings an acre. The committee discussed this point at length, thinking that 15 shillings would be the appropriate price; however, with the going price in neighbouring colonies at around 5 shillings per acre, they compromised on a minimum price of 12 shillings. Stanley also wanted the land fund to be used to support religion and education, but the committee suggested that this compromised the colony's fundamental principles. Stanley was satisfied and agreed to refer the Bill to the government.[55]

The planning of the colony occurred at a time in Britain when there was significant agitation for social and parliamentary reform, for things such as a broader extension of the franchise to make parliament more representative, and a separation of Church and State. A significant portion of the people who promoted and planned the colony were Dissenters, men and women who belonged to Protestant denominations opposed to the established privileges of the Church of England. Dissenters resented paying taxes that supported a State church, and they bridled at being denied careers in the civil service and entry into universities. Dissenters held to the principles of religious equality, believing that all denominations should have the same rights and should be supported voluntarily, rather than being aided by the State.[56] As historian Douglas Pike noted, their 'great strength' was in the 'middling classes of the industrial towns'.[57] While many of the disabilities they suffered were gradually being removed, most notably with the Reform Act of 1832, which extended the franchise to sections of the middle classes, many thought more needed to be done. For some, the colony offered an opportunity to further pursue these social and religious ideals. The influential George Fife Angas, a Baptist, wrote that the colony would 'provide a place of refuge for pious Dissenters' and even distributed leaflets promoting the colony among Dissenting congregations.[58]

Fully expecting the Bill's approval, the Association continued to promote the colony, and prospective colonists made preparations for departure. Shortly before the Bill went before parliament in July, the Association held a public meeting in Exeter Hall, a venue renowned for holding religious and philanthropic meetings, to explain the principles of the colony. They praised the opportunities that this settlement presented, in contrast to those in the existing convict settlements of Australia; they highlighted its support of the voluntary principle in religion; and they proclaimed the benefits that would come from early self-government.[59] Despite some opposition, the Bill was passed on 15 August 1834. To get the Bill passed, compromises had to be made; one of these was the addition of a clause authorising the Crown to appoint 'Chaplains and Clergymen', and to provide for their support, a provision that went against the Dissenters' opposition to State aid to religion.[60] Under the terms of the *South Australia Act 1834*, a governor would make laws, but a body of commissioners would have responsibility for the survey and sale of lands, at a minimum price of 12 shillings per acre. This fund was to be employed to support the emigration of respectable people to the colony; men and women under the age of 30 and in equal proportions. No convicts were to be permitted. When the colony reached 50,000, self-government was to be established. The cost of government was to be supported by two loans: one of £50,000 to cover the cost of sending emigrants, until the land fund itself was able to do so, and a second of £20,000 to support the cost of establishing the colony and its government. The Act stipulated that land to the value of £45,000 must be sold before settlement could take place.[61] By these means, the colony was touted as being 'self-supporting', imposing no burden on the British taxpayer. James Stephen was more cynical: 'It is simply a

Plan for selling the Lands of the Crown and applying the proceeds to the foundation of a colony to which at the expense of the Crown, poor persons are to be conveyed as emigrants'.[62]

With the passage of the Act one of the first tasks was to establish the South Australian Colonisation Commission, whose role was to put the much-laboured plans into action. Nine names, mostly prominent businessmen, were put forward and accepted by the Colonial Office, which also appointed two men of its own.[63] From these men the Anglo-Irishman Robert Torrens was elected as Chairman. A former military man who had been elected to parliament in 1831, he well understood the principles of the colony, having been involved with the planning of it from early on.[64] Earmarked for the position of Governor was Colonel Charles Napier, but the veteran of Waterloo was uncomfortable with the way the powers of the Governor were circumscribed by the Commission, so he withdrew his name. The man appointed was Captain John Hindmarsh, a former naval officer whom the Colonial Office described as 'zealous, good tempered' and 'anxious to do right'. Hindmarsh chose George Stevenson, a journalist and a man with some colonial experience, to serve as his private secretary.[65] After the Governor, the most important position in the colony was that of Resident Commissioner, whose role would be to represent the Commission in the colony itself, with extensive powers over surveys, the sale of land, and emigration. These were powers that in an ordinary Crown colony would usually have rested with the Governor. A lawyer, James Hurtle Fisher, was awarded the post. The important position of Surveyor General was given to Colonel William Light who, at the time, was serving with the military in Egypt.[66]

Although the Act stipulated that land could be sold at 12 shillings an acre, the Commission initially offered it for sale at the much higher price of £1. This proved to be too high to attract sufficient buyers so they agreed to lower it to 12 shillings. To help get land sales to the threshold £45,000, George Fife Angas – one of the Commissioners – agreed to purchase the remaining land orders through his newly established South Australia Company.[67] Two other financial hurdles also had to be satisfied: the raising of a loan to fund the cost of government, and the depositing with the treasury a 'guarantee' of £20,000.[68] While the Commissioners were negotiating with the Colonial Office about these matters, another issue unexpectedly arose: the welfare of the Aboriginal inhabitants of the colony.

The status and rights of the Aboriginal people had hardly been discussed in the planning of the colony and, indeed, the *South Australia Act* of 1834 had declared the land 'waste and unoccupied'. This disregard for Aboriginal land tenure was consistent with the attitudes reflected in earlier established colonies; but attitudes seemed to be changing. Many of the people in the reformist government of Lord Melbourne were evangelicals and had actively campaigned against slavery, which was abolished in 1833, and they now turned their attention to Aboriginal rights. Even as the *South Australia Act* was being passed, a Select Committee of Inquiry was being convened to inquire 'into the state and condition of the aboriginal tribes of countries ... under the dominion of Great Britain'.[69] More immediately relevant to the planners of the colony was a letter from Van Diemen's Land Governor, George Arthur, to the Colonial Office in which he reflected on the disastrous consequences of colonisation on the Aboriginal people of his colony. Referring to the proposed colony of South Australia, he advised that 'every effort ... ought to be made, to come to an understanding with the natives'. It was, he added, 'a great oversight that a treaty was not, at that time, made with the natives, and such compensation given to the chiefs, as they would have deemed a fair equivalent for what they surrendered'.[70]

Given the heightened sensitivity to the issue at the time, it is not surprising that the Colonial Secretary wrote to the Colonisation Commissioners in July 1835 quoting Arthur's report, and asking what provision was being made for Aboriginal people.[71] Rowland Hill, the secretary, wrote back with platitudes that failed to assuage Colonial Office concerns. In December 1835, Torrens, as Chairman of the Colonisation Commissioners, wrote to the Colonial Office requesting that 'various instruments be issued which must precede the proposed emigration'.[72] In his reply, the Secretary of State again raised the question of what was being done in regard to the 'present proprietors of the Soil or rulers of the Country?'[73] They were claiming a vast territory that might 'embrace in its range numerous Tribes of People whose proprietary Title to the Soil, we have not the slightest ground for disputing', adding that before approval could be given 'he must have at least, some reasonable assurance that He is not about to sanction any act of injustice towards the Aboriginal natives of that part of the Globe by demonstrating that no earlier and preferable Title exists'.[74] A flurry of proposals ensued, promising to protect Aboriginal lands shown to be in their 'actual occupation and enjoyment', negotiation for the purchase of lands, and appointment of a Protector of Aborigines specifically charged with looking after their welfare. Lord Glenelg was not persuaded that these matters could be resolved without altering the Act and suggested 'that the Settlement itself should be postponed until the necessary alterations in the Statute had been affected'.[75] Torrens was stunned; if the objections of the Colonial Office were not withdrawn he thought that 'the Colony was pretty well ended'.[76]

In response to these delays, prospective colonist Robert Thomas wrote to the Secretary of State and asked how a 'few strolling savages' could be allowed to further delay the start of the colony? It was mid-January 1836 and all the necessary funds had been raised, but the Colonial Office continued to press the Commissioners about how the rights and welfare of Aboriginal people would be ensured. Thomas's letter had an exasperated tone; the colonists were on the verge of establishing a home for the 'overabundant population of Great Britain in comfort and affluence' on lands now 'waste'. He confessed himself at a loss to understand how a people, few in number, ignorant of the 'arts of civilized life', and 'averse to cultivating the land' could be considered its 'actual proprietor'.[77] The Commissioners engaged in a sort of brinksmanship to push through Colonial Office objections. Torrens met with Sir George Grey and said that if these proposals to amend the Act, along with others relating to the land fund, were insisted upon, then the Board would resign immediately. The building pressure from colonists and the Commission had its effect. On 21 January 1836, the Colonial Office relented; in a letter to Torrens, the minister, Lord Glenelg, withdrew his remaining objections and apologised for any inconvenience caused. The delay, he explained, had been occasioned by 'the entire novelty of the scheme, by the peculiar structure of the Act of Parliament' and by a desire to avert 'the calamities' that

Aboriginal people had faced in the other British settlements of Australia.[78] With the issuing on 16 February of the Letters Patent, defining the extent of the colony, and the Order in Council on 22 February, authorising its government, the colonists now had the legal authorities they needed to make a start.

Chapter 2

Foundations, 1836–45

The first emigrant ships to leave for the new colony were South Australia Company ships, the *John Pirie* and the *Duke of York*, departing from London on 22 and 24 February 1836, followed by the *Lady Mary Pelham* on 30 March. These were small vessels carrying fewer than 30 passengers between them, but suited to whaling, for which they would be used once they arrived in the colony. The *Rapid*, a fast vessel purchased by the Commissioners for the use of the Surveyor General, Colonel William Light, should have sailed at this time but illness kept Light ashore until the beginning of May. The *Cygnet*, which carried Deputy Surveyor George Strickland Kingston and the remainder of the survey team, had already departed in March. The HMS *Buffalo*, carrying Governor John Hindmarsh and the Commission's representative in the colony, James Hurtle Fisher, left on 23 July 1836. Between February and September 1836, nine emigrant vessels left for the colony.[1]

The *Africaine*, with 82 passengers and 17 crew, sailed on 2 July 1836 and carried with it, in microcosm, many of the ambitions and ideals of the colonial venture itself. The vessel was privately chartered by Robert Gouger, the Colonial Secretary, and John Brown, the Emigration Agent. Gouger and Brown, with their respective wives, occupied two of the four first-class cabins aboard the ship; Captain Duff occupied the third while John Hallett occupied the fourth. Hallett, who travelled with his wife and children, was a man of capital and part-owner of the ship. For Gouger, it was the culmination of a dream begun five years before when he helped Wakefield publish his *Letter from Sydney*. Robert Thomas, whose letter to the Secretary of State back in January had helped pressure the government into allowing the colony to proceed, also travelled on the *Africaine*. His family occupied two of the eight intermediate cabins aboard the ship: one for him and his wife, Mary, and the other to accommodate four of their children.[2] Their eldest son, Robert Jnr, travelled separately aboard the *Cygnet* as a draftsman apprenticed to the Deputy Surveyor.[3] This was the sort of respectable, but ambitious, middle-class family that the promoters wanted to encourage. Robert was a moderately successful printer and stationer in London, and planned to pursue the same business in the colony. He had already entered into a partnership with George Stevenson, an editor, to establish the colony's first newspaper, *The Register and Colonial Gazette*, the first issue of which went to press a fortnight before they sailed. They had also been awarded the government printing contract.[4] Mary, a published poet and avid diarist, shared the liberal values of the colony's planners and saw opportunity for the advancement of her family. Robert and Mary brought out three servants: Mary Lillywhite, who shared the children's cabin, and two agricultural labourers, who travelled in steerage. There were 49 passengers in steerage, most of them travelling free as employees of the land-owning colonists.[5]

Passengers on these emigrant vessels shared what limited space there was with the miscellaneous supplies thought fundamental to starting a life from scratch. When passengers walked on the decks of the *Africaine*, they had to navigate their way past goats, a cow and its calf, crates of duck and fowl, as well as a sheep dog with its puppies.[6] Stevenson, Robert Thomas's business partner aboard the *Buffalo*, described similar scenes: 'On both sides of the main deck are rows of filthy hogs kept in pens, generally in a horrid state of dirt and uncleanliness. The emigrants can only walk alongside these animals and inhale the stench from them.'[7] Many emigrant accounts describe the monotony being broken by the occasional novelty of watching dolphins tracking the ship, the nautilus magically skimming across the surface of the sea, flying fish sometimes grounding on the deck, and the rare encounter with passing vessels.[8] Sickness also broke the monotony. With so many people crowded together, illness was always a worry. At the start of her voyage, Mary Thomas fretted over her youngest daughter, who was suffering from scarlet fever.[9] Robert Gouger worried over his consumptive and pregnant wife, Harriet, who suffered badly from sea-sickness. The 'opiate plaister' given her to help ameliorate her symptoms merely added nightmares to her list of discomforts.[10] Food could be a diversion. Early in his voyage, Gouger reported that the cabin passengers 'fared sumptuously', enjoying three-course meals and good-quality wine.[11] The fare for steerage passengers was not quite so fine: a relentless round of salt beef, salt pork and peas, bread and tea, augmented by dried fruits.[12]

Most of the emigrant vessels broke their voyage on at least one occasion. The *Africaine* stopped over at the Cape of Good Hope 12 weeks after leaving London. Other vessels, such as the *Buffalo* and the survey ship, the *Cygnet*, stopped at Rio de Janeiro, but it made for a longer voyage. Here passengers could go ashore, enjoy fresh food, re-provision for the remainder of the voyage, and shop for whatever necessities had not already been purchased and packed in England. When Arthur Gliddons was ashore at the Cape, he said the locals assumed they were sailing for Van Diemen's Land; they had heard nothing of 'South Australia'.[13] On 27 July 1836, five months after setting off from London, the *Duke of York* was the first vessel to arrive in Nepean Bay on Kangaroo Island; the *Lady Mary Pelham* arrived three days later and the *John Pirie* on 16 August.[14] The disembarking passengers may have been surprised when they discovered that a small population of sealers was living on the island with their Aboriginal wives and children.[15] After Flinders and Baudin had left South Australian waters in 1802, news of the island's potential spread among the sealing community and they started to visit the island regularly. Rebe Taylor, in her history of this community, suggests that there may have been as many as 30 men living on the island by the mid-1820s, many with wives abducted by them from Van Diemen's Land or the South Australian mainland.[16]

As Bill Gammage has noted, settlers need a dependable supply of fresh water to start a new life and they needed a suitable harbour to connect them to their old life; finding a combination of the two has always proved difficult in Australia.[17] In the absence of preparatory surveys, the South Australia Company had relied on the few existing accounts to identify potential sites for the capital. Sturt saw no potential in the mouth of the Murray and recommended Holdfast Bay. Péron, the assistant of French explorer Baudin, waxed lyrical about the virtues of Port Lincoln but Flinders was unimpressed by its dangerous entrance and barren soil, and was more inclined towards Kangaroo Island. On the strength of these early reports the South Australia Company sent their first vessels to Kangaroo Island's Nepean Bay.[18]

Light, who had been given detailed instructions by the Commissioners to select the site of the capital and survey the land, did not arrive at Nepean Bay until 20 August 1836. He was no stranger to the colonial world. Of mixed Portuguese Eurasian heritage, he was born in Georgetown, Penang, founded as an East India Company settlement by his father, Francis. A veteran of the Napoleonic Wars, Light was also a gifted artist and musician who had already travelled widely.[19] In South Australia, he had the unenviable task of commencing his surveys while eager settlers, growing in numbers, waited impatiently to make a start. Light quickly came to the view that while Nepean Bay was a fine harbour, the sources of fresh water were poor and the land would be difficult to clear.[20] While still waiting for his Deputy Surveyor, George Kingston, to arrive Light decided to explore the coast of Gulf St Vincent. On 7 September he landed at Rapid Bay and was 'enchanted' by the 'beautiful little valley', the fertile soil and the streams of fresh water.[21] Here was land suitable for a settlement, but there was no harbour. In late September he reconnoitered the Port River, which he thought would be suitable, but with challenging mangrove swamps and reports of another harbour that they were unable to find, he still had not quite solved his puzzle.[22] On 10 October, Light's *Rapid* rode out a storm in Holdfast Bay, near the mouth of the Patawalonga. Like Rapid Bay, this was promising land, not at a harbour, but serviceably close to one. The earlier discovery of the Torrens on the Adelaide plains helped fix the site of the capital and even the settlers, wrote Light, now 'think this is the place for the capital of a flourishing colony'. Further exploration of the Port persuaded him that this would serve them well; the 'harbour', he wrote on 22 November, 'is now found – more extensive, safe and beautiful, than we could have hoped for'.[23]

While at Holdfast Bay, Light received news that the remainder of his survey party had arrived, and more emigrant vessels were on their way.[24] On 4 November the *Africaine* reached Nepean Bay and, a few days later, was anchored off Holdfast Bay ferrying its passengers and cargo ashore in longboats. Mary Thomas reported that it was 'no trifling labour' conveying all their goods inland without any form of transport whatsoever.[25] Gouger reported on 17 November that 'all hands are employed in erecting tents, building huts, and landing goods and cargo'.[26] On 28 December 1836, Governor Hindmarsh came ashore at Holdfast Bay. That afternoon soon-to-be members of Council gathered together in a tent where His Majesty's Orders in Council were read out and the oaths of office administered. When this was done the Colonial Secretary, Robert Gouger, read out the Governor's Commission before an assembly of 200 colonists. The Governor's first Proclamation was also read aloud. The settlers were enjoined to act with 'order and quietness', 'respect the laws', be industrious, sober and moral, and to 'prove themselves worthy to be the founders of a great and free colony'.[27] Written with an eye to the new concerns of the Colonial Office for the welfare of Indigenous people throughout the empire, most of the document was devoted to the rights and protection of Aboriginal people. Aboriginal people, it made clear, were to be regarded as British subjects, protected by the law and any acts of injustice committed against them were to be punished with 'exemplary severity'.

That afternoon Hindmarsh introduced himself to the colonists. Mary Thomas wrote that he was 'delighted with our little village, as I may call it, which consisted of about 40 tents and huts'.[28] That evening, Gouger wrote in his journal of how rapidly 'my heart beat on this occasion – an occasion to which, during the years I have devoted to the prosecution of the enterprise, I dared sometimes to anticipate and rejoice in'. The next morning he made a new entry in his journal: the 'Commission had hardly left my tent', he wrote, when his wife went into labour and at '6 o'clock gave the province a new son! ... the first child born in the colony, after the establishment of the Government.'[29]

The constitutional division of authority between the Governor and the Resident Commissioner immediately presented difficulties

Figure 2.1: Charles Hill (Australia, 1824–1915), *The Proclamation of South Australia 1836*, c.1856–76, Adelaide, oil on canvas, 133.3 x 274.3 cm, Morgan Thomas Bequest Fund 1936. Courtesy of the Art Gallery of South Australia.

for the governance of the colony. As Governor, Hindmarsh's authority derived from the Crown; his commission gave him the responsibility to make laws and impose taxes. The Board of Commissioners derived its authority from the Act of Parliament and its agent, Resident Commissioner James Hurtle Fisher, consequently had authority over the survey of lands and the Emigration fund, including the power to appoint key colonial officers. Fisher, a lawyer, understood the power he held, while Hindmarsh bristled at his lack of power. Two factions formed, one around Hindmarsh, which was small but puffed up by the inclusion of George Stevenson, who was editor of the colony's first newspaper, and the other around Fisher, which included most of the significant colonial officers (such as Light and Kingston in the Survey Department; Brown, the Emigration Agent; and Gouger, the Colonial Secretary).

Hindmarsh complained that Fisher acted with almost no reference to him, failing to report on the progress of the surveys, the construction of roads and bridges, or even the fact that he had ordered Deputy Surveyor Kingston back to England aboard the *Rapid* with a request to increase the Survey Department.[30] In May 1837, he complained that Brown treated his 'authority and person with disrespect and contempt' and should be dismissed, and a few days later that 'Kingston's insolence' almost equalled that of Brown's.[31] In August, he suspended Robert Gouger, the Colonial Secretary, for what he described as a 'disgraceful pugilistic contest' with his own supporter, the Treasurer Osmond Gilles.[32] A couple of weeks later, he suspended Brown for defying his authority by not organising the burial of a pauper, something that Brown, probably correctly, claimed was not his responsibility. He even had a party of Marines take Brown into custody, which Brown claimed was illegal because he had no 'civil authority' to do so.[33] While personalities played a part in these disputes, ideology did so as well, with Fisher's faction seeing themselves as democrats faithfully observing the colony's foundational principles. In private letters to the colony's principal investor, George Fife Angas, Hindmarsh complained that Fisher had 'ridiculously exalted notions' of his authority, 'monopolized all power in his own hands', 'interfered in every and the most trifling act of government', and 'acts as though the proprietorship of the land gives him the right to all other power'.[34] While Hindmarsh was South Australia's first Governor, Fisher – in control of the funds – effectively led the colony's first government. Hindmarsh wanted him removed from office.[35]

By March 1837, with the survey of the town site at last complete, settlers, in anticipation, began to move into tents and reed cottages along the banks of the Torrens. By November 1837 there were about 300 houses in Adelaide, mostly clustered around the north-western corner of the future city.[36] The tent camp for new arrivals on the banks of the Patawalonga now migrated inland to the banks of the Torrens. By December the population was about 3,000 and the pressure to get the surveys completed, so that crops could be planted, became increasingly intense. Colonist John Adams reported that they were often short of common necessities, such as flour and meat, and 'were it not for the cockatoos and parrots', and kangaroo they sometimes got 'from the natives', they would 'have been badly off'. Everything had to be imported. Beef, he recalled, was 1 shilling per pound, when you could get it, while flour was 'almost impossible to procure at £80 to £100 per ton'.[37]

When Kingston was dispatched to England to appeal for more assistance with the surveys, he also carried with him a request from the leading colonists that Hindmarsh be dismissed. The

Commissioners concurred and presented their case to the Colonial Office. Lord Glenelg, who was sympathetic to the compromised position in which the Constitution of the colony had placed Hindmarsh, agreed, and he was recalled in 1838.[38] However, the Colonial Office also amended the Act to remove the division of authority that had been poisonous to the operation of government. When the next governor took office, he took over the powers formerly exercised by the Resident Commissioner.

When the new Governor, George Gawler, arrived in October 1838, the colony was in a parlous state with thousands of frustrated colonists drawing down their capital on expensive imports while they waited to get on the land.[39] The surveys were effectively stalled; according to Gawler there were 'scarcely any settlers in the country, no tillage, very little cattle and sheep pasturing', the 'landing places' were undeveloped, transport to and from the Port 'ruinous', and the colonial finances in a 'state of confusion'.[40] With 5,000 settlers already in the colony and thousands more on the way, Gawler considered that he had to act decisively to meet this 'great emergency of public affairs'. He needed to get people on the land and provide the services necessary for a rapidly growing population, and to effect this he needed to 'surpass his instructions' and make 'unauthorized' expenditure.[41] To hurry along the surveys, Gawler decided that moneys could be drawn against the land fund, dramatically increasing the numbers in the department and accelerating the surveys. Suffering ill-health and frustrated by arguments about the site of the capital and the progress of the surveys, Light resigned. The Commissioners appointed Lieutenant Edward Charles Frome as the new Surveyor General and gave him a staff of 15 sappers to help expedite the work, which he began in October 1839. Within a year the department, with Charles Sturt as Assistant Commissioner, had grown to nearly 200.[42] By December 1840, 6,000 settlers had moved onto rural sections and 2,700 acres were under cultivation.[43]

Gawler also embarked on a public works program; he authorised the construction of government offices, a police barracks and a gaol, and the development of the port to provide a more dignified and practical landing point for passengers and cargo than 'Port Misery' had hitherto offered.[44] Work on the project began in May 1840 and was completed in October of that year. The government built the road from Adelaide and one wharf; the South Australia Company built the terminal section of the road, its own wharf and a warehouse. Mary Thomas recalled the grand opening performed by the Governor and his wife, which was attended by 5,000 citizens.[45]

The colony's population had ballooned to almost 15,000 in less than four years, a small but growing proportion of which now included German settlers, primarily from the Silesian region of what was then Prussia. Escaping religious persecution in their homeland, these 'Old Lutherans' emigrated to South Australia under the guidance of their Pastor, August Kavel, and with the financial assistance of a sympathetic Dissenter, George Fife Angas.[46] About 500 emigrated in 1838 and 1839, settling initially in the village of Klemzig where, as gardeners, they provided much needed produce to the undeveloped settlement. The Germans were the first non-English speaking settlers to establish themselves in Australia as an organised group, which presented them and Governor Gawler

Figure 2.2: George French Angas, *Klemzic, a Village of German Settlers*, 1846. Courtesy of the State Library of South Australia. B 15276/12.

with a unique problem. As 'friendly aliens' they could not enjoy the civil and political rights of British subjects, such as owning land. At Kavel's request, Gawler passed an Ordinance in 1839 naturalising Kavel and nine other Germans. Further amendments in the 1840s extended these rights to other Germans coming into the colony.

Given how the question of Aboriginal rights had figured so significantly in Colonial Office deliberations about the colony, it was a conspicuously marginal issue during Hindmarsh's term of office. The apparent undertakings to recognise Aboriginal ownership of land, in some form or other, went unmet. The divided administration played a part in this: in 1837, when Acting Protector William Wyatt approached the Resident Commissioner to reserve some sections of land, Fisher responded legalistically that the Act 'admitted of no reservation of this kind'.[47] The appointment of a permanent Protector of Aborigines to oversee their interests also remained unsatisfied in the very period when it might have mattered most. At least they could say there had been precious little violence between Aboriginal people and settlers. All these things changed during the term of George Gawler's administration.

Upon his arrival in October 1838, Governor Gawler introduced himself to the Kaurna people of the Adelaide Plains by organising a 'feast' for them in the Adelaide Parklands.[48] Curiously, the formalities were redolent of a British treaty-making ceremony; the participants were dressed in their finery, fine speeches were made, gifts given and food shared.[49] Gawler's speech, translated into their language, announced to the Kaurna that they were to be taught the ways of Christianity and British civilisation.[50] Present at the festivities was interim Protector Wyatt, who had established an 'Aborigines Location' where huts were built and rudimentary gardens established to encourage 'habits of useful industry' among the Aborigines. Wyatt was replaced by Dr Matthew Moorhouse who took up his post as the first Crown-appointed Protector of Aborigines in July 1839. The office of Protector of Aborigines, an imposition of the Colonial Office, was intended to aid in the protection of Aboriginal people from the sorts of injustices that had characterised earlier Australian settlements. The Protector, essentially working alone, developed the Aborigines Location, where he hoped Aboriginal people would settle in pisé-style houses erected for them. However, Aboriginal indifference to the site meant that it never developed as the sort of civilising mission that had been imagined, so Moorhouse shifted his attention to educating the children.[51]

The little assistance Moorhouse received came from a group of German Lutheran missionaries from Dresden, sponsored by George Fife Angas. Clamor Schürmann and Christian Teichelman arrived with Governor Gawler in 1838. Initially, Schürmann taught at the first school established at the Aborigines Location in December 1839, while Teichelman evangelised the adult population and later attempted to establish a mission at Happy Valley. Samuel Klosé and Heinrich Meyer joined their brother missionaries in 1840. The experience of the missionaries was generally an unhappy one; with inadequate support from Angas and their home society, they found themselves forever compromised by their reliance on government assistance. Klosé took over as teacher at the Aborigines Location school in 1840, where he taught the children in their own language, and enjoyed considerable success. However, when a more permanent school was established in the city and he was asked to teach in English, he refused and was replaced. Schürmann in the meantime took himself to the frontier settlement of Port Lincoln. To support his work he agreed to serve as Deputy Protector in the district, but he resigned when he found himself working primarily as a guide and interpreter for the police. Heinrich Meyer established a school for Ramindjeri children at Encounter Bay, but received little support. By 1853 all four men had given up their mission to the Aborigines.

The question of Aboriginal rights to land, which had been so central to the concerns of the Colonial Office in the planning of the colony, was revived, and effectively resolved, in a dispute over the land surveys. In July 1840 a new set of surveys was completed and offered for selection by the purchases of preliminary land orders. Gawler instructed Moorhouse to set aside sections for the benefit of Aboriginal people. When news of this became public knowledge, there was an uproar; not only had the surveys been slow, and the choices seemingly limited, but now first choice was being given to Aboriginal people. Gawler defended his decision with surprising vigour, making clear that Aboriginal people were the original owners of the soil and reminding the complainants of all the undertakings they had made regarding Aboriginal rights. Yet, in the end, it amounted to little more than rhetoric. Aboriginal people, he argued, were too little 'advanced in civilisation' for 'treaties or bargains' to be fairly entered into, so what he had decided was to set aside sections for their 'future use and benefit', which were to be held in trust until such time as they chose to settle upon them as farmers.[52]

Two shocking events in 1840 and 1841 further tested the humanitarian ideals of the colony's foundation, this time in regard to Aboriginal people's status as British subjects. On 7 June 1840, the *Maria* left Adelaide bound for Hobart with 10 crew and 16 passengers, but just three weeks later it wrecked on the southern coast at Lacepede Bay. Everyone survived and the party, with whatever possessions they could salvage, started to make their way up the Coorong towards Encounter Bay. An Aboriginal clan known at the time as the Milmenrura initially assisted them; however, relations between the parties ruptured and all of the 26 survivors were killed. This was the largest death toll of Europeans in any single frontier incident in Australia's history. What motivated the killing is uncertain. One view at the time was that the Milmenrura, when offered no recompense for their assistance, started to take what they wanted and a violent confrontation ensued.[53] Another explanation is that it was started by the crew's 'loose conduct ... with the native women'.[54] When rumours of the massacre were received in Adelaide, Governor Gawler ordered the Police Commissioner, Thomas O'Halloran, to travel to the district and investigate. If he found the guilty parties, he was to try them on the spot, but was cautioned to hang no more than three. O'Halloran did indeed conduct a summary trial and two men were executed, their bodies left to hang as a warning to others. George Stevenson, editor of *The Register*, criticised Gawler's actions and reminded his readers that Aboriginal people were British subjects entitled to the protection of the law. Gawler's defence was that he had operated on the principles of martial law, and regarded the Milmenrura as a 'nation at enmity with her Majesty'.[55] For Gawler, legal niceties mattered less than a rapid and decisive response for punitive effect.

Hardly had the dust settled after the *Maria* massacre than Gawler faced a second crisis in Aboriginal relations. If the new settlers, now finally expanding into the country districts as the surveys gathered pace, were to establish their properties, they needed sheep and cattle to stock them, bullocks to pull their carts, and horses to speed their travels. These were provided by enterprising settlers driving stock overland to the colony from New South Wales. The explorers Sturt and Eyre were among the first to bring stock into the colony in 1838. Two routes were used: overland via Port Phillip, or via Sturt's route along the River Murray. By 1840, cattle, sheep and horses were being driven along the river to Adelaide. Men such as Sturt and Eyre had considerable experience in the bush and, eager for government posts, had reason to be circumspect in their dealings with Aboriginal people – others did not. Alexander Buchanan left Sydney for Adelaide in July 1839, and his journal records that he fired upon Aboriginal people on half a dozen occasions, killing at least eight. That such things were happening was an open secret; in October 1840, a correspondent to *The Register* reported that seldom did such parties arrive in Adelaide without some tale of 'butchering the natives along the way'.[56]

Aboriginal men, most notably the Maraura who occupied country near the New South Wales border, escalated their attacks and started confronting these parties with large forces. In April 1841, Henry Field and Henry Inman's party were attacked near Lake Bonney, resulting in the dispersal of 5,000 sheep and 800 cattle. For a struggling colony, this was a shocking loss and Gawler responded by dispatching Police Commissioner O'Halloran with a party of police and volunteers to assist the overlanders and help recover the stock. However, when the unexpected news that Gawler had been recalled by London was reported, the expedition was called back. In May, colonists petitioned newly arrived Governor George Grey to organise an expedition to assist Charles Langhorne, whose party was known to be approaching the district. Grey agreed to do so but, conscious of the controversy generated by Gawler's previous actions, he made every effort to observe the letter of the law, reminding the colonists that Aboriginal people were British subjects and ensuring that Protector Moorhouse accompanied O'Halloran's party. Langhorne's party was attacked, and four of his men killed, before assistance could arrive.

A further expedition was sanctioned by Grey in August, this time led by Protector of Aborigines Moorhouse and assisted by Sub-Inspector of Police Bernard Shaw with instructions to provide

Figure 2.3: Sir George Grey, c. 1885. Courtesy of the State Library of South Australia. B 3752.

protection for William Robinson's overland party. When they met up with Robinson, the overlander reported that his party had been attacked the previous day but had lost no men. Just across the border, in New South Wales, at a place called Rufus River, the Maraura, numbering in the hundreds, challenged the Europeans; on this occasion, the Europeans had a combined force of over 30 well-armed men. Moorhouse had clear instructions to avoid the use of firearms but, fearing that his party was getting within spear-range, he handed over command to Shaw. Without orders being given, the men started firing. Caught in a crossfire between the two European parties, the *Maraura* were trapped as they retreated into the river. The firing continued for half an hour, by which time at least 30, but probably many more, Aboriginal people had been killed. When Moorhouse's party returned in September, Grey ordered a Bench of Magistrates to inquire into the events. The actions were deemed 'justifiable'.[57] Grey had observed the letter of the law, but the outcome was the largest recorded massacre of Aboriginal people in the colony's history.

In the early months of 1842, the newly settled Port Lincoln district was experiencing an escalating series of clashes with the Battara people; shepherds were attacked and stock driven off, while stations were plundered and set on fire. By the end of March, five settlers had been killed and others wounded. Most settlers deserted their stations and retreated into the town of Port Lincoln for protection. Governor Grey was petitioned to provide them with military protection and he agreed to dispatch a unit of the 96th Regiment to aid the local police. While the presence of Red Coats may have been a source of comfort to the settlers, infantrymen cluttering noisily through the scrub were singularly ineffective in tracking down the alleged ringleaders of the recent attacks. Before too long the military were withdrawn, replaced by more effective Mounted Police, supported by settlers and aided by Aboriginal trackers. This would become the model of frontier policing in 19th-century South Australia.[58]

Violence on the frontier was just one of many pressing problems. At the beginning of 1841, the colony had seemed to be steaming ahead under Gawler's stewardship, but it was being driven almost entirely by deficit spending. As an inquiry later noted, 'Gawler, without authority, was expending more annually than the whole amount of capital the Commissioners were authorized to raise'.[59] In 1840 alone, with an income of £30,000, Gawler had spent £174,000.[60] Gawler maintained that spending on sorely needed infrastructure had been required and public works provided employment for idle men while they awaited land to be surveyed. Moreover, it prevented the ruin of private enterprises by enabling currency to circulate through the emerging economy. As news of Gawler's management of the colony's finances filtered back to London, the Colonisation Commissioners were mortified; the entirety of the £300,000 land fund had been expended. Seeing no way of covering the ballooning debt, the Commissioners saw no alternative but to hand the problem over to the government.[61] It was decided to recall Gawler and to re-organise the fledgling colony's administration. George Grey was appointed the new governor, and arrived in the colony in April 1841 with instructions to bring the colonial finances into order.

Grey's immediate political challenge in Adelaide was to balance the budget by reducing expenditure and increasing government income. He did the former in a variety of ways: halving the police force, abolishing minor government departments and reducing expenditure on the surveys – he could do this without harm because of the progress achieved during Gawler's time. He stopped capital works projects (such as the new Customs House being built at the Port, and the Adelaide Gaol) and he suspended assisted immigration. He raised funds by securing a loan from Governor Gipps in New South Wales, introduced customs duties on certain imported goods and imposed fees for depasturing stock on Crown lands.[62] His austerities nonetheless left many people without work. By October of 1841, a total of 555 men (or 2,427 colonists in total when dependents are factored in) were on Poor Relief – the scale of which he also reduced. His imposition of taxes – without representation – was further regarded by some as an affront to the democratic principles of the Province.[63] It goes without saying that these measures made him extremely unpopular.

Given the Commissioners' confident predictions of early self-sufficiency, and their insistence on the freedom to manage their own affairs, it is hard not to imagine Lord Stanley taking a certain guilty pleasure in the colony's discomfort. We get an inkling of this in his censure of Governor Grey for continuing to provide relief to the unemployed at the expense of the Crown. He suggested that the funds would be better employed in providing these 'destitute labourers' with free passage to other colonies, such as New South Wales, 'where the demand for labour is likely to be steady and effective'.[64]

In this age of sail, when messages moved in slow motion, praise and censure often passed like ships in the night. Grey was affronted by this criticism and wrote a passionate defence of his actions. The question he found himself having to answer, he wrote, was this: should he 'permit upwards of two thousand British subjects to starve or support themselves by rapine and pillage, which they threatened in very intelligible language that they would do?' On his arrival only about 3,000 acres were under cultivation yet 'the town assembled a population of 8,479 who were supported wholly or indirectly' by the government. Despite the hostility he faced, he had still made significant reductions in expenditure. In dispatches to England he reported that he had been threatened with personal violence, 'seditious language had been used' and he feared a 'popular outbreak'. He went on to point out that the colonists' complaints were not without foundation and that he himself had contributed more than one-third of his salary to charitable purposes. Grey concluded by pointing out that the measures he implemented had been 'crowned by complete success', with almost 20,000 acres now under cultivation, and the colony growing enough grain for its own needs as well as export. The number of men on government works, he added, had been reduced from 555 to about 60, and when the harvest commenced, most of them would be employed.[65] Rather than being required to dispatch the unemployed to other colonies, Grey pointed to a looming shortage of labour, and requested a resumption of emigration.

Crucial to the development of the economy was the discovery of copper, bringing Australia's first mining boom, which underpinned the colony's growth for many years. Among the men overlanding sheep and cattle along the River Murray in 1838 was Frederick Dutton. He and his brother William had pastoral interests in New South Wales and saw opportunities in the new colony. Men of capital, William brought property at Mount Barker in 1839 and Frederick, in partnership with Captain Charles Bagot, established the Koonunga run on rolling plains about 75 miles north of Adelaide.[66] Their family was well-to-do; their father had been a British vice-consul in Germany and the youngest brother, Francis, was educated in Switzerland and worked for a firm in Rio de Janeiro before joining his brothers in Australia. In 1842, Francis was mustering sheep on the Koonunga run when he found what he recognised to be a copper outcrop.[67] Copper was already being mined in the Adelaide Hills, but the lode was modest and difficult to extract. Bagot and Dutton quietly acquired the 80-acre section at auction and sent samples to England for analysis. After a long delay they learned that their samples averaged a remarkable 23% copper and were payable. Mining operations commenced at Kapunda in 1844. More were to be established in other places over the next decade.

The colony's founders had placed great store on the idea of early self-government and political independence, but a flawed Constitution had produced an administrative mess. In 1842, the British Government passed two Acts that more or less reset the direction of the colony's political development. The *Act to provide for the better Government of South Australia* (5 & 6 Vict. Cap 36) repealed the *Constitution Act 1834*, bringing an end to the hybrid Constitution, and giving South Australia the status of an ordinary Crown colony. Where previously the Governor had been assisted by a Council of Government made up of three Crown nominees,

Figure 2.4: George French Angas, *The Kapunda Copper Mine*, c. 1846. Courtesy of the State Library of South Australia. B 15276/31.

this Act created a Legislative Council comprising the Governor, together with three official and four non-official members nominated by the Crown. The Governor was still essentially an autocrat, with the sole power to propose laws, and ultimately responsible to the British Government rather than his Council.[68] The second significant piece of legislation was the *Waste Lands Act 1842*, which provided a uniform system of land regulation across the Australian colonies. Lands were now to be put up for auction at a minimum price of £1 per acre with half the proceeds supporting emigration and the remainder for local purposes.[69] It was through this Act that the Governor could reserve lands for the benefit of Aboriginal people, and it essentially provided the basis for the 'grace and favour' system of Aboriginal land entitlement well into the 20th century.[70]

In the fluid, almost elemental, circumstances of these foundational years, fortunes could rise and fall with capricious cruelty. For Robert Gouger who, emotionally and intellectually, had invested as much as anyone in the South Australian dream, the colonial reality was tragic. Just three months after the proclamation was read, his wife died of her illness and their son died several days later. After being suspended by Hindmarsh in August 1837, Gouger hurried back to England to seek redress before returning in 1838. Grey gave Gouger the position of Colonial Treasurer, but his mental and physical health declined and he returned to England, where he died in 1846. Robert and Mary Thomas took the risk of leaving behind a comfortable middle-class life for something better and at first their fortunes soared under Hindmarsh. Besides running the colony's first newspaper, they operated a general store in Hindley Street and built one of the city's earliest stone residences. However, Thomas's business partner's righteous editorial attacks against Gawler caused them to lose their government printing contract, and then the financial collapse of the early 1840s brought them to the verge of bankruptcy. Robert had to sell the newspaper and eventually got work in the public service, but his family at least enjoyed a comfortable middle-class life. The Duttons, on the other hand, with capital and colonial experience behind them, thrived. By as early as 1842 Frederick Dutton's herds were the largest in the colony, after those of the South Australia Company, and his Anlaby estate became one of the finest. Francis Dutton, while in

England to secure experienced labour for the Kapunda mines, sold his shares in the company for £16,000 and he returned to the colony in 1847 with both wealth and influence.[71]

In October 1845, Frederick Robe arrived in Adelaide to replace Grey, who had been posted to New Zealand. Governor Robe was inheriting a colony that was now on a sound financial footing and rapidly expanding. A city was starting to grow, close to the water of the Torrens and the terminus of the road that led up from the port. Laid out on a grid plan with the larger section south of the River Torrens and the smaller to the north, it contained, as it still does, generous public squares, wide roads and even wider terraces. For many, the crowning glory of the plan was the generous extent of parklands that encompassed it, which now contributes to the city's 'sense of difference'.[72] Many of the earliest houses in Adelaide were of wood or pisé construction, with thatched roofs. Over time, however, the easy availability of stone as a building material made stone-walled cottages the dominant style of housing.[73] On the surrounding plains, small villages at places such as Walkerville, Thebarton and Klemzig were established; others would soon appear – the beginning of Adelaide's suburban spread. The planning of the city was Light's most enduring legacy, but he never lived to see it take shape. He died at his Thebarton cottage in October 1839.[74]

By 1846, the colony was taking on a distinctive social character. Its population had grown rapidly to about 25,000, of whom some 43% were women – an unusually high proportion for a colony in its foundational stage.[75] South Australia stood by its 'no convict' principle in the belief that it would protect the colony's respectability and freedoms.[76] George Fife Angas's encouragement of migration by German Lutherans resulted in South Australia having the country's first significant proportion of settlers from continental Europe. While religious Dissenters, such as Angas, were significant in the planning of the colony, their numbers at this time were small, with Anglicans making up more than 50% of the population, but their influence would grow rapidly in coming decades.[77]

Chapter 3

Settling and Unsettling, 1846–56

'The country', wrote Mary Thomas in 1836, 'resembled an English park, with long grass in abundance and fine trees scattered about'.[1] Gawler also thought it resembled an 'English Park', with 'the trees beautifullfy grouped, very large and free from Brush-wood'.[2] Francis Dutton, in his book *South Australia and its Mines*, published in 1846, praised its 'beautiful park-like scenery' and seemingly detected a deeper design: 'the groups of trees planted by the hand of nature assume in hundreds of places, and for many acres in extent, a degree of elegant landscape arrangement, not to be exceeded by art'.[3] The design in this case involved many generations of skillful Aboriginal land management through the use of fire, although this was not appreciated at the time.[4] For those aspiring to the life of a country gentleman or woman, it was encouraging. Traveller William Leigh thought the land near Encounter Bay was much like 'the domain of an English noble'.[5] It was a landscape ideally suited not just to the agricultural and pastoral occupations of the settlers, but also to their social ambitions.

The bedrock of South Australian social and economic growth over the next 40 years was the Central Hills district, which extended from Kapunda in the south to Mount Remarkable in the north, reaching towards the Great South Bend of the River Murray in the east and towards Yorke Peninsula in the west. Easily accessible from Adelaide, with good soil and reliable rainfall, it was ideal country for grazing sheep and growing crops and below its surface lay mineral wealth.[6] Among the first settlers in the region were the Hawker brothers: James, George and Charles. In June 1841, they purchased a flock of 2,500 sheep from Frederick Dutton and began squatting on land near Mount Dispersion.[7] The process of establishing a station is driven primarily by the need to find a reliable source of water, and in their search they shifted several times that year before finally locating themselves near the Hutt River, at a station they called Bungaree. At first they lived under canvas and, in an inversion of the 'voyage out', subsisted on a diet of mutton with salt pork an occasional 'treat'. The shepherds they employed had a weekly ration of meat, flour, sugar and tea, and typically earned between 10 and 15 shillings a week. With the aid of a shepherd and hutkeeper, they set about building themselves a wattle and daub hut with thatched roof and a solid stone chimney. Gardens of potatoes and onions were soon planted, fences were erected and preparations made for shearing.[8] By the end of 1845, they had purchased and surveyed the land around the head station, which was now a small village, and secured an occupation licence that enabled them to run stock on the surrounding country.[9]

Although this region was suitable for agriculture, it was developed primarily as pastoral lands. The early settlers in the Central Hills Country, together with those who took up land in the Lower Lakes region and the lower South East, formed the basis of a colonial squattocracy that would dominate South Australia's social and political landscape for the remainder of the century. Wakefield's vision was not an egalitarian one; country land was sold at a 'sufficient price' at £1 per acre in 80-acre lots, designed to prevent labourers too easily becoming landowners, but for enterprising men of capital it was a once-in-a-lifetime opportunity. By 1891, a total of 130 landowners possessed half the freehold land in South Australia, and almost one-third of the land in the Central Hills Country. Most estates were in excess of 5,000 acres, while almost 40 were in excess of 25,000 acres, 'a landed interest that many a duke or baron in aristocratic 19th-century England would have envied'.[10]

Most of these men of property, besides overseeing the management of their own agricultural and pastoral interests, leased significant portions of their land to small farmers. Many of the German settlers in the Adelaide Hills and valleys of the Barossa, for instance, were tenant farmers tending their gardens and growing their crops on the lands of the South Australia Company. George Fife Angas had proposed such a scheme in 1835. He suggested that 'benevolent and opulent' landholders might rent 80-acre sections of land to 'poor farmers', with the lure of purchase down the track and, in the interim, the farmers would be advanced credit to help them develop their holdings.[11] By 1850, the South Australia Company alone had 467 tenants, contributing 20% of the colony's wheat crop. Douglas Pike suggests that this was a life many of the tenants came to regret; they had to 'clear, fence and crop the land, build houses and sheds, buy their seed stock and implements from the Company and deal with the Company's bank', but in the end were often 'no better rewarded' than those 'working for wages'.[12] Samuel Davenport had a Special Survey around the town of Macclesfield in country south of Mount Barker; besides running his own stock, growing fields of corn, and seeding acres of olive and fruit trees, he earned an income from renting sections of his land to aspiring farmers. For one of the sons of the industrial revolution, life in the colonies had a decidedly feudal quality.[13] His tenant farmers rented their land for about a shilling an acre and a set percentage of their grain crop. Whereas Davenport could afford to hire 'Ridley's Stripper' – a mechanical harvester drawn by horses – his men and women used scythes and reaping hooks, and when they came into his town they drank at 'his' inn and had their horses shod by 'his' blacksmith.

Judy Jeffery, in her study of small farmers in South Australia prior to 1869, suggests the ideal that migrants might, after a few years, earn enough to become landowners in their own right was rarely realised.[14] In an economy where shepherds' wages in 1850 may have been about £20 a year, it was 'almost incomprehensible', she argues, 'that a wage earner could save enough to buy 80 acres at a minimum of £1 per acre' (an acreage that in any case was often 'too small to be viable').[15] Those who did succeed tended to be people who had other skills that they could rely on; people such as George Uppil, a joiner by trade, who came out as an assisted immigrant and worked as a coach builder until he had acquired enough capital to buy land. Even then, he, like other small farmers, needed to supplement his farm income with other work, such as carting ore, to make ends meet.[16] Inquiring into the lives of these small farmers, Jeffery reminds us, is challenging, as most 'of those who failed in the difficult task of farming in an alien climate with insufficient capital have faded into anonymity, and even "success" was simply to provide a comfortable living for oneself and one's family'.[17]

One of the central pillars of systematic colonisation was the regulation of migration to ensure the ready availability of labour and the healthy reproduction of British society. South Australia lost exclusive control of emigration when it became a Crown colony in 1842, but the Colonial Land and Emigration Commission, which the British Government created and which served all the colonies, regulated migration in a similar way.[18] Colonial governments submitted reports on their labour needs and Emigration Agents scattered through the British Isles would endeavour to recruit as required.[19] The sort of assistance the emigrant was given varied over time, but in the 1850s men with sought-after skills would receive free passage for themselves and their families, while others had only a portion of their fare paid. The applicants were vetted by the Agents; character references and evidence of age and marital status were required, and the prospective emigrant had to be healthy and under the age of 35 for women and 40 for men.[20] Between 1847 and 1851, for example, over 20,000 people were given free or assisted passage to South Australia, 34% of whom were men and 39% women, while the remainder were children.[21] Most of those who emigrated were from England, Scotland and Wales, relatively few from Ireland, but a significant proportion from Germany. As Eric Richards has observed, the assisted migrants were mainly 'agricultural labourers and domestic servants ... typical products of industrialising mid nineteenth century England'.[22] The system put in place to regulate migration to South Australia ensured a greater parity of men to women than in any of the other Australian colonies, especially in the foundation years.[23]

The persistent problem was the time-lag between the request for labour and its supply; miners might arrive at a time when domestic servants were needed, or a flood of labourers would be unloaded at the Port just when a downturn in the economy meant there was no work for them.[24] Particularly prominent among the arrivals were single, female domestic servants, of whom a high percentage were from Ireland. The Female Immigration Depot was unable to cope and a network of regional depots was hurriedly established to take the excess and provide them with support until work could be found.[25] Ireland was not a preferred source of migrants to South Australia and their prominence was partly a consequence of the devastating famine occurring in Ireland at the time.[26] South Australian Governor Richard MacDonnell was not pleased about this. He complained to the Secretary of State that Britain had 'no reason for sending here, suddenly in one year, from Ireland, not merely more than half of the entire Female Immigrants, but nearly treble the number of United English and Scottish Immigrants'.[27] The percentage of Irish-born people in colonial South Australia, which was low in comparison to the other Australian colonies, reached its colonial peak of 10% in the 1861 census, but gradually declined over the remainder of the century.[28]

Despite the settlers' opinion that Aboriginal people possessed no proprietorial rights over the land, the fact remained that at the time of colonisation they *were* in actual occupation of South Australia, and their dispossession was a necessary condition of European settlement. In some parts of the British Empire, this was achieved through negotiation; in British North America, for instance, treaties were often entered into. In return for the surrender of the greater part of their lands, Aboriginal nations would be granted reserves to live on, sometimes provided with animals and equipment to allow them to farm, and often given annual cash payments. It was a process along these lines that the British Government tried to persuade the South Australian settlers to follow – but they chose not to. In the absence of negotiation, settlers, with the support of police, used violence against Aboriginal people who resisted encroachments upon their land.

Apart from his property interests close to Adelaide, Samuel Davenport was keen to expand his pastoral holdings and took out occupation licences in the lower South East. He travelled there occasionally to superintend his interests. In June of 1846, Davenport wrote of the 'open hostility' that characterised the district when he was trying to establish his sheep run near Rivoli Bay. Something, he wrote, that would only end when settlement was effected and Aboriginal people had been subdued or eradicated. He described the fear and anxiety he felt as he travelled in the district: 'twice I have been nearly shot; once has a waddie been hurled at me', this 'and more, that nobody may know of, have I endured'.[29] He complained about the character of the men who worked for him, and their treatment of Aboriginal people, remarking, these 'poor beings are much shot, and no one sees how to avoid it'.[30] Whatever anguish he might have felt, Davenport openly acknowledges the violence employed in the dispossession of Aboriginal people. In the more remote regions like this, where there were often no police, settlers would take the law into their own hands and retaliatory raids on Aboriginal camps were frequently designed to have a punitive effect. The process was often not very different when the police took the lead. In the same district in 1847 the Bunganditj people drove off hundreds of sheep from the South Australia Company's run. Mounted Police, who were now stationed at Mount Gambier, were called in and, with the assistance of the Company's manager and his shepherd, tracked the 'depredators' to a camp in thick scrub near Cape Northumberland. The attempts to arrest the Aborigines were repulsed by spear thrusts, and when one of the men was wounded, the police fired into the scrub, killing four men and wounding others. The Corporal in charge, not wishing 'to take more lives', called a halt to the shooting when it was clear that they would not surrender.[31] The pattern of employing punitive levels of violence to 'teach a lesson', be it on a large scale like at the Rufus River, or on a typically smaller scale like this, exemplifies the frontier tradition that emerged, and was broadly similar across all the Australian settlements.[32]

There was a weary resignation that violence on the frontiers of settlement was inevitable, and that the best the colonial government could do was employ strategies to mitigate it. Making plain to the colonists that Aboriginal people were British subjects, deserving the protection of the law, was one such strategy. This was predicated on a belief that if settlers understood that they were liable to legal sanction for crimes committed against them, they would be more circumspect in their behaviour. The extent to which this knowledge restrained their behaviour is hard to know, but the evidence suggests that it may merely have encouraged settlers to act more secretively.[33] On those occasions when it was reported, the legal system struggled to find a way of dealing with it. South Australia was early among the Australian colonies in allowing Aboriginal evidence without the sanction of an oath, but the disadvantages Aboriginal people suffered were legion.[34] The local magistrates and Justices of the Peace, who committed them to trial on charges such as sheep stealing, for instance, were usually friends and neighbours of the aggrieved settlers.[35] Juries were always made up of Europeans. Dragged in from the colony's frontiers, the prisoners typically had little understanding of the processes and often no knowledge of English. Over the course of the 19th century only half a dozen settlers were brought before the courts for capital offences against Aboriginal people, and only one was found guilty and hanged. In the same period, 24 Aboriginal people were hanged, mostly for crimes committed on the frontier.[36]

One of the administrative strategies employed to mitigate frontier violence was the introduction of a system of ration distribution. Initially, flour was distributed as a sort of compensation in the hope that it might reduce the desire, or the necessity, for Aboriginal attacks on settler's stock and property. Governor Robe expanded the system in 1847 when he established ration depots at strategic locations throughout the colony, usually police stations. The rations consisted of flour, tea and sugar; similar, but on a reduced scale, to the sort of rations supplied to shepherds. Meat was not included, however, because it was imagined that Aboriginal people would continue to hunt native game. The rations were distributed once a week and were occasionally supplemented with medical comforts and assorted items, such as fishing lines, pots, pans and blankets. The system is unlikely to have had much effect on moderating frontier violence, but over the course of the 19th century it became one of the principal sources of social welfare for Aboriginal people dispossessed of their land and forced to live on the fringes of white society.[37]

What passed for general Aboriginal policy in this period was a set of *ad hoc* strategies guided by an assumption that the fate of Aboriginal people lay in their eventual amalgamation into colonial society. In the language of the times, they were to be 'civilised and Chrisitianised'. Overseeing this task was a Protector of Aborigines. Between 1839 and 1856, Dr Matthew Moorhouse held this hopelessly daunting office, with rarely more support than a secretary, a school teacher and a remote Sub-Protector. The idea that Aboriginal people should be 'civilized and Christianised' was colonial dogma; often the only doubt was which should come first. For the German missionaries, there was no doubt that Aboriginal souls were their principle concern; the press not uncommonly criticised them for spending too much time teaching Bible lessons, and not enough time instructing them to till the land.[38] Faced with relatively little support, most of the Dresden missionaries had left the field by 1851. In Adelaide at this time, the Protector oversaw the operation of the Native School Establishment, which was now located in the city and operated as a boarding school. It had over 80 children whose scholastic progress was considered outstanding. The only problem, as Moorhouse saw it, was that once the students finished their education, they returned to their communities and their 'old ways'.[39] An apparent solution to this was found in 1851 when the Anglican Church, under the leadership of Archdeacon Matthew Hale, entered the mission field. With the support of the Government, a settlement was established at Poonindie, not far from Port Lincoln. The first Aboriginal people to settle at Poonindie were youths from the Native School in Adelaide. The Protector married them off and Poonindie became their new home.[40] Over time, Poonindie accepted Aboriginal people from the local region as well as others dispatched there by the Protector. For many years Poonindie functioned more like a village settlement than an institution. It had its own cricket team, and on a number of occasions played against St Peter's College, the prestigious Anglican school in Adelaide.[41] Bishop Augustus Short described it as 'a Christian village of South Australian Natives reclaimed from barbarism'.[42] By 1856, it was the only institution of its sort operating in South Australia.

The discovery of copper at Kapunda in 1842 eventually led to a mining mania. People ranging from shepherds to solicitors were kicking over rocks in the hope of finding that tell-tale glitter of green or, better still, gold. In 1845, a shepherd came to town with a sample of copper he had found in country north of Kapunda. He showed it to a solicitor, Henry Ayers, the secretary of the South Australian Mining Association, which, at the time, had discovered no copper, but had capital and aspirations.[43] Convinced that this was a significant find, two consortia emerged to compete for the land, but the task was more difficult than it had been when Bagot and Dutton had only to purchase a standard 80-acre section. Grey had tightened the land laws in regard to special surveys (that is, land outside the surveyed Counties), which had been available for purchase at £1 per acre at a minimum of 20,000 acres. Wealthy pastoralists had been rorting the system by 'picking the eyes out of the country'. Governor Grey now insisted that the land had to be in a single block, the good with the bad, and purchased cash down. Finding £20,000 quickly was challenging. The two consortia eventually divided the special survey into two equal parts and drew lots as to which they would get. The South Australian Mining Association, with the additional support of small businessmen, won the northern section, which developed into the Burra 'Monster' Mine, while the Princess Royal Mining Company got the southern section, which proved to be good pasture land.[44]

Mining began at Burra in September 1845 and became profitable very quickly; 7,000 ton of copper ore was mined in the first year, valued at over £100,000. The pickings were easy at first; rich ore lay close to the surface and had merely to be quarried, which meant production costs were low at a time when international copper prices were high. Finding good labour also proved relatively straightforward.[45] When assisted passages were reintroduced, among the first to arrive were Cornish miners, and miners from Germany were also recruited.[46] The town grew quickly and the demand for labour increased when a smelter was built in 1849. In 1851, even though the economy was in a slump, the mines employed 400 men and the smelters 1,000, and the value of the colony's mineral exports totalled £310,916, twice what was being earned from wool and four times more than grain. With a population of 5,000 people, Burra was then the seventh largest town in Australia and one of its largest industrial centres.[47] So significant were the mines that the *Sydney Morning Herald* sent a journalist to the town in 1851 to investigate its operations. The articles appeared in May of 1851 but, before the final instalment appeared, the *Herald's* 15 May edition carried a simple banner headline 'GOLD' – reporting on Edward Hargraves's discovery at Bathurst in New South Wales.[48]

News of the discovery reached Adelaide in June 1851, at a time when unemployment was relatively high. When reports that people were leaving for the New South Wales goldfields began to circulate, the press churlishly characterised these men as a class the colony was better rid of. The New South Wales diggings generated modest interest, but when news spread of extensive discoveries at Bendigo and Ballarat in Victoria, it excited mania. For the unemployed in Adelaide, the attraction of the goldfields was obvious and by the end of 1851 men of all classes, drawn by dreams of riches, were leaving in droves. So many miners left from Burra and Kapunda that by March of 1852 work had ceased. Shepherds took off to the diggings and left their flocks unattended, farmers hastily sowed their fields and left, and shopkeepers locked their doors and took off after them.[49] Two thousand people had left for the goldfields by the beginning of 1852, and by the time the mania began to subside a few years later it is estimated that 15,000 to 20,000 had tried their luck.[50] Many women and children were left to mind the farm, but many others were left with only the prospect of destitution.[51] The crisis had a cascading effect. As government revenue slumped, people were retrenched, and had little option but to join the exodus.[52] With so many drawing their cash from the banks before they left, currency started to run short, and banks faced the very real prospect of being unable to buy the gold off the returning diggers.[53] Fearing financial collapse, Governor Henry Young convened a meeting of his Legislative Council and sought the advice of the colony's leading bankers. It was decided that the only solution was to set up a Government Assay Office to receive the gold of returning diggers at a superior price to that being offered in Victoria, and to issue bank notes that would be declared legal tender.[54]

To reinforce this strategy the newly appointed Police Commissioner, Alexander Tolmer, just three weeks into his tenure and in charge of a rapidly dwindling force, suggested instituting a gold escort to assist the men in returning their gold to South Australia and, hopefully, to induce them to eventually follow it back themselves. The Governor approved the scheme and in the next few months Tolmer personally made three trips to the Victorian goldfields, where he exchanged bank notes for gold and escorted it safely back to Adelaide. Tolmer records a distinct camaraderie among the South Australian diggers, many of whom worked together at places like 'Adelaide Gully', and who assured him that they would certainly be returning home.[55] Tolmer's escort was also a mail service, carrying letters back and forth between the diggers and their family and friends in South Australia. With the return of Tolmer's second escort to Adelaide in May 1852, *The Register* reported that it carried gold worth £70,000, 'and 1,500 valuable letters from successful diggers … to their anxiously expectant wives, families and friends'.[56] The scheme had its desired effect and by the end of 1853 it had returned the colony's finances to a stable footing. The Assay Office was no longer needed and the gold escort ceased.

South Australia's first significant novel, *Clara Morison: A Tale of South Australia during the Gold Fever*, was published in 1854. Its author was Catherine Helen Spence, who had arrived in South Australia as a 13-year-old girl in 1839 when her family emigrated. As the title suggests, the novel is a romance set against the impact of the gold fever on South Australian society. The 'Clara Morison' of the title is an emigrant girl from a good family who came out expecting employment as a governess, but had to swallow her pride and accept work as a domestic servant. Through her eyes we see the lives of South Australians in the early 1850s and their social aspirations, mores and pretensions.[57] For a novel written just 18 years after settlement, it conveys a surprisingly powerful sense of South Australia as 'home'. The last section of the novel, told through correspondence between the South Australian diggers and their loved ones back in Adelaide, portrays a sense of patriotism among her 'Adelaide men'. One of her characters, Gilbert, writing to his sister from the diggings, tells her that she would be 'delighted to hear the Adelaide men talk of their own colony with pride and affection' and that 'all our diggers mean to return and spend their gold at home'.[58]

Ultimately, the true measure of a colony's evolution as an independent British community lay in its ability to govern itself. South Australia's population reached 50,000 in 1849; this was the number that the colony's 1834 Constitution had stated would be the trigger for self-government. The Act no longer had effect, but the desire for self-government in South Australia, as in the older established colonies, was strong. The rapidly changing nature of Australian settlement gave the British fewer reasons to deny those demands. As the number of free settlers in the Australian colonies grew, so did the sentiment against convict transportation, notably manifest in the Anti-Transportation Leagues being formed in the east. Secretary of State Earl Grey had ended convict transportation to New South Wales in 1840, and when an attempt was made to revive it in a modified form in 1849, mass protests conveyed a troubling air of sedition.[59] The British had the salutary example of British Canada's recent rebellion, which had only been resolved by granting them responsible government.[60] The land rush of the 1830s and 1840s and the Gold Rush of the early 1850s also brought prosperity, and free and thriving communities felt increasingly aggrieved that they were subject to autocratic rule.

It was becoming evident to the policy makers in Whitehall that semi-independent colonies within the Empire were preferable to independent republics outside it. A new imperial model was emerging of a community of self-governing colonies tied by trade, tradition and institutions to the mother country.[61] Earl Grey was amenable to the principle but wary of extending it too soon.[62] He sought the wisdom of James Stephen, who had only recently retired from the Colonial Office. Stephen's advice was that the subjects of Great Britain should be trusted to do the right thing. 'Responsible government', he wrote, 'can be applied with safety wherever the colonists constitute an intelligent, English, homogenous population, and therefore ... it may safely be applied to the Australian colonies'.[63] In February 1850, the Australian Government Bill was introduced into the House of Commons, allowing New South Wales, Victoria, Tasmania (then called Van Diemen's Land) and South Australia to introduce, in the first instance, 'blended legislatures' and giving them authority, if they wished, to introduce bicameral legislatures: a people's house and a house of review. More immediately, the *Enabling Act* of 1850 authorised the colonies to establish a Legislative Council comprising no more than 24 members, two-thirds of whom could be elected and one-third appointed.[64] In South Australia, the first popular elections for Council were held in July 1851, although the restrictive franchise of £100 ensured that only men of property sat in the Council when it met for the first time in August. These included pioneering pastoralists (such as Angas, Dutton and Davenport), alongside the original political schemers (such as Torrens, Hanson and Morphett).[65]

One of the first issues discussed in the new Council was the matter of State aid to religion. The early governors were concerned about the lack of State support for religion and, under Governor Robe, a scheme was introduced in 1846 to allow the government to provide financial support, but without making a distinction between the Church of England and other denominations. In the Council, a majority of those elected supported the voluntary principle, and they voted down an attempt to renew the church ordinance. As David Hilliard observed, this made South Australia the first colony in the British Empire to 'dissolve the last remaining vestiges of the traditional connection between church and state'.[66]

Apart from dealing with the ordinary business of government, the Councils in each of the colonies had the authority to determine the sort of representative government that they wished to implement, but they did so under the oversight of the Governor, who answered to the Secretary of State. The new Secretary of State at this time, Sir John Pakington, was uncertain whether or not the young colony of South Australia was ready for representative government. He expressed this opinion in a despatch to Governor Young, which Young withheld from the colonists, but which they found out about through the Victorian press.[67] When the Council met in 1853, the draft Constitution that the Governor presented was conservative; an appointed upper house and little concession to responsible government. Most Councillors objected to an appointed upper house, and wanted an elected, bicameral parliament. The Colonial Secretary, one of the Governor's nominees, told them that such a Constitution would be rejected by London so, on the principle that something was better than nothing, they agreed to send off the draft Constitution. They subsequently regretted the decision and, led by Charles Strickland Kingston, a significant faction of the Council continued to press for elected chambers, male suffrage and ballots. Meetings were held opposing the nominated upper house and a petition was sent to England, calling for further refinements to the Constitution.[68] The new and more liberal Secretary of State, Lord John Russell, was willing to accept further colonial modifications.[69] In June 1855, as the shape of the Constitution was being considered, Sir Richard Graves MacDonnell arrived to replace Young as Governor. Like his predecessor, he opposed the Constitution being proposed by the colonists and preferred a single-chamber Council with 36 elected and four nominated members.[70] Once again the leading colonists decried his interference in the formulation of their Constitution and the Colonial Office sided with them, informing the Governor that his proposal was 'inconsistent with the establishment of Responsible government' and that they saw 'no reason why South Australia should remain exempted from the operation of a system conceded to the neighbouring provinces of New South Wales, Victoria and Tasmania'.[71] In an attempt to get his way, MacDonnell dissolved the Council only to see liberals returned in about the same numbers as before, giving him no choice but to accede to the Constitution as redrafted by the Council.

In modern terms, South Australia's Constitution was the most liberal of any instituted by the four Australian colonies that had been given the authority to do so. The reasons for this lie in the respective circumstances of each colony. New South Wales, for instance, had long advocated colonial self-government, but with the longest history it also had a more deeply entrenched ruling elite. South Australia's Constitution provided for an upper house, the Legislative Council, comprising 18 members, six of whom had to face re-election every four years.[72] New South Wales had 21 members, elected for life at the end of a five-year term, while Victoria had 30 members with 10-year terms.[73] In South Australia, membership of the lower house, the Assembly, was restricted to people 21 years or older. Victoria and New South Wales had the same age restriction, but also property qualifications for both Assembly members and electors. The respective Legislative Councils all had property qualifications. In South Australia both electors and candidates were required to hold £50 of freehold property or an annual value of £20. In Victoria, by contrast, qualification as a Councillor required one to have £5,000 in freehold property or an annual value of £500, while electors had to have freehold property of £1,000 or an annual value of £100. As one commentator observed, 'in modern terms they created a house of millionaires'.[74]

Many of those who worked on the Constitution must have seen it as the realisation of ambitions that could be traced back to the first meetings of the National Colonisation Society in 1830. In Douglas Pike's summary of their achievement, they 'had the pick of the land', they had 'cheap, docile labour', their 'goals of civil and religious liberty had been reached', and they 'had their own government'.[75] As historian Angela Woollacott has observed, 'in the transition to self-government, Australian settlers and residents reconceived themselves as actors on the imperial and global stage, forging democratic modernity through constitutional innovation'.[76] South Australia was in the vanguard of these changes. It was the first to adopt adult male suffrage in 1856; Victoria followed in 1857, while Britain did not have full male suffrage until 1918. Victoria was the first to adopt the secret ballot in 1856, with South Australia following suit immediately after.[77] It pioneered other innovations, such as three-year parliamentary terms and electoral districts based on population, and would continue to implement important democratic reforms in the decades to come.[78] The *Constitution Act* was assented to in the British parliament in June 1856 and proclaimed in October 1856; the people of South Australia could now 'rule themselves'. As the *Times* in London observed, it was an 'odd position for a new community ... to awake one fine morning and discover that it is no longer a colony but a nation'.[79]

Chapter 4

Creating a Nation, 1857–87

When electors stood in their polling booths on 9 March 1857 and marked their ballot paper to elect the colony's first responsible government, they were among the first in the world to vote by secret ballot in a parliamentary election. Some still opposed the innovation, claiming that it stifled the democratic passions, preferring the former, more robust, procedure of a show of hands in a Town Hall meeting.[1] Voting was not compulsory and in a population of 109,000 people, 15,000 registered to vote and only about half actually did so.[2] All men, 21 years or older, had the right to vote in the House of Assembly; women were excluded but Aboriginal men were not. Members of the Legislative Council had to be at least 30 years of age, and voters had to meet a limited property qualification, making sure that members and their electors were thought worthy enough to review and restrain whatever the popular assembly might propose.[3]

The new parliament sat for the first time on 22 April 1857. Many of those elected to it had not only served in the previous Legislative Councils, but had been involved in the colonial project since its inception. Boyle Travers Finniss, for instance, who became the colony's first Chief Minister (or Premier as the position would later be known), was Deputy Surveyor General under Colonel Light and had been deeply involved in the colony's administration since 1847. Francis Dutton and Henry Ayers, who made their wealth in the copper boom of the 1840s, both served as Chief Minister in the 1860s. Samuel Davenport, with extensive pastoral and business interests, served in a number of early ministries and sat on numerous boards and committees. George Fife Angas was elected to the Legislative Council shortly after his arrival in 1851, and went on to serve in the upper house for 16 years. Pastoralists, businessmen and farmers so dominated the lower house that until 1890 only 25 members had been ordinary wage or salary earners.[4] The same classes dominated the upper house, although the spread of occupations and incomes was broader than in other colonial upper chambers because of the more liberal franchise.[5]

Interestingly, one of the first matters debated in the new parliament was the question of border security. To stem the flood of Chinese to the Victorian goldfields, that colony imposed a number of measures to discourage their entry, including a £10 poll tax on Chinese arrivals.[6] In an effort to circumvent this impost, the Chinese started to land in South Australia and travel overland to Victoria. The South Australian authorities were not entirely antagonistic to their presence; they were transiting to Victoria while bringing money into the local economy. The Victorians regarded South Australia's inaction as a sort of unseemly profiteering. The turning point came in 1857 when an estimated 15,000 Chinese landed at Guichen Bay in the lower South East, an embarkation point much closer to the Victorian goldfields. The South Australian Government, in an effort to placate its neighbours, imposed a poll tax to close this form of backdoor entry. The flow of Chinese arrivals ended very soon after this.[7] By 1861, there were just 40 Chinese resident in South Australia.[8]

Political instability was a feature of South Australian politics in the 19th century; in an era before political parties, allegiances shifted and changed as issues arose and subsided. Finniss's first ministry, for instance, lasted less than a year. Until political parties emerged in the 1890s, 47 different governments came and went in the first 36 years.[9] Not surprisingly, given the colony's origins and the classes from which its politicians were drawn, land became one of the principal concerns of the colonial parliament, and questions about its exploration, acquisition, survey, sale, distribution and occupation dominated the business of parliament for many years. Sometimes this concern produced genuinely innovative reform, such as the passage of the *Real Property Act* in 1858, which simplified the conveyancing of land. Known as 'Torrens Title', the system was adopted in other parts of Australia and internationally.[10] However, on many other occasions concerns about land were driven by more self-serving motives, such as how to get more and how best to profit from it.

In a decision perhaps indicative of the colony's ambivalent commitment to Aboriginal rights and welfare, the new Government did not refill the post of Protector of Aborigines when the incumbent resigned in 1857 and, with no little irony, rolled its few remaining functions into the Crown Lands and Immigration Office.[11] However, the increasingly visible evidence of Aboriginal destitution on the streets of Adelaide and the fringes of country towns led the Government to reconsider the issue. In 1860, a parliamentary Select Committee into Aborigines concluded that the Office of Protector should be re-established and encouragement given to the civilisation and Christianisation of Aboriginal people. There was a consensus that Aboriginal people were 'doomed to extinction' and whatever assistance was rendered served primarily to 'smooth the dying pillow'.[12] While the Government took no direct role in establishing schools or reserves, it provided land and financial subsidies to the philanthropic organisations that stepped forward. In the 1860s, the Aborigines Friends Association was granted land in the Lower Lakes region, where it established the Point McLeay Mission. In 1864, concerned citizens in the thriving copper and wheat district of Yorke Peninsula helped establish the Point Pearce Mission. The Lutherans also re-entered the mission field, establishing Killalpaninna in the far North East in 1869 and Hermannsburg in Central Australia in 1874.[13]

The experience of most Aboriginal people in South Australia during the late 19th century was not on missions, but in the pastoral industry. In the sheep and cattle industry developing in the colony's northern and western regions, Aboriginal people emerged as the principal source of labour in country where European workers were often hard to find. In the 1860s, to encourage this development, the Government modified its system of supplying rations by now granting them to remote pastoral stations to give out to the dependents of station workers. This was a system that not only subsidised the cost of labour, and kept Aboriginal people largely in their own country, but also made employers of that labour their de facto Protectors. While Aboriginal people on mission establishments traded off a certain independence for the apparent security offered by the 'reserve', those in the pastoral industry enjoyed a greater degree of independence, albeit subject to the uncertain goodwill of their bosses.[14]

By the time self-government was granted, the colony had recovered from the crisis of the early 1850s and agriculture flourished; by 1859, the colony had over 360,000 acres under cultivation – more than any other Australian colony – and wheat had surpassed copper as its principal export.[15] Besides meeting the demand of the burgeoning markets of the eastern colonies, Great Britain became an increasingly important export market.[16] Major new copper discoveries at Moonta in 1860, Wallaroo in 1861 and Burra in 1869 provided significant economic stimulus to the Mid North, and the colony in general. Where copper had made Burra the second largest population centre in South Australia in 1851, it likewise made Moonta, with a population of 12,000, South Australia's second largest town by 1875. To facilitate the import of coal and the export of ore, Wallaroo developed as the colony's most important seaport after Port Adelaide. The Mid North also became the focus of a burgeoning wine-making industry. By the 1860s, South Australia was producing over 2 million litres of wine, about one-third of which was exported to Great Britain and the other Australian colonies. German settlers, especially in the Barossa Valley, played an important role in the development of the industry. The pioneers included the Bavarian Johann Gramp, who settled at Jacob Creek in 1847, and the Silesian migrant Joseph Seppelt, who planted his vines in 1851. By the 1860s, Seppeltsfield had grown into an impressive estate.[17] Wool also continued to grow in significance and, although not as substantial an export earner as wheat, nor as significant a generator of employment, the demand was sufficient to spur the restless demand for new grazing lands. Most of the expansion was to the north and, to a lesser extent, the east coast. However, by the early 1860s the limits of easy land were being reached. The well-watered, moderately fertile lands exemplified by the Central Hills District were starting to give way to drier, scrubbier, more marginal country.[18]

While wheat farming grew rapidly in the central and northern districts of the colony in the years immediately after self-government, the same cannot be said of the south-eastern district. Pastoralists had early picked the eyes of the country, and what remained was poorly suited to agriculture. The region has an unusual ecology; poorly draining soils and high annual rainfall result in vast areas of the district flooding every year, making it useless for cropping and dangerous to pastoralism because of the prevalence of coast disease. Settlers in the South East, keen to see the district develop, felt neglected and wondered what they were getting for their taxes. In 1861, a secession movement developed. Driven principally by settlers in Victoria's Western District, who felt similarly neglected, the disgruntled coalition petitioned the Government to create a new colony of Princeland. With the Imperial Government unmoved by their complaints, and without widespread support in the region itself, the movement petered out, but the Government was alerted to the need to pay the district more attention.[19] Surveyor General George Goyder was well aware that the construction of a good drainage system would create new agricultural lands and open up new areas to stock holders. Work on the first drains, cut to improve the transport corridor and reduce the district's isolation, commenced in 1863, and by 1864 work was proceeding on swampy country south of Rivoli Bay. This was a long-term project that would continue for decades, but it did succeed in reclaiming vast tracts of land for agriculture and, eventually, forestry.[20]

Exploration is an important investment in the business of colonisation. When settlers first came ashore in 1836, the colony's coastline had been charted, but what lay beyond the horizon was still largely a mystery. Between 1839 and 1842, Edward John Eyre explored parts of the colony's interior: in the southern Flinders Ranges he came to the 'sterile and desolate shores' of Lake Torrens; to the west – crossing the peninsula that would be named after him – he reported that he found nothing of 'interest or utility to the colonists', hardly meeting with 'permanent water anywhere'; while on his last epic expedition across the Nullarbor Plain to King George's Sound in Western Australia, he traversed country that he considered among the 'wildest and most inhospitable wastes of Australia'.[21] The far north-eastern regions of the colony remained unexplored and Charles Sturt still wondered if this central region of the continent might yet reveal an inland sea. His expedition set off in August 1844, but by the summer of 1845 he was literally stranded on the edge of the Simpson Desert. By the end of 1845, with one of the party already dead and others suffering badly from scurvy, Sturt gave up the idea of one last push to the centre of the continent and the expedition retreated south.

Where previous expeditions such as those of Sturt and Eyre had generally been sanctioned by the Imperial Government, they were now the business of the colonies alone. By the 1860s, the lure of what seemed a rapidly diminishing reserve of 'undiscovered country', and the prestige and potential bounty that might be earned in claiming it, encouraged a degree of rivalry among the Australian colonies. The prize at this time was a transcontinental crossing of the continent from south to north. In 1857, the South Australian Government appointed Benjamin Babbage, a colonial engineer, to lead its Northern Exploring Expedition, to conduct a survey of the country between Lake Eyre and Lake Gairdner, and to press further north when that was completed. It was a large and cumbersome expedition carrying every conceivable scientific instrument and creature comfort.[22] Simultaneously, John McDouall Stuart, a surveyor who had accompanied Sturt on his northern expedition, was exploring the same region at the behest of two wealthy colonists: William Finke, who had made his money from mining and land speculation; and James Chambers, who had made a fortune from his carrier business and property holdings.[23] Both men wanted new lands for grazing and whatever mineral lodes could be discovered. With a party of just three men in total, Stuart explored land well north and west of Babbage and returned a local hero; while Babbage's sluggish Northern Exploring Expedition was considered a disappointment.[24] In 1859, the Government, frustrated by the ineptitude of its own expedition, decided it was more strategic to offer rewards of land for those who opened up new country and an additional incentive of £2,000 for the first successful crossing of the continent.[25] Spurred on by this, Finke and Chambers supported Stuart in a series of northern expeditions.

In 1860, Victoria entered the game. With funds from wealthy businessmen and eventual support from the Government, an

Exploration Committee was established to organise a scientific expedition to explore and traverse the interior of the continent. Warburton was touted early as a possible leader of the expedition, but local patriotism eventually saw an inexperienced senior policeman, Robert O'Hara Burke, appointed to lead the Victorian Exploring Expedition.[26] This would be the most lavishly equipped expedition so far undertaken in Australia, comprising 15 men, 27 camels and 23 horses.[27] As the expedition was being planned in the early months of 1860, Stuart, with only two companions and 13 horses, was attempting his first transcontinental crossing. In April, he reached the geographical centre of the continent and by June was as far north as Tennant Creek, but struggling to find water, running out of rations and having been once attacked by Aboriginal people, he decided to turn back.[28] As Stuart returned south to prepare for another attempt, the Victorian Exploring Expedition prepared to advance north.[29] By October and November of 1860, the South Australian and Victorian press were taken up with the excitement of what they termed the 'Great Australian Exploration Race'. Illustrations depicted Burke riding a camel and Stuart a horse, galloping neck and neck through the desert.[30]

On 16 December 1860, Burke and Wills left their depot at Coopers Creek and made for the north coast. Favoured by good weather, they came within a couple of miles of the sea by 9 February 1861, but unable to make it through the bog, they had to turn back.[31] Hurrying south to meet their support party, they reached Coopers Creek on 21 April, only to find that it had left nine hours before. They were stranded.[32] Meanwhile Stuart's fifth expedition tried again, only to be defeated by impassable country near Newcastle Waters in June 1861.[33] Concerns about the fate of Burke and Wills saw a relief party dispatched. Led by Alfred Howitt, it reached Coopers Creek in mid-September, only to discover that Burke and Wills were both dead, with King the only survivor.[34] Stuart's sixth expedition was already under way, leaving from Chambers Creek in northern South Australia in January 1861; it succeeded in reaching the shores of Van Diemen's Gulf on 24 July 1862.[35] The South Australian expedition, with Stuart so ill he was carried on a stretcher for most of the trip south, finally returned to Adelaide in mid-December.[36] On 21 January 1862, huge crowds gathered in

Adelaide to celebrate Stuart's achievement and, by tragic coincidence, on the same day in Melbourne 40,000 mourners watched the funeral procession of Burke and Wills.[37]

With the completion of the 'Great Australian Exploration Race' the central corridor from the salt lakes of the south to the mangrove swamps of the Top End was now finally known. But a question remained: what to do with it? Technically this territory north of the 26th parallel, which stretched from Queensland's western border to the eastern border of Western Australia, was part of New South Wales. However, being unsettled by Europeans, the British regarded it as a no man's land and the gift of the Colonial Office to grant as it saw fit. South Australian pastoralists were keen to possess it and they were a powerful lobby in parliament. Some of them had sponsored Stuart's explorations that had revealed rich grazing country both in the centre of the continent as well as in the Victoria River district. Queensland was also interested. It was geographically contiguous and their own pastoralists were attracted to the rich grazing lands of the Gulf country.[38] Both the South Australian and Queensland governments put their case to the British Government which, in the end, granted most of this 'no man's land' to South Australia. It gave Queensland the eastern portion comprising rich grazing land in the Gulf country. Although the South Australian Government accepted the offer, granted by Letters Patent in 1862, there were mixed feelings. Some regarded it as a potential white elephant, while others, well-schooled in land speculation and with a certain arrogant confidence in the Province's particular skills in colonisation, thought it an opportunity too good to miss.[39]

South Australia treated the settlement of the northern regions of the territory as a colonising exercise and in November 1863 passed an Act that was modelled to some degree on its own origins. The Act authorised the sale of 500,000 acres of country land and 1562 acres of town land. A down payment of £20 per 160-acre block was required with the remainder payable 14 days after allocation. A generous period of five years was allocated to the completion of the surveys. The money raised from land sales was to be devoted to the surveying and administration of the colony, but surprisingly little thought was given to the question of immigration. The sale of preliminary land orders began with a rush in both London and

Adelaide in March 1864.[40] Land speculators, however, dominated the sales, leading historian Peter Donovan to describe it as 'another "Great Land Job"'.[41]

Boyle Travers Finniss, who had been an assistant surveyor with Colonel Light, must have seemed a logical choice to lead the 40-strong surveying team. The Northern Territory Expedition set sail in April 1864 and began surveying the site of the prospective town of Palmerston in June. However, the site that may have seemed ideal in the dry season proved less than ideal in the wet season. So poor was the progress that Finniss was recalled in 1865 and the explorer McKinlay was dispatched to investigate the situation. He was scathing of Finniss's choice of site. By December 1866, £50,000 of the £70,000 raised from the land sales had been spent but little more had been achieved than the planting of 'survey pegs on floody lands that nobody wanted'.[42] The Government decided to withdraw the party while it re-evaluated the situation.

While the South Australian Government was being challenged by the realities of a tropical climate in the north, down south the colonists were experiencing their first serious drought. The effects of the drought, which coincided with an intense El Niño climate phase in the years 1864–66, were felt especially severely in the northern districts.[43] By this time pastoralists had penetrated well into the Flinders Ranges and as far north as Lake Hope. The greatest increase in sheep numbers occurred between 1857 and 1864, doubling from 2 million to 4 million, with much of that growth occurring in these newly opened districts.[44] While the colony had experienced drought before, the severity of this one was truly shocking. By September of 1865, a total of 83 stations reported the loss of at least one-third of their sheep. One station near Leigh Creek reported that it had only 150 cattle left of an original herd of 10,000.[45] The Pastoral Lands Commissioners toured the far North at the end of 1865 and reported that there had been no rain for two years, all vegetation fit for pasture was gone, and dust storms were blowing away what was left of the top soil.

As well as affecting the European settlers in the region, the drought was taking a terrible toll on the Aboriginal population. The drought exacerbated the competition for the diminishing resources of the country, and there was an increase in attacks on settlers' stock. In November 1865, Thomas Elder's property in the northern Flinders was attacked, with one man killed and six others wounded. Despite the losses suffered by the pastoralists, there was still sympathy for the plight of Aboriginal people. Elder himself rose in parliament to plead for assistance for the pastoralists and the Aboriginal people. In the middle of December 1865, a newspaper article looked beyond the drought to the deeper ecological implications. The author pointed out that while they could not avert the drought, the pastoralists' own overstocking of the country was reducing it to desert, causing not only the settlers' stock to perish, but also the native animals upon whom the Aboriginal people relied: 'we have destroyed their food, then abandoned their country, and left them to die'.[46] Dorothy Tunbridge's study suggests that the effects of drought, combined with overgrazing, resulted in the extinction of almost 80% of the small mammals of the region, an important food of the Aboriginal population.[47]

Figure 4.1: Mounted Constable Willshire with members of the Aboriginal police contingent, 1888. The contingent operated in Central Australia in the 1880s. Courtesy of the State Library of South Australia. PRG 280/1/2/119.

As the drought intensified, the Northern Pastoral Association, which had powerful supporters in parliament, lobbied the Government for relief, and the Surveyor General was ordered to investigate. Goyder produced a report that mapped the southern limits of the drought and, more indelibly, defined the boundary between land suitable for agriculture and land best suited to grazing. Broadly speaking, 'Goyder's Line' ran sharply north-west from the Great South Bend of the River Murray to Melrose near the head of Spencer Gulf, before dipping sharply south-west towards the top of Yorke Peninsula and incorporating Eyre Peninsula (see Figure 1.1).[48] Not only were the limits of easy agricultural expansion being reached, but the pastoralists of the Central Hills district were being blamed for 'locking up' good farming land. Anxieties were multiplied when it became apparent that potential farmers were starting to migrate to Victoria where more liberal land laws were in operation.[49] The Government had no choice but to find better ways of getting farmers onto the land.

After much discussion the *Waste Lands Amendment Act* was passed in January 1869. It was known as the Strangways Act after the Premier of the day, and was similar to legislation already in place in Victoria and New South Wales.[50] Under this Act, districts were set aside and designated 'Agricultural Areas' within which farm blocks not exceeding 320 acres were surveyed and put up to auction. Successful bidders were required to pay only 20% of the purchase price, with the remainder due at the end of four years. Credit purchasers were limited to 640 acres, which had to be contiguous, and were obliged to occupy the land within six months. The increase in the size of farm blocks, from the old 80-acre standard, was a significant change and a recognition of the nature of the environment itself. Most importantly, the availability of land on credit made it possible for many more people than ever before to have an opportunity to get onto the land.[51]

During the drought, the settlement of the Northern Territory went onto the back-burner. Instead of 'dreaming of empire' and talking about South Australia's 'position amongst nations', the editor of *The Register* suggested that bread-and-butter concerns, such as roads and water supply, needed to be satisfied.[52] In 1866, Premier Boucaut contemplated abandoning the settlement altogether, but the colony clung to its dream.[53] In 1867, Captain Cadell, famed for his pioneering of river transport on the Murray, was sent to search for a better site for a town settlement, but when he returned in 1868 the picture was no clearer.[54] The situation was becoming urgent as May 1869 was the date by which the land had to be made available to the purchasers, who were becoming both restless and threateningly litigious.[55] In November 1868, Premier Henry Strangways turned to the Surveyor General to get the job done. Goyder was given considerable support, and a new settlement site at Port Darwin was selected. He and his team departed Adelaide aboard the *Moonta* in December 1868 and dropped anchor in early February 1869. He managed to complete the survey of the newly situated Palmerston within a month. By the end of August his team had surveyed almost 660,000 country acres, as well as four town sites.[56] By the end of the year, some settlers began to trickle in, and in June of 1870 William Douglas arrived in Palmerston to take up his post as Government Resident.[57] Douglas had visions of tropical plantations and cheap labour imported from the north, a system he had witnessed first-hand when he had lived in the Dutch East Indies, but other priorities emerged to swamp his imaginings.

In 1855, South Australia appointed Charles Todd Superintendent of Telegraphs. After building the first line from the city to the Port, he negotiated an agreement with the Victorian Government to build a line to Melbourne, which was completed in 1858. In 1859, when New South Wales linked into the Victorian network, the three colonies had a communications system that allowed inter-colonial news to travel in hours rather than weeks.[58] South Australia had the additional advantage of being the first port connected to the network on the shipping route that brought the mail from London. The mail took three months or more to arrive from London, and Adelaide was now the place from which it could be transmitted, at a profit, to the east.[59] Over the course of the 1860s, most of the scattered colonies of the British Empire were gradually being linked by an international telegraphic network, and by 1870 it was a certainty that the British–Australian Telegraph Company would land a submarine cable in northern Australia. But by what route would it be connected to the population centres of south-eastern Australia? Queensland proposed a south-eastern line to Brisbane, while South Australia proposed a line directly south following Stuart's transcontinental route. South Australia intensively lobbied both the company and the British Government, and in June 1870 won the contract on the condition that it be completed by 1 January 1872.[60] Todd immediately set to the task of organising the construction of the line that was to be tackled simultaneously in three sections; one in the south, another in the centre and another in the north. In today's language this was a 'nation-building' project, hugely challenging and expensive. In Adelaide, craftsmen were contracted to build bespoke wagons to transport the specialised components, and in Port Adelaide a timber yard had the job of building 30,000 insulator pins in 10 weeks. In London, Agent-General Francis Dutton arranged for the purchase of over 1,800 miles of galvanised wire and all the necessary telegraphic equipment.[61]

The Central Australian work parties left Adelaide in August 1870, and in the middle of September the first pole was ceremonially erected in the Top End. Pressure for a timely completion was considerable. Work on the southern and central sections proceeded well, but the difficulties of working on the northern section in the wet season were so frustrating that eventually the contractors were fired and Todd himself rushed north to take charge.[62] When the cable-laying ship, the *Hibernia*, steamed into Darwin on 26 October 1871, there were only 40 days to complete the remaining 400 miles. The contractors failed to meet the deadline, which was compensated for by using a pony express to carry messages between the operational sections.[63] The Government's embarrassment was assuaged somewhat by the submarine cable itself failing in June 1872. With the break in the submarine cable eventually found and repaired, and the overland cable completed, the service became fully operational on 21 October 1872.[64] Described today as the 'Victorian internet', the telegraph accelerated the flow of international news, aided the economy by more rapidly disseminating commercial and price information, and generally transferred 'knowledge, instructions and human feelings from city, country, suburbs, capital cities and back again'.[65]

Wakefield and the colony's founders had imagined South Australia becoming a 'little England' and by the 1870s many of those ambitions had been seemingly achieved. By 1871 the population was 213,271, a youthful society with the native-born outnumbering immigrants.[66] It had grown quickly, exceeding Tasmania, Queensland and Western Australia not only in numbers but in economic development.[67] It was overwhelmingly English in origin, with the smallest percentage of Irish of all the colonies, but the highest percentage of Germans.[68] In its desire to produce a 'respectable' citizenry, it tenaciously adhered to its 'no convicts' policy. As late as the 1860s, it was vetting arrivals from Western Australia by making them fill out the colonial equivalent of 'embarkation cards' in which they had to swear that they were not convicts.[69] Wakefield believed that the shortage of women had been a source of moral degradation in the convict colonies and stressed the importance of achieving a balance of the sexes. By 1871, women comprised 48.7% of the population, the nearest to parity in any of the colonies.[70] Susan Marsden argues that this commitment to establishing a family-based society comprising equal numbers of young British men and women, was 'steadfastly maintained, especially through government policies which successfully favoured family-based rural settlement'.[71]

Wakefield had relatively little to say about religion, but the founders' instance on separating Church and State, and their encouragement of the Dissenting Churches had, by the 1870s, produced a distinctive religious culture in South Australia. The English novelist Anthony Trollope visited the Australian colonies in this period and noted that Adelaide was renowned as a 'city of churches', drawing attention to the many churches and chapels that marked the skyline, and the many religious denominations they served.[72] By 1871, the Church of England constituted about 27% of the population, the largest denomination, but Dissenters – namely Baptists, Congregationalists and Methodists – flourished. Methodists comprised over 23%.[73] David Hilliard suggests that the Church of England's influence was especially strong in Adelaide and the larger country towns, and among the gentry and upper classes, while South Australia's 'most potent religious movement' was the Methodists. Their strength lay in the Cornish-dominated mining communities of the Mid North, and the burgeoning northern agricultural communities. One observer described them as 'the rural church of South Australia'.[74]

By contrast with the other colonies, the Catholic proportion of the population was relatively small, its numbers peaking in the 1870s at about 15%. This might be partly explained by the comparatively small Irish portion of the population. A consequence of this small representation was the relative absence of sectarian tensions between the Church of England and the Catholics that were characteristic of New South Wales and Victorian society.[75] To the extent that there was a religious divide in South Australia, it was, Hilliard suggests, 'between the Anglican and the English non-episcopal churches, especially the Methodists'.[76]

While the 1869 Strangways Act was primarily intended to stabilise the agricultural sector, it stimulated a land rush. The implementation of the new scheme fortuitously coincided with a La Niña climate phase between 1870 and 1875, which brought bountiful rainfall to the newly opened agricultural districts.[77] According to historical geographer Michael Williams, a whole new sub-region of colonisation was opened up as farmers moved beyond the Central Hills district into the northern and eastern edges of the Agricultural Areas and the inter-range basins and plain of the Flinders Ranges.[78] Between 1869 and 1881, a total of 5,500,000 acres of land was purchased by cash or credit, exceeding by almost 1 million acres all the land sold prior to that period. Parliamentarians and others now began openly scoffing at Goyder's Line demarcating viable agricultural land and in 1874 one commentator confidently asserted that Goyder's Line had been 'shifted out of the colony'.[79] The boom was so encouraging that the cautionary distinction between Agricultural Areas and Pastoral Areas was disregarded, and by the mid-1870s farmers were taking up new lands beyond Goyder's Line.[80] They did so in what were serendipitously good seasons, which encouraged some to invoke the old English folk wisdom that the 'rain followed the plough'.[81] In October 1878, a northern newspaper reported that 'the "mad rush" of settlers into the remote northern hundreds seems not to be abating'.[82] The population in the Hawker region of the southern Flinders Ranges jumped from 6,000 to 21,000 by the end of the decade.[83] Commenting on this extraordinary period of growth and prosperity, the historical geographer Donald Meinig observed that South Australia 'put her faith in wheat as the single great medium of economic progress ... and it seemed to be vindicated'.[84]

The net loss of people through inter-colonial migration was reversed and in 1876 there was a net gain of 9,000. In that same year, assisted migration was resumed and over the next eight years 25,000 people were attracted to the colony. The social profile of this new wave of assisted emigrants was much the same as those that had preceded them, 'proportionately more English than the rest of Australia, and marginally fewer Scots and Irish'.[85] On arrival, those who had been 'nominated' by South Australian residents were taken in by family or friends. The already established German community saw their brethren continuing to be drawn to the colony and helped by their countrymen to settle in. The other arrivals were assisted by the Immigration Department, given temporary accommodation and free passage to country districts. In the mid-1870s, most immigrants were able to find employment within a few weeks of arrival.[86] Given the economic circumstances, it was farm workers that were in most demand, but many of the emigrants who arrived were seeking urban employment, and were castigated for refusing 'to go out of sight of the Post Office clock'.[87] An agricultural labourer who emigrated to the colony in the mid-1870s with the assistance of his union found work as a ploughman near Mallala, in the lower Mid North. He wrote glowingly of his experience: 'since I got here I have seen some beautiful wheat, good white bread and good meat, and fine brilliant sunshine'. His employer, he wrote, provided him with all the necessary comforts, and he even went out shooting with him. His prospects seemed good: 'Those who wish can soon have land of their own. Government land is £1.5s per acre to be paid off in six years by instalments'.[88]

Most of the small farmers taking up land in the new era of credit selection were not immigrants but South Australians: not necessarily farmers but not ignorant of local conditions. Although the Act allowed selections of up to 640 acres, most took up land a quarter to half that size.[89] This second wave of pioneers typically got started by building wattle and daub houses, before later erecting buildings in stone, a resource that was readily available in most districts.[90] Farming families were generally larger than their urban counterparts, with boys and girls helping with the labour, especially at harvest time.[91] Wheat farming was the obsessive focus of these northern pioneers.

Trollope wrote at length about the selectors who were taking up lands on these new wheat frontiers. He was ambivalent about their prospects. The 'cockatoos', as they were sometimes called, had an advantage over their social equals in Britain because they had the capacity to own land. In just a few years, land purchased by credit selection could be theirs but, he cautioned, their farming practices were poor. Their yields per acre were vastly inferior to those in England, a deficiency only partly compensated for by lower costs. Machines like Ridley's Stripper, for instance, meant that less labour needed to be employed. The selector's life, wrote Trollope, 'is not picturesque, but he cares for nothing', his family 'have plenty to eat and drink', and 'he is nobody's servant'; nonetheless, 'he is a very bad farmer'.[92] It puzzled him that the farmer did not manure the land or rotate his crops, 'he knows nothing of the word fallow', and he makes no attempt to give back to the land 'anything in return from what he takes from it and as a consequence the land deteriorates from day to day'.[93] 'Unless he mends his ways', Trollope warned, 'soon the land which he now ploughs will cease to give him the plenty he desires'.[94]

Trollope liked South Australia, especially the 'pleasant prosperous town' of Adelaide, which, at the time of his visit in 1871, had a population of 61,000 people.[95] He approved of the 'regularity and order' with which it had been laid out, and the fine buildings that were being constructed. He praised the newly constructed Post Office, which was about to become the hub of the new telegraphic network.[96] He concluded his account of Adelaide with the observation that 'no city in Australia gives one more fixedly the idea that Australian colonization has been a success, than does the city of Adelaide'.[97] South Australia had become the third largest colony on the continent by 1860, and in the decade between 1871 and 1881 its population grew from 185,626 to 279,865. By 1881, South Australia was also one of the most urbanised of Australia's colonies, with 33% of its population living in the capital, compared with 31% in Victoria and 30% in New South Wales.[98] But it was also a very distinctive 'city-state' style of concentration, unlike its larger neighbours, which had significant regional centres; South Australia's settled areas were unusually compact with Adelaide serving as the focus.[99] While South Australia was the most urbanised of

Australia's colonies it was, paradoxically, one of the most agrarian, with 60% of the workforce engaged directly or indirectly in agriculture and pastoralism.[100] As the invention of Ridley's Stripper signalled, an agricultural implements manufacturing industry developed early to service the farming industry and by 1875 there were 86 works producing farm implements.[101]

Transport was required to carry the grains and wool to market and, for a time, steamers working the River Murray catered to this need. Captains Cadell and Randell pioneered the use of paddle steamers on the Murray River in the 1850s, and the river trade grew in significance in ensuing decades.[102] Wool was by far the most important commodity that the river steamers carried. Wool bales were collected from locations along the river and transported to the river ports, such as Goolwa and Milang, where they would be unloaded onto trains to take them to Port Adelaide.[103] The river trade was at its peak in the late 1870s and early 1880s, at the very

Figure 4.2: View of Adelaide looking north, 1870. Courtesy of the State Library of South Australia. B 16004/1.

time the Government was borrowing heavily to develop the colony's railways.[104] The significance of river steamers gradually declined as the rail network expanded. In 1875, only 200 miles of track had been laid, but this increased in the next five years to 2,000 miles. By 1880 most farms were 'within a day's journey by cart of a railway station'.[105] Trains needed wagons to transport their loads, and farmers needed carts to get their produce to the trains, all of which encouraged the growth of firms building coaches and carriages.[106] To get these goods to their interstate and overseas markets, new port facilities, such as Port Pirie, were established and existing ones, at places such as Wallaroo and Port Wakefield, were improved.[107]

The growing population, and its concentration in Adelaide and the surrounding settled districts, stimulated commercial and cultural developments. Adelaide's retail centre, which had originally been centred on Hindley Street, migrated into Rundle Street. Iconic South Australian department store John Martin's was flourishing, as were other local retailers, such as Cox Foys, Miller Anderson's and Harris Scarfe's. Rigby's bookshop and newsagency began in 1859 and by the end of the century had become South Australia's leading publishing house.[108] In 1885, the Adelaide Arcade in Rundle Street opened for business. Leading Adelaide photographer Captain Sweet had his photographic studio in the Arcade, from where he sold city and country 'views', did portraits or accepted commissions to produce photographic views of the estates of South Australia's wealthy patricians.[109] Steiner and Wendt, who produced some of the colony's most distinctive silverware, also had a shop in the arcade. Sweet's photographs and Steiner and Wendt's creations were often featured in South Australia's displays at International and Intercolonial Exhibitions during this period. The hoi polloi may not have been able to afford Sweet's portraits for their walls or Wendt's fancy epergnes for their dining tables, but at least they could window shop and perhaps take pride in these signs of colonial progress.

It was in this period that North Terrace began to take shape as Adelaide's principal cultural precinct. The South Australian Society of the Arts' annual exhibitions, held in the Institute Building on North Terrace, had been a feature of the colony's art scene since 1856. In 1880, in an effort to help with the establishment of a permanent art gallery, the Government authorised the expenditure of £2,000 to assemble the nucleus of a national collection. When the Jervois Building, now the Mortlock wing of the State Library, was constructed in the early 1880s, it housed the Public Library and Museum, and also the new National Art Gallery of South Australia. Its first exhibition in its new home attracted over 90,000 visitors.[110]

The prosperity encouraged the Government to develop the colony's education system. From as early as 1851, the South Australian Government provided financial support to schools, although not church schools, and attendance was not compulsory.[111] The wealthy sent their children to Adelaide's prestigious private schools: St Peter's College educated the colony's Anglican elite, while Prince Alfred College catered to 'the children of well-to-do Methodists, rising in the social scale'.[112] It was not until 1875 that the Government introduced compulsory elementary education and henceforth provided most of the primary schools in the colony. The *Education Act* of that year required all children between the ages of seven and 13 to attend 'at least seventy days of school in each half year'.[113] The new system, however, did not take into account the realities of life for many children, especially those living in rural districts, where children's labour was an important element in the family economy, and the rules were changed in 1878 to allow a greater percentage of 'absentee days'.[114] With no provision for religious education in state schools, Sunday school was regarded as a place 'where children could receive an elementary moral education', while at the same time giving their parents a rest. They reached their peak of popularity at the turn of the century, with Methodist Sunday schools accounting for between one-third and one-half of total enrolments.[115]

At first, the colony's new education system reflected social norms, with the education of girls, for instance, slanted toward 'domestic duties' seen fitting for 'future wives and mothers'.[116] However, some saw deficiencies in this approach and argued for a 'superior', more academically oriented, school for girls.[117] The Government agreed and in 1879 the Advanced School for Girls was established in Adelaide, the first state secondary school for girls in Australia. The school educated some 600 girls to a high standard before closing in 1908, partly because of the competition from newly established private schools, such as the Methodist Ladies College, which followed its example. Helen Jones argues that the Advanced School for Girls was a model, 'a foundation stone', of the state secondary school system.[118]

The University of Adelaide was established by an Act of Parliament in 1874. Australia's third university after Sydney and Melbourne, and with foundation professors recruited from Great Britain, it was formally inaugurated in April 1876. The Government gave 5 acres of parkland on North Terrace as the site for the university and two wealthy patrons – W.W. Hughes, who made his money in copper, and pastoralist Thomas Elder – each donated £20,000 to fund foundation chairs.[119] Students had to make do with temporary teaching facilities until the University of Adelaide – the Mitchell Building on North Terrace – was officially opened in 1882.[120] Women were admitted to classes from the very beginning, and comprised 33 of the first 52 students, although it was not until 1881 that they were eligible for degrees.[121] The first woman graduate was Edith Dornwell, who received her degree in science in 1885. Like 13 of the first 14 women graduates, she had been educated at the Advanced School for Girls.[122] South Australia played a pioneering role in the education of women, something which Jones argues became a 'facilitating factor for change' in both raising the status of women and in securing political rights.[123]

The buoyant economic circumstances also meant that by the 1870s many working men and women were acquiring increased leisure time through the gradual winning, industry by industry, of the eight-hour day. When the Saturday half-holiday was also secured, the 'weekend' was invented.[124] The morally righteous in the community were concerned that the working classes might use this time wastefully by, for instance, drinking or gambling, so community leaders encouraged the pursuit of 'rational recreation'. The cornerstone of rational recreation was the Institute movement; a network of government- or council-funded buildings that provided space for the public to hold meetings and lectures, and served as lending libraries, all of which was designed to encourage the very Victorian notion of 'self-improvement'.[125]

Most working people, however, were more interested in sport and leisure activities. Colonial circumstances favoured such pursuits because the abundance of available land provided room for sporting grounds in both town and country. Light's provision of expansive parklands in the city also provided space for more leisurely forms of recreation. The Botanic Gardens, which were established early, were made open to the public in 1857, while the Zoological Gardens were opened in 1883.[126] With the damming of the Torrens Lake in 1881, Adelaideans had a pleasant water feature and a venue for boating, rowing and swimming. The spread of weekend leisure activities to Sunday – whether it be picnicking in the countryside or playing football in the parklands – offended many Christians, especially the Non-Conformists, who campaigned strongly, but vainly, to defend the sanctity of the Sabbath.[127]

As transport technologies improved, trams and trains encouraged the development of team sports, which facilitated, in turn, the emergence of suburban, country, inter-colonial and even international competitions. Cricket had arrived in the colony as an elite sport very early, and the South Australian Cricket Association was established in 1871. In 1874, the legendary W.G. Grace led an English Eleven team on a tour of the Australian colonies. They played a three-day match on the Adelaide Oval in March. Despite the fact that the South Australians were allowed 22 players, they were knocked over in the first innings for 62 and eventually lost by seven wickets.[128] The game of Australian Rules Football, which was developed in Victoria in the 1850s, was readily adopted by South Australians, and in 1877 the South Australian Football Association was established and the Victorian code of rules adopted.[129] By the early 1880s, matches between South Australian and Victorian teams had become a feature of the sporting calendar and were sometimes regarded as a symbol of growing inter-colonial unity.[130]

As Hilliard makes clear, the church was the 'centre of social life and recreational activities' for many people in the 19th century.[131] He suggests that because of their 'numerical strength and ubiquity', the Methodists in particular developed a distinctive subculture, encompassing Christian Endeavour groups, youth fellowships, church choirs, youth camps and sporting clubs. The annual Sunday school picnic was a highlight of the year. Usually held on a public holiday, such as Easter Monday, teachers would take their charges on an outing, perhaps to the beach or to one of the national parks in the

Adelaide Hills. Such events may have been especially important to working-class children for whom such outings were rare.[132]

By the 1870s, the Protestant Churches were becoming increasingly active in political campaigns, especially those involving social and moral issues, such as drinking and gambling, and they gave support to political candidates who endorsed their principles.[133] The Social Purity Society was established in 1882 by Congregationalist minister Joseph Kirby and campaigned on issues such as prostitution and the raising of the age of consent. Its members swore to 'protect ... all women and children from degradation ... and behaviour derogatory to women'.[134] The South Australian branch of the Woman's Christian Temperance Union was established in 1886 and campaigned to restrict the availability of alcohol, which members regarded as a leading cause of violence against women and of family poverty.[135] While easily portrayed as wowsers for their pre-occupation with moral and social purity, they nonetheless played an important role in advocating the protection of women from social and economic exploitation, and in the promotion of their social and political rights. Organisations such as these also provided women, who were excluded from voting and being represented in parliament, with a forum in which to articulate their aspirations. Prominent in the campaign to advance women's rights was novelist and journalist Catherine Helen Spence, whose growing influence was recognised by the Government with her appointment to the State Children's Council in 1886.[136] An important victory in this period was the passage of the *Married Women's Property Act* in 1883–84, which for the first time gave women control over their own property and earnings after marriage.[137]

For the first 30 years of representative government in South Australia, parliament was dominated by the pastoral–mercantile elite. At a time before political parties as we know them today came into existence, governments were made up of shifting and changing alliances among a small ruling elite. To the extent that there was a 'democratic opposition', it came from an alliance of workers and small farmers, the working men and women who suffered most during cyclical droughts and economic downturns. Under the leadership of a small-businessman and city councillor, John Clarke, they formed the Political Association in 1859. Besides advocating the payment of politicians, which would assist working people to enter parliament, they protested at the Government's use of the Land Fund to finance assisted immigration, which they blamed for driving down wages.[138]

With the growth of industry and manufacturing in the boom years of the 1870s, trade unions began to emerge. In 1872, what became the Waterside Workers' Federation was established in South Australia to represent the interests of maritime workers. A Shearers' Union was established in the 1870s and over the course of the next two decades made common cause with its interstate counterparts, coalescing as the Australian Workers' Union in 1894.[139] Miners, who had already demonstrated their capacity for militancy in a major strike at Moonta in 1864, formed their own political association in 1872.[140] To co-ordinate the campaign for fair pay and shorter working hours, the Labour League of South Australia was established in 1874. As a result of its campaign, the Colton Government passed a *Trade Union Act* in 1876, which gave workers the right to strike – the first Act of its type in Australia.[141] Improvements in transport and communication made inter-colonial travel for reasons of work more common; shearers worked sheds in different colonies, and maritime workers shared interests with their inter-colonial brethren. The common interests of workers throughout the colonies became a matter of collective concern, and the first Intercolonial Trade Union Conference was held in 1879. The captains of industry responded by forming their own umbrella organisations; in 1886, the South Australian Employers' Union was formed and shortly afterwards the ship-owners established their own association.[142] As in the rest of the country, politics was beginning to coalesce along class lines.

Where South Australia's prospects had been good in the 1870s, they were becoming increasingly gloomy in the 1880s as another El Niño phase in the early part of the decade saw drought set in once again.[143] Red rust was endemic, locusts swarmed and crop yields dropped to almost nothing, especially in the northern districts beyond Goyder's Line. On the northern plains of Willochra the average yield was 1.5 bushels per acre, and farmers, many of whom had no seed to plant their next crops, pleaded for government help.[144] Farmers began abandoning the North East; in 1883 and 1884, forfeits and surrenders totalled 600,000 acres. The total acreage under wheat in the colony dropped for the first time since the boom began in 1869, and the average yield fell to just 4 bushels per acre – the worst on record.[145] Other sectors of the economy were suffering as well. Increased costs of production led to the closure of mines at Burra in 1877 and Kapunda in the following year, and continued depressed prices in the 1880s saw the newer mines at Wallaroo and Moonta forced to lay off workers and eventually amalgamate.[146] The Province, which had made itself so hugely reliant on agriculture, slumped into depression; unemployment grew, government revenues shrank, and the colony's debt, accumulated during the 1870s to finance infrastructure development and public works, ballooned.

Far from the 'rain following the plough', it might be truer to say that 'drought follows the plough'. Environmental scientist Michael Glantz argues that increases in the 'frequency or intensity of agricultural droughts in marginal areas' are not necessarily the result of 'changing precipitation patterns', but, rather, of 'inappropriate … agricultural' and, one might add, grazing 'practices'.[147] In Australia, the practices that contributed most to 'the deterioration of the ecological equilibrium' were overgrazing, overcultivation, tree clearance, poor water management and the introduction of destructive pests, such as rabbits.[148] The drought and recession of the 1880s brought with it the sobering realisation that the land's finite capacity to provide the abundance that had previously come so easily had to be better managed.

Continued economic growth in the agricultural sector now required movement into regions that had previously been avoided as too difficult, such as the mallee country of the Yorke Peninsula and the Murray Lands, and into the more marginal soils of Eyre Peninsula. Light, sandy soils, dense scrub and increased distance from the coast rendered these areas only marginally profitable. One of the innovations that allowed for a relatively cost-effective form of scrub clearance was the technique known as 'mullenising'; once an area of scrub had been burned, a heavy roller dragged through the scrub by horses or bullocks could do 'the work of a dozen scrub cutters a day'.[149] However, it still left larger roots that interfered with the ploughing. The Government offered prizes for innovative agricultural implements to contend with such problems and a number were developed, but it was the Stump-Jump plough that proved most effective. A spring mechanism allowed the shears to be raised when they struck an obstruction, enabling them to continue ploughing once it had been passed. Some thought it a 'slovenly' solution, but it worked and was in general use by the 1880s.[150]

Australian soils are generally deficient in phosphates and organic matter, and it was clear that old farming methods of cropping the same patch of dirt over and over again led to rapidly diminishing yields.[151] For generations, South Australian farmers had stepped around this problem by simply moving into unfallowed lands. By the end of the 1870s those options were becoming increasingly limited as the choicest land outside of the established agricultural areas was the mallee country of Yorke Peninsula and the Murray Lands, the thinner, inland soils of the Eyre Peninsula, and the swamps of the South East. Diminishing yields, difficult lands and the realities of cyclical droughts required smarter agricultural practices. Science was seen as one response and a new agricultural college at Roseworthy was established in 1879 to investigate and help improve farming practices. The Principal, J.D. Cunstance, demonstrated the virtues of bone dust and guano – superphosphate – as an effective fertiliser that would improve the quality of soils and increase yields. In truth, the benefits of this form of fertiliser had been known for years, but hitherto farmers had ignored the 'experts'. Now the benefits were well-understood and the use of superphosphates gradually became standard practice in South Australian agriculture. Other scientifically driven innovations were employed: fallowing acreages, growing clover to help maintain soil fertility, and developing wheat varieties that were both drought- and rust-resistant. These adaptations helped enable an expansion into more marginal country.[152] Despite the 1890s Depression, the Government continued to develop its rail network, both to aid expansion into these new regions and to make it more cost-effective to get crops to market. This saw a new surge of settlement in the Murray artesian basin, and provided a link to a hitherto under-utilised resource, the River Murray itself.

For 'the driest state in the driest continent', South Australia was slow to undertake large-scale irrigation works. By its nature such work requires cooperative action, which governments are best placed to undertake. In the political and financial climate of the 1880s, the most the Government was willing to do was encourage private initiatives. Up until the 1880s, the River Murray was regarded primarily as a transport corridor, and was largely untapped as a source of domestic or commercial water. In Victoria, the Government had invited the Chaffey brothers from California to help establish an irrigation scheme. Taking advantage of this in 1887, the South Australian Government induced them to establish a similar scheme on the Upper Murray, with the offer of significant acreages and an agreement to lay out the town of Renmark. The emphasis was to be on fruit-growing and viticulture; however, while enthusiasm was high, progress was slow, with only 3,000 acres under irrigation by 1896.[153]

Before the drought set in during the early 1880s, the colony was at the height of its prosperity and its dreamers were expansive. In 1880, Victoria had staged the Melbourne International Exhibition to wide acclaim in its purpose-built 'Industrial Palace'. Talk immediately began about Adelaide staging its own International Exhibition, a 'world show that would deserve to reckon with those magnificent exhibitions in Paris, Philadelphia, and Melbourne'.[154] The Government supported the idea and everyone agreed that the logical time to hold it would be South Australia's Jubilee in 1886. The Treasurer pointed out that the cost would be considerable but, as Melbourne and Sydney had shown, the benefits of promoting trade and raising the Province's image on the world stage were worth the cost. By 1886, he added, the railway line to Melbourne would be completed.[155] With the economic downturn, enthusiasm for the International Exhibition began to wane. When plans of the proposed Exhibition Building were shown in parliament in November 1883, one member said that its grandeur 'wouldn't disgrace the Imperial Government'. What, he asked, was the figure illustrated atop the central dome, 'a distressed selector perhaps?'[156] Given the colony's debt, some suggested that the idea be abandoned altogether, and the money be spent on boosting the colony's manufacturing capacity and supporting employment strategies, while others suggested the exhibition would, in itself, be a stimulus to the economy.[157] The plans were temporarily shelved, but were revived again at the end of 1885. The plan now was for an International Exhibition to commence in June 1887, coinciding with the Queen's Jubilee celebrations, and for it to be funded by a mixture of government and private money.[158]

The Commemoration Day ceremony of 28 December 1886 marked the colony's Jubilee year and the *Weekly Chronicle* proudly reported that 50,000 'patriotic South Australians', travelling by tram and rail alone, had made the 'pilgrimage' to Glenelg.[159] Many visited the 'Old Gum Tree' where Governor Hindmarsh's proclamation formally establishing the colony had been read 50 years before. The festivities at Glenelg, on what was often referred to as South Australia's 'national day', were now well entrenched; South Australia's new gunboat, *The Protector*, would fire a 21-gun salute at midday, 'Old Colonists' would mark the anniversary with a luncheon, and citizens would enjoy the numerous carnival attractions and sporting events staged at the Bay. *The Register* took this anniversary as an opportunity to reflect on the character of the

Figure 4.3: Adelaide Jubilee International Exhibition Building, 1887. Courtesy of the State Library of South Australia. B10212/1.

community that had developed over the past 50 years. The enterprise and daring of the pioneers was such to give a 'tone to the whole community': 'there was developed a kind of national character – brave, earnest, patient, and self-reliant', qualities which had built 'a free, robust, and manly nation'.[160]

This strong feeling of South Australian nationalism ran side by side with a deep emotional attachment to the British Empire. On the day the Jubilee Exhibition was opened, the column inches devoted to praising this 'nation only fifty years of age' were almost equalled by the column inches devoted to eulogising Queen Victoria and the glories of the British Empire. When the Governor proceeded from Government House, at one end of North Terrace, to the Exhibition Building, at the other, he passed through a guard of honour formed by over a thousand troops of South Australia's Volunteer Defence force. When he arrived, the formal proceedings began with the singing of 'God Save the Queen' and when his speech concluded the throng sang the 'Song of Australia', South Australia's national song. South Australia's pride in its independence was not regarded as something that existed in opposition to its status as a British colony, any more than it existed in opposition to its position within the family of Australian colonies. Representatives from all the Australian colonies were present at South Australia's Jubilee; men who, in concert with their South Australian counterparts, were already beginning to imagine what a Federation of the Australian colonies might look like.[161]

Chapter 5

Making a State, 1888–1913

Every year since 1818 New South Wales had celebrated 26 January as the colony's Anniversary Day. Anniversary Day 1888 was different, as it was the hundredth anniversary of Captain Phillip's landing at Botany Bay and an effort was made for the first time to mark the occasion as a continent-wide commemoration of Australian settlement. For all its enthusiasm, New South Wales was in an economic slump and its plan to erect a State House was shelved for a more restrained Centennial Park reclaimed from the Lachlan Swamp. The high point of the week-long celebration was a State Banquet attended by invited dignitaries, including the governors of the seven Australasian colonies.[1] Most of the colonies joined in the celebrations. While everyone acknowledged the emerging 'Federal spirit', the spirit of unity was by no means universal. One Melbourne newspaper rather rudely proclaimed that it was not going to celebrate the day because it did not trace its ancestry to 'sturdy beggars and thieves'.[2] The Adelaide *Advertiser*, while acknowledging that 'bonds which unite us were strong', nonetheless observed that it was not 'in any sense the anniversary of a common birthday, because some of the colonies were established on quite independent terms'.[3]

While travelling through Australasia in the 1870s, English novelist Anthony Trollope remarked that the Australian colonies seemed 'determined to be separate'. He noted that when a minister rose in parliament, he might speak of a 'friendly colony' in the same way that a minister at home might 'call this or that nation a "friendly country"'. 'Australia', he observed, 'is a term that finds no response in the patriotic feeling of any Australian. They are Victorians, or Queenslanders, or men of New South Wales.'[4] What prompted these observations was a discussion of the duties imposed on goods imported from other colonies. While New South Wales was the most vocal advocate of free trade, the other colonies, especially Victoria, adopted protectionist policies. Customs posts were located at most of the important border crossings, be they by road, river, land or sea. Travellers entering Queensland from South Australia's arid North East were greeted by Customs Officers at Birdsville.[5] Railway passengers entering south-eastern South Australia by rail had to disembark at the border town of Wolseley to have their luggage searched and pay import duties if necessary. Colonies vigorously protected their local industries: Victoria, for instance, imposed a tariff of 450% on some South Australian wines.[6]

Border security was not just an issue for colonial trade; it was also a matter of colonial defence. From early in the history of the colony, South Australia had a volunteer militia. In 1854, when Britain and France declared war on Russia, South Australia passed a *Militia Act* to organise and equip a volunteer militia and Artillery Corp. They numbered over 2,000 in 1860, although some of the companies had more the appearance of social clubs.[7] With the removal of British military garrisons in Australia in 1870, the question of colonial defence started to be taken a little more seriously and in 1878 a permanent defence force was established.[8] In the same year work began on the construction of Fort Glanville, a gun emplacement at Semaphore, to protect the entrance to Port Adelaide. When completed in 1882, Fort Glanville became the headquarters of the colony's defence force. Only 19 men were on the payroll: a commander and 18 officers, who would lead a reserve of volunteers ready to be called upon as required.[9] South Australia also commissioned the construction of a warship, the HMCS *Protector*, which arrived for service in 1884.[10] Exactly how the colony's defence force would act in concert with the other colonies, if at all, had yet to be determined or tested.

Concerns over inter-colonial cooperation and coordination were longstanding. As early as the 1840s, during discussions about the prospects of self-government, the Colonial Office had suggested that Federation might be a wise way of dealing with potentially divisive issues, such as trade and tariffs. It was raised again in the 1850s after most of the colonies had achieved self-government but, having just gained their much sought-after legislative autonomy, there was no mood to risk compromising their gains.[11] A historian of Federation and former Premier, John Bannon, suggests that opponents of Federation tended to fall into two camps: the 'inopportunists' and the 'irreconcilables'. The former, he argues, thought Federation inevitable, but not until the colonies had matured politically and socially, while the latter opposed it on principle as 'endangering our colonial independence'.[12] From the 1860s, a number of mechanisms were put in place to contend with important intercolonial issues. Eleven Intercolonial Conferences were held between 1863 and 1890 to deal with matters such as tariffs and trade.[13] The establishment of a Federal Council of Australasia in 1883 was another attempt to achieve a more entrenched form of federal union. The Council met every few years to discuss issues of trade, tariffs and defence, but it had mixed support from the colonies. New South Wales was not a member, and even South Australia, which supported the body, attended on only a few occasions.[14]

As the colonies moved towards greater cooperation, the increasing polarisation of labour and industry was becoming more entrenched. Conflict came to a head in the late 1880s and early 1890s as unionists throughout the country sought to defend their rights to bargain collectively, while the owners of capital defended the principle of individual contracts. The flashpoint in 1890 was a dispute between Australian mercantile marine officers in Victoria, who wanted to affiliate with the Melbourne Trades Hall Council. The Steamship Owners' Association opposed this on the grounds that discipline aboard ships would be undermined if officers and seamen were allied under the same council. Meanwhile, in New South Wales, pastoralists were in dispute with the Shearers' Union over the latter's demand for a 'closed shop' – the principle that only union shearers could be employed. Maritime workers showed their support for the shearers by refusing to handle 'black wool'. The impact of the Maritime Strike began to cascade across the colonies. With shipping at a virtual standstill because of the strike, other industries were affected, such as mills that were forced to shut down because of a shortage of supplies.[15] In September 1890, a total of 5,000 workers were locked out at the Broken Hill mines for supporting the strikers, and in South Australia the smelting works at Port Pirie were shut down. The level of militancy rose when strike-breakers were introduced. On 28 October, a group of unionists at Port Adelaide surrounded and harassed strike-breakers coming off a boat. One of the strike-breakers drew a pistol and levelled it against the mob. Although he was disarmed, the incident led to several days of rioting at the Port. The Premier endeavoured to quell the disturbances with a massive show of force; 500 men, a combination of police and the colony's permanent defence force, marched to Port Adelaide. This escalating series of confrontations lasted 14 weeks, at the end of which the unions backed down.[16]

Organised labour increasingly came to believe that the best chance of achieving reform was through the political process and by 1890 the United Trades and Labour Council was agitating for 'labour candidates' to represent their interests in parliament. To this end, a United Labour Party was established in South Australia. Included in its platform was the payment of members of parliament, the protection of industry and the arbitration of industrial disputes. Success came in 1891 when it managed to have three members elected to the Legislative Council.[17] In response to this labour challenge, Richard Chaffey Baker, one of the leaders of the Council, formed the National Defence League in an effort to unify conservative interests in parliament.[18] Party politics in South Australia was being born, but before it was fully formed, Charles Cameron Kingston, a political radical from Adelaide's establishment, emerged to shape South Australian politics in the 1890s.

Kingston was the son of George Strickland Kingston, who had been an active promoter of the colony while it was planned and who arrived in the foundation years as Deputy Surveyor to William Light. George went on to become a wealthy man through his mining interests and became the first speaker of the colony's first House of Assembly.[19] His son, Charles, excelled at school, trained at the bar and entered politics as the member for West Adelaide in 1881.[20] His private life was marked by scandal – in 1885 he was accused of having an extra-marital affair – and his public life was no less tempestuous. In July 1892, while Chief Secretary in Thomas Playford's administration, Kingston introduced a ground-breaking

Figure 5.1: Charles Cameron Kingston, c.1890. Courtesy of the State Library of South Australia. B 1848.

Bill to establish a Board of Conciliation and Arbitration in order to avoid the sort of industrial chaos that had occurred during the Maritime Strike.[21] In an effort to undermine his Bill, Richard Baker introduced a parallel piece of legislation in the upper house, but one that reflected the conservative aims of the National Defence League. As a consequence of this tactic, the passage of the Bill was stalled as parliament went into its summer recess.[22] The long-standing animosity between the two men came to a surprisingly public climax when, in December 1892, Kingston had a package delivered to Baker's office containing a pistol and a note challenging him to a duel the next day at noon in Victoria Square. Kingston arrived at the appointed hour, but Baker remained in his office where his son was standing guard with a shotgun.[23] The police were waiting for Kingston and he was subsequently charged with inciting a breach of the peace and ordered to pay a surety to 'keep the peace "towards Richard Chaffey Baker and all Her Majesty's liege subjects" for twelve months'.[24] Exactly what purpose Kingston thought this melodramatic theatre might serve is hard to know.

Despite his perceived moral failings and occasional eccentric outbursts, Kingston continued to enjoy the confidence of his working-class supporters in the seat of West Adelaide, being re-elected to parliament in 1893. After this election John Downer formed a ministry but, struggling to maintain support, he resigned and the government benches were offered to Kingston, whose 'radical liberal Government' included 21 Liberal and eight labour members.[25] Kingston's ministry has been called the 'Cabinet of all talents', for the fact that it included three former Premiers: Cockburn, Holder and Playford.[26] With the support of this new coalition of interests, Kingston served as leader of this Government for the next six years, the longest incumbency of a Premier in South Australia until that point in time and, indeed, for many years after.[27]

Not long after the success of the Centennial Exhibition, Victoria's property market crashed. A general economic crisis began in late 1890 when a number of South American countries defaulted on their loans and Barings Bank in London teetered on the verge of bankruptcy. Credit suddenly dried up; banks and building societies, including the State Bank of South Australia, the colony's oldest bank, collapsed; and colonial governments were unable to raise loans on the British market.[28] The liquidity crisis was made worse by the fact that the prices of key exports such as wool and copper were at historic lows, and the effects of yet another drought were being felt in south-eastern Australia.[29] Most of the colonies slumped into Depression. It is estimated that at the height of the crisis Victoria's unemployment rate reached 28%. South Australia's fall was not as severe, but only because it had less distance to fall. These were difficult years. In February 1894, it was reported that almost 100 homeless people were sleeping rough in the Exhibition Grounds, and more on the banks of the Torrens. A meeting of approximately one thousand unemployed people was held in the City Market, and later a deputation of United Trades and Labour Council members met with Kingston to request action.[30] South Australia's population growth, which had been about 5% per annum in the 1870s, fell to about 1% per annum in the mid-1880s, a decline compounded by a pattern of net emigration. Over the course of the 1890s average wages dropped by 20%, and unemployment levels grew. Life on the land became harder; in 1885, there were 155 million acres in use, but within a decade this had fallen to 88 million. South Australia had lost its status as the 'granary of Australia'.[31]

These were the circumstances that Kingston's ministry faced when he took office in 1893; circumstances that encouraged a level of political reform and social experimentation that had hardly been witnessed before in South Australia. Despite his impeccable establishment background, Kingston pursued a radical program. In one speech he described himself as a 'State Socialist – as a man who recognises it is right for the State to interfere for the good of society'.[32] He was not one of the 'labour' men, but his leadership suited them and, with the help of their numbers in the upper house, they assisted him in getting a range of controversial measures through parliament. Many of his reforms were designed to temper the financial crisis, protect working conditions and alleviate the distress of the poor and unemployed. He boosted the government's revenue by introducing new taxes and increasing existing ones, while also reducing expenditure by cutting the salaries of the public service and parliamentarians.[33] In 1895, he created the State Bank, which it was hoped would provide a secure, state-backed source of funding for farmers, producers and development projects, at a time when credit was difficult to obtain.[34] He also introduced important factory legislation to safeguard working conditions, and a conciliation and arbitration system – later adopted federally – to umpire industrial disputes.[35] His Government's reforms were beginning to attract both national and international attention.[36] Irish nationalist and Home Rule advocate Michael Davitt visited South Australia in the middle of Kingston's term and was impressed by what he described as the 'progressive law-making ... of this go-ahead province'.[37]

One of Kingston's more radical initiatives was his Government's support for communal settlements in the newly established irrigation districts on the River Murray. The idea already had currency in Australasian labour circles and was promoted by journalist and socialist William Lane through his Queensland labour journal *The Worker*.[38] Lane failed to garner the necessary support in Australia, but when Paraguay offered 450,000 acres of land, he and a number of followers, including a significant number from South Australia, sailed to South America in July 1893 to establish their socialist utopia there.[39] The idea of communal, or 'cooperative', village settlements, albeit in a modified form, was nonetheless encouraged by Kingston. An Act was passed to allow the Government to advance £50 per head to groups, 'each with £50 capital, who might be settled on Crown land to the extent of 160 acres per person'.[40] The location of the settlements was the new irrigation districts of the River Murray, where these communities concentrated their efforts on fruit growing and vine cultivation. Davitt, who visited the settlements while they were still in the process of being established, described the experiment as 'evidence of the enlightened spirit' in which the colony was trying to 'solve the problem of the unemployed'.[41] Over the course of the 1890s, a total of 13 settlements were established on the River Murray, where they experimented with forms of communal government and collective labour. Despite the idealism, none of them survived much beyond Federation.[42]

Another issue taken up during Kingston's ministry was women's rights and, in particular, the question of women's suffrage. It was Dr Edward Stirling, a lecturer at the University of Adelaide, who in 1885 first introduced a resolution to parliament in support of suffrage for women. In this instance the proposal was limited to single and widowed women, and although the resolution won support, its effect was purely symbolic – a testing of the water, rather than a legislative proposal.[43] A year later, he introduced a Bill for women's enfranchisement, but it faltered. The campaign in support of women's right to vote was galvanised by Mary Lee, who was pivotal in the establishment of the Women's Suffrage League in 1888, which included men and women in its membership and elected Stirling as president.[44] Lee had migrated to Adelaide from Scotland in 1879 at the age of 58 to care for her ill son, and had become involved in the campaign through her work with the Social Purity Society.[45] She worked tirelessly over the next six years, writing on the issue in the press, speaking at public meetings and rallying support from other organisations, such as the United Trades and Labour Council. The Woman's Christian Temperance Union supported the campaign, as did influential author Catherine Helen Spence.[46] In 1891, Spence was a member of a delegation that met with Premier Thomas Playford, and she reminded him that, as an old colonist and taxpayer, she nonetheless had no more right to vote than a 3-year-old child. It was 'perfectly absurd', she argued, 'to condemn half the human race to silence on public questions'.[47]

Kingston, who had previously opposed women's suffrage, was persuaded to support a Bill shortly after he came to office. In September 1893, a Bill enfranchising women was passed by the New Zealand Parliament, giving further momentum to the campaign.[48] The League undertook a petition campaign that received the support of the major Protestant churches, who swung their

Figure 5.2: Catherine Helen Spence, c. 1900. Courtesy of the State Library of South Australia. B 36575.

'moral and social power' behind the campaign.[49] A 'monster' petition in support of women's suffrage, signed by 11,600 South Australians, was presented to parliament in August 1894 and, in the view of Helen Jones, 'contributed powerfully to the shift in formerly uncommitted public opinion'.[50] The Bill was eventually passed in December 1894, giving women not only the right to vote, but also to sit in parliament. Ironically, this latter provision was introduced by opponents of the Bill in the belief that it would be considered a 'step too far' and would ensure the Bill's defeat.[51] Kingston later described the Act as 'the greatest constitutional reform ever effected in the colony'.[52] In the next election both Mary Lee and Catherine Helen Spence were nominated as Labour candidates, but both declined to stand, believing that their social reform campaign was best furthered through non-partisan channels.[53] Women voted for the first time in the elections of March 1896 and the proportion voting for conservative and progressive candidates proved to be no different to that which had prevailed when men alone had the right to vote.[54] Helen Jones argues that although these 'pioneering social initiatives concerning women may have originated in England, the small, relatively homogenous society' of South Australia, 'with its strong liberal emphasis, often enabled reforms and innovations to be established more readily than elsewhere'.[55]

A famous visitor to the colony in the Kingston era was American humourist and novelist Mark Twain. He recorded his impressions of the 1895 visit in the epic travelogue *Following the Equator*. He thought South Australia a tolerant place: not only did it host a bewildering array of religions – he counted about '64 roads to the other world' – but it even tolerated a 'Yankee cabinet minister'.[56] In this Province, he wrote, 'the workingman is sovereign', he is 'a great power everywhere in Australia, but South Australia was his paradise'.[57] Furthermore, the place had a 'most un-English mania for holidays', and 'mainly workingmen's holidays'. He was in Adelaide on one of those holidays, Commemoration Day, which he described as 'the Province's national holiday, its Fourth of July, so to speak'.[58] He attended the Commemoration banquet with the 'Yankee' minister, John Jenkins, and was entertained by the ramblings of Old Settlers, 'living their heroic youth over, in these days of their honoured antiquity'.[59] These 'time-worn veterans', he wrote forgivingly, 'who had laid the foundations of their commonwealth so deep, in liberty and tolerance', deserved to 'hear themselves being praised for their honourable work'.[60]

This was, indeed, a time when the 'pioneers' were being celebrated in art and literature for their contribution to the country's development. As more and more entered their dotage, their memoirs, and stories about them, became a popular genre of literature, frequently appearing in books and pamphlets and serialised in newspapers. The novel *Paving the Way: A Romance of the Australian Bush*, written by pioneering settler Simpson Newland, was first published in 1893. It was serialised in the local press not long before Twain's visit.[61] The book is perhaps South Australia's best-known work of historical fiction and was re-issued many times over the next hundred years. The novel tells the early history of the colony through the adventures of a pioneering settler. As the author notes, the incidents described, though 'romantic, are mainly authentic', and range from the wreck of the *Maria* in 1840 to known frontier massacres of a later period.[62] In the introduction, the author poignantly cautions that 'the time has not yet arrived in the life of Australia when the historian or novelist can write with an untrammelled pen'.[63] In *Following the Equator*, Mark Twain, tongue in cheek perhaps, observes, 'Australian history is always picturesque ... It does not read like history, but like the most beautiful lies'.[64]

The pastoral and agricultural frontiers of which these pioneers had been in the vanguard were reaching their limits. By the first decade of the new century, new agricultural regions were opened up in the east and west, aided, once again, by the Government easing land regulations and funding infrastructure development. On Eyre Peninsula the Government extended the railway from Port Lincoln to Cummins, and by 1900 another 367,000 acres were under cultivation. In the 'Pinnaroo lands' of the Murray Mallee, a new railway was built from Tailem Bend to the Victorian border, and by 1908 the region around Lameroo and Pinnaroo was thriving. Many of the farmers moving into the regions were migrating from the upper North, which had been badly affected by the droughts of the 1880s.[65] The expansion was impressive but, once again, movement beyond Goyder's Line was proven foolish when, in 1914, another severe drought set in and crops failed. As historical geographer Michael Williams observed, there 'was a limit to what superphosphate, new wheat varieties, fallowing and new railways could do'.[66]

During this period, mining emerged again as an important stimulus to the South Australian economy. In the 1880s, when high-grade silver–lead–zinc deposits started to be mined at Broken Hill in New South Wales – just 50 kilometres over the border – South Australia benefited enormously.[67] By 1891 the town's population had grown to 20,000, and by 1893 there were nine major mines, the most important of which were those of the Broken Hill Proprietary Company (BHP).[68] Historian Geoffrey Blainey notes that the region was all but part of South Australia and its growth in the late 1880s was 'akin to a vast program of public works in a sick economy'.[69] With the decline of copper mining in South Australia, this was a new opportunity and many South Australian miners moved to Broken Hill. A corollary of this was the development of a significant Non-Conformist influence in the town, as well as in the labour movement.[70] A further consequence of Broken Hill's growth was the development of Port Pirie, on the northern end of Spencer Gulf, as a major industrial town. During the 1870s, the town had emerged as an important port servicing the burgeoning wheat and wool industry of the north. When a railway to Cockburn, on the South Australian–New South Wales border, was completed in 1887, it also became the destination for Broken Hill ore. In 1889, the British Block Company began smelting operations in the town, and in the 1890s BHP decided to move all its smelting operations there.[71] During the 1890s, the importance of Broken Hill – as well as Western Australia's new eastern goldfields – to the South Australian economy would not have been lost on the colony's leaders, heightening their sensitivity to issues such as cross-border trade and the benefits that might flow from Federation.

While Kingston was presiding over a period of radical reform in South Australia, he was also emerging as a strong proponent of Federation. At the Intercolonial Conference in Melbourne in 1890, the Premier of New South Wales, Sir Henry Parkes, called for a convention to begin devising a Constitution of an Australian Federation. The first National Australian Convention was held in Sydney in 1891 and South Australia was represented by John

Cockburn, the Premier at the time; Thomas Playford, the opposition leader; as well as John Bray, John Downer and Charles Kingston.[72] Kingston played a particularly significant role as a member of the Drafting Committee. With a Bill drafted, the delegates returned to their colonies to persuade their respective parliaments to pass the Bill into law. It would be another 10 years, however, before the process was eventually complete.[73] Interest in Federation waned as leaders focused their minds on dealing with the economic crisis of 1892–93.[74] As Bannon has argued, 'Federation was by no means inevitable'; at various times, union of only selected colonies seemed likely, or only a looser alliance akin to the Federal Council seemed possible, or there may have been no change to the status quo at all.[75] It was by no means a simple process because it meant leaders sacrificing autonomy and power and putting aside self-interest and short-term political gain.[76]

That South Australia emerged as one of the most active supporters of a federal union is somewhat surprising. Of all the Australian colonies, with the possible exception of New South Wales, South Australia had the most assertive sense of colonial nationalism, taking great pride in its distinctive history and its political autonomy.[77] Despite those sentiments, by the 1890s South Australia's leaders had no doubt that the colony's economic and political welfare was best served by Federation. They had become acutely aware of the colony's economic disadvantages and, in light of the sustained economic hardship the colony had endured for over a decade, Federation offered a prospect of reducing these 'points of economic vulnerability'.[78] One of the key concerns of the South Australian delegates at the Federation Conventions during the 1890s was the removal of inter-colonial trade barriers. Wine growers, for instance, were great supporters of Federation; during the 1890s wine production was booming and, while the export trade with Britain was strong, trade barriers continued to limit access to neighbouring colonies.[79] Other priorities included the better management of the River Murray, the construction of inter-colonial railways that would make South Australia a transport hub, and the transfer of the Northern Territory to the Commonwealth. Federation delegates also worked hard to see their recent social reform – the extension of the franchise to women and the establishment of a system of conciliation and arbitration – adopted by the proposed Commonwealth of Australia.[80]

Kingston, John Bannon argues, played a critical role in maintaining the momentum towards Federation, especially on those occasions when enthusiasm seemed to be waning; he was 'always pushing for progress and action, chiding and appealing to his colleagues, demanding deadlines, seizing initiatives, and generally refusing to let go of the concept of a united nation'.[81] Despite their personal and political differences, South Australian delegates to the Convention – most notably Richard Chaffey Baker, Sir John Downer and Thomas Playford – all contributed to the development of the Constitution.[82] La Nauze, in his analysis of the Convention, regarded them as a strong and talented team, 'one and all, sincere federalists'.[83] The Federal Convention, held to draft the new Constitution, took place in Adelaide in March 1897, Sydney in September of the same year and, finally, in Melbourne in March 1898, where the Bill was formally adopted. Put to the vote in 1898, it was initially defeated because New South Wales, while narrowly in favour, failed to reach a requisite quota. Put to the vote again in 1899, after some amendments to appease residents of New South Wales, the five colonies that held a referendum voted in favour (Western Australia held its vote a year later).[84] After Victoria, South Australia was the colony most strongly in support of Federation. In the 1898 referendum, South Australians voted two to one in favour of Federation, while in the successful referendum of the following year that proportion increased to four to one.[85] On 1 January 1901, South Australia, formerly a self-governing 'province' of Great Britain, became a state in the new Commonwealth of Australia.

As South Australians were endorsing the new Commonwealth, they found themselves involved in their first overseas war. British conflict with the Boer settlers of the Transvaal dated back to the early 1880s, and South Australian politicians and the press had offered to dispatch colonial military forces to fight as a show of 'Imperial loyalty', but nothing came of it.[86] In October 1899, however, when war broke out again, South Australia, like the other colonies, contributed troops. The most noteworthy were the mounted troops, who were considered well-equipped to handle the sort of guerrilla warfare that characterised the campaign. Harry 'Breaker' Morant was the most notorious of South Australia's volunteers. A bush poet who had only recently arrived in South Australia from Queensland, where he may have had some familiarity with Australia's 'guerrilla' wars, he took to his role of 'subduing the natives' a little too energetically. Morant and his comrade, Hancock, were charged with shooting Boer prisoners, found guilty of the charges, and executed. South Australians served in six contingents raised in the colony itself and in three composite battalions formed after Federation. By the time the war ended in 1902, a total of 59 South Australians had died in the conflict.[87]

In the first federal election held in March 1901, South Australians elected 12 representatives to the new Commonwealth parliament: six in the House of Representatives and six in the Senate. Many of those elected had played a significant role in the Federation campaign. In Edmund Barton's Federal Government, Frederick J. Holder was elected Speaker of the House of Representatives, Richard Chaffey Baker, the first president of the Senate, and Kingston, Minister of Trade and Customs.[88] It was a stressful term for Kingston in the first ministry as he navigated the nation's first Customs Bill through parliament. In 1903, he resigned from the Ministry, principally because of his objections to changes that Cabinet had made to the Conciliation and Arbitration Bill, though his health was also failing. He continued to serve in federal parliament as a backbencher, and was elected to his seat of Adelaide on two further occasions, but he died in May 1908. Prime Minister Deakin and other members of federal parliament took their place in the funeral cortège that made its way to St Peter's Cathedral on a rainy and sombre May day, in what was said to be one of the largest State funerals ever held in South Australia.[89]

In the closing years of the 19th century, while Kingston's ministry prevailed, the South Australian parliament was dominated by progressive liberals with the support of Labor Party members, but the seeds of 'party politics' were being planted. According to Dean Jaensch's history of state politics in this period, the 1902 election saw both the National Defence League (NDL) and the Labor Party emerge as 'fully organised and active parties'.[90] Labor fared badly in the election, which was dominated by NDL, now renamed the Australian National League (ANL). Labor bounced back in the

1905 elections. Although Richard Butler, a conservative, became Premier, he lost the support of the House in July of that year and Thomas Price was asked to form government. Price became the first member of the Labor Party to serve as Premier.[91] One of the policies of the Labor Party in this period was reform of the upper house, which was dominated by conservatives because of the restrictive property franchise, but the ANL's majority continued to frustrate this ambition.[92] For the conservative side of politics, an important change came in 1910 when the ANL became the Liberal Union and, like the Labor Party, members were now required, in the interests of party discipline, to pledge support for both the party and its platform.[93] By 1912, Jaensch argues, the familiar binary of the Labor Party representing 'a progressive working-class and urban-oriented' constituency and the Liberal Union representing 'a conservative middle-class and rural-oriented' constituency had taken shape.[94]

In federal–state relations, it was the management of the River Murray and the future of the Northern Territory that most tested South Australian politicians in this period. In the 1880s, the River Murray had been the 'great national highway' linking South Australia, Victoria and New South Wales, but by the 1890s it was becoming an increasingly unreliable one as irrigation systems and drought threatened to further compromise flows.[95] During the Federation debates, the question of how best to manage the River Murray was a prime concern of South Australians and it continued to be so in the early years of the new Commonwealth. At first, it was presented primarily as a struggle between the interests of navigation and those of irrigation. A conference held at Corowa in April 1902 proposed the establishment of a Royal Commission to inquire into the 'Conservation and Distribution of the Waters of the River Murray ... for the purposes of Irrigation, Navigation, and Water Supply'.[96] The Inquiry recommended the establishment of a Permanent Commission to manage the waters, a modest series of locks to enhance navigation, as well as an estimated water allocation for each state. It made clear that the interests of navigation should yield to those of general supply to settlers and for irrigation of land.[97] South Australians were outraged. The *Observer* reported the recommendations under the heading 'The River Murray Steal', and described it as an attempt at 'daylight robbery'.[98] It had been hoped that the new Commonwealth Government would devise a 'broad national solution', but it was largely left to South Australia, Victoria and New South Wales to determine a compromise. As discussions progressed over the next decade, the 'navigationists' were rendered irrelevant by the growing dominance of rail, while at the same time South Australia's own irrigation districts grew in significance.[99] A compromise was eventually reached with the River Murray Agreement of 1914, which led to the establishment of the River Murray Commission.[100]

While the River Murray was an asset that the state wanted to protect, the Northern Territory was a liability it wanted to be rid of. After the optimism of the 1860s, the development of the Northern Territory stagnated. Attempts to establish tropical plantations floundered as labour proved difficult to attract. In the 1870s, there were plans to import Indian labour, and an Act was passed in 1872 to facilitate the scheme, but nothing of significance eventuated.[101] Chinese labour was imported in the 1870s to service a short-lived gold rush, and they continued to be a significant proportion of the Territory population until the early years of the 20th century. Apart from working in the goldfields and labouring on the Pine Creek Railway, the Chinese established themselves in business and market gardening.[102] In 1888, the Chinese population of the Territory reached a peak of 7,000, while the European population struggled to reach 1,000.[103] In the same year, fearful of an 'influx' of Chinese into northern Australia, South Australia, in concert with the other Australian colonies, passed a *Chinese Immigration Restriction Act*, and the percentage of Chinese in the Northern Territory gradually declined.[104] Despite the demands for labour, such racial anxieties, especially in regions where European numbers were small, mitigated against any significant non-white immigration.[105] By the turn of the century, the only industry in the Territory that was doing reasonably well was the cattle industry.[106]

In 1910, after over £6,000,000 had been spent on the Northern Territory's development, its non-Aboriginal population stood at just 2,800, most of whom were Chinese. Almost as soon as the first federal parliament was formed, the Premier offered the Territory to the Federal Government on condition that it assume all its liabilities.[107] There was debate in the South Australian parliament about the conditions that might apply to the transfer, with pastoralists seeking the construction of a transcontinental railway to service the cattle industry.[108] From a national perspective, a transcontinental railway from east to west was a greater priority, and a condition for Western Australia entering the Federation.[109] After 10 years of haggling, the Act authorising the transfer of the Territory to the Commonwealth Government was passed by parliament in 1910.[110] The proposed north–south railway linking Adelaide to Darwin would take almost another hundred years to complete.

South Australia and the other colonies slowly emerged from the Depression and, despite a return of drought, economic conditions gradually improved.[111] *The Advertiser*, in welcoming the new century on 1 January 1901, reflected on the 'modern' world that was unfolding; just 50 years before, not a mile of railroad had been laid, and electricity was a mere 'scientific curiosity'. It noted that the frontier of terrestrial exploration at the time was Antarctica, but what of the future? 'Who will venture to say that the moon will not one day be as accurately mapped as the British Islands, and there will not be communication opened with the inhabitants of Mars?'[112] While Premier Price may not have been dreaming of mapping the moon, he was establishing the Metropolitan Tramways Trust, and beginning a network of electrified trams that would soon start spreading into the suburbs.[113] The motor vehicle was seen on South Australian roads. In 1910, there were fewer than 1,000 cars, but about 1,500 motorcycles.[114]

The sensation of the age, however, was aviation. The exploits of pioneer aviators, such as Frenchman Louis Bleriot, were reported widely in the press.[115] In 1910, John Martin's department store in Rundle Street put a Bleriot monoplane on display in its 'Magic Cave' – a basement grotto usually reserved for Father Christmas.[116] One of the earliest attempted flights in South Australia was undertaken by Lieutenant Wilkins, at the Cheltenham Racecourse in October 1911. The aircraft, a Vickers 1, which was intended for use on Douglas Mawson's Antarctic explorations, got off the ground but then crashed, rendering it effectively unusable for Mawson's Australasian Antarctic Expedition.[117] In December 1913, young English aviator Arthur Jones put on a series of successful exhibition flights at the Cheltenham Racecourse before a crowd of

15,000 people. 'Miss Duncan', who was invited to enjoy a 'trip to the clouds', thought the experience 'just lovely', and when asked if she was frightened, answered no, because she was already 'used to riding in motor cars'.[118] Many South Australians would already have seen film of aviators, as cinemas had emerged as a popular form of entertainment. In 1911, the *Daily Herald* reported that the 'picture craze' had captured the public imagination. 'The pictures', it reported, 'have come to stay', observing, 'it will require some extraordinary invention to supplant them in public favor'.[119] At first, movies were shown in rented halls but by 1912, South Australia's first purpose-built 'picture palace', the Pavilion, was operating in Rundle Street.[120]

By the 1890s, the era of land exploration had more or less run its course, but interest in the nature of the country itself – its flora and fauna, its geology and geography – encouraged further exploration for more purely scientific purposes. In 1891–92, Thomas Elder sponsored an expedition composed primarily of scientists to investigate the north-eastern corner of South Australia and adjoining regions of Western Australia and the Northern Territory. In 1894, the Horn Scientific Expedition travelled to Central Australia to study the region's natural history.[121] Sponsored by mining magnate and pastoralist William Horn, the expedition included Adelaide's first professor of physiology and women's rights campaigner, Edward Stirling; his university colleague, the botanist and geologist Ralph Tate; and, from the University of Melbourne, biologist Walter Baldwin Spencer.[122] It was on this expedition that Spencer teamed up with Central Australian telegraph officer Francis James Gillen, whose bush experience gave him an unrivalled knowledge of the Arrernte people. Spencer and Gillen's subsequent collaboration resulted in the 1899 publication of *The Native Tribes of Central Australia*, internationally regarded as a ground-breaking work of anthropology. When they travelled again to northern Australia, their exploits were front-page news.[123]

Another scientific explorer to come to prominence in this period was Douglas Mawson. Educated at the University of Sydney, Mawson was appointed lecturer in petrology and mineralogy at the University of Adelaide in 1905. He was particularly interested in the evidence of ancient glaciation recorded in the rocks of the

Flinders Ranges. A meeting with British Antarctic explorer Thomas Shackleton led to his inclusion in the Nimrod expedition in 1908. Mawson subsequently led the Australasian Antarctic Expedition, 1911–13.[124] His explorations, while producing many important discoveries, are best remembered for one expedition in which two of his colleagues tragically died, while Mawson, in a feat of heroic endurance, struggled back to the base alone.[125]

By the late 19th century the idea of 'White Australia', which conflated the concepts of race and nation, was emerging as an orthodoxy. Australia, in common with other Anglo nations (such as the United States, Canada and New Zealand), felt a need to defend its racial 'purity' against perceived internal and external threats. As Andrew Markus has pointed out, these ideas were buttressed by widespread acceptance of social Darwinism, and 'marked a high point of racial determinism in western culture'.[126] Within Australia the 'threats' to that purity were usually identified with the Chinese, the Japanese, and the Melanesian workers of Queensland. As a leading article in *The Bulletin* observed in 1901: 'Australia rejects the whole Asiatic, African and Kanaka tribe', because they work for lower wages, would 'introduce a lower civilisation' and because they would intermarry and create the 'beginnings of a mongrel race'.[127] It is no surprise that one of the first acts of the new Federal Government was to pass the *Immigration Restriction Act* of 1901. Quite apart from anxieties about the minorities already in Australia were fears of Asiatic nations invading the undefended and 'empty' north of the continent. In the words of Premier Tom Price, speaking in 1908, Australians needed to be ready to protect the 'largely undeveloped and sparsely populated' regions of the continent, such as South Australia's Northern Territory, from the 'jealous eyes of Eastern races'.[128]

Anxieties about White Australia did not develop in response to concerns about Australia's Indigenous population, but did help shape the Aboriginal policy of the era. From the 1860s onwards, Aboriginal welfare had become an increasingly marginal concern of the South Australian Government. Attitudes started to change in the 1890s when it became apparent that the number of Indigenous people, especially those of mixed descent, were increasing. What for generations had been an ideal of 'passive' assimilation was replaced by a belief that assimilation needed to be actively engineered. Most of the Australian colonies had passed Acts for the 'Protection and Control' of Aboriginal people by the end of the 1890s. The provisions of these Acts were designed to segregate Aboriginal people on reserves while controlling the lives of those who lived beyond the boundaries; regulations gave the government authority to restrict their freedom of movement, conditions of employment, rights to marry, and control of their children.[129] South Australia had attempted to introduce an Aborigines Act in 1899, but it failed to go to a vote. While there was a consensus that an Act of this sort was needed, provisions requiring employers of Aboriginal people to have a licence to employ them, and restricting their freedom of movement – ostensibly to protect them from exploitation – were opposed by the powerful pastoral lobby. Aboriginal people were the principal source of labour in the industry and, at a time of economic uncertainty, these provisions were regarded as a threat to their continued employment. Another 'Aborigines' Bill was introduced to parliament in 1911 and, on this occasion, it was passed, with the earlier controls on the conditions of Aboriginal employment removed.[130]

One of the key concerns in the Federation debates of the 1890s had been the question of national defence. Each of the colonies had volunteer militias and an assortment of naval vessels that, after Federation, were combined to form the basis of a national defence force. What began as routine concerns about coordinating national defence acquired great urgency as events unfolded in other parts of the globe. In May 1905, the Anglo world was surprised when the Japanese sank the Russian Fleet in the battle of Tsushima. At the same time, Britain was also increasingly alarmed by the gathering pace of German militarisation and especially its naval build-up.[131] Australia responded by ordering the purchase of new warships, both to augment its own defences and to aid Britain if necessary. It also began to build the nucleus of a national army. It did the latter by implementing a scheme of compulsory military training, under the *National Defence Act* of 1909. For South Australians, this meant dividing the state into two divisions, which were in turn subdivided into 12 regions, each with a training centre.[132] Implemented in 1911, it required youths between the ages of 12 and 18 to register as Junior or Senior Cadets, devoting a prescribed number of hours per year to training. Those between the ages of 18 and 25 were conscripted into Citizens Forces and, like cadets, were required to take part in regular drills, and also participate in camps where more rigorous military training was undertaken.[133] For many South Australians this involvement in military training probably constituted their earliest experience of national service within the new Federation. Indeed, for Prime Minister Alfred Deakin, this reorganisation of Australia's national defence was 'a means of breaking down the divisions between modern national and the older colonial sentiment'.[134] While many people opposed the coercion implicit in the scheme, condemning it as 'child conscription', most supported it, especially as the spectre of war in Europe continued to loom large in their imagination.[135]

For years now, the local press had been anxiously reporting stories that presaged a possible war in Europe. In 1909 came the 'Dreadnought crisis' with claims that Germany was secretly accelerating its construction of battleships and that the Empire needed to match to maintain its naval dominance.[136] European war looked close in 1911 when France and Germany confronted each other in Morocco in what was known as the 'Agadir Crisis'. Even more worrying was the outbreak of the First Balkan War in October 1912, when the Balkan states of Serbia, Greece, Montenegro and Bulgaria confronted the Ottoman Empire.[137] As these events were occurring, Australia's newly commissioned fleet of battle cruisers was being built in British shipyards and dispatched to southern waters.[138] At the end of December 1913, *The Advertiser* reported a speech of Australia's new Governor-General, Lord Denman, a veteran of the Boer War.[139] Denman spoke about the international situation and Australia's preparedness: 'They were living in an age of war and rumours of war', he told his audience, 'and it was impossible to say when trouble would arise again', but he had faith that Australians would contribute nobly to the 'Empire defence'.[140]

Chapter 6

War and Peace, 1914–35

Britain's declaration of war and Australia's pledge of combat troops that followed Germany's invasion of Belgium and France in August 1914 were greeted enthusiastically by many South Australians. On 9 August, the *Advertiser* reported that '[s]eldom has more fervent demonstration of loyalty and devotion to his Majesty the King been given in Adelaide' after an estimated 20,000 people gathered in Elder Park to listen to speeches and sing patriotic songs.[1] The Commonwealth *Defence Act 1903* prohibited the use of established military forces overseas, so the Australian Imperial Force (AIF) had to be raised by voluntary enlistment for service outside the country. South Australians rallied to the call and by the end of World War I a total of 34,959 men between the ages of 18 and 44 had enlisted for service. This constituted an enrolment of 37.6% of those who were eligible. Of those who enlisted, some 29,000 saw active duty outside Australia.[2] Two-thirds of these men were wounded in action and 5,565 were killed.[3]

South Australian recruits constituted the 10th Battalion, which was among the first infantry units raised for the AIF in the weeks following the declaration of war. Together with the 9th, 11th and 12th Battalions, the last of which also included South Australians, it formed the 3rd Brigade. This Brigade was the covering force for the ANZAC landing at Gallipoli on the morning of 25 April 1915 and was the first ashore. Two soldiers of the 10th Battalion – Lance Corporal Philip Robin, a bank accountant from Murray Bridge, and Private Arthur Blackburn, an Adelaide lawyer – are believed to have penetrated further inland than any other Australians that day.[4] Robin was later killed but Blackburn continued on to be commissioned as an officer and awarded the Victoria Cross for bravery at Pozières, in the 10th Battalion's first major battle after being redeployed to France. The 27th Battalion was raised in South Australia in early 1915 and left Australia in June. After training in Egypt, it landed at Gallipoli to relieve other units on 12 September. It too later joined the hostilities in Europe – notably the battle at Pozières in the Somme valley in July 1916 and the battles at Ypres in Flanders – and was followed to the western front by the 43rd and 32nd Battalions, which were also largely comprised of South Australian soldiers. On the eve of the catastrophic advance on German positions near Fromelles on 19 July 1916, Eric Chinner, a 22-year-old bank clerk from Peterborough stationed with the 32nd, wrote: 'I feel sure God will watch over me and pull me through'.[5] Almost two thousand Australian soldiers lost their lives and twice as many were wounded that night and the next day, in what military historian Ross McMullin has called 'the worst 24 hours in Australia's entire history'.[6] Lieutenant Chinner was among them, killed while trying to smother a bomb he dropped when hit by shrapnel.[7]

At least 220 South Australian women also served overseas as part of the Australian Army Nursing Service and the Queen Alexandra Imperial Military Nursing Service.[8] They were joined by female doctors, including Dr Laura Fowler Hope, who had been the first woman to graduate in Medicine at the University of Adelaide in 1891.[9] A further 423 nurses served in military hospitals in Australia. At the start of the war, senior Army officials were more inclined to use trained male soldiers in preference to female nurses for medical duties. Major General Howse, Director of the Army Medical Services, felt that the female nurse (as a substitute for the fully trained male nursing orderly) 'did little toward the actual saving of life in war ... although she might promote a more rapid and complete recovery'.[10] Yet the female nurses quickly proved their worth. They worked in hospitals, on transports, and in casualty clearing stations closer to the front line, serving in Egypt, Lemnos, England, France, Belgium, Greece, Salonika, Palestine, Mesopotamia and India.

Figure 6.1: The 9th and 10th Battalions of the AIF stationed near Cairo, 1915. Courtesy of the State Library of South Australia. SRG 435/1/281

South Australians who remained at home also made sacrifices. Services were disrupted, some essential goods were in short supply, and taxes were increased or new ones imposed to pay for the war, requiring families to be thrifty and resourceful. Women improvised in the home, entered the paid workforce in place of enlisted men, and many volunteered to assist the war effort by raising money, sewing sandbags and clothing for soldiers abroad, and patriotically buying only goods made in Australia and Britain.[11] Children also contributed by making fly-nets for horses in the Palestine campaign, donating their toys to French orphans, and collecting scrap metal for resale or recycling, which helped raise funds for the Red Cross and hospitals.[12] Needless to say, the absence of fathers, brothers and other relatives serving overseas had a profound effect on family life, and wives, mothers and children endured agonising periods of waiting for news about the fate of loved ones. 'How many an Australian mother is waiting, hollow-eyed and heavy-hearted, for news of her son', asked *The Register* on Mother's Day 1915, 'dreading each click of the gate lest it should herald a messenger with the fateful telegram, scanning the casualty columns in terror lest her beloved's name should figure in the lists of the lost.'[13]

Such displays of sacrifice and solidarity during the war are fondly remembered, but they tend to obscure tensions and divisions within society that were obvious at the time. Socialists and members of the left wing of the South Australian labour movement, for example, were not among those gathering in Elder Park to sing patriotic songs. They characterised the war as one of imperialist expansion rather than defence of freedom, initiated by colonial powers but fought by ordinary working people. Business and industry, they argued, profited from the war by filling government orders for military provisions; meanwhile workers had their wages capped and their taxes raised, and lost their jobs due to trade disruption. These were not unwarranted concerns; many businesses and investors prospered during the war while the unemployment rate in Australia rose from a pre-war level of 6.5% to 9.3% in July 1915.[14] The Commonwealth and state arbitration courts moved to freeze wages, so that they rose at less than half the rate of prices between 1914 and 1919,[15] while tax paid per head of South Australian population increased from £1 6s 8d to £2 13s 2d.[16] Other federal taxes followed, including succession duties on estates worth more than £1,000, a tax on admission to popular amusements, and a 'shirker's' tax on the incomes of unenlisted single and widowed men that was so unpopular it was never put into operation.[17]

During this time South Australian trade unions and workers proved unwilling to abandon their demands for fairer working conditions, as some assumed they should in the time of war. In 1916, miners in Broken Hill went on strike during a campaign for a 44-hour working week, and workers in Port Pirie, who were more concerned about the hiring of non-union labour, followed in 1917, affecting the wharves and coal-handling areas. Such was the importance of the work being disrupted that strike-breakers, including the town's mayor, participated in unloading shipments in place of the striking workers.[18] Later in the war, when the conscription of men was proposed, it was the labour movement and the South Australian branch of the Industrial Workers of the World (IWW) that led the campaign against the proposal. The Government used provisions under the Commonwealth's *War Precautions Act 1914* and laws against association to silence the agitators. IWW members were subject to police surveillance and could be arrested for publicly reading the IWW newspaper, *Direct Action*, visiting IWW headquarters or liaising with other members.[19] In August 1917, stalwart IWW members Ted Moyle and Hans Christopherson were arrested for speaking against conscription in Adelaide's Victoria Square without a permit, and a similar event in Broken Hill saw some 30 people arrested as each took to the stage to speak.[20]

Members of the IWW were not the only ones to feel persecuted by provisions of the *War Precautions Act*. The Act enabled the monitoring, restriction and internment of foreign-born or foreign-descended residents as well as the suppression of communications deemed seditious or 'likely to cause disaffection or alarm', 'jeopardize the success of operations' or damage trade and infrastructure. Under this Act South Australia's press and civilian postal communication were censored, causing significant disruption. South Australian newspaper editors quickly raised concerns about whether censorship of information was a legitimate wartime precaution or an act of political suppression. The *Advertiser* argued that military expediency was the only justification for suppressing negative stories, compared to the lesser motivation of protecting public opinion and mood. 'To assume the contrary', it contended, 'is, in fact, to treat the people as if they were mere children and not responsible citizens of a free democracy. ... The constant feeding of the public with optimistic reports of the military situation ... puts the war in an utterly false perspective in the people's minds, and incidentally tends to discourage recruiting.'[21]

As the editorial suggests, soldier recruitment was a concern at the time and was to become another highly divisive issue. Many men who remained at home during the war were ineligible to enlist, being either too young or too old, or failing to meet the physical requirements set by the AIF. Others declined to enlist because of religious or political beliefs, or because they felt it more important to maintain their jobs and support their families. Nonetheless, they all faced constant calls to enlist, often framed in sporting or adventure metaphors that urged men to 'Keep our wicket up!' or answer the 'Coo-ee!' of their soldier mates.[22] As the war moved into its fourth year, recruitment strategies became increasingly desperate and manipulative. South Australian men received letters from R.M. Orchard, minister in charge of recruitment for the Commonwealth Department of Defence, who wrote:

> If [Germany] succeeds, or is not broken utterly, Australia within one or two generations may easily become a German slave-province like Alsace, or Belgium, or Prussian Poland. ... [I]n view of these atrocities, can any man of military age and fitness quietly remain at home without deep dishonour?[23]

Men were further pressured by women, some of whom organised recruitment committees and shunned those who would not enlist. A postcard circulating in 1916 declared: 'Only the brave deserve the fair'.[24]

The issue was inflamed by the proposal of the Australian Prime Minister, William Morris (Billy) Hughes, to conscript men to fight overseas, which resulted in two nation-wide referenda: in October 1916 and December 1917. Many South Australians, led by the Adelaide Quakers and the Australian Freedom League, had objected to compulsory military training before the war, and fought for the repeal of its provision under the Commonwealth *Defence Act 1911*.[25] This stance was maintained during Hughes's campaign for conscription in 1916, when local trade unionists, bolstered by militant miners in Broken Hill, stridently resisted the proposal. When the referendum question was narrowly defeated, South Australia, with its negative vote of 57.6%, was second only to New South Wales. If national support for and against the proposal prior to the vote is any indication, class seemed to be the most influential factor in determining the outcome, with the Labor Party and many trade unions opposing conscription, while the Chambers of Commerce, employers' associations and political conservatives were in favour. In South Australia, the predominantly labouring-class residents of the copper-rich region encompassing the towns of Moonta, Wallaroo and Kadina mostly voted against conscription, for example, despite the majority being members of the Methodist Church, which firmly backed the proposal.[26] South Australia's relatively high proportion of German settlers were blamed by pro-conscriptionists for the strength of the 'No' vote in this state, but farmers concerned about the loss of rural labour and Catholics responding to the British repression of Irish Catholic rebels also voted against conscription.[27]

The referendum result was repeated in December 1917 when a noticeable drop in the negative vote in German-settled areas still left the state's 'No' vote at 56.1%.

The anti-German sentiment that flared during the conscription debates continued throughout the war, causing much heartache for settlers of German descent, who in South Australia constituted a much larger proportion of the population than in any other Australian state. Despite decades of cordial relations between residents of German and non-German origin, and the important economic contributions made by the migrants, the promotion of German culture was now forbidden. The newspaper *Sud-Australische Zeitung* published continuously in South Australia since 1850, was banned, and more than 50 schools using German as the chief language of instruction were closed and their teachers made redundant.[28] In parliament, John Verran, who had served as the state's pre-war Premier, demanded that people of German origin be removed from government departments and introduced a Bill to prevent them from voting in state elections unless their sons had enlisted.[29] Some German settlers felt compelled to change their surnames, and under the state's *Nomenclature Act 1917* sixty-nine place names of German origin – four times more than any other Australian state – were Anglicised, given Aboriginal names or altered to honour notable soldiers or battlefields, with Hahndorf becoming Ambleside, Bethanien changing to Bethany, and Lobethal to Tweedvale. Some of the towns reverted to their original names in 1935 but it took until the mid-1980s for the majority to do so. The career of German-born painter Hans Heysen, renowned for his magnificent gum tree landscapes, also suffered. Despite achieving commercial and critical acclaim prior to the outbreak of hostilities, Heysen's paintings fell out of favour during the war and remained so until a 1921 exhibition restored his position in public esteem.[30]

German settlers, and those originating from other combatant or neutral countries, who were not yet naturalised as British subjects (that is, citizens) faced more dire consequences. Classified as 'enemy aliens', they were subject to internment in a guarded camp established on Torrens Island near Port Adelaide. The camp was considered the worst of all Commonwealth internment facilities, a fact demonstrated in the few photographs of the camp that remain.

One depicts rows of draughty white tents situated on flooded, muddy ground, in which approximately three hundred men slept on wooden boards. Guards at Torrens Island lacked experience and were poorly supervised, which led to offensive and cruel conduct, such as the public whipping of two men who had attempted escape.[31] There were reports of even worse brutalities, including weapons being fired at internees.[32] The camp was closed in August 1915 following a damning investigation, details of which were suppressed at the time, and the internees were either released or moved to Holsworthy Concentration Camp in New South Wales. These were not prisoners of war, it must be remembered, but South Australian residents who were forcibly removed from their families and occupations on suspicion of disloyalty. This atmosphere of suspicion allowed for little appreciation of the sacrifices made during the war by German-Australians such as the Heinrich family of Mount Barker whose three sons served overseas in the AIF; the eldest, Richard, was killed in action while his two brothers were seriously wounded before returning home.[33]

The end of the war in November 1918 brought great joy but also challenges for the South Australian Government. How was it to reintegrate tens of thousands of ex-servicemen, some with severe physical injuries and traumatised minds, into society? Would sufficient jobs and housing be available for them? How might their newly acquired skills be best employed? The Government decided to marry the needs of the men with priorities of its own, namely the settlement and cultivation of land away from Adelaide. Under the closer settlement Acts, large estates in the state's north and elsewhere had been acquired by the government and the land divided for smaller-scale farming. With the introduction of the *Returned Soldiers Settlement Act 1915* and the *Discharged Soldiers Settlement Act 1917* some of these properties became available to ex-servicemen under favourable conditions. Commonwealth loans to the State Government were passed on to settlers for the purchase of stock and equipment, and the payment of these low-interest loans could be postponed until the farms became productive. Of the 7,000 who applied, about 4,180 ex-servicemen were granted land in the lower North, Mid North, Eyre Peninsula and Murray region.[34] Regrettably, many of the farms that they established failed due to the poor quality of the soil, the size of the allotments, the failure to adequately train and resource the farmers, and the lack of business acumen among them. Insufficient transport and food processing facilities also hindered getting produce to market. By 1924 one-quarter of the soldier settlers in the south-east of the state had abandoned, surrendered or transferred their blocks. In 1933, it was reported in parliament that the scheme had been a 'muddle, blunder and disaster'.[35]

Finding accommodation for the returning soldiers and the recommencement of house building was another government priority, as the domestic construction industry had come to a standstill during the war. By offering loans on generous terms, the State Bank financed the construction of thousands of homes in the early-to-mid 1920s, including nearly 400 that were built on the site of the former army camp at Mitcham.[36] This constituted part of what became the carefully planned 'garden suburb' of Colonel Light Gardens, which melded parks, gardens, homes, shops and schools into a neighbourhood designed to attract a diverse mix of residents.

Some of the demand for housing came from new immigrants, who arrived in South Australia in steady numbers after the war. British migrants, offered assisted passages made available by the British Government under the *Empire Settlement Act*, were particularly sought with the hope that they would bring agricultural skills and settle on the land. They came, but many instead chose to settle in the city, or moved there after their farms failed. Several contingents of Italians, Greeks and Yugoslavs also arrived in the mid-to-late 1920s. By this time, there were 314,330 residents of Adelaide, constituting more than 55% of the state's population, a degree of urbanisation matched in Australia only by Victoria.[37]

Three of the main sectors of the economy (mining, manufacturing and agriculture), into which many of the ex-servicemen and migrants entered, had been greatly disrupted by the war. Prior to the conflict, Germany and Belgium purchased millions of tons of copper, lead and zinc concentrates from Australia, much of it shipped from Port Pirie. After hostilities commenced, the Commonwealth Government passed laws to prevent metal exports going into enemy hands, so this trade ceased. The production of metals continued, however, and was quickly consumed by the manufacture of the instruments of war. The Port Pirie smelters passed into the control of the Broken Hill Associated Smelters in 1915, and they were soon producing one-tenth of the world's total output of lead, in addition to quantities of silver and zinc.[38] Employment followed and Port Pirie consequently became the second largest town in South Australia.

Other towns reliant on the mining industry also saw greater activity during and, depending on their resource, after the war. Opal was discovered by a 14-year-old boy at Coober Pedy in 1915. Many returned soldiers made their way to the area, where the unforgiving heat prompted the practice of creating 'dugout' homes burrowed underground rather than conventional houses. A practice perhaps influenced by the trench-digging experience of the war, these subterranean dwellings provided a constant temperature and respite from the climate above. Wartime demand also resulted in rising copper prices that revived the fortunes of copper towns on Yorke Peninsula, but only for the duration of the war.[39] Meanwhile, BHP expanded its mining of iron ore in the Middleback Ranges on Eyre Peninsula. For some years BHP had mined iron ore at Iron Knob, for use at Port Pirie as a flux in the smelting of the Broken Hill ores. With its Broken Hill mine almost depleted, in 1915 the company began steel production in Newcastle, using the rich iron ore deposits at Iron Knob. In the following year, it extracted and processed 188,000 tons of ore, and within five years half a million tons were being produced annually.[40] Despite this activity, South Australians saw relatively little benefit from mining. The contribution of the mining industry to the state's wealth was at its highest in the 1860s, when it constituted between 5% and 8% of the state's gross domestic product. This had fallen to 2% by the 1880s and remained between 2% and 4% until after World War II.[41]

Other industrial developments resulted from the interruption of normal trade during the war. One of the most important of these was the manufacture of motor car bodies. As a consequence of the Commonwealth Government's wartime import ban, two long-standing Adelaide-based saddlery and coach-building businesses were able to transform themselves into modern motor-body building enterprises, Holden's Motor Body Builders Ltd and T.J. Richards and Sons Ltd. Both built large new Adelaide factories, at Woodville and Mitcham respectively, and Holden, in particular, thrived; by 1926 it was producing more than one-half the national output of motor bodies and fulfilling orders for its major customer, General Motors.[42]

The state's agricultural sector did not fare as well. In 1914, it was devastated by one of the worst droughts ever experienced. In the wheat-growing season between April and November, an average of just 6.9 inches of rain was recorded in agricultural areas, resulting in a dramatic reduction in the crop yield.[43] Only 3.5 million bushels of wheat were harvested compared with 16.9 million bushels the previous season.[44] Stock-owners were not spared, and watched in despair as their cattle, sheep and horses died for lack of water and feed. Fortunately rain arrived in the following seasons and good wheat, barley and oat crops could be harvested; 34.1 million bushels of wheat were harvested in 1915–16, followed by 45.7 million bushels the following season.[45] The export of these commodities was hampered, however, by the lack of ships and disruption of trade

Figure 6.2: Workers assemble car chassis at the Holden Motor Body Works in Woodville, 13 February 1928. Courtesy of the History Trust of South Australia. GN06307.

routes due to the war. John Pratt of Two Wells, who had received help from the Drought Relief and Farmers' Assistance Board, wrote to the Crown Lands Office in December 1915: 'though I have had a real good harvest I won't have much left for myself. My only hope is that I can square you all up and get out of it. I am just about full up with farming.'

There were advances in the fields of science, transport and communications during the war and the following decades, and those achieved by South Australians remain a source of pride. The father and son team of William Henry and William Laurence Bragg, who had worked and studied at the University of Adelaide until 1909, received the Nobel Prize in 1915 for their research in the field of X-ray crystallography, the application of which led to later innovations in the production of pharmaceutical medicines and the revelation of the structure of DNA. Adelaide-born Howard Florey, who studied chemistry and medicine at the University of Adelaide during and after the war, began a remarkable career that culminated in him jointly receiving the Nobel Prize for the development of penicillin into an antibiotic treatment, which has saved the lives of millions of people around the world.[46] Mark Oliphant completed an Honours degree in Science at the University of Adelaide in 1922, and then moved overseas to become part of pioneering nuclear physics teams. During World War II, he was a key member of the group that developed the first atomic bomb. More modest, but still fondly recalled, was James Stobie's invention in 1924 of a steel and concrete pole used to support electricity and telephone lines, which solved the problem of the state's lack of suitable timber for the purpose. A few years later, Adelaide engineer Alfred Traeger invented a pedal-powered generator and wireless transceiver, which opened up communication in the outback and enabled the work of the Australian Inland Mission Aerial Medical Service, soon to be known as the Royal Flying Doctor Service.

In the fledgling age of air travel, South Australians Ross and Keith Smith made their acclaimed crossings, first from England to Australia (which took 28 days) in 1919 and then from Melbourne to Adelaide in under five hours in 1920. In 1924, airmail services between Adelaide and Sydney also commenced, helping to shrink the 'tyranny of distance' that had defined the lives of Australians for so long. Personal travel was still largely undertaken on foot and by train, tram and bicycle, however. Improvements were made to the public transport system with the electrification of trams, renovation of the Adelaide Railway Station, and completion of the rail line between Adelaide and Alice Springs. Motor cars also came into wider circulation, with the number of registered vehicles increasing from 11,120 to 79,637 between 1920 and 1928.[47] Living in a flat and dry state with a relatively limited rail network, South Australians adopted the motor car more quickly than their interstate counterparts. By 1921, there were 24 motor vehicles (excluding motorcycles) per 1,000 residents, a rate one-third higher than the second most enthusiastic state, Victoria.[48] As the presence of cars grew, so did demand for better road conditions. The *Highway Act* of 1926 initiated a Federal and State Government joint venture that saw many unsealed roads and water-bound macadam pavement gradually repaved with bitumen and lit by electric streetlights. A speed limit of 15 miles per hour, guard rails and warning signs had already been introduced in South Australia to make roads safer amid increasing fatalities. Horse-drawn transport that had served Adelaide's population for nearly a century would soon disappear. It accounted for about 27% of road traffic in 1924 but less than 6% four years later.[49]

Such improvements in transport and technology were cause for optimism, but were overshadowed by the generally depressed state of the economy after the war. Indeed, a national Royal Commission on the Basic Wage in 1920 found that the real value of wages had been significantly eroded and required increasing by 50% for it to match the standard set by Justice Higgins in the 1907 Harvester judgement.[50] Manufacturing industries, which had seemed so promising prior to Federation and had been producing more in proportion to the state's population than either Victoria or New South Wales, were slipping well behind by the early 1920s.[51] Distance from interstate and overseas markets and the lack of ready access to coal supplies, essential for the generation of power, were major factors curtailing development. Coal needed to be imported from New South Wales by the South Australian railways at a price more than twice that paid by the New South Wales railways in 1927.[52] As a consequence, South Australian rail freight charges and the cost of power were much higher, leaving South Australian manufacturers at a competitive disadvantage.

Other structural weaknesses in the economy were apparent. South Australia continued to rely heavily on agricultural and pastoral production for income and tax revenue, which left it vulnerable to volatility in the international commodity markets. Such reliance also required extensive public investment in transport and port facilities. The State Government spent £11.4 million on upgrading its railways between 1923–24 and 1927–28, and more still providing housing, roads and electricity to the growing urban population.[53] In the short term, these assets provided little monetary return on investment, but they required large-scale public borrowing of overseas capital. As a result, the Government was spending and borrowing more money per capita than any other state; in 1930–31 its repayments of interest on overseas loans alone absorbed 45% of the State Government's income for that financial year.[54] This situation might have been tenable had not South Australian farmers been hit by twin disasters in the mid-1920s: widespread drought and catastrophic falls in the price of wheat and wool. The price of wheat fell because of chronic oversupply in international markets after 1925, while the decline in the price of wool was largely due to competition from synthetic textiles, such as rayon, that were used more extensively after the war.[55] Accordingly, the average wholesale price of wheat dropped by one-third between 1925–26 and 1929–30, and then a one-third again between 1929–30 and 1930–31.[56] The value of the state's wool production fell from £4.9 million to £1.5 million over a similar period.[57] Financial institutions responded to the crisis by withholding credit and increasing interest rates, which left farmers, businesses and the heavily indebted State Government exposed.

Since more than one-third of South Australians directly or indirectly owed their incomes to the agricultural and pastoral industries in the 1920s, it was only a matter of time before the secondary and tertiary sectors of the economy were affected. Farmers, factory owners and businesses could not afford to pay workers, and job losses, wage cuts, and declining consumer purchases were the result. Factory production weakened accordingly, with the gross value of goods produced plunging from £13.1 million in 1927–28 to £6.6 million in 1931–32.[58] All these factors were exacerbated by a credit squeeze and the State Government's desire to reduce public spending. It meant that what became known as the Great Depression occurred some 12 months earlier in South Australia than elsewhere in the country.

According to data collected by trade unions, unemployment in South Australia reached its peak in 1932 when 35.4% of union members were without work. If other records, such as the Census, and the under-reporting of female and youth unemployment are taken into consideration, the actual unemployment rate was likely to be closer to 40%.[59] The Census of June 1933 indicated that over 70% of unemployed people had been totally without work for more than a year, and over 45% had been out of work for more than three years.[60] South Australia maintained the highest level of unemployment throughout the country from late 1927 until early 1935, with Adelaide the worst-affected capital city.[61]

The majority of work-willing people were still in some kind of employment, though they were not necessarily much better off. Approximately one-half of those in employment were working on 'short time' (on average 12 hours less than a full week's work) at the worst point of the Depression.[62] According to the 1933 Census, two-thirds of all male wage and salary earners had received less than £155 in the previous 12 months, well under what was considered to be the basic wage at the time.[63] The real basic wage itself had already been cut by 10% in early 1931 by the Commonwealth and state Arbitration Courts in an effort to restore profits and reduce government spending. Hence, there was an extraordinary number of South Australians who could be defined as the working poor.

The industrial sector of the economy – including the building trades, small manufacturing and motor-body building industry – was the hardest hit. According to the 1933 Census, 42.3% of all males normally employed in the industrial sector were out of work.[64] Holden was a casualty. It produced 46,981 motor bodies and employed some 4,000 workers in 1927, but by the end of 1929 it was being forced to halt production for weeks at a time due to insufficient orders and to diversify into the production of golf-club heads, steel filing cabinets and packing-cases.[65] In 1931, only 1,630 motor bodies were built, and Holden's plight led to a take-over by its largest customer, General Motors.[66]

Working people were not the only class to feel the impact of the Depression. Hundreds of businesses were forced into bankruptcy, crippled by the diminished purchasing power of consumers and the inability of banks to extend credit. Others experienced a sharp decline in income. The 1933 Census suggested that 43.5% of South Australian employers earned less than the minimum wage payable to their employees.[67] Large companies fared better, as most had capital and assets to draw upon and were generally not tied exclusively to the South Australian economy. As a percentage of the total value of output, profits actually improved quite significantly in relation to wages during the Depression, and large companies generally continued to pay dividends to shareholders.[68] They sought to exploit the weakness of their competitors by either acquiring them or merging with them to improve market share.

Those without work during the Depression were not idle during the day, at least not until despondency set in. One man who recalled riding 30 miles for a day's work digging a garden noted: 'You were busy all the time because you would go out looking for work. But you knew you weren't going to get any because fellows were being put off.'[69] Another remembered:

> We would leave in the morning with two pieces of bread with some dripping and pepper and salt on it wrapped in a piece of paper. You didn't have lunch-wraps or anything like that. It would be newspaper. And we walked down to Holden's and got there early in the morning. By the time the gates opened at the side, there would be as many as two thousand men waiting. The gate would open and the fellow would come out and say: 'You, you, and you. That's all for today.' Three or four out of a thousand or two thousand men. You'd just turn around and walk home.[70]

Some men left their families to seek work in the country, though conditions there were not much better and in many cases considerably worse. Some of the state's unemployed found work and lodgings at the Kuitpo Industrial Colony, which was established on land near Willunga by the Methodist minister Samuel Forsyth, and others worked on forestry and reservoir projects initiated by the State Government. More typical was the experience of unemployed men who sought work in Port Augusta and found themselves sleeping in concrete pipes near the rail yards.[71] Farmers, pushed to breaking point by depressed prices, were certainly not hiring. In 1930–31, the price of wheat fell to about 70% the cost of production, so savings had to be made on the land.[72] Oil-guzzling cars and tractors were taken out of service and replaced by horses, which doubled in value because of the demand.[73] Fruit and vegetables could generally be grown in the garden and traded for meat if necessary, but there was little money to buy clothes, which were therefore patched or sewn new from flour bags that were dyed as dark as possible to conceal the brand.[74] It was in this context of need and making do that Mary Jane Warnes of Koomooloo Station east of Burra established the first South Australian branch of what became known as the Country Women's Association. Most farmers drew on advanced government payments for crops not yet harvested, or savings, to pay their creditors, though many repayments were missed. More would have been forced off the land if their banks and lenders had been confident that they could recover their money by selling the properties for a decent price.

The Great Depression is an apt phrase because it applied equally to the economy and to the mindset of the unemployed. As Ray Broomhill has demonstrated in his study of the unemployed in Adelaide, the routine of organised work had come to dominate the physical, social and psychological life of individuals in industrial societies, and was the basis for self-esteem and the maintenance of gender identities.[75] Unemployment was emasculating for men unable to fulfil the role of breadwinner prescribed by society at the time. Their wives were often careful not to ask for assistance with the housework or care of the children for fear of exacerbating their sense of failure. Unable to afford subscriptions or membership fees, the unemployed left social and sporting clubs, and often withdrew from their friends because they could not afford to entertain or reciprocate if kindness was extended to them. Marriages were delayed or broken while it was impossible to envisage a secure future for a family, and sex even within marriage became fraught as the birth of an unplanned child could lead to financial ruin. As a consequence, the marriage rate in South Australia declined by one-third between 1926 and 1931, and the annual number of births dropped by 26% between 1928 and 1934.[76] Women tended to cope with this situation better than their husbands. While they were often denied paid employment, as it was deemed that jobs must go first to men or young single women, their status and perceived importance in the family generally increased as their skills and economies in the home became indispensable for the family's survival.

The South Australian Government was at a loss as to how to respond to the economic crisis. Richard Layton Butler led a Liberal Government in the early phase of the Depression but lost office in 1930 to the Labor Party, under the leadership of Lionel Hill. Hill's administration survived for little over one year before the party split over support for the Premiers' Plan, which involved large cuts in government expenditure, wages and pensions. Hill's stance was deemed to be unduly influenced by the state's Governor, Alexander Hore-Ruthven, British born and raised, who insisted that British creditors must be paid at the expense of public spending, and a group of wealthy businessmen who accompanied Hill to the Premiers' meetings in Melbourne.[77] The split forced Premier Hill into coalition with the conservatives until 1933, when the Labor Party suffered a crushing electoral defeat.

The Butler and Hill governments introduced drought relief and debt adjustment legislation to assist farmers, which subsidised the cost of farming and made it harder to initiate foreclosure and bankruptcy proceedings against them, thus making farmers less of a risk to creditors.[78] The State Government also implemented some job-creation projects and supported those initiated by district councils. But, as in other states, its main support for the unemployed came in the form of relief known as the 'dole' – essentially a food and goods ration – supervised by the Children's Welfare and Public Relief Department and then, after 1930, by the newly established Unemployment Relief Council. Reports of these organisations show that about 21,000 persons were receiving some form of government relief per quarter in 1931, up from 6,121 in 1925.[79] In Government prior to 1930 and then in Opposition, the conservatives' position was to insist that men perform work such as street cleaning or park maintenance in order to receive the ration, but Hill's Government overturned this requirement; expecting a full day's work for much less than the equivalent of the basic wage was deemed unconscionable.

The dole was dispensed in the form of coupons rather than cash, and applying for it was a humiliating process that demanded the unemployed prove their deservedness. Applicants (nearly all of whom were men) had to be out of work for at least four weeks if married and eight weeks if single, and have a Justice of the Peace certify that they were destitute in order to begin the process. The applicant was then visited by a policeman who reported on their economic circumstances: rent, mortgage, debts and current accounts were all scrutinised. The officer looked for evidence of wealth in the form of assets – a piano, paintings, good china or a car – which were expected to have been sold prior to an application for relief being made, but also for signs of respectability; well-mannered and sober people in a tidy house were deemed more trustworthy. Once approved, the unemployed had to wait in a queue every fortnight for ration coupons, at which point they were interrogated about any earnings they had made over the previous fortnight, which might then disqualify them from relief.[80] The Relief Council looked for evidence of fraud at every turn; in 1932–33, three full-time police officers were employed at considerable cost to investigate possible cases, but their work resulted in fewer than 200 convictions.[81] For most people, relief was the last, humiliating resort and not the easy way out. The ration itself was meagre and was reduced as the Depression wore on. Its initial weekly value for adult Adelaide residents was set at 5 shillings 6 pence (children received half a ration), and for those in the country between 5 shillings 6 pence and 7 shillings.[82] By March 1931, its value had been reduced to 4 shillings 11.25 pence (which matched a general reduction in prices), consisting of coupons for poor-quality meat, bread, vegetables, fruit, groceries and milk, and a fixed weight of firewood and candles. This was one-fourteenth of the value of the 'living' wage at the time.[83]

As Ray Broomhill has argued, 'the ordering of the crisis during the Depression made it clear that the welfare of the unemployed was generally subordinate to the overriding concern for political stability, economic orthodoxy and the protection of established financial interests'.[84] The Labor Party in government – or at least Hill's faction that prevailed until the split – was certainly no great friend of the urban worker and, if anything, favoured country-based job-creation schemes, farm relief and rural loan reconstruction initiatives long associated with the ambitions of conservative politicians. This can be partly attributed to the relatively weak industrial base of the labour movement prior to the Depression, and the severe rural bias in the electoral system that made Labor dependent upon winning a large share of the small farmer vote to gain office. The more obvious explanation is that the Labor Government's hands were tied; in greater debt relative to its size than any other state government, it could do little more until international commodity and financial markets improved. It certainly was not alone in failing and fracturing; in an extraordinary move in New South Wales, Labor Premier Jack Lang was removed from office by the Governor after choosing to default on loan payments, and James Scullin's federal Labor Government, which cut public spending and wages on the advice of its largest creditor, the Bank of England, suffered the defection of key ministers and was dismissed by the people at the first opportunity.

Socialists, communists and syndicalists were active throughout this period. They viewed the economic crisis as vindication of their long-proclaimed prophesy that capitalism would inevitably collapse. When the Commonwealth Court of Arbitration delivered its decision to cut real wages by 10% in January 1931, worker representatives who were present in the court, upon gathering their senses, huddled together to sing the 'Red Flag' and issued three cheers for what they expected to be the coming revolution.[85] The two main revolutionary groups in Adelaide, the Industrial Workers of the World (IWW) and the Communist Party, attempted to recruit the unemployed to their cause, though they might have achieved more (and attracted wider membership) had they coordinated their actions and presented a united front. Communist agitators led public protests, and IWW leaders Jack Zwolsman, Ted Moyle, Ted Dickinson, Jim McNeill and Aboriginal orator Ted O'Reilly regularly addressed crowds of people in Victoria Square and Botanic Park, and drew some 5,000 people to a meeting in August 1930 to oppose the Hill Government's proposed wage cuts and tax increases.[86] Again, however, their fierce rhetoric failed to influence government policy or further destabilise the political system. They spent much of their time in jail, or engaged in debates about freedom of speech, or in scuffles with members of the Citizens' League of South Australia, a right-wing political group led by ex-serviceman Edward Daniel Bagot, which sought to break up Leftist gatherings.

Communist and IWW members were more effective when they supported unemployed men and their families in practical ways, such as when they stood within doorframes and opposed the eviction of those who could not meet their mortgage or rent payments. (In 1932–33, two out of every three mortgagors who had borrowed money from the State Bank were in arrears, and half of these were more than a year behind in their payments.[87]) On one occasion, an IWW mob not only prevented an eviction but succeeded in shaming the police into contributing money to funds being raised for the family that was being removed from their home.[88] Without the means for accommodation, some families were forced to live in tents by the banks of the River Torrens or seek shelter in public places, such as Jubilee Oval and the Exhibition Building.

The largest and most violent mass protest that took place during the Depression occurred on 9 January 1931 following the Government's decision to substitute mutton for beef in the ration. Approximately one thousand men, women and children marched from Port Adelaide to the city with banners, placards and red flags, and were joined there by a further one thousand unemployed men who started from the Labour Exchange. Together they marched past Parliament House and arrived at the Treasury Building in King William Street, by which time some were armed with paving stones, wooden spikes and iron bars. Wally Bourne, who participated in the march, recalled:

> [W]hen the door was opened – two big double doors at the Treasury – instead of the minister being there to greet us, there was the police force in all its glory, and behind us – in the half an hour that we'd been waiting there – behind the people, in the square itself, was the mounted police. In other words we were completely ambushed … [W]hen the police came out swinging their batons, they were horribly surprised to see that the unemployed workers were also swinging their batons and taking the blows of their batons on their arms. Now that battle … raged right across the squares. The mounted police were hunting down who they regarded as ring leaders. A lot of them took refuge in a hotel that used to be on the corner. Mounted police actually rode their horses into that hotel chasing two particular chaps …[89]

The *Advertiser* noted that the brawl outside the Treasury Building lasted 20 minutes with 'blood flowing freely on both sides'.[90] As Bourne attests, further violent clashes occurred in Victoria Square as the protesters were beaten back. Twelve men were arrested (six of whom were identified as members of the Communist Party) and 17 were admitted to hospital, including 10 policemen. That evening, a similar-sized protest took place in Port Adelaide, resulting in another violent confrontation with police and further arrests and injuries. The press and the Hill Government blamed communist agitators for the riot,[91] rather than viewing it as a genuine manifestation of despair on the part of the unemployed or as being caused by the over-zealous actions of police officers.

Other protest marches and violent action took place before and after the 'Beef Riot', most notably on the wharfs at Port Adelaide, where union workers attacked 'scab' labour. But, with the exception of the events of 9 January, none was of sufficient size or intensity to pose a real threat to the established order. This can be partly explained by the failure of leadership on the part of the disjointed and occasionally distracted revolutionary organisations that were unable to attract a sizeable following, but also the unwillingness of the trade unions to view the needs of the unemployed as a primary concern. Perhaps more important was the psychological impact of unemployment itself, which left individuals feeling isolated and demoralised, and thus less likely to participate in a mass movement for revolutionary change.[92] Government interventions (such as the ration, job creation projects and legislative attempts to grant renters and mortgagors more leeway in making payments) also proved to be just enough to prevent deep antipathy and desperation taking hold. Many unemployed men with dependent wives and children feared losing the dole, or their prospect of getting publicly funded work, by involving themselves in political activism.[93] Protest and militant action was therefore mainly left to single men and the unemployed of Port Adelaide, a tightly knit and long-standing working-class community.

Protest emerged in other fields of society. Under the 1911 *Aborigines Act* the state's Chief Protector of Aborigines had been given considerable power over the rights and freedoms of Aboriginal people. He was, for instance, made legal guardian of every Aboriginal and 'half-caste' child until the age of 21, regardless of the presence of parents or relatives, with the power to remove them as he saw fit. He had the authority to transfer Aboriginal people or 'half-castes' to reserves or institutions, to move Aboriginal camps from municipalities or towns and to proclaim 'prohibited areas'.[94] Aboriginal people increasingly resented life 'under the Act', and a range of advocacy groups emerged on the local and national stage to demand reform. In South Australia, the most radical was the Aborigines Protection League. Formed in 1926, it began a national petition campaign calling for the establishment of a 'Model Aboriginal State', to be governed by Aboriginal people themselves. Prominent in the early stages of the campaign was Aboriginal inventor and polymath, David Unaipon. Effectively a demand for land rights and self-determination, this proposal failed to gain much support at the time, but it paved the way for the introduction of South Australia's pioneering land rights legislation in the 1960s.[95] The idea for the Aboriginal 'state' may have had its origins in the establishment of South Australia's North-West Reserve in the early 1920s, set aside to protect the traditional people of the region from forced cultural change. These developments eventually led to the establishment of the Ernabella mission on the eastern edge of the reserve in 1937. Set up by medical doctor Charles Duguid, then President of the Aborigines Protection League, the mission was ground-breaking in seeking to be a 'buffer' between Aboriginal people and Europeans, and in advocating for no interference in tribal customs.[96]

In the time of such struggles, South Australians sought diversion and amusement through whatever means available to them. Those who could afford a receiver listened to radio programs after Adelaide's first two stations, 5DN and 5CL, commenced broadcasting in 1924. Interestingly, the Aborigines Protection League used this new medium to promote their cause. The cinema entertained others, including those lucky enough to experience Adelaide's first 'talkie' film, *The Jazz Singer* starring Al Jolson, at the Wondergraph theatre in March 1929.[97] Enchanted by the new technology, a writer in the *Advertiser* claimed that 'through the programme ... the onlooker, who is also the listener, realises thoroughly that the age of miracles is not yet past'.[98] (The success of films with recorded sound did meet some opposition, however, ranging from religious groups, who foresaw difficulty in censoring inappropriate material, to theatre musicians, some of whom were reduced to street busking and living on the breadline as their services became redundant.[99]) The poems and stories of 'battlers' and larrikins written by C.J. Dennis, who was born and raised in rural South Australia, were widely read and made into films. And city residents young and old delighted in the Christmas Pageant, first held in 1933 and sponsored by John Martin's Department Store as a means of bringing cheer and stimulating retail sales at the nadir of the Depression. Held in November, the Pageant has been a much-loved feature on the calendar every year since except for a short period during World War II.

Taking advantage of the Sunday and half-Saturday holiday, and even 'short time' when it was forced on them at work, South Australians also enjoyed taking to the road on their bicycles, picnics by the Torrens or in the park, and visiting the beach. Men were allowed to swim topless for the first time in the late 1930s, following a victorious campaign waged by *The News* against council by-laws that required males to wear neck-to-knee bathing costumes. Women, however, had to wait considerably longer before they too could swim in comfort. The wool and textile industries bemoaned the loss of business created by new bathing suits that required only a fraction of the raw material to produce. The gradual raising of hemlines in women's skirts produced the same effect, occasioning the Australian Wool Board secretary, S.L. Officer, to foresee a 'serious matter for the country' if fashion trends were to continue.[100]

By and large, South Australians did not respond to their financial problems by turning to alcohol, the consumption of which actually declined by almost one-half between 1927 and 1932. Convictions for drunkenness also fell by 63% over the same period.[101] Instead, they found hope and inspiration at the racetrack, where the wonder horse Phar Lap battled exceptional odds to win an unprecedented series of races between 1929 and 1932, including the Melbourne Cup, and at Adelaide Oval, where Don Bradman took up residence with the state cricket team after leaving New South Wales in 1934 and proceeded to flay interstate and international bowling attacks.

It was at the Adelaide Oval where the most unsavoury moment of the infamous 1932–33 'Bodyline' Test series between the English and Australian cricket teams occurred. On 14 January 1933, the second day of the Test match, a record crowd of 50,962 people were appalled to witness a barrage of dangerous and intimidatory short-pitch bowling directed at the bodies and heads of the Australian batsmen, including captain Bill Woodfull who was hit over the heart. The following day, another Australian batsman, Bert Oldfield, suffered a fractured skull when he was hit by an English delivery. Officials were required to separate the seething crowd from the English players, particularly their captain, Douglas Jardine, who had devised the tactic to curtail the effectiveness of players such as Bradman. The Australian Cricket Board accused the English team of 'unsportsmanlike' play, and the English responded by threatening to cancel their tour. The Australian and English public consequently exchanged insults, and South Australia's Governor, Alexander Hore-Ruthven, visiting London at the time, expressed concern that trade between the two nations would likely be affected.[102] The standoff was settled only when the Australian Prime Minister, Joseph Lyons, met with members of the Australian Cricket Board and secured the withdrawal of their complaint by outlining the severe economic hardship that could be caused in Australia if the British public boycotted Australian goods.[103] The Board's original position was vindicated, nonetheless, when the rules of cricket were subsequently modified to ensure that 'bodyline' or 'leg theory' tactics could never again be employed in a cricket match.

Economic laws of supply and demand, and the rules of lending and borrowing, were less easy to amend, but the economic depression and unemployment crisis in Australia and overseas did eventually abate. South Australia's fortunes were improved by increased demand and prices for its agricultural products in the mid-1930s, the devaluation of the Australian pound and the gradual recovery of its primary export markets, particularly the United Kingdom. Reforms in the banking sector and the regulation of loans also saw lending institutions again extend credit to businesses and governments, further stimulating the economy. Still, it took a clever strategy devised by the state's Auditor-General, J.W. Wainwright, which promoted industrial development through government assistance, and the onset of World War II, for manufacturing to recover fully and for surplus labour to be either absorbed into the armed forces or war-supply industries. By this time a new political order had emerged in South Australia. It was the 32-year rule of Liberal and Country League governments led by Premiers Richard Butler and Thomas Playford, whose policies were very much informed by the perceived causes and consequences of the Depression, and the catastrophe of World War II, that were the defining features of the next era of South Australian history.

Chapter 7

Industrialisation and the Playford Legend, mid-1930s to 1965

The economy and social structure of South Australia underwent a profound transformation between the mid-1930s and 1965, while the political party that formed government remained unchanged. This era saw South Australians fight in World War II and coincided with the unprecedented period in office of Premier Tom Playford and the Liberal and Country League (LCL). During this time South Australia's population almost doubled and became more ethnically and culturally diverse in the process. The state's reliance on primary industries (mainly wheat and wool production) for employment and income gave way to rapid growth in the manufacturing sector that was based in Adelaide and newly emerging industrial towns, such as Whyalla. Industrialisation was pursued with the zeal usually associated with the fulfilment of five-year plans in Stalinist Russia and saw factory employment in South Australia grow by 168% between 1939 and 1965, an increase greater than that achieved in any other state over the same period.[1] Coal mines and power stations were also developed in the north of the state, providing a secure and cost-efficient source of energy, and the ready availability of funds for building construction enabled South Australians to move into new rental properties or take up home ownership like never before. In the process, the city of Adelaide was utterly transformed. The flat plains and market gardens between the city centre and the coastal suburbs in the west were filled in, and the newly developed northern and southern suburbs, among them the British migrant havens of Elizabeth and Christies Beach, extended the city's limits.

This transformation, largely viewed as progress, has been attributed to the vision and energy of Premier Tom Playford, and its spoils helped keep him and the LCL in power until 1965. Entering parliament in 1933 and holding the key positions of Premier and Treasurer from 1938, Playford had a reputation for acting unilaterally while his charm and effective negotiating skills allowed him to 'get things done'. But while Playford's resolve and canny political skills were crucial in some respects, the roots of South Australia's transformation and the LCL's electoral success lie elsewhere.

Figure 7.1: Sir Thomas Playford, c. 1938. Courtesy of the State Library of South Australia. B 7756.

Foremost, they lie with the architects of the industrial development of the state, particularly Auditor-General J.W. Wainwright, who held that position from 1934 until 1945. Wainwright's influence on Playford's predecessor, Richard Butler (who served as Premier during 1927–30 and again during 1933–38), and Playford himself far exceeded the remit of his position. Remembered for his hard-working, self-effacing but rather humourless manner – some regarded his glass eye, the result of a childhood accident, as the kinder of the two[2] – Wainwright prepared a series of meticulous and convincing arguments for State intervention in the economy that promoted the manufacturing sector. Other leading advocates of industrialisation included businessmen Edward Holden and Frank Perry, who enjoyed unfettered access to the Premier and sometimes sat alongside Wainwright on government advisory committees and commissions of inquiry. Together they engineered low-cost housing for workers and concessions to industrial firms. Tens of thousands of workers who took jobs in factories and stoked the fires and oiled the cogs of industry also deserve greater credit than they have generally been given in this story. Playford played his part by recognising when others had good ideas and by trusting them, even if this placed him at odds with his previously held views and the *laissez faire* liberals in his own party.

When Butler assumed office for a second time after the defeat of the Labor Government in 1933, he initially felt that salvation from the Depression lay in further expanding agricultural production, the state's traditional source of wealth. However, the volatility of commodity markets and the wider scope for growth in the industrial sector convinced his key advisor, Wainwright, otherwise. Manufacturing in South Australia was stymied by high energy prices due to the necessity of transporting coal from New South Wales, and its distance from the primary markets in the eastern states. Wainwright believed that both industrial firms and migrant workers could be attracted if wages – the primary expense of manufacturing – and the cost of living in South Australia could be kept lower than in the other states. Government provision of infrastructure and concessions would also be required to entice industry development. The threat by General Motors-Holden in 1935 to relocate its manufacturing plant from Woodville in Adelaide to

Fishermans Bend in Victoria because of South Australia's higher rate of taxation and wharfage charges brought this last issue into sharp focus. It was the catalyst for the Government reducing these rates and charges and offering further inducements to other industries. In a number of cases the Government enacted legislation that guaranteed assistance to companies subject to them establishing specific manufacturing facilities. Butler, for example, gave BHP secure mineral rights and committed his Government to build a water pipeline from the River Murray to Whyalla in exchange for the company agreeing to build a blast furnace in that city.[3] (As a backbencher, Playford was a stern critic of the scheme.[4] He changed his mind upon becoming Premier and benefited politically a great deal from its success.) Twenty years later, in 1958, BHP agreed to build a £30 million steel works in Whyalla in return for exclusive rights to prospect for iron ore in the Middleback Ranges and long-term mineral leases.[5]

Wainwright understood that more sustainable means of attracting and retaining industry in South Australia depended on keeping wages and the cost of living below those of Melbourne and Sydney. The basic wage was set by the Arbitration Court which received submissions from employers and unions, but its determination was partly tied to the cost of living, over which government could assert some influence by applying price controls and intervening in the housing market to lower the cost of accommodation. The former was facilitated by the onset of World War II, during which the Commonwealth Government capped the price of many goods in order to prevent profiteering. The South Australian Government assumed this responsibility in 1948 and retained price controls on hundreds of products long after most other Australian state governments had removed them.[6]

Providing cheap public housing was an even more effective strategy as it lowered the cost of living, stimulated the building industry and attracted migrant workers to the state after World War II, when housing shortages were experienced across the country. Moreover, as the new homes were intended for the working class, it helped to placate workers who were being asked to accept comparatively lower nominal wages. As Ernest Anthoney, LCL member in the House of Assembly, cynically suggested: 'what better insurance can we have against the growing menace of Bolshevism than a proper housing scheme'.[7] Wainwright, again, was at the forefront of the housing proposal, arguing that 'some hundreds' of low-rent houses would save industry and state and local government about £330,000 per year directly in wages because of reduced cost-of-living increases.[8] He worked in concert with Keith Wilson, co-founder of the Political Reform League, and Horace Hogben, an accountant and LCL member in Butler's Government after 1933, who were additionally concerned about the sub-standard and relatively short supply of accommodation that resulted from the building industry coming to a standstill during the Depression. The derelict nature of the existing housing stock was confirmed by a government inquiry in 1939 that identified 6,870 decaying slum dwellings in Adelaide that housed nearly 30,000 inhabitants.[9]

Following intense lobbying of the LCL Government that included Playford, then still a backbencher who opposed the proposal,[10] a Housing Trust was established in 1936 with the remit to build low-cost homes for rent by South Australian workers. Subsequent Acts of parliament gave government authorities the power to order the improvement or demolition of sub-standard dwellings and enabled easier terms of finance for prospective home-buyers who wished to free themselves from landlords.[11] While working-class families benefited from these reforms, their plight was not the primary motivation for the establishment of the Housing Trust. If it were, poor people would not have been excluded from renting Trust homes. The Housing Trust meticulously scrutinised applicants and only chose those with unblemished records as tenants, excellent references and a demonstrable ability to meet fortnightly payments. Those who had irregular work and income or who were deemed unlikely to maintain the cleanliness and appearance of a dwelling were turned away.

While relatively few houses were built during World War II due to scarcity of materials and labour, under the direction of Chairman Jack Cartledge and General Manager Alex Ramsay the Housing Trust became the state's de facto economic and metropolitan development authority after 1945.[12] Building was initially restricted to Adelaide, but was extended to Whyalla in 1940 as BHP's blast furnace and ship-building facilities became operational, and to Port Pirie and Port Augusta in 1941, Millicent in 1942 and Mount Gambier in 1945, following industrial and infrastructure developments in those country centres.[13] In 1946, the Trust also began to build homes for sale, targeting middle-class home-buyers and enabling the Trust to invest the profits in further construction. On average it built over 3,250 houses and flats each year between 1950–51 and 1966–67,[14] peaking in 1954 when Trust homes accounted for 47% of all residential dwellings built in South Australia that year.[15] Over the period 1945–70, the Trust provided a remarkable 31% of house and flat completions in South Australia. The comparable percentages for state housing authorities in other states in the same period were 21% in Western Australia, 18% in Tasmania, 15% in Queensland, 14% in New South Wales and 11% in Victoria.[16] The Trust was able to build the homes cheaply and quickly by utilising bulk-purchased materials and in some cases prefabricated structures, and by employing only a limited number of architectural designs that minimised space and adornments. This resulted in some rather austere and repetitive streetscapes, especially before the gardens matured and the dirt roads were paved.

Beginning in 1954, the Housing Trust also developed industrial estates, acquiring land for industrial firms and occasionally building factories, thus determining where they too would be situated. It was the only state housing authority to become involved in such activity. It coordinated the provision of water, sewerage, electricity and other services on industrial estates, and facilitated the extension of roads or rail lines to them if required. It then concentrated the construction of rental accommodation adjacent to these areas. The planning and building of the satellite town of Elizabeth, located 27 kilometres north of the Adelaide CBD, epitomised this model of industrial development.

Established in 1955 and originally intended to house those working at Salisbury's Weapons Research Establishment and other northern suburb industries, Elizabeth soon became a self-sustaining industrial town and merged into the outskirts of Adelaide. International manufacturing firms, such as Pinnock and Kenwood, took up residence, and General Motors-Holden, the state's largest private employer, was also enticed to the area by the Housing Trust's generous provisions. In developing Elizabeth, the

Trust was granted greater powers to oversee the complete planning and provision of the town. This included setting aside land for schools; planting public gardens; and establishing sporting facilities, a shopping centre and a town square – public amenities that were generally lacking in other residential areas developed by the Trust, much to their detriment. Chairman Cartledge also persuaded the Playford Government to permit the Trust to build a free local borrowing library, the first such facility in the city, which was opened in 1957.[17] Despite the intention behind each carefully planned public amenity, residents still brought their own notions about how to use them. The civic hall, for example, saw more games of bingo than concerts or plays.[18] The shops in the town centre were well patronised, though, mostly by women who otherwise found themselves stranded at home, miles away from Adelaide and for many years without public transport, while their partners went to work.

Figure 7.2: Mr Raymond Pinnegar, the Housing Trust's first tenant in Elizabeth, with members of his family outside their new home, November 1955. Courtesy of the State Library of South Australia. B 62138.

Elizabeth absorbed much of Adelaide's additional population when the city as a whole was experiencing its most rapid growth and highest rates of immigration since the 19th century. Between 1954 and 1966 the population of the northern Adelaide Plains, incorporating the Elizabeth and Salisbury areas, increased almost ten-fold to 68,711.[19] There was a shortage of housing in most Australian capital cities, but British migrants could secure employment and a home in Elizabeth within a couple of weeks of arrival, which many preferred over being accommodated in a hostel for months at a time. The Housing Trust was active in recruiting such migrants and, through an office it established in London, ran a Migrant House Purchase Scheme that attracted many British couples and families.[20] By 1966, British-born residents constituted 44.5% of Elizabeth's population, making it one of the most 'British' residential areas in Australia.[21] Amelia Redmond, who rented a Trust home, provides a sense of what it was like for the new arrivals:

> We were offered a house in Elizabeth Downs ... It was a lovely spanking new place but at the end of civilisation. Houses were put up so quickly there were no roads, lights, paths or driveways. You stepped from a sea of red mud into the lounge ... At night it looked like we were on the edge of nowhere. ... We walked everywhere – there were no buses – only the trains and the nearest station was Broadmeadows way over to the west – a long way when the roads were unmade. You got taller as your shoes picked up the red mud – it dried like concrete.[22]

By the mid-1960s, however, the city had taken shape. Elizabeth now had a new shopping centre, a department store, a swimming pool and two theatres. Moreover, as Redmond recalls, 'our high school was tops in the late [19]60s and into the '70s, matriculations were one of the highest in Adelaide ... [and] the buses took on a new look and came more than twice a day'.[23]

Her claim about the success of Elizabeth's high school was true, and is testament to the endeavour of migrant parents who encouraged (and sometimes bullied) their children to succeed and make the most of their opportunities, a story that has been repeated with each new wave of migrants who settled in the state. These included Germans and Dutch who also settled in Elizabeth in high numbers, Italians and Greeks, and Central and Eastern Europeans (such as

Poles, Latvians, Lithuanians and Czechs), who arrived as Displaced Persons soon after World War II. The latter were initially accommodated in outlying migrant hostels in places such as Smithfield, Mallala and Willaston before being distributed throughout country areas and Adelaide. These hostels were usually crude rows of corrugated iron and asbestos shelters or converted barracks on recommissioned Defence Force property. Displaced Persons needed to sign and fulfil two-year work contracts in order to be chosen to come to Australia, and had little choice about where they were settled during this time. These migrants became both essential workers in the now-thriving manufacturing and construction industries, and a key new market for the products that were being manufactured, grown and built.

World War II provided another means of stimulating the economy, especially the manufacturing sector, and enabled jobs to be found for those still wanting in the late 1930s. Essington Lewis, the Managing Director of BHP, who was South Australian born and educated, exploited the opportunities that the onset of war provided. He cannily predicted an increased demand for iron and steel products and shipbuilding as war in Europe and Asia loomed, and negotiated with the Butler and then Playford governments to establish such facilities in Whyalla.[24] Once just a tiny country town, its population grew from about 1,100 in 1939 to nearly 8,000 by the end of the war.

During the war, Wainwright (who served the Commonwealth as South Australia's Deputy Director of War Organisation of Industry) and Playford actively lobbied Lewis (who became Director-General of Munitions from June 1940) and Norman Makin (Minister of Munitions) for government war contracts.[25] They argued that Fremantle and Sydney were unsuitable locations for war-related industries because they were most likely to be attacked, whereas South Australia's southern-most position kept it relatively safe from enemy action. They also noted that Adelaide's advanced motor vehicle industry and the facilities of the South Australian railway workshops could manufacture munitions equipment. Finally, they pointed to South Australia's largely under-employed, regionally distributed population, which was available to work in war-related industries.[26] The Commonwealth Government was convinced, and three major munitions plants were built in Adelaide's west and north at Finsbury, Hendon and Penfield (in the district of Salisbury) in 1940 and 1941. The Penfield works consisted of 1,405 buildings covering an area of 3,672 acres and employed approximately 6,400 people.[27] Along with the Islington railway workshops, which produced shells and components for Beaufort bombers, they formed the backbone of the state's industrial contribution to the war. By 1942, at least 87 metropolitan manufacturers were also under contract to the Ministry of Munitions. General Motors-Holden became engaged entirely on defence projects, manufacturing aircraft components, armoured vehicles, marine craft, torpedoes and weapons, and its workers – some 5,000 at its Woodville plant – became government employees for most of the war's duration.[28] Factories in regional centres (such as Peterborough, Port Pirie, Murray Bridge and Whyalla) also manufactured products for the war and soaked up the state's surplus labour.[29]

The large munitions factories were refitted after the war and became the basis of further industrial development. By August 1946, every available building except two at the Finsbury works had been acquired or leased by private industry, these being mainly devoted to engineering, automotive and whitegoods production.[30] In 1947, the entire plant at Hendon was purchased by Philips Electrical Industries, which moved its production headquarters from Sydney and was soon employing nearly 3,500 workers.[31] Philips was the country's largest producer of electronic components and its Hendon plant became a major centre of technological skill development and research. The enormous Penfield complex was occupied by the Commonwealth's Department of Defence after the war for the development and testing of weapons, particularly rockets.

The war exposed South Australia's reliance on imported coal as a source of energy and became the catalyst for a decision that furthered the development of industry in the state. When Playford took office, the Adelaide Electric Supply Company (AESC) had a virtual monopoly on power supply in Adelaide and some rural areas. It largely relied on the importation of black coal from New South Wales as its source material, the cost for which was transferred to private consumers and manufacturers. This monopoly, as well as the disruption to coal supplies due to striking miners in New

South Wales that caused crippling 'black outs' in South Australia during and after the war,[32] compelled Playford to seek control of energy production. He wanted AESC to generate power from the lower-grade so-called 'brown' coal reserves at Leigh Creek in the Mid North. Claiming it was unsuitable for use in its boilers, the company refused to comply. Following Wainwright's advice, the Government proposed limiting the price that could be charged for electricity and capping dividends paid to AESC shareholders, measures that were also firmly resisted by the company.[33] Tensions between both parties led to a Royal Commission (Wainwright served as one of the three commissioners), which recommended the acquisition of AESC by the state.

Playford's decision to pursue this course of action divided parliament and the broader community and threatened to split his own party, which was founded on the principles of private enterprise and limited government interference. Of the 17 witnesses who gave evidence to the Royal Commission, only two – a representative from the Communist Party and Australian Labor Party (ALP) leader R.S. Richards – pushed for acquisition. Edward Holden, who served as a Liberal in the Legislative Council during 1935–47 and was one of Playford's key allies and chief beneficiaries of the industrialisation plan, refused to vote for the government take-over, as did the leader of the LCL in the Legislative Council, Collier Cudmore, who famously labelled Playford a 'Bolshevik'.[34] Naturally AESC also rejected the proposal, with director Stanley Murray buying advertising space in country newspapers to make the company's case to shareholders living in the LCL's heartland.[35] The Bill to absorb AESC and establish a Trust to take over its assets and operations, although supported by the ALP in the House of Assembly, was defeated in the Legislative Council by LCL member Sir Walter Duncan's casting vote in December 1945.[36] However, with minor amendments and some political wrangling, the Bill was passed in 1946. Over the next seven years AESC was entirely absorbed into the new Electricity Trust of South Australia (ETSA), which also took over operation of the Leigh Creek mine in 1948. Within a decade it became the state's primary source of coal,[37] and South Australian consumers were enjoying some of the lowest-priced electricity in the Commonwealth.[38]

Playford could now promise interstate and overseas industrial firms secure access to reasonably priced power. He could also entice them by pointing to South Australia's reputation for industrial peace. This was not an idle boast. For all but one decade between 1913 and 1997 South Australia recorded the lowest number of working days lost to strikes in the country.[39] The number of days lost in South Australia fluctuated between one-third and one-half of the national average, reaching the lowest point in the 1930s when an annual average of only 19 working days per 1,000 workers were lost (compared to 852 days in New South Wales, 155 days in Victoria and 244 days in Queensland – South Australia's main competitors in attracting industrial development).[40] The insecurity fostered by the Depression, and the failure of union action to alleviate the plight of workers, certainly contributed to this. But the earlier and later trends point to further deep-rooted reasons for the moderation of the labour movement. These include the state's effective system of compulsory arbitration and the corporate sector's encouragement of labour compliance by making strategic concessions regarding wages and conditions at key moments.[41] The religious and ideological orientation of the South Australian workforce – composed of a higher proportion of moderate-minded Methodists and Non-Conformists and a relatively smaller number of traditionally more militant Irish Catholics compared to other states – also cannot be overlooked.[42] After coming to power, Playford took additional steps to ensure cordial relations between workers and their employers, and that unions, in particular, were in step with his plans for industrial development.[43]

Agriculture was not ignored during this time and, like manufacturing, received a boost. In the 1950s, most farming districts underwent a quiet revolution with the adoption of new methods and the almost complete replacement of horse teams with tractors. Barley assumed much greater significance, and in some years surpassed the area planted with wheat. Contour banks were constructed, which diminished the threat of sheet wash and gully erosion. Medics and subterranean clover, whose value as a fodder crop was first discovered and enthusiastically promoted by a South Australian farmer, Amos Howard, were incorporated into rotations of temporary pastures and grain crops.[44] This added nitrogen and structure to the soil, and provided feed for livestock. As a result, grain yields improved substantially and the size of South Australia's sheep flock increased by two-thirds between 1950 and 1959, a rate of growth not seen since the early 1860s.[45]

The ironstone and sandy soils in higher rainfall areas that had earlier been judged too infertile for farming were also brought into cultivation – the final expansion of South Australia's agricultural frontier. Research demonstrated that sizeable areas of mallee scrub and heath in the upper South East, the Fleurieu and Southern Eyre Peninsulas, and western Kangaroo Island could be transformed into productive pastures with the supplement of superphosphate and specific quantities of trace elements, such as zinc, copper and manganese.[46] Through their application, as well as state-sponsored improvements to the drainage of the South East, some 1.25 million acres of scrub and heath were turned into pasture. A government land-settlement program for ex-servicemen reclaimed 620,000 acres, mainly in the South East and on Kangaroo Island. A separate, privately financed scheme developed 400,000 acres into farming properties in the upper South East. 'In the process', wrote the editors of the *Atlas of South Australia*, 'the former Ninety Mile Desert faded from map and memory, and became the more pastoral Coonalpyn Downs'.[47]

Yet it is for the expansion of manufacturing, power production and urbanisation that Premier Playford, and the era, is best known. It was Playford's determination to seek accommodation between workers and their bosses, to 'nationalise' the electricity company, retain price controls long after the war had ended, and intervene in the housing market that led ALP Opposition leader Mick O'Halloran to ruefully quip that Playford was 'the best Labor Premier South Australia ever had',[48] and suggest that 'Playford can often do more for my voters than I could if I were in his shoes'.[49] O'Halloran never had the chance to test his assertion. A 1936 reform to the *Constitution Act* abolished multi-member electorates and redistributed electorates in the state so that country seats outnumbered the more populated city seats by a ratio of 2 to 1. The 'Playmander', as this electoral malapportionment became known, effectively consigned the ALP to Opposition for more than 30 years. The ALP attracted more votes than the LCL after preferences were distributed in the 1953 and 1962 elections, and consistently won the majority of metropolitan seats and those centred on industrial towns, but could not break the LCL's stranglehold in the more socially conservative country areas. The 'Playmander', above any of the particular achievements of the Premier, kept the LCL in power. Playford's stranglehold on the premiership was so complete that the most serious opposition to his policies came from his own LCL members in the Legislative Council – themselves elected through an undemocratic process that required both candidates and voters to own property in order to qualify to stand or cast a ballot. Led by Collier Cudmore, they became the de facto opposition to Playford and his colleagues in the House of Assembly.[50] Cudmore was a stout defender of the function of the Council as a house of review, and insisted that LCL councillors convene separately from their lower house LCL colleagues to decide on government proposals. Much to the displeasure of Labor councillors, Cudmore actually sat in the seat traditionally occupied by the leader of the Opposition in the chamber.[51] Ironically, the LCL's hold on 'country' seats came to an end partly as a result of the Government's success in establishing Elizabeth and other industrial areas on the urban–rural fringe, bringing their traditionally Labor-voting blue-collar populations within the boundaries of rural electorates.

Like O'Halloran, some historians, and certainly popular memory, have been kind to Tom Playford, to the extent that all the achievements of his period in office have been largely credited to him.[52] Yet, as has been shown, the plans and implementation of the mechanisms for industrialisation and urbanisation predated his premiership and were designed and executed by others, chiefly a remarkable cohort of clever public servants, such as J.W. Wainwright and the Housing Trust's Jack Cartledge and Alan Ramsay. (Wainwright was a humble man and the fact that others took the spotlight would not have bothered him. When he died in 1948, he left directions that there be no advertisement of his death or burial, and that his body be taken to the cemetery in a plain coffin in his own car. As his biographers note, his efficiency died with him: the car broke down and had to be towed.[53]) World War II also made possible a scale of industrial development and income generation that would have been otherwise impossible, regardless of the determination and energy of a Premier.

To be sure, the South Australian economy and social structure – not to mention the city of Adelaide and towns such as Whyalla and Port Pirie – were utterly transformed in this period. Yet this transformation largely mirrored what was happening in other states. It has thus been suggested that, rather than charting distinctive development, the main achievement of the Playford governments was to ensure that South Australia matched the rising standard of living, industrialisation and modernisation that was occurring elsewhere in Australia, at a time when high Commonwealth-set tariffs protected industries and jobs, Commonwealth-provided welfare initiatives rewarded war service and enhanced the purchasing power of the poor, and conspicuous consumption became a way of life.

A focus on the achievements of the Playford era also risks overlooking the social and environmental costs of the pursuit of economic and industrial development. Statistics testifying to the tremendous growth of Adelaide's suburbs only obliquely reveal the geographical class divide promoted by uneven Housing Trust activity, and obscure entirely the dull and repetitive streetscapes and uninspiring architecture that resulted and which now blights parts of the city. Nor do they illustrate the many suburbs that, unlike Elizabeth, failed to be provided with parks, social amenities, libraries, and even electricity and sewers for a time.[54] Indeed, as Jenny Stock notes, while 'development' was given top priority, areas of lesser concern to the Premier (such as education, health, social welfare, and the arts) atrophied or got by with less than optimal funding.[55] Playford maintained that once people had money in their pockets they could choose whether or not to support the arts, and that the provision of welfare to the poor was the matter for private charity not the public purse.[56] He could hardly be accused of Bolshevism on these fronts. Equally, while tens of thousands of migrant workers settled in South Australia, a considerable number were not retained as insufficient attention was paid to their needs and desire to maintain their own cultural and language traditions. The Premier famously rejected a proposal to introduce foreign language training into schools because, in his words, 'English is good enough'.[57] Playford's attitude towards the natural environment as a place to knock down, pave over, fence in and pollute if a buck could be made, was equally renowned.[58]

Nor should the much-lauded growth in South Australia's manufacturing sector escape critique. Manufacturing certainly grew but generally remained confined to particular industries that were already prevalent before the Playford period, such as metal industries (including motor body manufacturing) and whitegoods production, with a corresponding lack of non-durable goods industries, such as textiles, clothing and paper. As Dean Jaensch has observed, the industrial development strategy originally intended to reduce dependence on rural industries thus created a 'new overdependence' on a narrow manufacturing sector that was vulnerable to shifts in consumer demand and, because it relied on foreign capital, the whims of corporate bosses based in the United States, Europe and Japan, who cared little about the local social consequences of their decisions.[59] When consumer credit and foreign capital dried up in the 1970s, and especially at the turn of the century when car manufacturers began to replace their Adelaide plants with those in countries where labour costs were cheaper, Adelaide's northern and western industrial suburbs were hardest hit. The very success of the Housing Trust in situating workers close to industrial areas in the 1950s and 1960s came to constitute a grave problem. These suburbs became characterised by endemic unemployment and associated social problems, while housing and rental prices fell and residents who had the means – often those with the most talent and potential to become community leaders – left.

When the LCL lost power in 1965 and Playford retired from parliament in 1967, these problems had not yet manifested, although they might have been foreseen. The long boom was still continuing. Before examining how subsequent governments dealt with these problems, it is worth exploring other aspects of the Playford era, particularly the impact of World War II, and how social behaviour, education, technology, the role of women, and policies and practices concerning Indigenous people evolved during these three decades.

Chapter 8

War and Society in the Playford Era, 1939–65

In early September 1939, the declaration that Australia was at war was not welcomed as enthusiastically as it was in 1914. Only one generation separated the two great wars of the 20th century and many South Australian families were still grieving their losses from the first. The Commonwealth Government became more involved in everyday life – recruiting soldiers, and censoring the press and private communications – but as Australian troops did not leave for Europe until January 1940 and the war was confined to that continent, South Australians largely went about their business as normal. The ever present threat of bushfire, such as the Black Friday fires of January 1939 that raged through Victoria, south-eastern South Australia and the Adelaide Hills, destroying more than 1,500 homes and killing 71 people, was perhaps just as keenly felt.[1] But this attitude changed by the time Hitler's armies conquered France in mid-1940 and German planes began to bomb cities in Britain. The stakes were raised further once Japan attacked the US naval base at Pearl Harbor and began swiftly advancing through Asia and the Pacific. In less than two months the Japanese occupied the Malay Peninsula and the supposedly impregnable British fortress of Singapore, in the process capturing an entire division of Australian troops and medical units, some 15,000 personnel, more than one-third of whom subsequently perished as prisoners of war.

On 19 February 1942, only four days after the fall of Singapore, the Australian mainland came under direct attack with the bombing of Darwin, causing the loss of nearly 250 lives, and Japanese midget submarines penetrated Sydney Harbour in May, firing torpedoes that killed 19 sailors aboard HMAS *Kuttabul*. In South Australia, a German raider laid mines off the south-east coast near Beachport in 1941 and later a German submarine fired at local shipping near Kingston SE.[2] Australia's military hierarchy began to secretly prepare contingency plans for invasion, including considering a proposal to prioritise defence of the vital industrial regions between Brisbane and Melbourne, excluding South Australia, but this was rejected by Labor Prime Minister John Curtin and the Australian War Cabinet.[3]

The Commonwealth Government assumed greater powers with each escalation of the war, and further dedicated the nation's financial and human resources to defeating the enemy. From 1942, this included assuming responsibility for collecting income tax – a power it did not rescind after the war, much to the annoyance of the states – and the conscription of eligible men for service within Australian territory. Unlike in World War I, conscription did not encounter insurmountable objections since the Australian mainland was under attack and US conscripts were now stationed in Australia and helping to defeat the Japanese. The South Australian branch of the Australian Labor Party (ALP) was one of four state branches to give Curtin approval to broaden the definition of 'home defence' to incorporate the south-west Pacific,[4] which saw conscripts fight in the islands adjacent to and including Papua and New Guinea. Women were also employed in various auxiliary services to the military in numbers that far exceeded their participation in World War I. These included the Australian Women's Army Service, established in October 1941 with the aim of releasing men stationed in Australia from particular military duties so that they could be assigned to combat units overseas; the Voluntary Aid Detachment, where women served as clerks and nursing orderlies in Australian army hospitals; and the Women's Auxiliary Air Force, in which South Australian women served as aircraft ground staff, wireless telegraphists, signals operators and drivers. The Navy employed women as well, initially as civilian telegraphists, but then through the uniformed Women's Royal Australian Naval Service, which was formed in 1942.[5]

Facing much greater danger were nurses, such as Vivian Bullwinkel, born in Kapunda in the Mid North and raised in Broken Hill, who served in combat zones with the Australian Army Nursing Service. Bullwinkel was posted to a medical unit in Singapore in early 1942 but during its evacuation her transport was bombed, and she, along with 21 other nurses, spent 18 hours in the ocean before surrendering to the Japanese. Her companions were brutally executed shortly after coming to shore but Bullwinkel, badly wounded and feigning death, was able to escape into the jungle. She was captured again two weeks later and spent the next three-and-a-half years as a prisoner of war in camps on Banka Island and Sumatra.

Nearly 1 million Australian men and women served during World War II – 557,799 outside Australia. These included 54,660 South Australian men, constituting 9.14% of the state's total population and 43% of those eligible to join the Australian Imperial Force.[6] The rate of enlistment was slightly lower than in other states, which can be partly explained by South Australia's essential role in the provision of war materials and food, which required labour.[7] Diaries and letters collected by the Australian War Memorial and the State Library of South Australia provide moving accounts of what the servicemen and women witnessed while stationed overseas or as prisoners of the Germans, Italians and Japanese. Despite the brutality of conflict and captivity, flashes of humour sometimes emerge, as in the diary of Don McLaren, written as a prisoner of war in Singapore and later in Burma and Japan. On 22 March 1942, he wrote:

> I just can't believe the Japs. Today was the first time we had any food. None of us had a scrap to eat for three days. It's funny though, we just go past being hungry. We did grab some tufts of grass and chew on them, and equally amazing it tasted nice and sweet. This has also given us something to laugh about. Someone said, 'Where is Donny McLaren?' The answer was 'He's down the back paddock feeding.'[8]

South Australian Indigenous men served in all three branches of the Australian Defence Force, as well as the civilian corps, received pay that was equal to non-Indigenous servicemen (which was rarely the case in civilian employment), and for the first time were entitled to be promoted to commissioned and non-commissioned officer ranks. Private Timothy Hughes, a Kaurna-Narangga man who served in the 2/10th Battalion, was one of the celebrated 'Rats of Tobruk'. He later won the Military Medal for bravery under fire while attacking Japanese positions at Buna, in Papua, and went on to serve in the New Guinea and Borneo campaigns.[9] Indigenous women also enlisted in the Australian Women's Army Service and the Australian Army Medical Women's Service.

Back home, women were invited to take the place of men in the workforce and became involved in munitions production. Most did so voluntarily, happy to support the troops and eager to earn pay that was much higher than normally available for 'women's work'. It has been argued that the war provided an opportunity for many women to enter the paid workforce for the first time and that most were reluctant to give up their jobs once men returned from the war. Both cases have been overstated. A large number of South Australian women were already undertaking paid work before the war, though not necessarily in factories. A 1941 study of 800 women applying for work at a small arms factory at Hendon, for example, found that only 47 had never been employed in some capacity. The largest group (some 268 women) came from domestic employment, while most of the others were factory workers (180), shop assistants (88) and waitresses (74).[10] The author deduced that they were attracted by the higher wages offered by munitions work, although, depending on the role, this was still only 60–90% of what men earned for the same job. The manager at the Penfield munitions plant noted that women 'were used to the greatest degree practicable, and proved themselves superior to men for most of the work in the filling sections, and in certain operations in cordite manufacture'.[11]

Such work was dangerous for both male and female employees. At least one death was directly caused by accidental explosion at Penfield,[12] and several other explosions causing personal injury were reported. These injuries were often downplayed, but confidential incident reports tell a different story. One fire at Penfield was observed by a senior chemist whose report described an operator 'injured by acid splatters and glass fragments on the face and arms'; the manager, attempting to minimise the impact of the incident, reported the man 'may not suffer permanent injury', though added 'the sight in his left eye may be lost'.[13] Such sacrifices are rarely recalled during modern-day ANZAC commemorations.

Figure 8.1: Two women welding ammunition boxes to be used during World War II, 1943. Courtesy of the State Library of South Australia. B 7798/423.

In order to stabilise the workforce and production, the Government demanded that workers and employers also sacrifice certain freedoms. After February 1942, workers in 'protected industries' that produced essential war materials were prohibited from changing employment or joining the Defence Force, while their employers were prohibited from dismissing them (except for serious misconduct) or altering existing modes of work without permission.[14] Other types of workers were liable to have their employment redirected to jobs chosen by the state's Director of Manpower (a misnomer, given that women were being increasingly called upon). During the war many rural workers moved into large towns and the city in search of higher wages and more sophisticated lifestyles, thus stripping farms and orchards of essential labour, so some workers were directed into agricultural employment and food processing and other unattractive, lower-paid jobs instead of being allowed to work in munitions production.[15] The shortage of food became a dire problem due to the scarcity of labour and materials, and because large quantities of food were sent to feed Allied troops and British civilians. As a consequence, rationing of basic foodstuffs was enforced for various periods between 1942 and 1950. *The Australian Women's Weekly* did its best to help by publishing recipes for 'Eggless, Milkless and Butterless Cake' (described as 'delicious', which seems unlikely), and 'Mock Sausages', for which left-over porridge and onions were substituted for meat.[16]

An even greater price was paid by groups who were deemed to be 'disloyal'. The Communist Party was banned between June 1940 and December 1942 – a period that extended nearly 18 months after Communist Russia had joined the Allies in the fight against Germany – and South Australian residents of German, Italian or Japanese origin were interned because they were suspected of supporting fascism. The Loveday internment camp, located near Barmera in the Riverland, was one of the largest in Australia and at its peak in May 1943 housed more than 5,000 internees and prisoners of war. These included German Jews who had recently arrived in Australia after fleeing persecution in Europe, and who were forced to bunk alongside professed Nazi sympathisers of German origin because internees were housed in 'national' groups inside the camps. One Italian internee, Francesco Fantin, an anarchist, was tragically bashed to death by an ardent Italian fascist, whose views he did not share but with whom he was forced to reside.[17] Also interned were Lutheran pastors, including one from Immanuel College, which was raided and forced to close in 1942.[18] (Immanuel College had actively supported Australia's war effort, raising funds for the Red Cross, teaching first aid and digging air raid trenches. By 1942, 63 Immanuel 'Old Boys' and seven 'Old Girls' had enlisted to fight and serve.[19]) About one-quarter of the internees chose to work during their period of confinement at Loveday, growing vegetables and raising pigs and poultry, and harvesting opium poppies for morphine production that fulfilled most of the Australian Military Forces' requirements.[20] The majority made appeals for release, knowing that their families were suffering and sometimes starving without them, but some felt safer behind the wire given the anti-German, anti-Italian and anti-Japanese sentiment being expressed in the community.

In many ways, the South Australian experience of war mirrored that of other states, for it was a national crisis and elicited a national response. Civilians practised sheltering from air raids and some built bomb shelters in their backyards; volunteers watched for enemy aircraft during the day and suburbs were 'blacked out' during the night in an effort to confuse enemy bombers. Identity discs were pinned to the clothing of children, lest they be lost, wounded or worse in an attack. Family and friends fretted for their loved ones serving abroad, and mourned those who did not return. Finding pleasure while soldiers suffered was frowned upon, and profligate spending on inessential items deemed wasteful when savings could be directed to purchase War Bonds. Playford's Government was particularly 'wowserish' in this regard, banning horse-racing and betting shops in July 1942, which the other states then tried to emulate – albeit by suspending racing for just one Sunday each month – only to experience a resulting increase in drunkenness as frustrated punters took to the pubs.[21]

The war also had consequences that were more vividly manifest in South Australia than elsewhere. The Depression, which started earlier and arguably lasted longer here, came to an end as government expenditure on war materials stimulated the economy and unemployed men enlisted or were conscripted into the armed forces or civilian militia. The fortunes of the state's farmers also improved due to increased international demand for their products. As one agricultural journal lamented, 'It is saddening to reflect that it was left to human slaughter to solve the problems of overproduction and unprofitable prices'.[22] Similarly, South Australia's manufacturing sector profited more than most from wartime contracts and the decision to situate munitions plants and shipbuilding in the state. After the war, defence technology research and long-range weapons testing facilities were established at the site of the Penfield munitions plant and at Woomera in the Mid North, which attracted a range of highly skilled migrants to South Australia, especially from Britain.

The mass movement and permanent relocation of people through both external and internal migration was one of the most significant consequences of the war. Young people left country and rural areas in droves to take advantage of war-related work opportunities in the burgeoning industrial towns and cities. New urban centres, such as Whyalla and Salisbury (where the Penfield munitions plant was located), were created, while some small farming settlements effectively disappeared. Soon after the war, tens of thousands of European Displaced Persons settled in South Australia, where they were joined by Italians, Greeks and Brits who had abandoned their war-ravaged countries. Between 1947 and 1954, this resulted in South Australia experiencing the nation's highest proportional increase in population due to migration. The arrival of so many migrants from Italy and other parts of Catholic Europe meant that the state's Roman Catholic Church lost its predominantly Irish character and expanded numerically so that by the early 1980s it had become the largest denomination in South Australia. (The Catholic proportion of the population rose from 12% before the war to 20% by 1981.[23]) This had ramifications for Government, especially when making or amending policy concerned with social and moral issues, especially those of a sexual nature. In the short term, the Playford Government needed to find ways to peacefully incorporate such a large number of migrants – many of whom did not fit the 'White Australia' mould – in a short period of time. In 1949, it sponsored a state-level Good Neighbour Council to support a network of community groups in organising social gatherings and providing practical advice to migrants about assimilating into the 'Australian way of life', a scheme that subsequently became a national movement.

Amid concerns about how to settle migrants after the war were anxieties about how to get women to 'settle down', with all the connotations that this phrase entails. During the war years, young women were freed from familial and marital constraints, and many took advantage of opportunities to earn money outside the domestic sphere. In doing so they gained a degree of economic, social and sexual independence. In other parts of Australia, this independence was most clearly expressed through romance and sex with American soldiers, which generated a great deal of attention in the press and condemnation from the pulpit. This was less of an issue in South Australia, where fewer American GIs were stationed during the war. Nevertheless, significant energy was exerted to discipline the behaviour of South Australian women. This mainly came in the form of discourses that positioned 'loose' women as hindering the 'boys at the front' and aimed to shame them into practising self-control. More coercive measures were also employed; in the first six months of the war, some 1,485 women and girls were warned by female police officers for improper conduct, and 280 parents were approached concerning the conduct of their daughters.[24] Later, in September 1942, the National Security (Venereal Diseases and Contraceptives) Regulation came into operation, whereby women were threatened with detention in a lock hospital if they were suspected of carrying or transmitting venereal disease – suspicion that might simply arise from being seen consorting with a variety of men. The new regulations also banned mail advertising of contraceptive devices and advice on how to use them in an effort to control what the Government considered to be excessive sexual activity. The possible use of contraceptives as prophylactics against sexually transmitted diseases seems to have been conveniently ignored, giving weight to the argument that this measure was driven by concerns about morality rather than health.[25]

Anxiety about the increasing sexual independence of women and moral decay was heightened further in the period of economic prosperity after the war that lasted nearly three decades. The 'long boom', as it has been called, was the result of a myriad of factors, the most important of which were the economic stimulus created by the initiation of major national infrastructure projects; the Commonwealth's generous financial support of returned servicemen and their families, mothers and the unemployed; high levels of consumer spending after a long period of enforced saving (due to rationing and wartime austerity); and the extraordinary level of migration that fuelled the building industry and provided a new market for products. In addition, the Commonwealth Government's high tariff wall and a healthy British demand for goods ensured steady job creation, rising incomes and thick company profits. Women benefited through increased opportunities for paid work and higher wages, and a degree of independence and sexual freedom followed this, but not to the extent that is often imagined and feared by social conservatives. For the decade after 1945 the average crude birth rate (that is, the number of babies born each year per 1,000 people) was 23.8, compared to 17.3 for the previous decade.[26] This 'baby boom' – driven by post-war prosperity coupled with the joy of soldiers returning home – tied women to the home as child care facilities were virtually non-existent. Thus, for the majority of South Australian women, the pre-war condition of marriage and maternity continued to be the norm, and this generally entailed giving up paid employment, whether by choice or compulsion, at least until the mid-1960s. Women still constituted only 21% of the South Australian workforce in 1947 (less than 0.3% higher than in 1933), rising to just 21.2% in 1954 and 23.6% in 1961.[27]

While the liberation of women still had some way to go, the rise of consumerism prompted by the booming economy was certainly not a mirage, and it was through conspicuous consumption, rather than one's class or place of employment, that individuals began to define themselves. This was most true for young people aged between 12 and 18, who were freed from the necessity of leaving school or finding full-time paid work at an early age. Parent-provided pocket money and paid casual employment allowed them to purchase clothing, music and other paraphernalia that identified them first as 'teenagers', and then as a specific type of teenager – perhaps a 'bodgie', a 'widgie' or a 'mod'. The 'teenager', an entirely new social category, became the focus of the fashion and entertainment industries. The styles and demeanours adopted by young people (strongly influenced by American popular culture), and the increasing amounts of free time they enjoyed, served to alienate some from their parents, who had scrimped and saved their way through war and the Depression. Predictably, the incompatibility of the experiences of young people and their elders contributed to a mid-1950s moral panic about juvenile delinquency, which saw police urged to crack down on idle youths who gathered in Adelaide's milk bars.[28]

For the most part, though, teenagers and young adults were not gathering in milk bars to plan their crimes; they were dancing in their bedrooms, reading magazines, attending concerts and going to the ‘drive-in’ theatre, an outdoor experience in which couples and families watched films projected on a screen from the (dis)comfort of their own cars. The first drive-in, the Blueline, was opened in 1954 at West Beach, and by September 1957 there were six suburban drive-ins and one in Port Pirie.[29] Other popular leisure and recreational pastimes for young and old included playing and watching cricket and tennis, and joining swimming and surf life-saving clubs, which experienced their heyday in the late 1960s and early 1970s.[30] Port Adelaide supporters relished their team winning the South Australian National Football League premiership on 13 occasions between 1936 and 1965 (including six times in a row between 1954 and 1959).[31] Their team’s victory in 1965, by a slim margin against Sturt, was witnessed by a record 62,543 spectators.[32] The Royal Adelaide Show remained a high point on the social calendar for city and country folk alike, although for the latter it was also an occasion to conduct serious business. The Show was cancelled between 1940 and 1946, when the showground at Wayville served as a mobilisation, training and demobilisation centre for the armed forces, but it was warmly embraced by the public immediately afterward. It transformed from a strictly agricultural and homewares show in 1954 with the addition of side-show rides and games, and the introduction of show bags in 1958.

Figure 8.2: Wheelbarrow race at the Royal Adelaide Show, 1938. Each team includes a man, woman and horse as well as the wheelbarrow. Courtesy of the State Library of South Australia. B 7798/492.

The emergence of the drive-in theatre was a consequence of the tremendous increase in motor car ownership in the 1950s and 1960s, which was itself a result of the economic boom. South Australian factories helped produce the first car that was built entirely in Australia, the FX Holden, which became available at the end of 1948. The success of this and subsequent car models, coupled with wages rising faster than the cost of living,[33] contributed to the doubling of new motor vehicle registrations in South Australia between 1952 and 1965.[34] No other technological innovation matched its impact on reshaping towns, cities, streets and homes in the 20th century. Garages and carports were attached to houses, roads were widened, the first motels and caravan parks were opened, suburban shopping centres were built, and land between the major public transport arteries was developed for housing. After the war, once employees won the right to a full weekend off work and two weeks' paid annual leave, private transport also took South Australians further afield than ever before – to the Flinders Ranges and the Riverland, for instance, instead of just Glenelg and Semaphore, and to 'chop picnics' in the Hills and camping in the bush. Motor vehicles became such a priority that when the journey through the city and the hills south-east of Adelaide became unbearably congested, not even the property and two-storey mansion of Federal Immigration Minister Alexander 'Alick' Downer could be spared from the path of a newly constructed freeway.[35]

Television, introduced to the state in 1959, would come to have a similar impact on changing the ways in which South Australians spent their leisure time. For most of the Playford era, however, South Australians still relied on radio and the daily newspapers to keep them informed and amused. Popular radio programs included *Life with Dexter, Blue Hills* and, for children, *The Argonauts Club*.[36] Throughout most of his tenure Premier Playford also made weekly radio broadcasts to the public in the manner of US President F.D. Roosevelt's 'fireside chats', a technique also adopted by Robert Menzies when he was the leader of the Opposition in federal parliament. The advent of television, and especially the televised interview rather than speech, did not suit Playford nearly as well, and he could not match the performance of the ALP's emerging star, Don Dunstan, in this regard.[37]

The most influential newspaper at this time was, and still is, *The Advertiser*, with Lloyd Dumas as managing editor. Dumas envisaged increased sales and profits for the paper if the Playford Government's industrialisation plan was successful and prosperity ensured, so *The Advertiser* backed it to the hilt.[38] In 1965, political scientist Katharine West claimed that 'no non-Labor Leader in post-war Australia has had such dedicated support from an influential daily newspaper as Playford has had from the *Advertiser*'.[39] Dumas's journalists (as well as radio station 5AD and later television station Channel 7, both owned and operated by Advertiser Newspapers) were rewarded with privileged access to the Premier and occasionally advance notice of government initiatives. The cosy relationship evoked derision from the ALP but it endured throughout Playford's period in office and remained mutually beneficial for both parties.

The daily afternoon newspaper, *The News*, managed from 1953 by 22-year-old Rupert Murdoch (his first experience of running a newspaper) and edited by Rohan Rivett, proved to be less cordial. In 1959, it became embroiled in a legal case that enthralled the public and caused considerable embarrassment for the Playford Government. The case centred on a young itinerant Aboriginal man, (Rupert) Max Stuart, who was found guilty and sentenced to death for the rape and murder of a 9-year-old white girl near Ceduna on the state's far west coast. Stuart pleaded not guilty at his trial, alleging that police had used threats and violence to extract a confession from him, and a submission to the High Court was made on these grounds after an appeal against his sentence to the Full Court failed. Stuart was supported by Catholic priest and prison chaplain Tom Dixon and anthropologist Theodor Strehlow, who spoke with the condemned man in his native Arrernte. Neither believed that Stuart could have composed the confession he had signed as it was written in formal, grammatically correct English, which the presiding police officers insisted Stuart had used. It was also argued that Stuart did not have access to a proficient interpreter during his trial. The High Court appeal failed, as did an application for special leave to appeal to the Privy Council; Stuart remained condemned to hang.

Murdoch and Rivett were not convinced that justice had been served, and, for reasons of principle or because the scandal provided

Figure 8.3: Rupert Maxwell Stuart in custody, 1958.
Courtesy of News Ltd/Newspix.

means to sell more newspapers, *The News* criticised the handling of the case, called for a Royal Commission and then criticised the proceedings of that inquiry, which were indeed dubious – one of the three commissioners was Stuart's trial judge, while another had presided at his Full Court hearing. The commissioners criticised aspects of the police procedures but found the trial verdict justified and rejected Stuart's allegations of police assault.[40]

In the meantime, sufficient doubts had been raised about the prosecution of Stuart to evoke public sympathy and attract attention interstate and overseas. Sydney's *Daily Telegraph* warned in a front-page editorial that 'It should not be forgotten that the millions in the newly-independent Asian countries are particularly sensitive to the civil rights of black minorities',[41] and senior jurists and politicians in Britain were drawn to comment on the case.[42] The police, the judiciary and the Playford Government – which had ultimate responsibility for the actions of the police, appointed the Royal Commission and supported the continuance of capital punishment – were fiercely criticised. Playford eventually buckled and in October 1959 convinced his cabinet to commute Stuart's penalty to life imprisonment. Stuart served 14 years in jail and, after serving further time for committing minor offences and violating conditions of his parole, eventually became a respected elder in his community and chairman of the Central Land Council. It was in this capacity that he welcomed the Queen to Alice Springs in 2000 by presenting her with a painting of an Arrernte Dreamtime story.[43] Respected journalist and biographer Stewart Cockburn claimed that the controversy surrounding the Stuart case resulted in the loss of the Liberal and Country League (LCL's) majority in the 1962 election and sowed the seeds for its defeat in 1965.[44] More tangibly, it led to reforms of police and court procedures, exposed the disadvantage of Indigenous people in the criminal justice system, and ignited a public campaign that eventually saw the repeal of the death penalty in South Australia in 1974.

Another Max featured in an earlier case that similarly captured attention interstate, in this instance exposing South Australia to be the morally and socially conservative society it was often accused of being. In 1944, Max Harris, just 23 years old and a precocious writer and editor of the literary and art journal *Angry Penguins*, published a series of poems purported to have been penned by Ern Malley, whom Harris proclaimed as one of the 'giants of contemporary Australian poetry'.[45] In reality, the poems had been written (or, more accurately, cobbled together from phrases extracted from an assortment of texts, including a report about mosquito control) by two interstate poets, who sent them to Harris to see if he could tell the difference between good modernist poetry and nonsense. Harris fell for the hoax and became the subject of ridicule. Worse was to come. Police objected to the content of some of the poems in the issue (including Harris's own) and the editor was charged with having published 'indecent, immoral or obscene' material. The prosecuting police officer was unable to explain exactly how some of the poems were obscene other than to identify individual words, such as 'incestuous' and 'genitals', and, in one case, because the setting of the poem was a park after dark, and the officer, in his professional experience, had 'found that people who go into parks at night go there for immoral purposes'.[46] The judge nevertheless agreed that the poems were indecent, chided Harris for his preoccupation with sex, and found him guilty, with a fine of £5 and £21 costs.[47] An unrepentant Harris retorted that 'Adelaide, which prided itself on its cultural standing, would remain a source of ridicule to the rest of the world and an example of unenlightened and bigoted provincialism until its archaic and barbaric law was changed.'[48] He had a point, though South Australia was not alone in banning literature deemed to be obscene.[49]

It was not only sexually explicit topics that were censored or banned. Shortly after the inaugural Adelaide Festival of Arts in March 1960, the American musical comedian Tom Lehrer was forbidden by Chief Secretary Sir Lyell McEwin from singing five songs in his repertoire at a forthcoming concert at the Adelaide Town Hall.[50] McEwin drew on powers given to him by the *Places of Public Entertainment Act*, in a section dating from 1913 that allowed the prohibition of a performance for the 'preservation of public morality, good manners, or decorum, or to prevent a breach of the peace'.[51] One of the songs, entitled 'I Hold Your Hand in Mine', told the story of a man who cut off his girlfriend's hand and carried it with him, a topic that might not immediately lend itself to comedy or song but which nevertheless was apparently enjoyed by audiences elsewhere.[52] Lehrer pointed out that the opera *Salome*, in which the title character is presented the head of John the Baptist on a platter, had just been performed to great acclaim during the Festival, and was hardly less ghoulish,[53] but he was forced to obey the order as police officers were stationed at the doors during his performance.[54] He did, however, amuse his audience by quipping that he 'really did not wish to pick a quarrel with the SA Government as [he] knew it had one of the finest 18th century Governments in the world'.[55] Even the conservative *Advertiser* editorialised in Lehrer's favour, labelling the ban 'one of the most nonsensical pieces of censorship that this city has suffered from in a long time – "suffered" because it is going to make us look rather less than adult'.[56]

At this time, adults in the other states of Australia, except Victoria, were allowed to drink in pubs past 6 o'clock in the evening and gamble on lotteries and, for those interested in horse-racing, by means of an off-course totaliser. This was not the case in South Australia where Tom Playford's governments refused to amend or introduce legislation allowing such activities. Tasmania had extended hotel trading hours until 10 o'clock in 1937 and New South Wales followed suit in 1954, but South Australia did not change its law until 1967, by which time Playford's LCL was no longer in office. State lotteries and betting through a Totalisator Agency Board (TAB) were not allowed until 1966 and 1967 respectively. The service of alcohol, spectator sport and leisure activities, such as movie screenings in cinemas, were also prohibited on Sundays, as this was preserved as a day of religious worship; though such regulations were not unique to South Australia at the time. Playford's religious faith (albeit expressed with greater restraint than his puritanical Baptist mother) and his personal abstinence from alcohol, as well as his party's occasional reliance in parliament on a number of pious and church-backed Independent members, partly explains the stance taken by his Government on such issues. The LCL appeared to be in step with public attitudes, at least until the late 1950s, when calls for the relaxation of drinking and gambling laws became more strident, particularly among the recently arrived European migrants who objected to the prohibition of pleasures they had enjoyed in their countries of origin. As LCL member of parliament Condor Laucke recalled:

> I went to the Premier before the 1965 [state election] campaign began and said: 'Sir Thomas, I cannot hold Barossa unless you promise to end 6 o'clock hotel closing and permit a State lottery and reasonable TAB facilities. My new English constituents are angry that they can't go down to their 'local' and have a few beers in the evenings after work and dinner. And they miss their football pools. They miss their gambling.'[57]

Barossa was one of the two seats lost by the LCL in 1965, thus consigning the party to Opposition for the first time since 1933.

The fight for the right to be served alcohol – at any time of day – was an even more prolonged process for Indigenous people, whose lives continued to be tightly regulated by the state during the Playford era, despite a shift in philosophy concerning how to govern them. The *Aborigines Act Amendment Act 1939*,[58] saw the state move away from the policy of 'protection', which many regarded as encouraging paternalistic control, segregation and dependence, to the new policy of assimilation, which sought to 'absorb' Aboriginal people into the broader community.[59] Reserves and the powers of the Protector remained, including the power to remove Aboriginal children from their families, but the legislation created a mechanism by which Indigenous individuals could apply for 'exemption' from provisions of the Act and the Protector's control. If Aborigines could prove they were sufficiently 'civilised' they were permitted to live among white people, buy alcohol and qualify for government welfare, such as pensions and maternity allowances. (Full citizenship rights, such as the ability to vote in federal elections or be counted in the Census, were not conferred, however.) In doing so, they had to effectively renounce their Aboriginality, as they could no longer live among their kin on Aboriginal reserves or qualify for government benefits that were designated solely for Indigenous people.

The exemption system received a mixed response from Indigenous people. As Judith Raftery has noted, some saw it as a pathway to enhanced social and economic opportunities for themselves and their children, while others thought the price of separation from kin and banishment from reserves outweighed the perceived benefits.[60] Many, even if they sought exemption, resented their surveillance by the State and white members of the community. Hotel owners could demand to see an exemption certificate before serving alcohol and the Government could revoke their exemption if they did not 'behave'. Most could agree that it was insulting that an Indigenous person must 'cease to be an aborigine' before being considered equal to white people under the law. As Cyril Coaby recalled:

> I never held a permit. I didn't like the wording, 'cease to be an aborigine'. Although I wanted the alcohol, which I could get easily through having an exemption, I think my pride was stronger than my need for alcohol. No way in the world would I give up my Aboriginality for anything. I considered it an insult to my mother. I'm so glad now when I look back. I don't hold it against anyone [who sought exemption], I'm not aiming at people, if they wanted to better themselves, because you had to have it for some things.[61]

Ngarrindjeri woman Vi Deuschle was more forthright: 'Aboriginal people saw assimilation as a form of genocide, because it was expected by Europeans that Aborigines would move into mainstream society and forego their own Aboriginal identity.'[62]

The 1939 Act was also contentious in other ways. It broadened the definition of an Aboriginal person to include anyone 'descended from the original inhabitants of Australia', which brought people of fourth- and fifth-generation Aboriginal descent under control of the Act. This was a considerable shock to those who were taken to be 'white' and who previously enjoyed the rights of an ordinary citizen. Another clause in the Act prohibited 'white' men (a category that now included exempted Indigenous men) from associating sexually with Aboriginal women unless they were married – a measure notionally designed to prevent exploitation, but which effectively sought to control their sexuality in a way that was not applied to white women.

It took until the mid-1950s before the South Australian Government began to meaningfully assist Aboriginal people to move away from missions and reserves. The provision of housing, education and other services gave them opportunities to improve their standard of living and also the chance to be accepted in white society. The first government-built house intended for Indigenous people was leased to an Aboriginal family in 1954, though only 104 more such dwellings existed by late 1962.[63] Meanwhile, increasing numbers of Indigenous children were accepted into the state school system. As Peggy Brock has noted, the changing expectations of Aboriginal living standards fostered by the doctrine of assimilation put immense pressure on privately run Aboriginal institutions, which lacked the financial resources to improve their accommodation and educational services. Their failure to do so, and shifting public expectations of government responsibility for Aboriginal affairs, led the South Australian Government to assume financial and administrative responsibility for all Aboriginal institutions in the 1960s and 1970s.[64]

In practice, the doctrine of assimilation and the exemption system failed to facilitate the peaceful integration of Aboriginal people into white society, in part because it was reliant on a shift in non-Indigenous attitudes that the 1939 legislation could not enforce. Assimilation required white people to accept Aborigines living among them, to lease them accommodation, and willingly provide employment and equal wages. In many cases they failed to do so. Yet, inevitably, it was Aboriginal people who were blamed for failing to 'shape up' and fit in.

War service provided a means for some Aboriginal men and women to improve their skills and receive training, enabling them to break out of the pattern of unskilled and seasonal employment in which they were trapped. Leon Kent, originally from Koonibba, for instance, enlisted in the Royal Australian Air Force (RAAF) and trained at various technical colleges, where he became proficient in electronics and the operation of radar. He graduated as a ground radar mechanic and after an operational tour converted to airborne radar. Following the war he served with the RAAF as a member of the British Commonwealth Occupation Forces in Japan, and was stationed in Hiroshima where the atomic bomb had been dropped.[65] Timothy Hughes, who had been awarded the Military Medal for bravery while fighting in Papua, also made a good life for himself after the war, leasing a block of land at Conmurra under the War Service Land Settlement Scheme and later serving as Chair of the Aboriginal Lands Trust between 1966 and 1973, during which time he was appointed MBE (Member of the Order of the British Empire).

Remarkably, the fame and achievements of Hughes's mother, Gladys Elphick, came to exceed his own, and it is through the effort and determination by people such as her that the advancement of Indigenous people was finally realised, although not in Playford's time. Gladys grew up on the Point Pearce Mission, where aged 17 she married a shearer named Walter Hughes. They had two sons before her husband died. In 1939, she moved to Adelaide and married a soldier named Frederick Elphick. During the war, Gladys found work, like many women, producing munitions at the South Australian Railways' Islington workshops, and fretted for the safe return of her eldest son. After the war, she joined the South Australian branch of the Aborigines Advancement League and in 1964 became the founding president of the Council of Aboriginal Women of South Australia, where she worked to advance the status of Indigenous people and campaigned for the 'Yes' vote in the 1967 referendum concerning Indigenous citizenship. The Council employed a social worker, established various sporting clubs and arts groups, and encouraged women to learn the art of public speaking in order to convey their ideas confidently. It also founded a women's shelter and health service in Adelaide.[66] It is through this work, and her membership of the South Australian Aboriginal Affairs Board, that 'Aunty Glad', like her son, was appointed MBE, and came into regular contact with the new breed of politician, such as Don Dunstan, who were replacing those of the Playford era. As will be seen, they had new visions for South Australia, which in the context of an emerging discourse about civil rights, and in haste to fulfil desires that had been suppressed throughout the long period of single-party rule, saw the state regain its reputation for social and democratic innovation.

Chapter 9

The Dunstan 'Decade', 1965–79

With regard to politics at the national level, the period spanning the late 1960s and the 1970s is remembered as an era of unfulfilled promise. The short-lived Labor governments of Gough Whitlam were derailed by ministerial impropriety and economic mismanagement, and the Liberal governments of John Gorton, William McMahon and Malcolm Fraser largely failed to inspire. The opposite is true of South Australia, which, under the leadership of Don Dunstan, came to occupy a more prominent position in Australian politics than any other time in the 20th century. Dunstan spent the first 10 years of his political career in Opposition combating Tom Playford, who prioritised industrialisation and economic development over social concerns, and came to office when older and more conservative men, such as Robert Askin in New South Wales and Henry Bolte in Victoria, seemed to embody the character of state politics. Dunstan was cut from a different cloth and broke new ground by promoting Aboriginal rights, civil liberties, environmental issues and equality of opportunity for women, and by reinvigorating the arts. In doing so, he not only helped set the agenda for the modernisation of politics at federal and state levels, but also oversaw a period of profound cultural transformation in South Australia.[1]

South Australian pride in these achievements took some time to manifest, and they are more commonly celebrated now than they were then. For those who were challenged by Dunstan's conception of social democracy, his libertarian views and penchant for theatrical gesture, he was a radical and a show-off leading the state to economic ruin. But there were others who shared his vision of a modernised, socially just state and they revelled in the enthusiasm and flamboyance that Dunstan brought to politics, be this expressed through bold sartorial choices (such as the pink shorts he once wore to parliament) or his appearance at Glenelg Beach to hold back a tsunami that, it was foretold, would be sent by God to punish South Australians for their increasingly wicked ways.[2] Described as 'the Nureyev of Australian politics' by one commentator,[3] Dunstan was proud of the interest his governments' initiatives aroused from interstate and enjoyed the praise he received. 'Modesty is not your forte,' shouted a Liberal member to the Premier across the parliamentary floor. 'That is quite true,' Dunstan replied. 'False modesty, however, never was.'[4]

The period we are calling the 'Dunstan Decade' spanned more than 10 years and includes almost two terms of government in which Dunstan was not in charge. Small 'l' liberals in the Liberal

Figure 9.1: Premier Don Dunstan waves to the crowd from the balcony of the Pier Hotel at the Glenelg foreshore on 19 January 1976, after a clairvoyant predicted a tidal wave would arrive at noon to destroy the city. Courtesy of News Ltd/Newspix.

and Country League (such as Steele Hall, Robin Millhouse and Murray Hill) shared Dunstan's enthusiasm for law reform and social change, and key personnel in his own party (such as Len King, Hugh Hudson and Peter Duncan) proved willing allies. Yet even in Opposition, and when serving as a minister in Frank Walsh's Labor Government from 1965 to 1967, Dunstan was the most vocal proponent and principal instigator of reform. The Australian Labor Party (ALP) won the 1965 election by wresting two seats from Tom Playford's Liberal and Country League (LCL), and Dunstan, at 39 years of age, was given the portfolios of Attorney-General, Minister of Aboriginal Affairs and Minister of Social Welfare. Within two years he had overseen landmark reforms in his portfolio areas of lotteries and gaming, and liquor licensing, the latter of which saw the extension of alcohol trading hours in pubs and restaurants. In a popular move, the Government also amended the *Public Service Act* to extend annual leave for public servants to four weeks and remove all hindrances to the employment of married women. Equal pay for women performing comparable work to men in the public service was also promised, and phased in over five years. On such employment matters the private sector was expected to follow suit.

When Walsh was compelled by ALP rules regarding age to retire as leader before the next election, Dunstan won a tight ballot for the leadership. Dunstan's premiership lasted less than one year before the LCL again formed government despite winning just 44% of the popular vote (compared to the ALP's 52%) in the 1968 election. This was due to typically conservative country-based electorates outnumbering those located in Adelaide by a ratio of 2 to 1 – despite the city having over twice the population – and the stated intention of Independent MP Ian Stott to vote with the LCL in exchange for being made Speaker of the House of Assembly. Dunstan made the tactical decision to delay resigning until the first sitting of the new parliament, some six weeks after the election, in order to draw maximum attention to the democratic failure of the electoral system, which had yet again resulted in the defeat of the majority supported party. Dunstan's protest helped undermine the legitimacy of the incoming Steele Hall Government and made it sensitive to the need for electoral reform.[5]

Reform was duly achieved when the Steele Hall Government passed legislation establishing a 47-seat House of Assembly, which, while retaining a degree of rural malapportionment, provided much fairer urban representation. This virtually guaranteed its defeat at the next election. The LCL-dominated Legislative Council, however, resisted any attempt to alter its own system of election. Indeed, voting for the Council remained non-compulsory and a property qualification applied to the franchise until the Dunstan Government secured the amendment of the *Constitution Act* in 1973. Three years later, further revisions entrenched the independence of the Electoral Boundaries Commission and established a maximum tolerance of 10% variation of enrolments between electorates. (Prior to this, it was possible for a suburban seat, such as Enfield, to represent nine times as many residents as the country seat of Frome.) South Australia had thus gone from having arguably the most undemocratic electoral system in the country in the early 1960s to the fairest.[6]

The Hall Government's other main legacy was to pass legislation in December 1969 that enabled women to legally obtain abortions under prescribed conditions (an outcome often credited to the Dunstan Government), thus making South Australia the first Australian jurisdiction to do so.[7] This was achieved following the passage of similar legislation in the United Kingdom, lobbying by the Abortion Law Reform Association of South Australia led by Jill Blewett, and widespread publicity of the torment of mothers whose babies were born with severe physical defects due to their consumption of Thalidomide, then marketed as a harmless anti-nausea medication.[8] It was also the product of generational change within society as well as parliament, where regardless of political affiliation all the members of parliament aged between 30 and 50 voted in favour of the reform Bill.[9] Hall's Cabinet both reflected and promoted generational change, with the average age of its members being 11 years younger than those of the final Playford ministry. They included the first woman to hold a ministerial position, Joyce Steele, who along with Jessie Cooper had become South Australia's first female members of parliament in 1959.

Yet it was Dunstan who best embodied the concerns of the generation born after World War II. Coming of age in a buoyant post-war economy, they were accustomed to consumption rather than thrift and embraced more permissive social mores. Their greater access to secondary and tertiary education fostered a more critical view of attitudes and laws that curtailed the freedoms and career prospects of individuals, particularly those of women. Dunstan was of the same mind, and achievement of equality of opportunity for all and protection and advancement of civil liberties became the rationale of the governments of which he was a part.

As Attorney-General, Dunstan's reformist agenda was evident when he introduced the first anti-discrimination legislation in Australia, predating comparable legislation in other states and the Commonwealth by nearly a decade. The *Prohibition of Discrimination Act 1966* criminalised discrimination in employment or the provision of services and accommodation on the grounds of race, skin colour or country of origin. It aimed to facilitate the integration of Aborigines into society and the workforce and protect the rights of the large number of non-British migrants who had settled in South Australia after the war. Dunstan had already signalled his commitment to racial equality in the 1950s when he opposed laws that prevented Aborigines from being served alcohol and 'consorting' with non-Indigenous people. Reforms in 1962 under Playford removed many restrictions on Aborigines, but laws and institutions governing Indigenous people continued to be framed by the discourse of assimilation, whereby Aboriginal people were expected to adopt the attitudes and behaviours of 'white' people.[10] Dunstan, by contrast, sought the integration of Aboriginal people into white society on their own terms, and recognised that Indigenous people needed the protection of the law, access to their own land and to be conferred the right of self-determination if they were to prosper. The *Prohibition of Discrimination Act* went some way towards this, although cases of discrimination were notoriously difficult to prove. The *Aboriginal and Historic Relics Preservation Act* (proclaimed in 1967) then gave recognition to the inherent worth of Indigenous culture by providing for the protection of Aboriginal scared sites, burial grounds, and rock-wall paintings and carvings.

Even more significantly, South Australia took a national lead in land rights with the passage of the *Aboriginal Lands Trust Act* in 1966, which consolidated all existing Aboriginal reserve lands and placed them under the authority of a Trust composed entirely of Aboriginal representatives. The day-to-day running of the reserves, formerly the domain of government-appointed superintendents, was also given to Aboriginal Reserve Councils, so that for the first time since European settlement Aboriginal people had the power to regulate entry to their lands.[11] The Aboriginal Land Trust's control was not absolute – permission of the Minister for Aboriginal Affairs was still required before land could be sold or leased to other parties, and a proposed provision for transferring all mining and mineral rights to the Trust was rejected in the Legislative Council before the Bill passed – but the reform was a significant step towards self-determination. This model did not suit the Pitjantjatjara people of the far north-west of the state, who argued for inalienable corporate freehold title to their traditional lands. Following deliberations by a Parliamentary Select Committee, a government-sponsored Bill was drafted to this effect in 1979, but an election brought a change in government before it could be considered fully. Despite fears that the proposal would lapse, negotiations with the new Liberal Government and ALP support saw the *Pitjantjatjara Land Rights Act 1981* come into effect, providing the most far-reaching form of Indigenous land rights in Australia. Similar legislation that conferred ownership of traditional lands on the Maralinga Tjarutja people was then passed under John Bannon's Labor Government in 1984.[12]

Following the measures to prevent racial discrimination, South Australia again led the other states and territories by introducing a *Sex Discrimination Act 1975*, which prohibited the discrimination of women and men due to sex-based stereotyping of their capabilities or marital status. The Act established the position of Commissioner for Equal Opportunity within the public service to investigate complaints of discrimination, and a Sex Discrimination Board to make appropriate orders for redress if required. The Board was also empowered, on its own initiative, to launch inquiries into discriminatory practices and issue 'cease and desist' orders.[13] Dunstan answered the call of the women's movement by establishing women's policy units and advisors within the public service and by funding 'radical' women-led initiatives, such as the Hindmarsh Women's Community Health Centre and a Rape Crisis Centre.[14]

These initiatives could not, however, overcome the inequality that women experienced in regards to work in the home: the disproportionate amount of cooking, cleaning and child care that they performed, which limited opportunities for career and educational advancement.

Nonetheless, some advances for women were made on the domestic front. The Adelaide Women's Liberation Movement – formed in 1969 with Anna Yeatman, Anne Summers and Julie Ellis prominent participants – drew attention to the objectification of women, and its members successfully lobbied for the establishment of women's health and welfare services.[15] Indeed, it is important to recognise here, as in other areas, such as Aboriginal advancement, that the government was responding to long-standing demands for change and the committed activism of ordinary people and local groups, who deserve much credit. Rape within marriage was made a criminal offence – another 'first' for South Australia – and more women gained access to child care facilities following the provision of federal funds and broadened criteria for admission. The Commonwealth Government's decision in 1975 to permit no-fault divorce also theoretically freed women from abusive or loveless marriages, and the introduction of the oral contraceptive pill in the early 1960s promised greater sexual freedom for heterosexual women, if not necessarily more satisfying sexual experiences. Divorce, however, was not a realistic option for women who were economically dependent on their husbands, and use of the contraceptive pill was curtailed for at least a decade by concerns about its safety and side-effects and because many doctors refused to prescribe it to unmarried women.

Sex was even more fraught for gay men, who until the mid-1970s could be imprisoned or threatened with employment termination, violence or blackmail if their sexual proclivities became known. Public awareness of the threats they faced peaked following the death of Dr George Duncan, a university lecturer who drowned on 10 May 1972 after being bashed and thrown into the Torrens River near a known meeting spot for gay men. Members of the Vice Squad were seen in the vicinity of the crime and were accused of the man's murder, but gay men who might have substantiated this claim were afraid of testifying lest their identities be disclosed.

Three constables who refused to answer questions at a subsequent inquest were suspended from the police force and later resigned.[16] Consequent reporting of issues related to the case allowed for sympathetic portrayals of homosexuality to emerge and inspired gay activists to lobby politicians for law reform.[17] This, in turn, encouraged Murray Hill to introduce a private member's Bill in July 1972 to decriminalise homosexual activity. Most members of parliament spoke in favour of reform, arguing that moral transgression ought not to be confused with criminality, but many still espoused their personal distaste for homosexual acts. LCL member Stan Evans stated that the 'whole thought of homosexuality abhors me', Attorney-General Len King called it 'intrinsically evil' and Labor's Don Hopgood had a 'feeling of personal revulsion'.[18] Leaders of the Methodist, Anglican and Catholic Churches agreed: all made it plain that they regarded homosexuality as immoral and a sin, but that the law was not the best instrument to bring redemption.[19] Amendments insisted upon by conservative members of the Legislative Council weakened the Bill before it was approved,[20] but a new Government Bill was passed by a reconstituted parliament in 1975, thus facilitating the complete decriminalisation of homosexual acts between consenting men. Equivalent outcomes were not achieved until 1980 in Victoria, 1984 in New South Wales, 1989 in Western Australia, 1990 in Queensland, and for more than two decades in Tasmania.

Attitudes towards sex, and what was deemed to be obscene or 'against God's law', were becoming more liberal in general. This was not unique to South Australia, but was perhaps more remarkable in this state than elsewhere, given the social and moral conservativism of the Playford era. The poet and publisher Max Harris and the singer-comedian Tom Lehrer, whose work was censored in earlier decades, would barely have recognised the place. The play *The Boys in the Band*, which *The Advertiser* described as 'full of ripe language and four letter words' and 'set around a homosexual's birthday party', was allowed to be performed in Adelaide in April 1970 after a viewing by Attorney-General Robin Millhouse, who insisted on only two small cuts.[21] (Earlier performances of the play in Melbourne had resulted in three actors facing obscenity charges in the Magistrate's Court.[22]) Six months later, Dunstan and his

Attorney-General, Len King, moved to relax censorship conditions and South Australia became the first state to permit the sale of Philip Roth's 1969 novel *Portnoy's Complaint*, even as other Australian state governments vowed to prosecute anyone attempting to sell the book.[23] In another Australian first, nude sunbathing was permitted along a 3-kilometre stretch of Maslin Beach, just south of Adelaide, in February 1975. Despite some initial opposition from local residents,[24] the beach soon became very popular.

State and council by-laws that prevented participation in organised sports and other such activities on Sunday were also relaxed. The first Sheffield Shield cricket match to be played across a Sunday was at Adelaide Oval in November 1969; this was, according to W.M. Kitto, Secretary of the 'Lord's Day Observance Society', 'an appalling crime against God'. In a letter to *The Advertiser*, he warned that the '[d]isregard for the sanctity of God's holy day, however evident throughout the nation, if persisted in, must bring retribution and every kind of disaster'.[25] If retribution came it was not immediately apparent, although on the second day of the match a ball bowled by Greg Chappell hit a small bird mid-pitch, killing it instantly, before proceeding to strike the stumps of the flummoxed batsman, Western Australia's John Inverarity.[26]

The sanctity of the Sabbath was not the only aspect of organised religion being tested. Each of the largest Christian denominations experienced sharp declines in weekly church attendance, Sunday School enrolments and membership of church youth organisations, and they divided internally over issues such as the permissibility of premarital sex, use of the newly available contraceptive pill, women's liberation and whether or not war in Vietnam and the stockpiling of nuclear weapons were morally acceptable.[27] The Second Vatican Council issued instructions for the reformation of Catholic Church services and minor aspects of doctrine, which rankled traditionalists but gave hope to progressives; however, many of the latter were disillusioned when the Pope maintained the Church's stance against birth control. Prior to the 1960s, one in four South Australians professed a Methodist faith, and it was possible for a young Methodist 'to live an entire religious and social life within a large and self-contained non-drinking Methodist subculture: Sunday school, Christian Endeavour, Order of Knights or Methodist Girls'

Comradeship, youth fellowship, church choir, youth camps, basketball and tennis clubs'.[28] But it was the young who now deserted the church, at odds with the authority it claimed and the relevance of its teachings.[29]

While the pews emptied, the classrooms filled as South Australians improved their level of formal education. This in turn transformed the expectations, capacities and attitudes that students possessed upon graduating. Increasing numbers of students entered the school system after World War II as the result of the 'baby boom' and the almost unprecedented level of immigration. The sustained post-war period of high wages, low unemployment and relatively low inflation then enabled young people to stay in school longer and, if they could pay for tuition or win a scholarship, consider going on to university studies. The number of secondary school students increased by 78% between 1961 and 1970, and the enrolment of South Australian university students more than doubled between 1961 and 1972, even before the Whitlam Government abolished university fees and created extra capacity in the system.[30] The state's second university, named Flinders, which opened in 1966, accommodated some of them. These figures reflect the number of new students entering the system but also improved rates of retention, with twice as many students completing Year 12 in 1966 than in 1960. (This was partly facilitated by raising the minimum school leaving age to 15 years in 1963.[31])

The Playford and Walsh–Dunstan governments had different approaches to managing these trends and education policy in general. Playford was widely criticised for failing to properly fund the education sector. Many teachers left the system while potential replacements were deterred by large classes and the prospect of working in poorly resourced schools.[32] Walsh's Labor Government immediately increased education expenditure, implemented a textbook subsidy scheme for students and improved the training of new teachers. Returning to power in 1970, Dunstan appointed Hugh Hudson as Minister for Education who, in that position, oversaw a range of further reforms. These included employing more clerical assistants and teacher aides in the classroom, bringing teachers' long-service-leave entitlements into line with those of public servants, and making the wage and retirement conditions of females equal to those of their male colleagues.[33] Hudson also pre-empted the Whitlam Government in increasing funding to non-government schools and distributing the subsidy according to need rather than an undifferentiated per capita basis.[34] Religious instruction in state schools, which had been legislated for in 1940 and 1947,[35] was curtailed, and disabled children were required to attend school on a compulsory basis for the first time. These changes enticed teachers back into the system and arrested the state's falling educational standards.[36]

The reforms continued following the increased availability of Commonwealth funding for education after Whitlam's Labor Party took office in 1972. Sex education, which included instruction about contraception and family planning techniques, was introduced into the school curriculum, although parents retained the right to prevent their child from participating. Less emphasis was given to assessment by examination, especially for students who did not intend to progress to university. The Leaving Certificate examination was abolished in 1974, although the Matriculation examination endured for longer.[37] The system of separating and directing students to either academic or technical high schools was also almost completely replaced by the provision of co-educational, comprehensive secondary schools, and students were promised greater choice about the schools that they could attend by the gradual elimination of school and neighbourhood 'zones'. This was in line with the government's philosophy of facilitating equal opportunities for students, regardless of where they lived or their family background. Unsurprisingly, the state government also strongly campaigned against Prime Minister Fraser's proposal to reintroduce university fees. Overall, funding for education constituted the greatest component of spending by the Dunstan governments and increased at a greater rate than areas such as health and housing. In 1969–70, for example, 32.1% of all government spending was directed towards education and rose to 39.1% by 1977–78.[38] This level of spending also exceeded the national average by over 2 percentage points.[39]

Like education, spending and innovation in the social welfare sector had waned under Playford but became a priority for the Labor governments after him. When Labor came to power in 1965, social welfare expenditure in South Australia was lower than in any other Australian state.[40] (This assessment excludes consideration of social housing, although under Playford its provision was mainly for those with good and steady incomes rather than the poor.) At this point, social welfare was still predominantly administered through the Children's Welfare and Public Relief Board and its department, with schools, hospitals, prisons, charitable organisations and the churches expected to pick up the considerable slack. These institutions tended to reflect and uphold conservative social, religious and patriarchal values, and their staff lacked formal qualifications in social work and followed practices that belittled the needy.[41] Upon coming to power the Walsh Government abolished the Board and created a new Department of Social Welfare (later titled Community Welfare) with Dunstan the responsible minister. A Social Welfare Advisory Council was established, which unlike the previous Board was composed of members with expertise in dispensing welfare,[42] and new criteria for staff appointments were introduced alongside training and professional development for existing staff. Conspicuously, a new department chief was recruited from Victoria, and the department was reorganised and decentralised with offices being based in local communities so that the needs of those communities could be better understood and met.[43] Coinciding with these structural changes was a shift in the philosophy underpinning the provision of social welfare whereby aid was stripped of its charitable connotations and financial hardship not seen as the outcome of vice or laziness. These changes, and the welfare support programs that followed (such as those targeting juvenile offenders, children in state care and the elderly), required a substantial increase in funds. Accordingly the budget for the Department of Social Welfare increased from $4 million in 1970 to $28 million in 1979.[44]

It should now be apparent that Dunstan's personal interests shaped the government priorities to a large extent during his time in office. This was most obvious in the support given to the arts in its many forms, which in the late 1960s and 1970s transformed South Australia from a cultural backwater to an internationally renowned centre of artistic production and innovation. During his tenure as Premier, Tom Playford had shunned the funding of professional arts companies and theatres, wondering why ordinary people should subsidise the cost of opera tickets when most would rather watch films in a cinema where they were expected to pay the full price of admission.[45] It was left to wealthy businessmen and arts enthusiasts to organise the first Festival of Arts in 1960, but this event, subsequently held on a biennial basis, was unable to support the activities of permanent professional companies or provide a large modern theatre or concert hall for performances to be held. Playford reluctantly pledged funds for the construction of such a venue in 1963 but the responsibility for building and operating the facility, and raising some of the money to cover these costs, was left to the Adelaide City Council.[46] A site at Elder Park, on the banks of the Torrens and adjacent to Parliament House, was eventually chosen and building began in 1970. In the meantime, the Walsh–Dunstan and Steele Hall governments had committed further funds and each had a hand in making possible the opening of what became known as the Adelaide Festival Centre in 1973. The addition of a playhouse and a permanent home for the State Theatre Company at the complex was Dunstan's initiative alone.

So too was the commitment of millions of dollars to arts companies and the creation of a range of statutory bodies to oversee the development of artistic practice in South Australia, most of which have survived to this day. In addition to the Festival Centre and the State Theatre Company, the South Australian Film Corporation and the State Opera Company were established in 1972 and 1976 respectively. Two major cultural festivals, the Fringe and Come Out festivals, also came into existence. The South Australian Craft Authority and the Jam Factory Workshops were founded in the mid-1970s, Carclew was established as a major youth arts centre and in the late 1970s three regional art centres were built. These provided a base for what became Country Arts SA, a network of medium-sized arts centres, galleries and smaller performing arts centres, as well as outreach programs throughout regional South Australia.[47]

Dunstan's commitment to the arts can be traced to his earlier life spent at the piano, writing (including for the *Angry Penguins Broadsheet* edited by Sidney Nolan and Max Harris) and in the theatre. He was an accomplished amateur actor in his youth, during which time he came into contact with Colin Ballantyne, who was a leading figure in the 'Little Theatre' movement and had long campaigned for state funding of professional performing arts. (Ballantyne directed a production of *Twelfth Night*, in which Dustan played Malvolio opposite the director's wife, Gwenneth.) In 1959, Ballantyne was a prime mover in the Arts Enquiry Committee for South Australia, whose recommendations in 1961 prefigured many of Dunstan's later initiatives.[48] He subsequently became the State Theatre Company's chairman following the Dunstan Government's statutory take-over of that organisation in 1972.[49]

Of course, artists and performers need not be fed by the government purse, although patronage helps. Prior to the 1960s, two distinct and influential Adelaide-established literary movements flourished: the Angry Penguins, which included Max Harris and Geoffrey Dutton among their number; and the Jindyworobaks, founded by Rex Ingamells, which sought to fashion a uniquely Australian literature that borrowed from Aboriginal culture and storytelling and evoked the Australian bush.[50] The artist Margaret Preston, born in Port Adelaide and living in the city at various points in her life, was similarly influenced by Aboriginal designs and motifs and native flora, though she interpreted them through Modernist viewpoints that originated in Europe. She was the country's finest female artist in the interwar period, and produced paintings, prints and pottery that were exhibited in galleries throughout Australia. These achievements were arguably surpassed by Robert Helpmann, born in Mount Gambier and trained at Nora Stewart's dancing school in Adelaide, whose career as a performer and director spanned over 60 years. Recruited by the English Vic-Wells Ballet (which became the Royal Ballet) in the 1930s, he performed opposite and under Margot Fonteyn in many productions, acted alongside Vivien Leigh and in the Old Vic Company, choreographed numerous ballets and directed for the dramatic stage and opera, including those performed at Covent Garden in London.[51] He was drawn back to Adelaide when appointed Artistic Director of the 1970 Festival of Arts, securing Rudolf Nureyev to dance in the production of *Don Quixote* and Benjamin Britten to conduct the South Australian Symphony Orchestra. He approved of Dunstan and the support given to the next generation of creative people.

Figure 9.2: Dancer, choreographer and actor Robert Helpmann as the Rake in 'The Rakes Progress' at the Royal Opera House, 3 March 1958. Courtesy of Getty Images/ Central Press/Stringer.

Dunstan's investment in the arts and increased spending on education and social welfare would have proved more difficult had it not been for the industries and business that grew during the Playford era, creating jobs and providing much needed tax revenue. The economy grew at a slower rate in the 1970s and the Dunstan governments were criticised for poor management. Taking office at the end of the decade, the new Liberal Premier David Tonkin opined: 'We simply cannot afford to lapse back into the coma that affected South Australia in the 1970s. We cannot afford to be a social laboratory whilst neglecting the material progress and achievement necessary to fund the experience.'[52] This criticism was largely unwarranted. While unemployment, inflation and diminished export income became serious issues, these were national problems whose solutions or even amelioration were largely beyond the capacity of state economic policies,[53] unless, as in the case of Western Australia and Queensland, large mineral deposits and natural resources were discovered and exploited. Industries and businesses throughout the country suffered from sharp rises in the price of oil and reduced international demand for their products, as well as the Commonwealth Government's decision to reduce tariffs and subsidies that protected Australian enterprises.

Workforce participation rates in South Australia actually exceeded the national average for every year between 1971 and 1978.[54] Jobs were created, mostly in the public sector, which employed an additional 38,900 workers between June 1971 and June 1979.[55] While the level of unemployment was markedly higher at the end of the decade than at the start, the unemployment rate fell in four of the eight financial years that Labor was in office during the 1970s.[56] South Australian workers earned less than their interstate counterparts, but the same was true during the Playford era and this was offset by the lower cost of living. There is thus little evidence to suggest that the economy suffered unduly from the Dunstan governments' pursuit of social objectives or that their problems were self-inflicted. Nor could Dunstan be accused of unfairly taxing the rich in order to pay for services for the poor. Taxes on wealth, such as land tax and succession duties, which provided over 25% of state taxation revenue in the late 1960s, fell to 16% of tax receipts (excluding payroll tax) by 1977–78.[57]

Industrial development stalled in the 1970s largely due to decisions made in earlier decades that had resulted in the over-concentration of employment and investment in two areas: motor vehicle/automotive parts and household appliance manufacturing. Together these industries accounted for 29% of the state's manufacturing workforce in 1969–70, twice the national average.[58] These industries were highly sensitive to fluctuations in consumer spending and interstate demand, so they suffered during the economic recession of the mid-to-late 1970s. US-owned car manufacturers, such as Chrysler and General Motors Holden, which had large production plants in Adelaide, were also slow to react to consumer demand for smaller and cheaper cars during this time, and lost market share to Japanese manufacturers. They then invested heavily in the automation of their plants, which saw workers replaced by robots. The result of these decisions in the boardrooms of Detroit were job losses in Adelaide, which then spread to the associated metals and components industries and the businesses that serviced them. These enterprises were threatened further by the reduction of Commonwealth-imposed tariffs on foreign-made vehicles and parts, but the Dunstan Government lobbied successfully on their behalf to lessen the impact. Federal subsidies that supported shipbuilding in Whyalla were withdrawn, however, leading to the closure of the shipyards in 1978 and associated job losses and flow-on effects.[59]

Natural gas was discovered in the Cooper Basin in the mid-1960s, and royalties earned by the state from companies that exploited this resource increased markedly in the late 1970s and 1980s.[60] Santos, a small exploration company at the time, profited most from its discoveries and entered into lucrative agreements with the State Government to build a 790-km gas pipeline from the region and to supply gas to state-owned utilities. Profits and royalties from the production of copper ore also increased, but South Australia largely missed the benefits of the mineral boom and activities of foreign mining companies that enabled the mineral-rich states of Western Australia and Queensland to leap ahead in economic and population growth in the 1960s and 1970s. Royalties paid by mining companies between 1970 and 1979 increased 19-fold in Queensland to $58 million, and nearly four-fold in West Australia to $57.8 million, but less than three-fold in South Australia to just $4.5 million.[61] The exploitation of South Australia's substantial deposits of uranium, used in the production of radioisotopes and nuclear power, would have improved this situation but was opposed by sections of the community and within the Labor Party. Western Mining Corporation had discovered uranium, copper and gold ores at Roxby Downs in 1975, but Cabinet voted to ban the mining, treatment and export of uranium until adequate health safeguards

Figure 9.3: Merchant vessel *Iron Monarch* shortly after being launched from the shipbuilding facility at Whyalla, 1943. The shipyards were closed in 1978. Courtesy of the South Australian Maritime Museum.

could be demonstrated. Dunstan travelled overseas in late January 1979 to investigate the latest developments in processing technology, raising the possibility that the ban would be lifted, but on his return he announced that safety questions remained and that the ban would stand.[62]

This issue demonstrated the increasing power of environmental activists and local community groups in South Australia, who grew more sophisticated as the decade progressed. They drew attention to the degradation of the environment and the effects of mining and industrial processes on ecosystems and population health, claims that were increasingly supported by scientists and doctors. Port Pirie attracted particular attention because of its proximity to lead smelters and concerns over the disposal of radioactive waste from a former uranium treatment plant. The city's air and soil were found to contain unacceptably high quantities of sulphur dioxide and lead, resulting in its children possessing elevated levels of lead in their blood, which placed them at risk of neurological retardation.[63] Industrial and agricultural practices elsewhere were shown to have resulted in both accidental and deliberate discharges of chemicals and waste into soil and waterways, the over-clearing of vegetation and indiscriminate use of pesticides.[64] In the late 1970s, BHP was forced to cease piping noxious wastes from its Whyalla operations into the waters of upper Spencer Gulf, but not all offending parties were called to account.

There are different opinions as to whether the government was sufficiently proactive in recognising such problems and devising solutions. Matthew Jordan argues that federal and state governments only began earnestly to enact effective pollution controls once environmental degradation was seen to impede economic growth and international covenants were signed to control air and water pollution without disrupting foreign trade.[65] Nevertheless, the Hall Government signalled an early interest in these matters in February 1970 when it appointed a Committee on Environment to investigate ecological and sustainability issues. The Committee raised concerns about rising levels of pollution, and unsustainable land use and population growth, and recommended the establishment of a Department of Environment.[66] Achieved under Dunstan in February 1972, the Department was the second such government ministry in Australia, and the first at state level. A flurry of legislation followed, including the *Coast Protection Act 1972*, the *National Parks and Wildlife Act 1972* and the *Beverage Container Act 1975*, which encouraged recycling by imposing a 5c refundable deposit on bottles and cans, an initiative that remains unique to this state and the Northern Territory. Under the *Mining Act 1971*, miners were required to pay a small royalty on extracted quarry material into a fund to rehabilitate quarries and former mine sites abandoned by previous operators. Planning regulations were also introduced with the aim of protecting delicate ecosystems and habitats during urban and land development. Community-based groups concerned with conservation, such as the National Trust of South Australia and the Nature Conservation Society, continued their hands-on conservation work and prodded the conscience of government. Their influence was bolstered by the formation of a Conservation Council in 1971 and South Australian branches of The Wilderness Society, the Australian Conservation Foundation, Greenpeace and Friends of the Earth. An Adelaide Parklands Preservation Society was also founded in 1975 to fight for the maintenance of the city's renowned parklands.

In order to address some of Adelaide's environmental issues and ease the pressure exerted by the city's growing population, the Committee on Environment's final report called for the establishment of at least one new city in South Australia.[67] Moves were already being made in this direction and in 1972 the Dunstan Government announced the construction of Monarto, a new city to be situated about 80 kilometres south-east of Adelaide. The newly established Commonwealth Department of Urban and Regional Development contributed funds, and tens of millions of dollars were spent acquiring land, which forced some farmers off their properties, as well as drawing up plans and conducting the necessary surveys. However, the state's rate of population growth stalled in the 1970s – increasing at only half the level of the previous decade[68] – and industries and government departments that were expected to relocate to Monarto voiced their reluctance. Dunstan maintained confidence in the project, but construction was put on hold. In 1980, a newly installed Liberal Government, having no need to save face, abandoned the project entirely. In place of the new city an open-range zoo was eventually created, as if to give credence to critics' claims that Monarto was Dunstan's 'white elephant'.

Environmental campaigners were joined in the 1960s and 1970s by a growing group of activists who fought for gender equality, Aboriginal rights, nuclear disarmament and peace. The latter came to the fore after the Commonwealth Government agreed to send combat troops to fight communist insurgents in South Vietnam in

1965 and a 21-year-old South Australian conscript named Errol Noack became the first national servicemen killed in the conflict in 1966. The core group of the anti-Vietnam War movement in South Australia, the Campaign for Peace in Vietnam (CPV), was formed in July 1967 after the Liberal Government's pro-war and pro-conscription policies had been seemingly endorsed by the electorate at a federal election. Neal Blewett, Geoffrey Harcourt and Derek Healey, then lecturers in Politics and Economics at the University of Adelaide, were prominent figures in the group, which favoured education of the public over provocation as a course of action. Within two years CPV could claim about 2,500 members and was very successful in raising money to pay for radio, press and television advertisements that promoted its cause.[69] During the 1969 federal election campaign the group energetically supported the return of South Australian Labor candidates who opposed the war. The state saw a swing of 11.7% to Labor (the national average was 7.2%), and the ALP won eight of the state's 12 House of Representatives seats in the federal parliament, including each of the five marginal seats that it contested, suggesting that anti-war sentiment and the CPV's activism was influential.[70]

In November 1969, the Australian peace movement united to organise a campaign against the war on a model borrowed from the United States. A Vietnam Moratorium Campaign (VMC) consisting of various pacifist and Leftist groups, anti-conscriptionists, church members and students was set up in each state to coordinate a series of nation-wide public demonstrations. Numerous CPV members became core participants of the new collective, but the former group continued its work and soon distanced itself from the more militant and confrontational tactics employed by the VMC. This became apparent at the time of the first moratorium march in May 1970, when radical members of VMC staged a separate event against so-called US imperialism that ended in fist fights between the protesters and soldiers dressed in civilian clothes – the only instance of serious violence anywhere in the country on this occasion.[71] The second moratorium march on 18 September 1970 resulted in confrontations with police in most capital cities. In Adelaide, police officers insisted on dispersing about six thousand demonstrators who had occupied the busy intersection of King William Street and North

Terrace at 3:45pm in the afternoon.[72] The state Labor Party initially supported the proposed protest, but withdrew approval once it became clear that radicals within the movement were unwilling to compromise on tactics.[73] Dunstan did, however, urge the police not to engage the protesters even if they disrupted traffic,[74] an instruction that was given scant regard as mounted police and officers on foot dragged protesters away. By the end of the day, 130 people had been arrested in the most violent confrontation between police and demonstrators in South Australia since the Beef Riot of the Great Depression.[75] They included the principal spokesmen for the VMC, Brian Medlin, a professor of Philosophy at Flinders University, who was subsequently imprisoned for three weeks, and Lynn Arnold, who two decades later would become Premier of the state.

Despite the visibility of the anti-war movement, fighting a war against communism overseas made sense to many South Australians, at least in the 1960s, because for decades they had been urged to help rid Australia of communist 'traitors' and 'wreckers' at home. Right-wing groups, such as the Citizens' League of South Australia, broke up communist meetings during the Depression, and Tom Playford's LCL Government upheld Commonwealth laws that banned the activities and association of communists during World War II (though leading communist trade unionists remained active). In September 1951, 47.3% of eligible South Australians voted in favour of the Liberal Government's unsuccessful proposal to constitutionally enable the banning of the Communist Party of Australia during peacetime. A few years later, South Australian soil became one of the 'battlegrounds' of the Cold War as the British Government was given permission to test atomic devices at Emu Field (in 1953) and Maralinga (1956–63), located 800 kilometres north-west of Adelaide. The tests did not arouse much opposition at the time, mainly due to the secrecy in which they were conducted, but decades later public outrage followed revelations that British and Australian servicemen and ordinary citizens had been exposed to hazardous radiation, and Aboriginal people who occupied the Maralinga lands had been similarly affected and dispossessed of their land as well.[76] Now that nuclear warfare had become a tangible possibility, South Australians had reason to feel anxious – even a sense of dread – at a time when the robust economy and long period without any major war should have meant they felt more relaxed and comfortable than ever before.

Across Australia the Labor Party was damaged by allegations that communists had infiltrated the party's ranks, its powerful union affiliates and even the office of the federal leader, Dr Herbert Evatt. These alleged links, real and imagined, enraged Catholic members and moderate supporters of the ALP. A secret Catholic 'movement', controlled by B.A. Santamaria with the support of Archbishop Daniel Mannix, was formed to oppose communists within labour organisations and to get Catholics elected to leadership. Once 'the Movement', as it became known, was discovered, acrimony ensued. After the Federal Executive of the ALP challenged the Movement, a number of the state ALPs split, with Catholic and anti-communist members forming a new political organisation called the Democratic Labor Party (DLP). At a federal level, this new party was influential in denying Labor office in the 1961 and 1969 federal elections by directing its preferences from voters to the Liberal Party. In South Australia, there was a similar degree of subversion, but owing to the prominence of anti-communist Catholics, such as Mick O'Halloran within the ALP's parliamentary leadership, coupled with the state containing the lowest proportion of Catholics in the Commonwealth, the gains made by the Movement were relatively modest.[77] Adelaide's Catholic Archbishop, Matthew Beovich, also declined to encourage Catholic constituents to vote for the DLP, in contrast to his counterparts in some other states.[78] A South Australian branch of the DLP was established in 1955 but it was the least successful branch in mainland Australia.[79] The state ALP did not split over the issue, as happened in Victoria and Queensland; no trade unions affiliated with the DLP and no prominent Labor person defected to the party.[80]

In the 1960s and 1970s, Don Dunstan and his government largely avoided being portrayed as communist sympathisers, although the Premier became the target of DLP attacks in the lead up to the 1970 state election after addressing an anti-Vietnam War rally alongside a communist spokesman.[81] The Premier's socially permissive views and his sexual proclivities were more commonly the source of condemnation from right-wing and religious circles. In any case, the LCL in Opposition was not in a strong position to capitalise.

Conflicts between the two wings of the LCL – progressive and conservative – especially over how to respond to Dunstan's efforts to reform the electoral system and the Legislative Council, led to Steele Hall being replaced as leader of the party, and the formation around him of a Liberal Movement, effectively a 'party within a party'.[82] Eventually there was reconciliation, and the adoption of a new name in 1976 – the Liberal Party – by which time Hall had transitioned to federal politics. Two of his key allies, Robin Millhouse and Janine Haines, remained outside the fold and in 1977 became state and federal parliamentarians, respectively, as members of the newly formed Australian Democrats.

As exemplified by the Vietnam protest episode, Dunstan had more difficulty dealing with the hierarchy of the state's police force than with the DLP or anti-communist crusaders. In September 1977, Peter Ward, a journalist for the *Australian* newspaper and Dunstan's former Executive Assistant, reported that the police's 'Special Branch' maintained secret dossiers on thousands of citizens who had not demonstrated any involvement in criminal activity.[83] The Premier was assured by Police Commissioner Harold Salisbury on several occasions that no such dossiers existed, and this information was relayed to the parliament and a Royal Commission on Intelligence and Security that had been appointed by Gough Whitlam. An inquiry into Ward's allegations by Supreme Court Acting-Justice J.M. White, however, found that the dossiers did indeed exist and were 'scandalously inaccurate, irrelevant to security purposes and outrageously unfair to hundreds, perhaps thousands, of loyal and worthy citizens'.[84] Furthermore, the dossiers betrayed a right-wing bias as there were many compiled on union officials and all but two state and federal Labor Party parliamentarians, but relatively few non-Labor politicians had been investigated.[85] There were also files on anti-war and anti-apartheid activists, members of the Council for Civil Liberties and participants in Women's Liberation. An unrepentant Salisbury argued mistakenly that he was not obliged to divulge the complete operations of the Police Force because he came under the authority of the Crown, not the government of the day.[86] On 17 January 1978, Dunstan dismissed Salisbury for misleading the parliament and the public, and a subsequent Royal Commission into the affair under Justice Roma Mitchell reported that his dismissal was justified. However, Salisbury was popular with Adelaide 'Establishment' figures, including members of the Liberal Party and journalists working for the Murdoch press, who accused Dunstan of acting hastily and improperly because he had something to hide.[87] Approximately 10,000 people gathered in Victoria Square to protest against the Commissioner's dismissal – a number greater than the crowd that assembled during the largest Vietnam moratorium march.[88]

The Salisbury affair encapsulated the way in which South Australia had changed since the Playford era, both in its style of government and the degree to which the media and the public were prepared to question established authority. Moreover, it demonstrated how the protection of civil liberties, and the right to privacy and to dissent, had become sacrosanct. It was now seen that government should uphold these freedoms and rights. South Australian governments of the Dunstan decade trod a fine line in embracing such notions of citizenship and democracy while maintaining their own authority. Throughout his tenure, Dunstan was acutely aware of the limits of the community's tolerance for more radical forms of social legislation. He first proposed the decriminalisation of homosexuality to Cabinet in 1965, for example, but legislative reform in this regard was shelved until the ALP felt the community would support it;[89] it took the death of Dr Duncan and a Private Member's Bill to galvanise community sentiment. The fact that Salisbury's dismissal occasioned such an outcry from conservatives at the end of the decade suggests that their patience had reached its limit.

The stress of dealing with the Salisbury affair, the death of his wife in 1978 and continual rumours about his sexuality (including accusations that he gave a homosexual lover preferential treatment in employment)[90] placed a great strain on Dunstan's health. He returned from the overseas uranium fact-finding mission with a debilitating viral infection, and was hospitalised on 8 February 1979 after collapsing in the House of Assembly. In a hospital room, wearing pyjamas – theatrical till the end – Dunstan shocked the assembled press with his resignation from parliament. He had been the Member for Norwood for nearly 25 years and led the government for a total of nine years and 11 months.

Dunstan was succeeded by Des Corcoran, an experienced politician of sturdy resolve who favoured moderation and pragmatism. In light of forecasts that predicted an increase in the unemployment rate and further decline of the state's economy, Corcoran unwisely went to the polls a full year before the end of Labor's term in office. Following a vitriolic campaign against his Government waged by Rupert Murdoch's press and employer associations, which were concerned about the economic downturn and spooked by the ALP's plan to alter industrial relations laws in favour of workers, Labor was defeated at the polls by the Liberal Party on 15 September 1979.

Chapter 10

Triumph of the Market, 1980–2001

The last two decades of the 20th century saw neo-liberal economic principles permeate much of the work of government and 'free market' forces determine the fate of South Australians in ways they had not for more than 50 years. The privatisation of public assets, the deregulation of the financial system and corporate affairs, uranium mining, the taxing of gambling profits, and the hosting of major events came to be seen as the means to drive economic growth and job creation. Employment in, and expenditure on, the public service decreased in real terms, ostensibly to enable competition between private enterprises to flourish, but also to decrease the burden on taxpayers and to encourage individuals to take greater responsibility for their own welfare. Thus, unlike the Dunstan era in which the principal innovations came in social policy, the most important experiments during the 1980s and 1990s were economic and fiscal in nature, and not all of them worked. One in particular saw the government-owned State Bank move beyond its traditional function to acquire what came to be very poor performing assets located interstate and overseas. The resulting losses, amounting to some $3 billion, were worn by South Australians, who, by some indicators, were materially worse off than they had been at the end of the Dunstan 'decade' and had good reason to wonder if the experiment had been worth it.

David Tonkin's Liberal Party won the 1979 state election on the back of strong support by the Chamber of Commerce and Industry and other employer associations, and the promise to 'Stop the Job

Rot'. From the outset, then, the economy was framed as the primary issue of importance for government. Tonkin encouraged the Public Accounts Committee to act with zeal in its review of departmental expenditures, and urged his ministers to cut costs in their departments.[1] Reversing a trend established in the final years of the Playford Government and continued under Labor, the size of the public service was reduced, while spending on health, education and social services declined. The Government sought to build confidence within the business sector in the hope it would lead to job creation. To this end, Tonkin contracted out some public works to the private sector, ended preference for unionists in government employment, and pledged to overturn the ban on uranium mining. Curiously, wealthier members of society benefited from other changes that were introduced, such as the abolition of death duties and gift duties, and the reduction of land tax, stamp duty and payroll tax,[2] which might have otherwise continued to provide healthy revenue streams for government.

In accordance with his election promise, Tonkin announced the mining of uranium would be allowed. On a visit to Britain to woo large mineral exploration companies, he told the London Chamber of Commerce that South Australia's 'mineral and energy reserves had been rendered almost worthless by the Labor Government's anti-uranium policies' but the lifting of the embargo would bring a wealth of benefits to capitalists and workers alike.[3] March 1982 saw the introduction of the Roxby Downs Indenture Bill, which was designed to give legislative approval to a complex agreement between the government and Western Mining Corporation and British Petroleum over royalties, environmental safeguards, the construction of roads and town facilities, power supply and radiological protection. However, the passage of the Bill was blocked in the Legislative Council by Labor and the Democrats until ALP Councillor Norman Foster, foreseeing electoral calamity for Labor if the Bill did not pass, voted in favour of the legislation. One month later the mining companies announced that the Olympic Dam deposits of uranium and copper at Roxby Downs were among the largest in the world, and the federal ALP changed its uranium policy, as Foster predicted, to allow the export of uranium as long as it was extracted in tandem with other minerals, such as copper and gold, as would be the case at Roxby Downs.[4]

Some of the public amenities that Adelaide residents have come to cherish were established during Tonkin's premiership. They include Linear Park, which follows the River Torrens from the foothills to the sea, and the O-Bahn, a bus expressway built on a German model (conspicuously never again replicated in Adelaide nor any other Australian city) that follows the same river from the city to Tea Tree Plaza in Modbury. Adelaide's airport at West Beach, opened in 1955, began servicing international flights for the first time in 1982, thus obviating the need for international travellers to transit via one of the interstate capital cities, and Adelaide's first world-class hotel (the Hilton on Victoria Square) commenced business. Life became a little easier for people with disabilities, who were now protected under extended anti-discrimination legislation, but a little more fraught for those who liked to drink alcohol and drive, as police gained the power to conduct random breath-testing of motorists. Earlier initiatives of the Dunstan governments, such as the establishment of an Ethnic Affairs Commission and the granting of land rights for the Pitjantjatjara people, also came to fruition.

The Tonkin Government's legitimacy rested, however, on its promise to arrest the state's declining economic fortunes, and failure to do so was the primary reason for its loss of office after only one term. In 1981, the state's unemployment rate was 8.4% (as opposed to the national average of 6.7%),[5] considerably higher than when Tonkin took office. Concerned that the rate would continue to rise and hoping to capitalise on the Roxby Down announcements, Tonkin called an early election to be held in November 1982. The South Australian Institute of Teachers and the Public Service Association, most affected by the spending cuts and policies of retrenchment, campaigned strongly against the Government, and Tonkin's team was soundly defeated by the Labor Party led by John Bannon

Bannon had the misfortune to lead the state through two of the deepest economic recessions since the Great Depression. They coincided with the beginning and end of his premiership. His governments faced the challenge of reducing the state's extraordinarily high levels of public debt and unemployment – now the highest of the mainland Australian states – at a time when the Reserve Bank of Australia was imposing high interest rates on borrowing and the Commonwealth Government in Canberra was opening the Australian market to foreign competition. It is not surprising that the *Australian Financial Review* reported Bannon's election victory under the headline 'A New Captain Surveys a Sinking Ship'.[6] Output and employment in the manufacturing sector had declined in the 1970s as international competitors ate into the Australian market, and this decline was hastened in the 1980s with the withdrawal of some of the Commonwealth Government's protective tariffs and subsidies. Between 1981 and 1991, some 17,000 jobs were lost in this sector (15.9% of South Australia's manufacturing workforce).[7] Labor, and particularly Bannon, who assumed the roles of Treasurer and Minister of State Development in addition to Premier, initially won plaudits for restructuring the state's economic base and balancing the budget, and was rewarded with election victories in 1985 and 1989. The strategy the Government pursued, however, became increasingly risky.

Bannon was adept at managing fiscal policy: raising and cutting taxes and charges on financial transactions, petrol, cigarettes and alcohol depending on the circumstances; and facilitating land sales and property development that attracted stamp duty. Taxes on gambling and gambling establishments also became a lucrative source of government revenue once legislation allowing the operation of a casino and poker machines was passed by a conscience vote in parliament in 1983 and 1992 respectively.[8] In each case, the financial benefits and arguments about an individual's right to choose how to spend his or her money were deemed to outweigh the detrimental effects of gambling and gambling addiction on families and the wider community

'Major projects' were also pursued. Two of the most popular resulted from successful bids to stage an annual Formula One Grand Prix through the streets of central Adelaide, which attracted overseas television coverage and tens of thousands of visitors each November, and to build and maintain submarines and naval frigates for the Royal Australian Navy. The Grand Prix was held for 10 years, beginning in 1985, before the event was 'poached' by Victoria, while the Navy contracts have provided training and employment for thousands of South Australians for nearly three decades. More contentious was the Adelaide Station and Environs Redevelopment project, which began in 1984 and involved the erection of a five-star hotel and a convention centre adjacent to the Adelaide Railway Station and its new casino. Critics were dismayed that normal planning requirements were bypassed in order for the project to be approved, and reminded the government that the land was part of the city's Parklands, which should be preserved in perpetuity. Nevertheless, the buildings in this new precinct undoubtedly served to facilitate tourism and trade. A large public–private venture to develop the Golden Grove housing estate in the north-east of Adelaide also attracted criticism, in this case due to the terms of the agreement between the South Australian Urban Land Trust and property developer Delfin. The Indenture endorsed a profit level of 32% per annum, and guaranteed that the state's Housing Trust would buy back at least 25% of the developed allotments at a price that incorporated this rate of return. While both the government (through the Land Trust) and Delfin would share the profit, it was estimated that Delfin's return on its investment over the life of the project would be between 1,500% and 3,000%.[9] Hugh Stretton, a respected historian and planner and deputy chair of the Housing Trust board, correctly argued that the deal represented 'a serious reversal of the long standing policy of using public enterprise to restrain land prices in this metropolis'.[10] Other government-backed planned developments (such as a 680-acre tourist resort and golf course at Wilpena Pound within the confines of the Flinders Ranges National Park;[11] marinas at Glenelg, Kingston Park and Sellicks Beach; and a 170-room hotel tower and revolving restaurant at Mount Lofty – to be serviced by a cable car running through the Adelaide Hills from Waterfall Gully) drew even greater opposition from local residents and conservation groups and were eventually blocked.

None of these projects promised as long-lasting benefit as the Multifunction Polis (MFP), a high-tech, environmentally sustainable 'city of the future' that the South Australian Government hoped to develop with the backing of international investors. The concept was devised by Japanese entrepreneurs and called for technology focused research and development facilities, educational institutions, recreational amenities and environmentally sustainable housing to be constructed in close proximity to each other so as to be mutually supporting. The government would provide land and tax concessions, but individual companies would be responsible for construction and for attracting workers and inhabitants – the expected population was between 100,000 and 250,000 people. Swampy land at Gillman near Port Adelaide was offered as the site, and in 1990, through a competitive tender process, South Australia was selected from other states to be the location (after Queensland, the favoured location, rejected the proposal). The MFP promised to attract wealthy and highly educated migrants, and reorient the state's economy from increasingly non-competitive automotive and whitegoods manufacturing to high-tech industries and educational services.

Unfortunately, none of this came to pass. The project had its detractors from the start, and both the Japanese and the South Australian Government found it difficult to 'sell' the concept to overseas companies and the public. The development's name, and its ever-changing objectives, did not help, nor did promotional material that obliquely promised 'a place of providing, gathering, and reproducing information of diverse aspects, strata, and form, as well as relaxation, comfort, surprise, joy, entertainment and intellectual stimulation'.[12] But it was the crash of the Japanese economy in the early 1990s that signalled the end of the MFP before it began. The project was officially abandoned by the South Australian Government in 1997, having cost the Australian taxpayer an estimated $150 million in planning, promotion and administration costs.[13] A much more modest Technology Park, along with a campus of the University of South Australia and a modern environmentally sustainable residential development, was established just a few kilometres east of the proposed MFP site at Mawson Lakes.

The MFP was not the only major project that proved to be less lucrative than first imagined. The Olympic Dam uranium mine was scaled down before it was finalised at the end of 1985 because of its developers' failure to win significant export contracts, and the second stage of the project was put on hold in December 1990 due to a fall in world copper and uranium prices.[14] Industry proponents and the Liberal Party argued that uranium-processing facilities and a nuclear-power generation plant needed to be established for the economic benefits of South Australia's reserves to be fully realised; simply supplying the raw material for export was insufficient.[15] The Labor Government refused to countenance such proposals, and it became even less likely following the catastrophic 1986 meltdown of a nuclear reactor at Chernobyl in the Ukraine.

After the 1985 election, the Bannon Government was returned with a greater parliamentary majority and the Premier with an extraordinarily high approval rating. Critics on the Left have argued that this popularity was wasted because the ALP failed to tackle social inequality more boldly.[16] Yet it *did* pursue a social democratic agenda. Bannon insisted that each government agency consider the social implications of its operations and nominate particular projects for funding on the basis of social justice objectives.[17] He also became the first state Treasurer to require his department to prepare annual reports on the specific allocation of funding for programs and services designed to benefit females.[18] The equal opportunity legislation of the 1970s was extended to make it unlawful to discriminate against people because of sexual preference, pregnancy or age.[19] The Government's spending on health and education (as a proportion of total budget) matched that of the Dunstan era, even without the benefit of the Whitlam Government's largesse;[20] its promotion of the arts and commitment to environmental protection never wavered; and it ushered in legislation that improved occupational health and safety and introduced a universal workers' compensation scheme, named WorkCover, that was fairer and more efficient. Most of these initiatives were opposed by employer associations and the Opposition in parliament. Moreover they were achieved when the Commonwealth Labor governments were tightening funding to the states.[21] Between 1982 and 1992, for example, the portion of state government revenue derived from Commonwealth grants fell from 66% to 55%,[22] and this funding was increasingly tied to Commonwealth Government priorities rather than being available for use by the state government to pursue its own projects.[23]

This determination to fund social services without substantially increasing the taxes and charges paid by South Australians within a circumscribed fiscal environment led the Bannon Government to adopt its most contentious economic strategy. It involved the 'commercialisation' of publicly owned assets and government-run instrumentalities so that they paid for some or all of their own operational expenses and ideally yielded a profit that could be used for other purposes. The State Government Insurance Commission (SGIC), for example, moved beyond selling personal home and motor vehicle insurance to become involved in property development and underwriting risky commercial ventures.[24] The Electricity Trust of South Australia (ETSA) was also run in a manner that enabled it to meet its costs and, after accounting for depreciation of its assets, return a profit to government of over $50 million in 1987–88 and 1988–89 and over $100 million in 1989–90.[25] This was achieved by charging consumers prices that were slightly higher than necessary and shedding 13% of its workforce between 1987 and 1991.[26] Whether this could be viewed as financially prudent partly depended on the size of one's power bill, or whether one's job was lost. Certainly less successful was the Department of Woods and Forests' investment (thorough its production and marketing arm, the South Australia Timber Corporation) in a New Zealand-based project that lost over $20 million, and its joint stake in a venture to develop a timber product called Scrimber, which cost it and the SGIC $30 million each.[27] Complicating these matters was the Government's refusal to divulge details about such investments to parliament on the grounds of the 'need to maintain commercial confidentiality', an inevitable response from a government whose authorities were behaving like businesses, but which contradicted the principle of government accountability.[28]

None of these arrangements had the potential to raise as much money and create as many jobs – or to fail as spectacularly – as the reorientation of the publicly owned State Bank of South Australia to engage commercially in the newly deregulated financial sector. The bank was formed in 1984 through an Act of Parliament and involved the merger of the Savings Bank of South Australia and the State Bank of South Australia. The primary functions of these banks had been to protect the savings of, and provide low-risk loans to, South Australian residents. It was a traditional approach to banking that had kept them solvent since the 19th century. The new State

Bank's brief, however, was to 'act commercially and to foster the economic development of South Australia'.

Under its entrepreneurial managing director, Tim Marcus Clark, the State Bank embarked on a heady period of expansion both in Australia and overseas. The Commonwealth Government was loosening banking regulation and allowing unprecedented competition between financial institutions, with restrictions lifted on international exchange transactions and foreign banks given licences to operate in Australia. Property developers and business entrepreneurs took advantage of credit that was now relatively easy to come by. The State Bank was willing to lend to higher-risk clients in order to compete with the other more established banks. It bankrolled a retail and office complex in Rundle Mall that became known as the REMM-Myer Centre and acquired a number of financial services and money lending companies, such as Beneficial Finance Corporation, which 'on paper' were capable of making substantial profits. From 1985 until 1990, the State Bank of South Australia Group increased its total assets by an average *annual* rate of 43.9% – an extraordinary level of growth – and it delivered dividends to the Government accordingly.[29] This rate of growth was vastly superior to equivalent financial institutions, such as the State Bank of NSW, which reported an annual increase in assets of 18.5%, and the 'big four' banks – Westpac, National, ANZ and the Commonwealth Bank – which grew at an average annual rate of 17.7%.[30]

As economist Graham Scott has noted, the State Bank's loan book was 'unusual to say the least': relatively few loans were made in the traditional sectors of agriculture, mining and retail/wholesale trade compared to the loans issued by other large banks. Almost half of its approved loans were to 'finance, investment and insurance' and to 'property and business services'.[31] In both of those categories, the overwhelming proportion of the loans was for property, especially office buildings and shopping outlets, which were in demand and able to achieve high rents and rates of return. However, once the market was flooded with surplus property, and the price 'bubble' burst, the value of these investments plummeted – halving in some cases – and investors were left unable to pay their loans.[32] The Auditor-General's report of 1993 stated that the bank had incurred losses of about $540 million on the loan to the REMM Group alone for the Myer building, and that the Bank was preparing to write off a further $129.5 million due to the decline in value of facilities associated with the development.[33]

The bank's extraordinary rate of asset growth, out of step with other major banks, should have alerted the bank's board and senior management, and the government – which ultimately guaranteed the bank's loans – that Tim Marcus Clark's strategy was flawed. The Opposition belatedly began to ask questions about this in February 1989, occasioning Treasurer Bannon, who relied on advice from the bank's Board of Directors, to declare that the bank was not at risk, and Marcus Clark to chastise doubters for undermining confidence in the bank for the sake of political gain.[34] In January 1991, following a sharp fall in the bank's profits and recognition that its subsidiary, Beneficial Finance, had acquired an inordinately large number of bad debts, Bannon appointed the firm J.P. Morgan to assess the bank's position. Its report revealed the bank's debt to be in the vicinity of $1 billion, with likely further losses of $2 billion due to non-performing loans. Bannon was genuinely crestfallen when making this announcement and stated that until that point he had no idea of the extent of the problem.[35] In February 1991, the Government promised $970 million to cover the bank's losses, and a further $2 billion was committed to the 'bail-out' over the next 18 months. All of the Government's good work had been undone: after patiently reducing the state's debt from 23.5% of Gross State Product in 1982–83 to 15.4% by 1989–90, it had now soared to 27%.[36]

As Premier and Treasurer of the Government that owned the bank, Bannon bore the brunt of the public outcry. He insisted, however, that 'the State Bank Act … specifically precludes, and rightly so, the Government being directly involved in direction and management of the bank's affairs'.[37] As much as this annoyed his critics, this was true. The Act effectively provided a commitment for the Government to underwrite the bank's potential losses with taxpayers' money without giving it any real power to manage its activities.[38] Yet Bannon's defence was somewhat weakened by revelations during a subsequent Royal Commission that he had requested the bank to moderate its interest rates in the lead-up to the 1989 election, secretly advancing the bank $2 million on the condition that it postpone a rise in interest rates until after the poll. Critics also argued that since the Government placed 'pressure' on the bank to yield high returns and dividends to the Government, this constituted tacit approval of its high-risk investment and acquisition strategies.[39]

Peter Duncan, who served as Don Dunstan's Attorney-General during 1975–79 and whose relationship with Bannon soured over an internal party matter soon after, was unequivocal about where the blame lay:

> Just as Wakefield, Light, Kingston, Playford and Dunstan can be seen as builders of South Australia, so Tim Marcus Clark and John Charles Bannon will be seen as the demolishers. ... Mr Bannon, of course, has sought to off-load any real blame ... This cannot be accepted and certainly will not be the judgement of history.[40]

Duncan's outrage and confidence in historical opinion was misplaced. It certainly would have been wiser for Bannon to probe the bank's activities more diligently, but a Royal Commission into the State Bank's collapse found that the bank had 'embarked upon a process of misleading the Government about the true state of affairs, largely by omission, but in some instances deliberate omission in the face of explicit questioning'.[41] It was also reasonable for Bannon to believe that the bank's Board of Directors should have been maintaining oversight and holding Marcus Clark to account; as it happened, the board members largely lacked any experience in banking and were dazzled or intimidated by the mercurial managing director. The Reserve Bank of Australia was similarly supposed to be closely monitoring the bank's activities; it was concerned about the bank's unprecedented growth and exposure to a collapse in property prices, but made insufficient effort to alert Bannon. The bank and its subsidiaries, especially Beneficial Finance Corporation, which incurred 42% of the losses, were also audited annually by external firms. Why did their reports fail to recognise the extent of the risks that were being taken and the losses that were being incurred? Each of these points was made in the final reports of the Auditor-General and the Royal Commission led by Samuel Jacobs QC, who were charged with determining the reasons for the State Bank's failure. At each step, the risks were downplayed by those involved in managing or monitoring the bank because they wanted the extraordinary rates of growth and profit to continue, the boom in the property and financial services sectors to endure, and employment in the construction industry to be maintained. 'Greed is good', insisted Gordon Gekko, capturing the zeitgeist of the 1980s in one of the era's defining films,[42] and especially so when the benefits might be so widespread.

South Australian residents who tended to agree with Duncan's assessment, and proved only too willing to punish Bannon and the Labor Party at the next election, might also have reflected upon their place in this story. Had they been prepared to pay higher taxes and charges, or, alternatively, to accept slightly lower standards of health care and schooling, and to drive on roads that were a little less safe and under the eye of fewer police, then perhaps the Government might have chosen to chart a more cautious approach to balancing the budget. Wanting more but wishing to pay less is, after all, another form of greed. Instead, they were content with blaming Bannon and he was forced to fall upon his sword. He resigned as Premier in September 1992 shortly after outlining the full cost of the Government's bail-out, leaving Lynn Arnold to lead the party to a crushing defeat in the December 1993 election. The Labor Government in Victoria suffered a similar fate when its State Bank collapsed in an almost identical fashion, in its case undone by the bad debts accumulated by its merchant bank subsidiary, Tricontinental.[43]

As damaging as it appeared at the time, the State Bank collapse may yet be surpassed as the Bannon era's defining legacy by a quiet revolution in land management that was transpiring hundreds of kilometres away from Adelaide's corporate heart. It was precipitated by concerns about environmental degradation that had begun to cause irreparable harm to fragile ecosystems and impinge on the state's agricultural and pastoral industries. Too much natural vegetation had been cleared in South Australia, especially in marginal country, exposing the most productive top soil to erosion and exacerbating soil salinity. The Bannon Government's response to these problems was to add vast new territory to the national parks system and prepare legislation to prevent farmers from clearing land. It was immediately challenged by a Kangaroo Island farmer supported by farmers' associations in the High Court and invalidated;[44] however, new legislation passed without legal challenge in 1985. It required landholders to apply for permission to clear native vegetation and to be financially compensated under a 'heritage agreement' if their application was refused. Some farmers were thus paid not to use their land, just as agriculturalists would later be paid not to use their entitlements to draw water from the River Murray to preserve its availability for purposes elsewhere. In addition, landholders became eligible for assistance in the form of rate relief and fencing subsidies, as well as tax deductions on expenditure related to soil conservation measures.[45] These were expensive and initially very unpopular initiatives, as were the decisions to halt the development of marinas in Adelaide and a cable car and hotel tower at Mount Lofty on environmental grounds, and hence they were brave; their benefit will only be truly appreciated by future generations of South Australians.

Land care drew attention to rural communities and farmers, many of whom were doing it tough. The number of productive horticulture, agricultural and pastoral enterprises in South Australia declined by almost one-third (from 21,402 to 14,565) between 1982 and 1989 while the value of agricultural and pastoral products slipped from 63.4% to 56.6% of overseas exports over the same period.[46] As geographer Les Heathcote has observed, this reflected the reduced profitability of the agricultural and pastoral industries in the face of increasing international competition and domestic costs; the impact of natural disasters, such as the 1983 Ash Wednesday bushfires, flood and prolonged drought conditions; and the Government's increasing concern about environmental degradation.[47] In particular, the Commonwealth's reduction of protective tariffs allowed for the importation into Australia of cheap (often subsidised) produce from overseas that undercut the price of local foodstuffs. Following the Gulf War in 1991, the invasion of US-subsidised produce into traditional Australian grain markets in the Middle East became another cause for dismay.[48] Increased pastoral rents and state government charges for drilling wells, irrigation water and waste management did not help; neither did the Commonwealth's increase in export meat inspection charges, the sales tax on oil and lubricants, and the fuel excise, and Canberra's maintenance of a virtually static subsidy on superphosphates over a period in which the price increased five-fold.[49] A Rural Assistance Scheme continued to provide both state and Commonwealth funds for natural disaster relief; however, it increasingly became a means to assist uncompetitive primary producers to leave the land rather than stay on it.[50] Farmers thus had every reason to feel abandoned by the ALP, but they found little solace in the Liberal Party, which had dropped 'Country' from its name in the 1970s and felt no compulsion to meet the demands of rural dwellers now that the electoral malapportionment had been corrected: its neo-liberal stance on economic issues and trade was even more extreme than that of Labor.

The Liberal governments of Dean Brown (December 1993–96) and John Olsen (1996–2001) became synonymous with the privatisation of public assets and outsourcing of the provision of public services and amenities to private enterprise. Accordingly, the portion of the state's workforce employed in the public sector fell from 18% to 12%.[51] The Engineering and Water Supply Department was corporatised as SA Water Corporation, with capital works and maintenance transferred to the private sector, and the government's computer and data-processing systems were outsourced to overseas-based companies. Some public transport services were put out to tender, the administration of Modbury Hospital and the Mount Gambier Prison was given over to private operators, and a new private hospital was established adjacent to the Flinders Medical Centre.[52] Some of the services formerly offered by the Department for Family and Community Services were also contracted out to private agencies, such as the Salvation Army and Centacare Catholic Family Services, which were seen to be more innovative and flexible in responding to the needs of 'clients'.[53] Some, but certainly not all, of those who lost their public service jobs were employed by the private sector, though their conditions of work and entitlements were altered.

The Labor Government had initiated the privatisation of large-scale public assets in order to repay the money lost in the State Bank collapse. In July 1992, Bannon announced that the Government would sell its majority share in the gas explorer and distributor Sagasco Holdings (forgoing $15 million earned in dividends each year in order to save the state more than $25 million per annum in interest payments on debt),[54] and the following year it announced that the State Bank would be divided into a 'Good Bank' (which was profitable) and a 'Bad Bank' (which retained the non-performing loans and assets), with the good one to be sold.[55] The profitable bank, renamed BankSA, was bought by Advance Bank in 1995, later to be acquired by St George Bank, which itself soon merged with Westpac – the change of hands typifying the predatory nature of the banking sector at the time.

The State Government Insurance Commission and Pipelines Authority of South Australia were also sold in 1995, to be shortly followed by SA Meat Corporation, the Ports Corporation Bulk Handling Facilities, and the Department of Woods and Forests' native plant nurseries and commercial timber processing and marketing operations. South Australians were assured, however, that the Electricity Trust of South Australia (reorganised and renamed ETSA Corporation), which made considerable annual profits, would remain in public hands. Olsen reaffirmed this promise going into the October 1997 election but he broke his word soon after, stating the need to repay debt accrued by the former State Bank – an excuse that was wearing thin among the public. The Liberal Party lost 13 seats in the state election (10 of them to Labor), suggesting that the public was now more concerned about social and economic costs associated with privatisation and deregulation: the retrenchment of public sector workers, the government's diminished capacity to intervene in the market and moderate the price of goods and services, the declining provision of services to 'customers' living in 'non-profitable' remote areas, and the trade of valuable sources of government revenue for the sake of short-term debt reduction. Don Dunstan, who had kept a relatively low profile since resigning as Premier in 1979, was one of the most vocal critics of this approach, writing essays for the *Adelaide Review* and delivering speeches that admonished the 'ideological nonsense' and 'blind faith of economic rationalists' within both the state Liberal and federal Labor governments.[56]

Having lost its majority in parliament, the Liberal Government required the support of Independent members of parliament in both the lower and upper houses to pass legislation enabling the sale of

ETSA. In desperation, Olsen offered a long-term leasing arrangement rather than an outright sale, giving the impression that this would allow the state to retain some control of this asset. Independent Nick Xenophon, who had the crucial casting vote in the Legislative Council, was unmoved, but two Labor MLCs resigned from their party and voted with the Government, enabling the legislation to be passed. Mike Rann, the Labor leader since 1994, then switched from opposing the sale to proposing an extended lease of 99 years (instead of the 25 being suggested by the Government) in order to secure a better sale price.[57] ETSA's privatisation ultimately involved the disaggregation of its business, with the power generation, transmission, distribution and retail assets taken up by distinct investors. The South Australian Government retained freehold ownership of the power generation and distribution infrastructure, with the investors acquiring long-term leasehold interests in the assets. AGL, a Sydney-based energy company, acquired the retailing component of ETSA, and began preparing for competition with other retailers once a national electricity market became operational in 2003.

From a political perspective the sale of ETSA proved disastrous, stretching the public's trust in government beyond breaking point, fracturing relationships within and between the political parties and severely damaging the credibility of Premier Olsen. Following revelations that he misled a judicial inquiry investigating a separate government commercial contract, he resigned as Premier and Leader of the Liberal Party in October 2001 and was replaced by John Kerin, who could not arrest the party's fortunes at a state election held less than four months later. Moreover, the privatisation of ETSA failed in a commercial sense, as other electricity retailers could not be enticed to enter the South Australian market, which meant that AGL was able to set prices unchallenged by competitors. On 30 September 2002, the company announced that standard power prices would rise by nearly 25% in the new year.[58] According to one study, this and subsequent price increases, coupled with the loss of ETSA's dividends returned to government, cost South Australians between $2 billion and $3 billion over the next 10 years.[59] Competition did eventually emerge but electricity prices were not significantly reduced because of it. The sale of ETSA had thus effectively transferred government debt to the public it served.

Stories about the economy and finance, typically found in the middle sections of a newspaper, thus became front page news items in the 1980s and 1990s. Owing to the professionalisation and commercialisation of organised sport during the period, they also increasingly became the subject of reports printed on the back. The Formula One Grand Prix and subsequently programmed annual races featuring motor cars and bicycles, which aimed to attract tourists to the state, typified the marriage of commercial and sporting interests. So too did the development of a national Australian Rules Football League (AFL), into which entered two South Australian teams, the Adelaide Crows and Port Adelaide. The AFL promised to pit the best players and teams in the land against each other on a weekly basis, thus creating an irresistible product for a lucrative national audience. Television and media companies were soon bidding hundreds of millions of dollars to acquire the rights to broadcast games with the prospect of earning even higher revenue from selling advertising during the telecasts, and sponsors clamoured to associate their brands with successful teams. Marketable players and coaches, such as the Adelaide Crows's Mark Ricciuto and Malcolm Blight, negotiated contracts worth hundreds of thousands of dollars per season. The net result was unparalleled exposure for the game and its sponsors and unprecedented fame and fortune for its star players. Public excitement for the AFL bordered on hysteria when the Crows won the AFL premiership in 1997 and 1998 and Port Adelaide in 2004. But this transformation came at a cost. State League football (the SANFL), sporting a proud tradition spanning over 100 years, was brought to its knees, barely able to attract 2,000 spectators to matches. The price of admission to AFL games also became prohibitive for poorer families, and some of the best viewing areas at the grounds were reserved for 'corporate boxes' rather than ordinary spectators. Furthermore, in part to make the game more palatable for a mass audience, particularly women, its rules were modified to make it less physically dangerous and more free-flowing, to the disappointment of those who liked to see football remain a true test of a player's courage, strength and grit.

AFL provided an opportunity for Indigenous athletes to have their skills recognised, and South Australian-born players such as Andrew McLeod and Gavin Wanganeen achieved a level of public

Figure 10.1: Andrew McLeod of the Adelaide Crows kicks in front of Port Power's Kane Cornes during an AFL match, 1 May 2010. Courtesy of Getty Images/Morne de Klerk/Stringer.

admiration foreign to Indigenous males. Indigenous people suffered, and continue to suffer, markedly higher rates of disease, unemployment and alcoholism than non-Indigenous people, and accordingly had much shorter life expectancies, for which they were generally held culpable and admonished for failing to look after themselves. Yet the longer-term socio-political and economic factors that led to poor health and welfare outcomes for Indigenous people – not least of which were the dispossession of their land, forced dependence on the State, and institutionalised forms of racism – were plain to see for those who cared to look. This was nowhere more apparent than in South Australian jails and police watch-houses, where Indigenous men and women were 20 times more likely than non-Indigenous people to be in custody and 30 times more likely to die – shocking in itself, but also twice the national average.[60] Two national inquiries conducted in the late 1980s and 1990s concerning Aboriginal deaths in custody rejected the notion that Indigenous prisoners were meeting misadventure at the hands of police or correctional officers; they were more likely to be committing suicide or dying from acute health issues.[61] It also found that many Indigenous offenders might have avoided incarceration in the first place, having been more likely to be arrested for minor offences, and placed in remand (rather than on bail) while waiting trial, compared to non-Indigenous offenders.[62] Moreover, a high proportion of the Indigenous prison population had family experience of forced child removal by the state (43 of the 99 Indigenous people who died in custody in Australia between 1980 and 1989 had been removed from their parents as children, for example),[63] suggesting that the trauma of family separation may have contributed to their destructive behaviour.[64]

The Royal Commission into Aboriginal Deaths in Custody thus became one of the first official forums to acknowledge the social and psychological ramifications of state-sponsored Indigenous family separation that took place in South Australia until the 1960s. Records are incomplete, but documentation and surveys of select groups suggest that between one-in-ten and one-in-three Aboriginal children were separated from their parents and placed in the care of government or church-run institutions or fostered out to white families.[65] The figure depends on whether one only counts children who were forcibly removed by the State or also those who were given up by their parents under duress and/or after being misled to believe that the separation would be temporary. For example, a submission by the SA Lutheran Church to the National Inquiry into the Separation of Aboriginal and Torres Strait Islander Children from Their Families (the 'Bringing Them Home' Inquiry) noted that a large number of South Australian parents relinquished their children to the care of the Koonibba Lutheran mission in order to protect them from being taken by the Protector of Aborigines and placed in institutions further away. (At Koonibba the parents were permitted limited and supervised access, although distance remained an impediment.)[66] The ultimate purpose of removal was to control the reproduction of Indigenous people with a view to 'merging' or 'absorbing' the children into the non-Indigenous population and severing connection to their culture. It also served to prepare Indigenous boys and girls for manual and domestic labour, which was in short supply in remote areas.[67]

In the 1990s much was learnt about the 'Stolen Generations' – the name given to those who experienced child removal – although claims that the policies were racially motivated (rather than based on sound child welfare principles) and that those 'stolen' were necessarily disadvantaged were contested, most notably by Prime Minister John Howard and a small number of conservative politicians, media commentators and historians. Their version of history contradicted the testimony of 535 Indigenous people who made direct submissions to the Bringing Them Home Inquiry and spoke of the enduring effects that the child removal policies had on their lives. They told of being forced to relinquish their culture and language and being taught to feel ashamed of their race and heritage, which prevented them connecting with family members later in life and resulted in feelings of worthlessness and isolation. And they spoke of how their trauma and, in some cases, physical and sexual abuse while in 'care' – now manifested as depression, or anger, or distrust or stunted intellectual growth – affected their relationships with their own children and the wider community. While the Commonwealth Government steadfastly refused to make an apology on behalf of those who enacted and enforced the child removal policies, the South Australian Government joined other state parliaments in issuing statements of sorrow and regret following the release of the *Bringing Them Home* report in 1997, and established a range of services that aimed to reconnect members of the Stolen Generations with their biological families and culture.

The other main racial group to attract public attention during this period were those born in Asia, particularly Vietnam, who migrated to South Australia in unprecedented numbers following the Commonwealth Government's abandonment of the 'White Australia' immigration policy and the end of the Vietnam War in the 1970s. Between 1981 and 1996, only the United Kingdom provided more migrants to South Australia than Vietnam. The Vietnamese-born population grew from 2,379 to 10,667 people,[68] and migrants from Malaysia and the Philippines composed the next most rapidly growing populations. In contrast, the Italian, German, Greek and Dutch-born populations of South Australia – some of the longest-standing and largest ethnic groups in the state – were declining in number. Most of the Vietnamese arrived as refugees or through humanitarian and family reunion programs following the imposition of a communist government in South Vietnam in 1975. Some, including Hieu Van Le, who 37 years later would become the state's Governor, fled for their lives aboard rickety fishing boats and washed up on Australia's northern shores, prompting panic among politicians and the public. These 'boat people', as they became known, were accused of bringing disease and dangerous ideologies with them, and draining the welfare system, none of which had a basis in fact. Nevertheless, the Commonwealth Government led by Malcolm Fraser allowed them to reside in the community and quickly processed their claims for asylum. In South Australia they made new lives and then sponsored family members to join them. They were largely successful, despite arriving when the economy and the availability of work were in decline. This contrasted with the context of the arrival of Displaced Persons after World War II who enjoyed almost three decades of full employment, affording them enhanced opportunities for prosperity and upward social mobility.

When a second wave of unauthorised boat arrivals from South-East Asia crashed upon Australia's shores at the end of the 1980s and the start of the 1990s, the Federal Government adopted a much more punitive approach. It established a system of mandatory detention for onshore asylum seekers, which saw adults and children incarcerated in detention centres, sometimes for many years, while they awaited the processing of their claims. One of the most notorious centres was located on the desert plains at Woomera, 485 kilometres north east of Adelaide. Between 2000 and 2002, the Woomera facility attracted international media attention when detainees staged a sequence of hunger strikes, sewed their lips together, and burned buildings and breached the perimeter fence during a riot protesting their treatment. These incidents occurred in the wake of the Howard Government's toughened stance on 'border protection', which reinforced the system of detention despite mounting evidence of its traumatic effect on detainees, especially children, and the fact that between 70% and 99% of detainees were eventually found to be legitimate refugees (the acceptance rate varied according to the country of origin and the time of arrival).[69] The Woomera facility was quietly closed in April 2003 after the

Figure 10.2: Nguyen Hoang Thanh is reunited with his wife, Mai Thanh Thuy, and two children at Adelaide airport in 1988. Nguyen Hoang Thanh had escaped from Vietnam by boat in 1982 and was selected for re-settlement in Australia under the Indo-Chinese Refugee Program. Their arrival reflected a shift in the ethnic composition of migrants to South Australia in the final decades of the 20th century. Courtesy of the National Archives of Australia. A12111, 2/1988/20A/1.

Government moved the detention and refugee assessment process to islands off the Australian mainland and thus further away from the prying eyes of those wishing to monitor the treatment of the detainees and assist them in making their cases.

The Asian-born migrants who came to South Australia were bucking a trend, as the poor economic situation and employment prospects in the state proved a disincentive for overseas and interstate migrants to settle here. Between 1991 and 2001, the South Australian population grew by just 3.9%, compared to an increase of 11.5% for Australia as a whole. By comparison, the populations of Western Australia and Queensland grew by 16.5% and 20.6% respectively.[70] The mean age of the South Australian population increased from 33 to 37 years during this period, and the proportion of people aged 65 years and over (and thus more likely to be drawing a pension rather than working and paying tax) increased from 12.9% to 14.6% of the state's population.[71] In each case this was significantly higher than the national average.[72] As the rate of births and deaths remained relatively stable over the period, the stagnation and ageing of South Australia's population was due to young people leaving to seek better opportunities elsewhere, and the state's inability to attract overseas and interstate migrants. (In the period 1991–2001, for example, 40,774 more people migrated interstate from South Australia than vice versa.[73]) Without an increasing population to serve, the outlook for South Australian businesses looked bleak, and the government recognised it would be increasingly difficult to provide services (particularly health-related) to an ageing population while it had limited revenue-raising capacity. Retaining the state's best and brightest young people, and attracting skilled and energetic migrants to the state, thus became a key priority for politicians and business leaders in the new millennium.

Chapter 11

Age of Anxiety, 2002–present

The apprehension engendered by the 'Y2K' bug – an embedded 'fault' in computer software that threatened to shut down electronic communication and navigation systems and cause planes to fall from the sky at midnight on 31 December 1999[1] – was prescient of a mood that came to define the next decade and beyond. Outside of the Great Depression and wartime, South Australians had seemingly never before been so anxious and uncomfortable: about their looks, their diet, their level of happiness, their health, their incomes, their job prospects, their sons and daughters moving interstate and the foreigners, especially refugees and non-Christian migrants, who replaced them. But herein lies the paradox. At a time when so many people felt poorer, threatened, stressed, unhealthy and worse off than others, the reality was that South Australians were more prosperous and secure, and living longer, healthier lives than ever before. Young people might have left the state, causing alarm, but they were inclined to return to raise families, bringing with them acquired skills and experiences that could be used profitably.[2] And despite Adelaide being derided by some as drab and backward, it was ranked the fifth 'most liveable' city in the world by an esteemed international magazine according to a comprehensive set of criteria.[3] If South Australians had a problem, it was seeing the glass half empty when it was almost full.

Technologies such as the internet and 'smart' phones – and their associated global news services, entertainment channels and social media apps – have played a role in magnifying personal insecurities.

South Australians now have unprecedented access to information about the affairs of others, at least as they are reported, tweeted and blogged in bite-sized, Photoshopped packages. Offering a representation of reality rather than reality itself – be this concerning the size of a woman's waist or the dangers of a city street – this information fosters false comparisons and unrealistic expectations, and manufactures desires that cannot be satiated or can be satiated too easily. Moreover, the sheer quantity of information that is now available is overwhelming to some people, leading to feelings of frustration and impotence as they confront the impossibility of processing, let alone acting on, it. The technologies that deliver this information, now so central to the social and working lives of South Australians, are very recent inventions. In 2001, only 35% of Australian dwellings had access to the internet, nearly all via a slow 'dial-up' service, and Apple Corporation's pioneering internet-enabled 'smart' phone was not introduced to the Australian market until July 2008.[4] Yet they are now almost universally utilised, especially by people under 65 years of age.

International and national events since the start of the millennium certainly gave cause for concern, but the fears were disproportionate to the events' actual impact on the lives of South Australians. Terrorist attacks on the mainland of the United States in September 2001 and then bombings in London and on the island of Bali, where Australians like to holiday, drew reprisals against countries that were seen to support terrorists; thus began a 'war on terror' that Australia joined but which in turn made Australians targets. The Australian Government placed its own citizens under closer surveillance and eroded privacy laws, and increased expenditure on defence and intelligence services. Critics of this approach have argued that the civil rights of all have thus been diminished for the sake of identifying internal enemies who barely exist, and note that more Australians have been killed or wounded by shark attacks than by terrorist activity on Australian soil, and an even greater number perish by drowning in the bath.[5]

The Global Financial Crisis, as it became known, has had more tangible effects. It manifested in 2007–08 as the consequence of US banks issuing mortgages to 'sub-prime' borrowers who were unable to repay their loans. This debt was in turn re-packaged and sold to other financial institutions and investors who did not fully appreciate the risk their purchase entailed. As the borrowers defaulted on their loans, the value of these investments plummeted along with the price of real estate. Some of America's largest banks were broken and it became more difficult to obtain credit, affecting the viability of businesses and companies and the value of share markets around the world. Due to the restriction on credit and the uncertainty fostered by these events, private and business spending and investment slowed, serving to exacerbate the pressure on businesses, their ability to hire workers, and the government's collection of tax revenue. Within three years, the economies of most developed countries had gone into recession, housing prices diminished by up to one-third and unemployment rates doubled or tripled.[6]

Australia remained relatively unscathed during this turmoil due to the strength of its more tightly regulated banking system; the insatiable appetite of developing countries, such as India and China, for commodities that Australia produced; and the quick decision by the Commonwealth Government to guarantee bank deposits and stimulate the economy by spending. The 'stimulus package' came in a number of stages, including $10.4 billion in late 2008 in the form of direct payments to pensioners, carers and families, and extra assistance to first home buyers and builders; and $42 billion committed in February 2009 that was delivered as direct cash payments to individuals, tax breaks for small business, and spending on school and university buildings, energy efficiency initiatives, and road and rail infrastructure projects. In 2009–10 alone, this spending in South Australia was estimated to have generated 11,000 jobs and contributed $1.06 billion to South Australia's Gross State Product.[7] The lesson of the Great Depression was thus heeded here, if not in parts of Europe; the Australian economy continued to grow, albeit modestly, and employment rates remained reasonably steady.[8]

South Australian-based industries and projects that relied on foreign ownership or investment were, however, affected, as these owners and investors were forced to contract or pursue more cautious strategies. Australian exporters also became less competitive as the value of the Australian dollar increased by more than one-third – a consequence of Australia's relatively stable economy and booming resources sector – which meant that Australian goods and commodities became more expensive in the international market and foreign-made goods cheaper to import.[9] Combined, these factors sounded the death knell for car manufacturing and the associated metals and components industries in South Australia, and contributed to the loss of 16,500 manufacturing jobs between the start of 2007 and the end of 2012.[10] With car manufacturing having such a long history in the state, and being tied to the fortunes of so many South Australian families, the closure of the General Motors Holden and Mitsubishi assembly plants had an emotional and psychological impact that went beyond the material. In reality, the withdrawal of the companies had been a long time coming, as it was cheaper to manufacture vehicles in developing countries where labour costs were lower and workplace regulation less stringent. Mitsubishi closed its Adelaide plant in 2008 and General Motors Holden was only able to continue production due to generous financial assistance from the Federal Government. It accepted $275 million in 2012 with a pledge to invest approximately $1 billion to continue car production in Australia until 2022.[11] Just 12 months later the company announced that it was cutting production and later declared its wholesale withdrawal from Australian manufacturing, to become effective in October 2017.[12]

The indefinite postponement of the scheduled expansion of BHP Billiton's Olympic Dam mining project near Roxby Downs in August 2012, which was expected to have injected $30 billion into the South Australian economy, was less foreseen. Just a year earlier the project had been described by the Government as a 'game-changer' for the state, with the benefits to include royalties of $350 million per year and the creation of 25,000 new jobs.[13] The Liberal Party tried to blame the company's decision on the federal Labor Government's introduction of a tax on mining 'super profits', but this was denied by the company, which cited mineral-extraction costs and global economic conditions instead.[14] The gloom surrounding this announcement exacerbated the anxiety that South Australia was falling further behind Queensland and Western Australia, whose energy and mineral resources were being fully exploited and which in turn were increasing tax and royalty revenue and attracting workers from interstate and overseas.

Yet these situations were never as bleak as portrayed. South Australia's economy – fortified by other forms of manufacturing – maintained steady growth throughout the 2000s and certainly outpaced the dire performance of the 1990s. Between 2002–03 and 2011–12, the Gross State Product grew from $53 billion to $92 billion, a 65% increase, the same as Australia's non-mining states.[15] During this time annual exports grew by 36%, rising to $11.4 billion.[16] By both indicators, South Australia was the envy of much of the western world. Manufacturing remained a major contributor to South Australia's economic, export and employment base, accounting for 10% of the workforce, around 37% of the value of exports, and 32.5% of research and development expenditure.[17] It continues to underpin and generate jobs in other industries (such as services, resources and construction) and includes a myriad of activities in addition to production (such as design, logistics, customer relations and research) that are not counted as manufacturing jobs in the statistics. Clearly, manufacturing in the state could not be left to wither on the vine and so, stung into action by the collapse of the car industry, the South Australian Government developed a range of initiatives to stimulate the development of high-tech and high-value-added manufacturing and to enable the retooling or transitioning of manufacturers that supplied the automotive industry.

The Olympic Dam expansion will also eventually come to fruition; the valuable ore remains in the ground and will be mined when improved extraction methods and commodity prices make it more profitable to do so. In some ways the delay is a blessing, as the South Australian community now has an opportunity to get a better deal from the project. Having been let down by BHP Billiton in 2012, the government will be in a stronger position to negotiate an indenture agreement, and it might be possible to avoid some of the negative consequences of the rapidly expanding mining sectors in other states, such as damaging inflationary impacts and the crowding out of other economic activity in the non-mining sectors.[18] Furthermore, as Jane Andrew and John Spoehr have asserted, less rapid mining growth is arguably a better outcome for the manufacturing sector, which might have been starved of local engineering, construction and electrical skills had the Olympic Dam expansion proceeded as planned.[19]

Such optimistic thinking, of course, runs counter to the mood of the times. It is therefore not surprising that South Australian governments elected since 2002 have tended to be modest in their promises, limited in their vision and frugal with their spending to avoid provoking further disappointment or calamity. They had little other choice. Labor came to power under Mike Rann in 2002, despite losing the popular vote. It was able to form government only because elected Independent members pledged their support. It had to appease the wishes of these members, secure the cooperation of backbenchers, and build a supporter base that would ensure its success in subsequent elections. Labor also needed to re-establish its credentials as a financial manager after its reputation was corroded by the collapse of the State Bank when last in office. There was thus little money for much-needed infrastructure projects and a succession of budget surpluses were announced as Treasurer Kevin Foley assiduously pursued the restoration of South Australia's AAA credit rating.[20] Once achieved, and with Labor's electoral fortunes secured, the onset of the Global Financial Crisis threatened to apply further brakes.[21] Yet the Commonwealth Government's stimulus package delivered road and rail projects, and upgrades to school, university and medical facilities, to which the South Australian Government contributed funds. The State Government also sponsored its own projects, such as constructing a desalination plant powered by renewable energy and redeveloping the Adelaide Oval and Royal Adelaide Hospital, forcing it to borrow heavily and again lose its AAA credit rating. This time the long-term benefits were perceived to outweigh the short-term pain, and the credit rating downgrade in 2012 did not trouble financial commentators and the general public to the extent it had in earlier years.

Under Rann's leadership the Government's social, economic, environmental and cultural priorities were encapsulated in a series of Strategic Plans that also identified the 'key performance indicators' that would measure whether its goals had been met. This provoked scorn among those who doubted that a society could or should be run like a business, but was well-received by the public and successful in promoting reform and improvements, mainly because it made the achievements of government reasonably transparent and the Government (prompted by independent auditors) was honest in its assessment of its and other stakeholders' performance.

Maintenance of law and order was one of the strategic priorities that received the most attention due to the Rann Government's populist pledge to increase the size of the police force along with the duration of imprisonment for those found guilty of serious crimes. Against the advice of criminologists who sought the expansion of prison diversion and educational programs for young or non-violent offenders, the Government promised to 'rack 'em, pack 'em, and stack 'em' in prison until the lessons of the law were heeded.[22] It also quarrelled with the Director of Public Prosecutions, who was accused of not pursuing particular cases with sufficient vigour; outlawed motorcycle gangs, preventing the association of their members and the fortification of club premises; and instigated harsher penalties for 'hoon drivers', including the confiscation of their vehicles. This in turn resulted in High Court challenges to the respective laws on the grounds that they eroded the judiciary's power to determine appropriate punishments based on the specific circumstances of individual cases, or to review or challenge decisions.[23] Discourse surrounding these matters probably only served to elevate the public's anxiety about their safety. More than two-thirds of the 3,500 respondents to a 2007 survey believed either that their community was less safe than it was five years previous or that safety had not improved, while almost 40% believed that efforts to control 'bikie' gangs had been ineffective.[24] A similarly sized survey conducted the previous year showed that almost 70% of respondents felt either 'quite unsafe' or 'very unsafe' when frequenting train stations and bus stops or walking through Rundle Mall or the parklands in the evening; more than one-quarter felt unsafe in their suburbs at night and 8% felt unsafe in their own homes.[25] This, despite the level of victim-reported crime falling by 37% between 2000–01 and 2010–11, and public-order offences (those that resulted from proactive police activity) also decreasing.[26] The state's rate of prison recidivism (that is, the rate of re-entry of offenders into the prison system within two years of being released) was also the lowest in the nation.[27]

When other socio-economic categories were considered, however, South Australia frequently found itself at the other end of the scale. Of the mainland states, it contains the highest proportion of households in receipt of government pensions and welfare payments (29.2% in 2011–12 compared to the national average of 24.8%),[28] and South Australian households earned the lowest average gross income.[29] There is also a vast difference between the incomes earned by the wealthiest and poorest households, a gap that has persisted for many decades and is getting wider. Since 1994–95, the poorest 40% of South Australian households have consistently shared in 15% or less of the total household income in the state, while the top 20% have held about 45% of total household income.[30] When 'wealth' (which includes assets and superannuation accumulated over a lifetime) is considered rather than just annual income, the disparity is even more marked. The poorest 40% of Australian households share of total net wealth decreased from just 7% to 6.3% between 2003–04 and 2009–10, and South Australia mirrored this trend despite having a demographic profile favouring home ownership.[31] Overall, we might speculate that South Australians are now wealthier than they have ever been but this wealth is less evenly distributed. If income and assets alone could be said to define 'class', the oft repeated notion that South Australia is a 'classless' society is clearly unsustainable, if it ever held truth at all.

Access to steady and fulfilling employment is part of this equation. Rates of unemployment have fluctuated since the start of the millennium, and were significantly affected by the Global Financial Crisis, the Government's stimulus package, the resources boom and oscillations in the exchange rate. The construction industry was buoyed by stimulus spending between 2008 and 2011 but has fallen since, while jobs in manufacturing mostly declined over the entire period.[32] By June 2015, the seasonally adjusted unemployment rate touched 7.9%, a full two percentage points higher than the national average, although the difference has more than halved since that time.[33] The outlook is not positive, with more job losses following the closure of Holden's Elizabeth plant, and the ceasation of steel manufacturing in Whyalla and coal mining at Leigh Creek, but the unemployment figure will likely remain well below the 12.7% it reached during the early 1990s recession, when interest rates and inflation were also much higher.[34] New jobs will continue to be created in the health and community services sector, with strong demand especially for nurses and aged care workers to service South Australia's 'ageing' population.[35] These figures hide much higher rates of youth unemployment, and under-employment, whereby casual and part-time workers who would like (and often need) to work more are unable to do so. Female workers are more likely than males to fall in the latter category, with data collected since 2002 suggesting that 14–20% of female employees wanted more work.[36]

Like the rest of the nation, South Australia has experienced a significant increase in female labour-force participation over the past few decades. Women comprised just 36.4% of the workforce in 1976, but are now approaching parity with men, constituting 47.1% of those employed in July 2017.[37] However, gender-based segregation persists, as female employment is generally clustered around occupations that attract lower wages and are considered low-skilled, and provide limited or no professional development opportunities.[38] Moreover, this work is predominantly part-time or casual, which allows for fewer employment-related benefits.[39] As of July 2017, 52.1% of all women workers in South Australia were in part-time or casual employment compared to 31.4% in 1976.[40] The earnings of South Australian women employed on a full-time basis stood at 86.9% of men's earnings as of May 2017,[41] and their total take-home earnings compared to men's declined from 68.1% in 2004 to 67.3%.[42] Thus, overall women's earnings have fallen relative to men's in the last decade – reversing the trend of the previous decade.

Inevitably, these shifts in the composition of the workforce have resulted in significant changes in the structure of households and have affected relationships between men and women. Fewer men are now the primary 'breadwinner' for their families, which has impacted on their status and self-esteem. They are also expected to do more unpaid work in the home and caring for children, although surveys suggest that they still do not do their fair share.[43] Depending on one's point of view, the increased economic independence of women stemming from their higher rate of participation in the workforce can be seen as a contributing factor to, or a symptom of, the decline in the rate of marriage, the rise in the divorce rate and the increase in the average age for women giving birth for the first time, all of which have occurred over the past few decades.[44] In South Australia, single-person households rose from 19.2% to 27.9% of all households between 1986 and 2011, with the majority of lone-person households comprised of women.[45] Over this period there was also a 68% increase in households comprising a single parent with a dependent child or children. As Ray Broomhill and Rhonda Sharp note, the disintegration of the nuclear family and rapid rise in single-parent households over the past two decades has been one of the major causes of impoverishment.[46]

Women fill four-fifths of the positions in health care and social assistance industries,[47] and are being relied upon to tend South Australia's 'ageing' population. Indeed, one of the most profound changes to occur over the past century has been the astonishing increase in the life expectancy of Australians, which between 1950 and 2012 improved from 66.5 years to 79.9 years for men, and 71.7 years to 84.3 years for women.[48] This is mainly due to improved medical care and the early detection and treatment of illnesses and disease, none of which comes cheap. Accounting for inflation, overall health expenditure in South Australia increased by 54.6% between 2003–04 and 2013–14, much higher than the growth in population or the state's income.[49]

Needless to say, this is a concern for government. With pensions to provide for and the medical expenses of a person aged over 65 years costing about four times as much as those under 65 years,[50] there are fears that within a few decades the economically active members of society will not be able to afford to pay (in the form of taxes) for the 'inactive'. However, health economists differ in their perceptions of the relationship between ageing, health and cost.[51] Some believe the impact has been overstated and that there is a shift in health costs to an older age bracket rather than longer periods of ill health or increased health-service usage; data suggests that South Australians are living free from illness and disability for longer periods, rather than just dying later.[52] They also point to the often ignored contributions made by older people in society. Economists in the United Kingdom, for example, quantified the net contribution made by people aged over 65 to the UK economy in 2010. They found that senior citizens added £76 billion to the economy through spending, £34 billion through providing informal care, £10 billion through volunteering, and £10 billion through charity and family donations. In addition to paying about £45 billion in tax, these contributions exceeded the cost of providing health care and pensions by some £40 billion.[53]

The Australian Government's response to the impending 'crisis' has been to raise the age of retirement by two years and encourage employers to hire workers aged over 55. Under Premier Jay Weatherill, who replaced Rann in 2011, the discourse surrounding ageing in South Australia has been framed more positively, with the contributions of older residents recognised and the growth of employment in the health and social assistance sector welcomed to counterbalance the decline of manufacturing jobs.[54] Challenges remain, however. For example, most elderly people prefer to be cared for in their own homes, but the number of family members willing or able to provide this care is diminishing, especially as more women take up paid employment.[55] One thing is certain: those entering the ranks of senior citizenry won't allow their needs to be ignored, having acquired political skills and confidence in their formative years spent protesting for the rights of women, Indigenous people, army conscripts and other such causes, and having already 'done their bit' caring for older family members and friends.

Aboriginal people have been largely excluded from the debate about ageing because so few of them are attaining the age of retirement. Indigenous Australians have higher death rates than non-Indigenous Australians across all age groups, with those in the 35–44 age group dying at about five times the rate of non-Indigenous people.[56] Accordingly the life expectancy of an Indigenous boy or girl born this decade is, respectively, 10.6 years and 9.5 years lower than the national average.[57] Just 3.7% of South Australia's Indigenous population is aged over 65, compared to 16.2% of the state's non-Indigenous population.[58] Nevertheless, overall health outcomes are improving and the gap in life expectancy between Indigenous and non-Indigenous Australians has narrowed over the past few decades.[59] Both the Commonwealth and South Australian governments have committed substantial funds (currently 1.5 times that spent on non-Indigenous people on a per capita basis)[60] to provide improved access to primary and tertiary health care services, and to better prevent and manage the devastating impact of chronic disease and substance abuse within Indigenous communities. It is proving a more difficult task to overcome the underlying social and economic factors that largely explain the poor health of Indigenous people relative to the rest of the population, namely the patchy provision of education that is culturally relevant and appropriate, inferior employment opportunities and the psychological damage that has resulted from being dislocated from country and family.

With so much discussion about ageing and mortality, it is easy to overlook that one of the other major transformations to take place in South Australia since the beginning of the new millennium has been the focus on providing opportunities for youth and on building vibrant, exciting communities in which young people want to live. Changes to development regulations have seen a boom in the construction of apartments in Adelaide's CBD and inner suburbs, which has brought young people and professional couples into the city centre and the establishment of new cafes, restaurants and shops to cater for them. Amendments to licensing laws have also enabled small bars and eateries to open in the formerly deserted laneways and side-streets of the CBD – a model pioneered in Melbourne (itself borrowed from cities such as Barcelona) to great effect. Through innovative programs, such as Renew Adelaide, young entrepreneurs have been allowed to open rent-free 'pop-up' shops, cafes, galleries and studios in formerly unoccupied and sometimes derelict commercial spaces, enhancing both the safety and amenity of the streets in which they are located. And the range of festivals on offer, increasingly throughout the year rather than just clustered into 'mad March', now cater to seemingly all tastes and proclivities.

Cultural and commercial activity in Adelaide's centre, and its youthful visage, has also been boosted by the resident population of international students, which has tripled since 2002 and now stands above 34,000.[61] Currently about 40% of the students are from China, with India, Malaysia and Vietnam the next most prominent countries of origin.[62] The majority of the students are enrolled in university or vocational courses and desire to be located close to the CBD-based campuses. They have thus had a significant role in reshaping the accommodation market in the CBD, and, as they pay much higher fees than domestic students, have propped up the higher education sector, which has been starved of funding since the mid-1990s. A high proportion of graduates subsequently apply for permanent residency (which an Australian university degree and English language proficiency facilitates), and some have become conduits for initiating and improving business and trade relationships between South Australia and their countries of origin. Due to the growth in international students, 'educational services' has become one of South Australia's most valuable export products in its own right.

Based on present trends and the capacity for growth, in a social, economic and political sense, Asia and the broader Indo-Pacific region will become more important to South Australia than will the United Kingdom, European Union and North America. China has already become the state's largest export destination, receiving between one-fifth and one-third of all exports by value (the proportion depends on the exchange rate and price of commodities at the time in question), and East Asian nations and India account for another one-third.[63] China and India are particularly interested in the state's minerals, energy and natural resources, 'clean' technologies (such as renewable energy and wastewater management systems) and education sector. Chinese markets for tourism, wine, agribusiness and advanced manufacturing are also strong, as is India's interest in aerospace and defence industries.[64] To this point, governments and business leaders in Asian nations, with the exception of Japan, have been more interested in buying raw materials, goods and services than investing in their production in South Australia. In 2012, only 5% of Chinese investment in Australian enterprises occurred in South Australia (some US$523 million), compared to 33% in Queensland (US$3732 million) and 56% in Western Australia (US$6383 million).[65] More recently, Chinese investment has turned to electricity production in Victoria and real estate acquisition and development in New South Wales, so South Australia's share of investment has dropped to 2–3%.[66] The State Government has led numerous trade delegations to Asian countries, and hosted overseas business leaders here, with the aim of increasing the state's share. Limited knowledge within South Australia's business community and public service of Asian cultures, customs and languages is proving an impediment – a legacy of Australia's historical determination to see itself as a white, European nation.

Food security – especially food grown in pristine environments – is becoming a major issue for Asian nations, so South Australia is well positioned to benefit from increased demand and investment in this area. This prospect remains only while the state's agricultural and pastoral environments remain productive and relatively unsullied. Given the current rate of climate change, this is anything but certain. South Australia's mean decadal surface temperature (the average temperature measured over a decade) has increased by nearly 1.5°C since 1950,[67] resulting in less rain over agricultural districts and less inflow into dams and water storages. The greatest change occurred between 2000 and 2009, when the average temperature was 0.58°C higher than during the previous decade.[68] If this trend continues, drought will occur with greater frequency and severity, rainfall will be more erratic and weather systems more destructive, and food production and biodiversity will be severely affected. The warming of the atmosphere has been attributed to the 'greenhouse effect', to which humans contribute by releasing heat-trapping gases into the atmosphere, especially through the burning of fossil fuels such as coal and oil for energy production. Energy use accounts for two-thirds of 'greenhouse gas' emissions, while the release of gas from industrial processes and livestock account for the majority of the rest.[69]

Australian governments and industries have taken longer than their European counterparts to acknowledge the need to curtail the use of fossil fuels and invest in the production of energy-efficient machines and renewable and non-polluting energy sources. In the Australian context, South Australia has been a leader in this regard, and has reduced its greenhouse gas emissions at a faster rate than the national average (and, on a per capita basis, by 19.5% in total between 2002 and 2013).[70] This has largely been accomplished through investment in 'wind farms' that generate electricity, which consumers can purchase instead of electricity produced by coal- or gas-fired power stations. When the Rann Government took office, South Australia had only one functional wind turbine and no substantial solar-power generation. The wind farm was located at Coober Pedy and amounted to 0.2% of national capacity.[71] Twelve years later wind- and solar-powered sources, respectively, produced 34% and 7% of electricity generated in the state,[72] and South Australia was producing 54% of the nation's wind power.[73] While Rann took credit for this transformation and certainly provided some financial incentives, the state's interest in wind power began in earnest under John Olsen, spurred by the Federal Government's introduction of the Mandatory Renewable Energy Target (MRET) in 2000.[74] The MRET mandated a 2% increase in renewably generated electricity, providing a market impetus to commercial investment in wind power. South Australia reached 54% of national capacity in 2006 with six operational wind farms, two of which had received planning approval before Labor came to power.[75] A further 10 wind farms were built by 2014.

Other 'clean' energy sources have not been exploited to the same extent. Despite Rann Government initiatives to install solar panels on school and government buildings, and the introduction of the first solar feed-in tariff in the nation, uptake of solar installations in the state remained negligible through to 2010.[76] In the next four years, the state improved its solar photo-voltaic capacity 11-fold due to the influence of an upwardly revised MRET target and federal government incentives.[77] Among the states and territories it now ranks fourth in solar photo-voltaic generation, but it does have the greatest proportion of households with rooftop panels (26%).[78] The majority of the nation's investment in geothermal energy exploration also occurs in South Australia; however, this source has yet to be successfully tapped.[79]

Fossil fuels are cheaper to use than renewable and non-polluting sources of energy, but their cost has traditionally not reflected the environmental damage caused by releasing carbon into the atmosphere. On 1 July 2012, the federal Labor Government placed a price on carbon emission, and greatly increased its expenditure on supporting the development of 'clean' energy production, in an effort to make 'clean' energy more attractive to consumers. As part of its response to the Global Financial Crisis, it also provided rebates for the installation of solar panels, free energy-efficient lightbulbs and subsidised roof insulation in private homes and businesses, all with the aim of reducing energy requirements. However, following a campaign waged by the Liberal Party, backed by mining and industry lobbyists, that obfuscated the scientific findings regarding global warming and turned public opinion against the government's initiatives, the 'carbon tax' was repealed and investment in 'clean' energy research and development was significantly scaled back. The responsibility for changing energy-consumption patterns in South Australia thus once again fell to the state government, which has considerably fewer resources at its disposal.

The quest for alternative sources of energy, coupled with the need to create jobs and stimulate the economy, revived interest in nuclear power generation and the domestic exploitation of South Australia's world-leading reserves of uranium. (This is somewhat incongruous given that the use of nuclear power generation is being phased out in highly industrialised Germany, the world's fourth biggest economy, which has mandated even more ambitious emission-reduction targets than Australia.[80]) In May 2015, a Royal Commission into the Nuclear Fuel Cycle was established to investigate the risks, feasibility and viability of uranium enrichment, nuclear power generation and radioactive waste storage in South Australia. The Commissioners' interim findings, released in February 2016, cast doubt on the cost effectiveness of the former, but were bullish about the prospects of South Australia storing high-level radioactive waste from overseas. Despite admitting that there was no existing market to ascertain the price that a customer might pay for the permanent disposal of their radioactive material, the Commissioners envisaged revenue to be $257 billion over the life of a waste-storage facility (with costs estimated to be $145 billion) and predicted the creation of up to 4,500 jobs in construction and 600 permanent jobs in the operation of the site and associated infrastructure.[81] Such prospects seem to have initially swayed public opinion, with a poll suggesting stronger support than opposition,[82] although even the most enthusiastic commentators have expressed disappointment that the state might settle for being a 'dump' instead of taking its rightful place at the forefront of nuclear technology.[83]

The Royal Commissioners' enthusiasm and public support marks a dramatic reversal of long-held opinion on these issues. The South Australian Parliament maintained a complete ban on the mining and processing of uranium in the state until as recently as 1982 due to concerns about radiation 'leakage' and detrimental effects on population health. Then, in 2003, in virulent opposition to a federal government proposal to store nuclear waste in outback South Australia, Premier Rann promised to declare the proposed site a national park and then took the Federal Government to court after it rushed to acquire the land before state parliament could pass its own enabling legislation.[84] The appeal was dismissed, but a further appeal before the Full Court of the Federal Court was successful. (Both sides were conspicuously silent when the lucrative Olympic Dam uranium mine, located near the proposed nuclear waste site, reported its fifth serious radioactive waste liquid spill for the year in December 2003.[85]) Opinion is likely to swing again, given that a site for the most recently proposed facility has not yet been chosen and, once it is, will probably offend many, not least those who live near it or close to the ports, rail, roads and towns along and through which the radioactive waste must travel.

The decision regarding whether or not to invest in nuclear power generation and/or radioactive waste storage will largely depend on the kind of future that South Australians envisage for themselves and the state, and what they make of the present. Those who have lost faith in the ability of human beings to change their patterns of consumption or to develop more efficient machines, or who cannot foresee any other significant opportunities for economic growth, will be inclined to support the proposal. These are attitudes befitting an age of anxiety. But they are out of step with the spirit in which the past was made. The men and women who sailed to South Australia in ships from the northern hemisphere, and who pushed cattle and sheep into the dry interior and planted crops in places where it rarely rained, had greater ambition. So too those who endured the deprivation of Depression and wartime and came out the other side demanding more of themselves and each other. The scientific breakthroughs that made the desert bloom, and the social and democratic innovations that attracted national and international attention, were not achieved by or for people who were resigned to their fate. More still remains to be done, and can. The future need not belong to people who are afraid.

NOTES

Preface

1. Douglas Pike, *Paradise of Dissent: South Australia 1829–57*, Melbourne: Melbourne University Press, 1957.
2. Paul Sendziuk, 'No Convicts Here: Reconsidering South Australia's Foundation Myth', in Robert Foster and Paul Sendziuk (eds), *Turning Points: Chapters in South Australian History*, Adelaide: Wakefield Press, 2012, pp. 33–47.
3. Derek Whitelock, *Adelaide: A Sense of Difference*, 3rd edn, Melbourne: Australian Scholarly Publishing, 2000.
4. Mark Peel, 'A Place to Grow: Making a Future in Postwar South Australia', in Robert Foster and Paul Sendziuk (eds), *Turning Points: Chapters in South Australian History*, Adelaide: Wakefield Press, 2012, p. 89.
5. John Hirst, 'South Australia and Australia: Reflections and their Histories', in Robert Foster and Paul Sendziuk (eds), *Turning Points: Chapters in South Australian History*, Adelaide: Wakefield Press, 2012, p. 130.

Chapter 1 An Imaginary Dominion, 1802–35

1. *The Southern Australian*, 28 July 1840.
2. Chris Clarkson *et al.*, 'Human Occupation of Northern Australia by 65,000 Years Ago', *Nature*, 547, 20 July 2017, p. 306.
3. Josephine Flood, *The Original Australians: Story of the Aboriginal People*, Sydney: Allen & Unwin, 2006, pp. 178–200.
4. Tim Flannery, *The Future Eaters: An Ecological History of the Australasian Lands and People*, Sydney: Reed Books, 1994, pp. 76–84.
5. Susan Marsden, 'South Australia', in Graeme Davison, John Hirst and Stuart Macintyre (eds), *The Oxford Companion to Australian History*, Melbourne: Oxford University Press, 1998, p. 598.
6. Paul Monaghan, 'Structures of Aboriginal Life at the Time of Colonisation in South Australia', in Peggy Brock and Tom Gara (eds), *Colonialism and its Aftermath: A History of Aboriginal South Australia*, Adelaide: Wakefield Press, 2017, pp. 23–4.

7. Charles Sturt, *Two Expeditions into the Interior of South Australia* [1833], Facsimile Edition, Sydney: Doubleday, 1982, p. 124.
8. Ibid., pp. 125–6.
9. Judy Campbell, *Invisible Invaders: Smallpox and Other Diseases in Aboriginal Australia 1780–1880*, Melbourne: Melbourne University Press, 2002, pp. 105–35.
10. Ibid., pp. 1–28.
11. Flood, p. 17.
12. Ibid., pp. 17–18.
13. R.W. Ellis, 'The Aboriginal Inhabitants and their Environment', in C.R. Twidale, M.J. Tyler and B.P. Webb (eds), *Natural History of the Adelaide Region*, Adelaide: Royal Society of South Australia, 1976, p. 115.
14. Gawler to G.F. Angas, 10 July 1840, Angas Papers, State Library of South Australia, PRG 174/1.
15. Philip Clarke, *Where the Ancestors Walked: Australia as an Aboriginal Landscape*, Sydney: Allen & Unwin, 2003, pp. 65–7.
16. Bill Gammage, *The Greatest Estate on Earth: How Aborigines Made Australia*, Sydney: Allen & Unwin, 2011.
17. Bill Gammage, 'The Adelaide District in 1836', in Robert Foster and Paul Sendziuk (eds), *Turning Points: Chapters in South Australian History*, Adelaide: Wakefield Press, 2012, p. 8.
18. Ibid., p. 10.
19. Dorothy Tunbridge, *The Story of the Flinders Ranges Mammals*, Sydney: Kangaroo Press, 1991, pp. 29–33.
20. Robert Foster and Tom Gara, 'Aboriginal Culture', in Eric Richards (ed.), *The Flinders History of South Australia: Social History*, Adelaide: Wakefield Press, 1986, p. 71.
21. G.F. Angas, *Savage Life and Scenes in Australia and New Zealand*, vol. 1, London: Smith, Elder & Co., 1847, p. 155.
22. Edward Eyre, *Journals of Expeditions of Discovery into Central Australia and Overland from Adelaide to King George's Sound in the Years 1840–41*, vol. 2, London: T. and W. Boone, 1845, p. 293.
23. Foster and Gara, p. 73.
24. Ibid., pp. 73–4.
25. Ibid., pp. 71–3.
26. Graham Jenkin, *Conquest of the Ngarrindjeri: The Story of the Lower Murray Lakes Tribes*, Adelaide: Rigby, 1979, pp. 13–15.
27. 'Aboriginal Occupation', in Trevor Griffin and Murray McCaskill (eds), *Atlas of South Australia*, Adelaide: Wakefield Press, 1986, p. 3.
28. Philip Jones, *Ochre and Rust: Artefacts and Encounters on Australian Frontiers*, Adelaide: Wakefield Press, 2007, pp. 353–61.
29. D.J. Mulvaney, 'The Chain of Connection: The Material Evidence', in Nicolas Peterson (ed.), *Tribes and Boundaries in Australia*, Canberra: Australian Institute of Aboriginal Studies, 1976, pp. 72–94.

30. Peter Hiscock, 'Creators or Destroyers? The Burning Questions of Human Impact in Ancient Aboriginal Australia', *Humanities Australia*, 5, 2014, pp. 43–5.
31. Clarke, p. 16.
32. Ibid., pp. 17–18.
33. Rebe Taylor, *Unearthed: The Aboriginal Tasmanians of Kangaroo Island*, Adelaide: Wakefield Press, 2002, p. 20.
34. Ibid., pp. 6–20.
35. Jean Fornasiero, Peter Monteath and John West-Sooby, *Encountering Terra Australis: The Australian Voyages of Nicolas Baudin and Matthew Flinders*, Adelaide: Wakefield Press, 2004, pp. 154–7.
36. Ibid., p. 167.
37. Henry Reynolds, *A History of Tasmania*, Melbourne: Cambridge University Press, 2012, p. 24.
38. Geoffrey Bolton, *Land of Vision and Mirage: Western Australia since 1826*, Perth: University of Western Australia Press, 2008, pp. 5–7.
39. Ibid., pp. 7–23.
40. Sturt, p. 246.
41. Philip Temple, *A Sort of Conscience: The Wakefields*, Auckland: Auckland University Press, 2002, pp. 89–135.
42. Douglas Pike, *Paradise of Dissent: South Australia 1829–57*, Melbourne: Melbourne University Press, 1957, pp. 52–5.
43. Ibid., p. 32.
44. Ibid., pp. 54–5.
45. Ibid., pp. 55–60.
46. Ibid., pp. 58–62.
47. Jim Main, 'The Foundation of South Australia', in Dean Jaensch (ed.), *The Flinders History of South Australia: Political History*, Adelaide: Wakefield Press, 1986, p. 5.
48. Pike, p. 62.
49. Ibid., p. 63.
50. Main, p. 6.
51. Pike, p. 64.
52. Cited in R.D. Lumb and K.W. Ryan, *The Constitution of the Commonwealth of Australia Annotated*, Sydney: Butterworths, 1974, p. 210.
53. Main, p. 7.
54. Alex C. Castles and Michael C. Harris, *Lawmakers and Wayward Whigs: Government and Law in South Australia 1836–1986*, Adelaide: Wakefield Press, 1987, p. 29.
55. Ibid., p. 8; Pike, pp. 68–9.
56. David Hilliard and Arnold D. Hunt, 'Religion', in Eric Richards (ed.), *The Flinders History of South Australia: Social History*, Adelaide: Wakefield Press, 1986, pp. 195–6.

57. Pike, p. 23.
58. Hilliard and Hunt, p. 197.
59. Pike, pp. 70–1.
60. Ibid., pp. 115–17.
61. *South Australia Act 1834*.
62. Main, p. 9.
63. Pike, pp. 97–8.
64. Ibid., pp. 92–5.
65. Ibid., pp. 103–4.
66. Ibid., pp. 105–6.
67. Jim Main, 'Social Foundations of South Australia: Men of Capital', in Eric Richards (ed.), *The Flinders History of South Australia: Social History*, Adelaide: Wakefield Press, 1986, p. 97.
68. Main, 'The Foundation of South Australia', p. 10.
69. House of Commons, *Parliamentary Debates*, 1 July 1834, p. 1061.
70. Arthur to Spring Rice, 27 January 1835, National Archives, UK (henceforth NA), CO 280/55.
71. Rowland Hill to Grey, 23 July 1835, NA, CO 13/3.
72. Stephen to Gardiner, 10 December 1836, NA, CO 13/3.
73. Ibid.
74. Grey to Torrens, 15 December 1835, NA, CO 13/3.
75. Glenelg to Torrens, 11 January 1836, NA, CO 13/4.
76. John Brown, Diary, 12 January 1836, pp. 90–1, State Library of South Australia, PRG 1002/2.
77. Thomas to Stephen, 16 January 1836, NA, CO 13/5.
78. Grey to Torrens, 21 January 1836, NA, CO 13/3.

Chapter 2 Foundations, 1836–45

1. H.J. Finnis, 'Before the Buffalo: The Story of South Australia 1800–1836', *Pioneers' Association of South Australia*, 39, 1964, pp. 14–21.
2. Beth Duncan, *Mary Thomas: Founding Mother. The Life and Times of a South Australian Pioneer*, Adelaide: Wakefield Press, 2011, p. 31.
3. Ibid., p. 21.
4. Ibid., pp. 24–5.
5. Ibid., p. 31.
6. Penelope Hope, *The Voyage of the Africaine: A Collection of Journals, Letters and Extracts from Contemporary Publications*, Melbourne: Heinemann, 1968, p.24.
7. Letter from Mary to George, 14 October 1838, cited in Duncan, p. 30.
8. John W. Adams, *My Early Days in the Colony*, Balaklava, S.A.: E.J. Walker, 1902, p. 4.
9. Duncan, pp. 27–30.
10. Hope, p. 40.
11. Ibid., p. 40.

12. Ibid., pp. 21–5.
13. Hope, pp. 77–9.
14. Finnis, pp. 14–16.
15. Philip A. Clarke, 'The Aboriginal Presence on Kangaroo Island, South Australia', in Jane Simpson and Luise Hercus (eds), *History in Portraits: Biographies of Nineteenth Century South Australian Aboriginal People*, Canberra: Aboriginal History Monograph 6, 1998, pp. 14–22.
16. Rebe Taylor, *Unearthed: The Aboriginal Tasmanians of Kangaroo Island*, Adelaide: Wakefield Press, 2002, pp. 12–43.
17. Bill Gammage, 'The Adelaide District in 1836', in Robert Foster and Paul Sendziuk (eds), *Turning Points: Chapters in South Australian History*, Adelaide: Wakefield Press, 2012, p. 7.
18. Mel Davies, 'Establishing South Australia', in Pamela Stratham (ed.), *The Origins of Australia's Capital Cities*, Melbourne: Cambridge University Press, 1990, p. 166.
19. Derek Whitelock, *Adelaide 1836–1976: A History of Difference*, Brisbane: University of Queensland Press, 1977, p. 6.
20. Geoffrey Dutton, *Founder of a City: The Life of Colonel William Light*, Melbourne: F.W. Cheshire, 1960, pp. 170–89.
21. David Elder (ed.), *William Light's Brief Journal and Australian Diaries*, Adelaide: Wakefield Press, 1984, pp. 62–3.
22. Ibid., pp. 66–9.
23. Ibid., pp. 79–81.
24. Ibid., pp. 71–2.
25. Duncan, p. 45.
26. Hope, p. 94.
27. Proclamation reproduced in Brian Dickey and Peter Howell (eds), *South Australia's Foundation: Select Documents*, Adelaide: Wakefield Press, 1986, p. 77.
28. Hope, p. 121.
29. Quoted in Hope, pp. 127–8.
30. Hindmarsh to Lord Glenelg, 1 June 1837, State Records of South Australia (henceforth SRSA), GRG 2/5.
31. Hindmarsh to Lord Glenelg, 30 May and 1 June 1837, SRSA, GRG 2/5.
32. Hindmarsh to Lord Glenelg, 19 August 1837, SRSA, GRG 2/5.
33. Hindmarsh to Lord Glenelg, 22 August and 11 September 1837, SRSA, GRG 2/5.
34. G.L. Fischer (ed.), 'Captain John Hindmarsh's Letters to George Fife Angas. Part II: 1837–1839', *South Australiana*, 1(2), September 1962, pp. 52, 60–1.
35. Hindmarsh to Lord Glenelg, 12 June 1837, SRSA, GRG 2/5.
36. Duncan, p. 66.
37. Adams, p. 11.
38. A. Grenfell Price, *Founders and Pioneers of South Australia*, Adelaide: Mary Martin Books, 1978, pp. 107–13.

39. J. Rutherford, *Sir George Grey: A Study in Colonial Government*, London: Cassell, 1961, p. 22.
40. Gawler to Lord Glenelg, 22 January 1839, SRSA, GRG 2/5.
41. Gawler to Lord Glenelg, 26 October 1838, SRSA, GRG 2/5.
42. Douglas Pike, *Paradise of Dissent: South Australia 1829–57*, Melbourne: Melbourne University Press, 1957, pp. 176–7.
43. Rutherford, p. 22.
44. Price, p. 149.
45. Duncan, pp. 105–8.
46. Ian Harmstorf and Michael Cigler, *The Germans in Australia*, Melbourne: AE Press, 1985, pp. 12–16.
47. Henry Reynolds, *The Law of the Land*, Melbourne: Penguin, 1992, p. 118.
48. Alan Atkinson and Marian Aveling (eds), *Australians 1838*, Sydney: Fairfax, Syme & Weldon Associates, 1987, p. 222.
49. Amanda Nettelbeck and Robert Foster, 'Food and Governance in the Frontiers of Colonial Australia and Canada's North-West Territories', *Aboriginal History*, 36, 2012, p. 21.
50. Protector William Wyatt's translation of Gawler's speech published in the *South Australian Gazette*, 3 November 1838, cited in Atkinson and Aveling (eds), p. 223.
51. Robert Foster, 'The Aborigines Location in Adelaide: South Australia's First "Mission" to the Aborigines', *Journal of the Anthropological Association of South Australia*, 28(1), 1990, pp. 11–37.
52. *Southern Australian*, 28 July 1840.
53. *Adelaide Chronicle*, 30 June 1841.
54. *South Australian Register*, 26 September 1840, p. 2. These theories and others are discussed in Robert Foster, Rick Hosking and Amanda Nettelbeck, *Fatal Collisions: The South Australian Frontier and the Violence of Memory*, Adelaide: Wakefield Press, 2001, pp. 17–20.
55. Foster, Hosking and Nettelbeck, pp. 13–28.
56. *South Australian Register*, 3 October 1840.
57. Robert Foster and Amanda Nettelbeck, *Out of the Silence: The History and Memory of South Australia's Frontier Wars*, Adelaide: Wakefield Press, 2012, pp. 32–9.
58. Ibid., pp. 40–54.
59. Rutherford, p. 22.
60. Ibid., p. 23.
61. Price, pp. 98–105.
62. Rutherford, pp. 23–6.
63. *South Australian Register*, 17 September 1842.
64. Lord Stanley to Grey, 1 March 1842 and 2 August 1842, *Papers Relative to South Australia*, no. 19 of 1842, pp. 67–8, and no. 54 of 1842, pp. 141–4.

65. Ibid.
66. Rodney Cockburn, *Pastoral Pioneers of South Australia*, vol. 1, Adelaide: Publishers Limited Printers, 1925, pp. 34–5.
67. Ibid., pp. 180–1.
68. Gordon D. Combe, *Responsible Government in South Australia: From the Foundations to Playford*, revised edition, Adelaide: Wakefield Press, 2009, p. 14.
69. Ibid., p. 15.
70. Reynolds, pp. 138, 148.
71. Geoffrey Blainey, *The Rush that Never Ended: A History of Australian Mining*, 4th edn, Melbourne: Melbourne University Press, 1993, pp. 104–6.
72. Whitelock, p. 29.
73. Stefan Pikusa, *The Adelaide House 1836 to 1901: The Evolution of Principal Dwelling Types*, Adelaide: Wakefield Press, 1986, pp. 3–19.
74. Price, p. 138.
75. Christopher Nance, 'The South Australian Social Experiment 1836–71: A Study of Some of the Aspects of South Australia's Early Social Development', MA Thesis, Flinders University, 1977, pp. 213–14.
76. Pike, p. 284.
77. David Hilliard and Arnold D. Hunt, 'Religion', in Eric Richards (ed.), *The Flinders History of South Australia: Social History*, Adelaide: Wakefield Press, 1986, pp. 197, 229.

Chapter 3 Settling and Unsettling, 1846–56

1. Penelope Hope, *The Voyage of the Africaine: A Collection of Journals, Letters and Extracts from Contemporary Publications*, Melbourne: Heinemann, 1968, p. 114.
2. Gawler to Lord Glenelg, 26 October 1838, State Records of South Australia (henceforth SRSA), GRG 2/5.
3. Francis Dutton, *South Australia and its Mines with an Historical Sketch of the Colony* [1846], Adelaide: Austraprint Facsimile Edition, 1978, pp. 83–4.
4. Bill Gammage, 'The Adelaide District in 1836', in Robert Foster and Paul Sendziuk (eds), *Turning Points: Chapters in South Australian History*, Adelaide: Wakefield Press, 2012, p. 7.
5. W.H. Leigh, *Travels and Adventures in South Australia 1836–38* [1839], Sydney: Currawong Facsimile, 1982, p. 169.
6. Eleanore Williams, *A Way of Life: The Pastoral Families of the Central Hill Country of South Australia*, Adelaide: Adelaide University Union Press, 1980, p. 5.
7. Frankie Hawker and Rob Linn, *Bungaree: Land, Stock and People*, Adelaide: Turnbull Fox Phillips, 1982, p. 15.
8. Ibid., pp. 20–6.

9. Ibid., pp. 33–40.
10. Williams, p. 2.
11. A.I. Diamond, 'Some Aspects of the History of the South Australian Company: The First Decade', MA thesis, University of Adelaide, 1955, pp. 333–4.
12. Douglas Pike, *Paradise of Dissent: South Australia 1829–57*, Melbourne: Melbourne University Press, 1957, p. 330.
13. B.S. Baldwin, 'Letters of Samuel Davenport, chiefly to his father George Davenport, 1842–1849, Part VIII: 6 August 1847 – 27 September 1849', *South Australiana*, 19(2), 1980, pp. 87–141.
14. Judy Jeffery, 'The Small Farmers in South Australia 1836–1869: An Assessment', *Flinders Journal of History and Politics*, 11, 1985, p. 53.
15. Ibid., p. 58.
16. Ibid., p. 56.
17. Ibid., p. 59.
18. Robin F. Haines, *Emigration and the Labouring Poor: Australian Recruitment in Britain and Ireland*, 1831–60, New York: Macmillan, 1997, p. 1.
19. Christopher Nance, 'The South Australian Social Experiment 1836–71', MA thesis, Flinders University, 1977; pp. 79–80.
20. Ibid., pp. 85–7.
21. Pike, p. 311.
22. Eric Richards, 'Migration', in Wilfrid Prest, Kerrie Round and Carol Fort (eds), *The Wakefield Companion to South Australian History*, Adelaide: Wakefield Press, 2001, p. 352.
23. T.L. Stevenson, 'Population Change Since 1836', in Eric Richards (ed.), *The Flinders History of South Australia: Social History*, Adelaide: Wakefield Press, 1986, pp. 172–3.
24. Nance, pp. 79–80.
25. Marie Steiner, *Servant Depots in Colonial South Australia*, Adelaide: Wakefield Press, 2009, p. 3.
26. Ciarán Ó Murchadha, *The Great Famine: Ireland's Agony 1845–52*, London: Bloomsbury, 2013, pp. 135–57.
27. MacDonnell to Earl Grey, cited in Steiner, p. 12.
28. Susan Woodburn, 'The Irish in New South Wales, Victoria and South Australia, 1788–1880', MA thesis, University of Adelaide, 1979, pp. 301–2.
29. Baldwin, p. 102.
30. B.S. Baldwin, 'Letters of Samuel Davenport, chiefly to his father George Davenport, 1842–1849, Part VI: 29 April – 1 August 1846', *South Australiana*, 16(2), 1977, pp. 142, 156.
31. Journal of the Mount Gambier Police Station, 17 August 1847, SRSA, GRG 5/151/1.

32. Henry Reynolds, *Forgotten War*, Sydney: NewSouth Publishing, 2013, p. 126.
33. See, for instance, Robert Foster and Amanda Nettelbeck, *Out of the Silence: The History and Memory of South Australia's Frontier Wars*, Adelaide: Wakefield Press, 2012.
34. For a comprehensive summary, see Alan Pope, *One Law for All: Aboriginal People and Criminal Law in Early South Australia*, Canberra: Aboriginal Studies Press, 2011.
35. Foster and Nettelbeck, pp. 82–4.
36. Pope, pp. 174–91.
37. Robert Foster, 'Feasts of the Full-Moon: The Distribution of Rations to Aboriginal People in South Australia 1836–1861', *Aboriginal History*, 13(1), 1989, pp. 63–79.
38. Christine Lockwood, 'A Vision Frustrated: Lutheran Missionaries to the Aborigines of South Australia 1838–1853', in Peter Monteath (ed.), *Germans: Travellers, Settlers and their Descendants in South Australia*, Adelaide: Wakefield Press, 2011, pp. 25–36.
39. Robert Foster, 'The Aborigines Location in Adelaide: South Australia's First "Mission" to the Aborigines', *Journal of the Anthropological Association of South Australia*, 28(1), 1990, pp. 23–7.
40. Lockwood, pp. 29–30.
41. Peggy Brock and Doreen Kartinyeri, *Poonindie: The Rise and Destruction of an Aboriginal Agricultural Community*, Adelaide: Aboriginal Heritage Branch, 1989, p. 46.
42. Augustus Short, *A Visit to Poonindie and Some Accounts of that Mission to the Aborigines of South Australia*, Adelaide: William Kyffin Thomas, 1872, p. 11.
43. Ian Auhl, *The Story of the 'Monster Mine': The Burra Burra Mine and its Townships 1845–1877*, Adelaide: Investigator Press, 1986, pp. 13–23.
44. Ibid., pp. 23–41.
45. Ibid., pp. 63–73.
46. Ibid., pp. 18, 76.
47. Ibid., pp. 1–12, 68.
48. Ibid., p. 3.
49. W.R.C. Jaques, 'The Impact of the Gold Rushes on South Australia 1852–1854', BA (Hons) thesis, University of Adelaide, 1963, pp. 5–16.
50. Ibid., p. 57.
51. See Therese McCarthy and Paul Sendziuk, 'Deserted Women and the Law in Colonial South Australia', *Journal of Australian Colonial History*, 20, 2018, pp. 95–114.
52. Jaques., p. 16.
53. Ibid., pp. 19–29.
54. Ibid., pp. 35–42.

55. Alexander Tolmer, *Reminiscences of an Adventurous and Chequered Career at Home and at the Antipodes* [1882], vol. II, Adelaide: State Libraries Board of South Australia facsimile, 1972, p. 152.
56. Ibid., p. 133.
57. Paul Depasquale, *A Critical History of South Australian Literature 1836–1930*, Adelaide: Warradale Pioneers Books, 1978, pp. 70–3.
58. Catherine Helen Spence, *Clara Morison*, Adelaide: Rigby Ltd, 1971, p. 235.
59. J.B. Hirst, *Convict Society and its Enemies: A History of Early New South Wales*, Sydney: Allen & Unwin, 1987, pp. 212–14.
60. J.M. Ward, *Colonial Self-Government: The British Experience 1759–1856*, London: Macmillan, 1976, pp. 181–90.
61. Ibid., p. 211.
62. Ibid., pp. 291–2.
63. Ibid., p. 293.
64. Gordon D. Combe, *Responsible Government in South Australia: From Foundations to Playford*, revised edition, Adelaide: Wakefield Press, 2009, p. 17.
65. Pike, pp. 426–35.
66. David Hilliard and Arnold D. Hunt, 'Religion', in Eric Richards (ed.), *The Flinders History of South Australia: Social History*, Adelaide: Wakefield Press, 1986, pp. 201–2.
67. John M. Williams, 'The Making of the South Australian Constitution: Fear, Optimism and Reform', in *The Politics of Democracy in South Australia: A Special Conference Marking 150 Years of Democracy*, Adelaide: State Electoral Office, 2008, p. 14.
68. Ibid., p. 15.
69. Ibid., p. 14.
70. Ibid., p. 15.
71. Labourchere to MacDonnell, 20 December 1855, cited in Anna Munyard, 'Making a Polity: 1836–1857', in Dean Jaensch (ed.), *The Flinders History of South Australia: Political History*, Adelaide: Wakefield Press, 1986, p. 71.
72. Williams, 'The Making', p. 15.
73. Ibid., p. 16.
74. Ibid.
75. Pike, p. 480.
76. Angela Woollacott, *Settler Society in the Australian Colonies: Self-Government and Imperial Culture*, Oxford: Oxford University Press, 2015, p. 99.
77. Ibid., pp. 100–1.
78. Rob Manwaring, *A Collaborative History of Social Innovation in South Australia*, Adelaide: Hawke Research Institute for Sustainable Societies, 2008, p. 30.
79. Cited in Reg Hamilton, *Colony: Strange Origins of One of the Earliest Modern Democracies*, Adelaide: Wakefield Press, 2010, p. 232.

Chapter 4 Creating a Nation, 1857–87

1. Carol Fort, 'Election Day, 1857', in *The Politics of Democracy in South Australia: A Special Conference Marking 150 Years of Democracy*, Adelaide: State Electoral Office, 2008, p. 20.
2. Ibid., p. 22.
3. Keith Seaman, 'The South Australian Constitution Act of 1856', in Dean Jaensch (ed.), *The Flinders History of South Australia: Political History*, Adelaide: Wakefield Press, 1986, pp. 91–2.
4. P.A. Howell, 'Constitutional and Political Development, 1857–1890', in Dean Jaensch (ed.), *The Flinders History of South Australia: Political History*, Adelaide: Wakefield Press, 1986, p. 116.
5. Ibid., p. 117.
6. M.P. Rendell, 'The Chinese in South Australia and the Northern Territory in the Nineteenth Century', MA thesis, University of Adelaide, 1952, p. 24.
7. Ibid., pp. 25–41.
8. Ibid., p. 14.
9. Howell, pp. 108–16.
10. Peter Moore, 'Torrens Title', in Wilfrid Prest, Kerrie Round and Carol Fort (eds), *The Wakefield Companion to South Australian History*, Adelaide: Wakefield Press, 2001, pp. 544–5.
11. Judith Raftery, *Not Part of the Public: Non-Indigenous Policies and Practices and the Health of Indigenous South Australians 1836–1973*, Adelaide: Wakefield Press, 2006, p. 81.
12. Ibid., pp. 83–90.
13. Christobel Mattingley with Ken Hampton, *Survival in Our Own Land: 'Aboriginal' Experiences in 'South Australia' since 1836*, Adelaide: Wakefield Press, 1988, pp. 183–201.
14. Robert Foster, 'Rations, Co-existence, and the Colonisation of Aboriginal Labour in the South Australian Pastoral Industry, 1860–1911', *Aboriginal History*, 24, 2000, pp. 1–26.
15. Michael Williams, *The Making of the South Australian Landscape*, London: Academic Press, 1974, p. 32.
16. K.R. Bowes, *Land Settlement in South Australia, 1857–1890*, Adelaide: Libraries Board of South Australia, 1968, p. 65.
17. Noris Ioannou, *Barossa Journeys: Into a Valley of Tradition*, 2nd edn, Sydney: New Holland Publishers, 2000, pp. 109–10.
18. Bowes, pp. 140–1.
19. R. McL. Harris, 'The "Princeland" Secession Movement in Victoria and South Australia 1861–67', *Australian Journal of Politics and History*, 17(3), 1971, pp. 365–76.
20. Williams, pp. 178–210.
21. Edward Eyre, *Journals of Expeditions of Discovery into Central Australia and Overland from Adelaide to King George's Sound in the Years 1840–41*, vol. 2, London: T. and W. Boone, 1845.

22. Erwin Feeken, Gerda Feeken and O.H.K. Spate, *The Discovery and Exploration of Australia*, Melbourne: Nelson, 1970, p. 158.
23. John Bailey, *Mr Stuart's Track*, Sydney: Picador, 2010, pp. 37–9, 87–95.
24. Feeken, Feeken and Spate, p. 158.
25. Ibid., p. 160.
26. Tim Bonyhady, *Burke and Wills: From Melbourne to Myth*, Sydney: David Ell Press, 1991, pp. 34–40.
27. Ibid., pp. 70–82.
28. Bailey, p. 149.
29. Bonyhady, p. 117.
30. Ibid., pp. 118–19.
31. Ibid., pp. 123–30.
32. Ibid., p. 134.
33. Bailey, p. 211.
34. Bonyhady, p. 177.
35. Bailey, p. 258.
36. Ibid., p. 280.
37. Ibid., pp. 282–3.
38. Jack Cross, *Great Central State: The Foundation of the Northern Territory*, Adelaide: Wakefield Press, 2011, pp. 1–14.
39. Ibid., pp. 13–15.
40. Frank Clune, *Overland Telegraph: The Story of a Great Australian Achievement and the Link Between Adelaide and Port Darwin*, Sydney: Angus and Robertson, 1955, pp. 66, 88–96, 116–19.
41. P.F. Donovan, 'South Australian Imperialism', *Flinders Journal of History and Politics*, 3, 1973, p. 52.
42. Clune, pp. 122–31.
43. Don Garden, *Droughts, Floods & Cyclones: El Niños That Shaped Our Colonial Past*, Melbourne: Australian Scholarly Publishing, 2009, p. 25.
44. Bowes, pp. 62–3, 140.
45. J.C. Foley, *Droughts in Australia: Review of Records from the Earliest Years of Settlement to 1955*, Melbourne: Bureau of Meteorology, 1957, p. 160.
46. *Advertiser*, 13 December 1865.
47. Dorothy Tunbridge, *The Story of the Flinders Ranges Mammals*, Sydney: Kangaroo Press, 1991, pp. 17–22.
48. G.W. Goyder, 'Surveyor-General's Report on Demarcation of Northern Rainfall', *South Australian Parliamentary Paper*, no. 78 of 1865; and 'Report of Surveyor-General on Northern Runs', *South Australian Parliamentary Paper*, no. 82 of 1865.
49. D.W. Meinig, *On the Margins of the Good Earth: The South Australian Wheat Frontier, 1869–1884*, Adelaide: South Australian Government Printer, 1988, pp. 22–4.

50. John Hirst, 'Selection', in Graeme Davison, John Hirst and Stuart Macintyre (eds), *The Oxford Companion to Australian History*, Melbourne: Oxford University Press, 1998, p. 579.
51. Meinig, pp. 26–7.
52. *South Australian Register*, 27 April 1865, p. 2.
53. Cross, pp. 112–13.
54. Clune, pp. 144–9.
55. Cross, pp. 150–2.
56. Clune, pp. 151–7; Cross, pp. 143–4.
57. Cross, pp. 166–8.
58. Peter Taylor, *An End to Silence: The Building of the Overland Telegraph Line from Adelaide to Darwin*, Sydney: Methuen, 1980, pp. 17–24.
59. Clune, pp. 66, 88–96.
60. Taylor, pp. 36–41.
61. Ibid., pp. 50–1.
62. Cross, p. 176.
63. Clune, pp. 211–16.
64. Ibid., pp. 225–30.
65. Ann Moyal, 'Telecommunications in Australia: An Historical Perspective, 1854–1930', *Prometheus*, 1(1), 1983, p. 28.
66. Wray Vamplew (ed.), *Australian Historical Statistics*, Sydney: Fairfax, Syme, Weldon Associates, 1987, p. 26.
67. Christopher Nance, 'The South Australian Social Experiment 1836–71: A Study of Some Aspects of South Australia's Early Social Development', MA Thesis, Flinders University, 1977, p. viii.
68. Ibid., p. 44.
69. Commissioner of Police, Correspondence relating to the *Convict Prevention Act*, GRG 5/2/1865/1374, SRSA.
70. Nance, p. 214.
71. Susan Marsden, 'South Australia', in Graeme Davison, John Hirst and Stuart Macintyre (eds), *The Oxford Companion to Australian History*, Melbourne: Oxford University Press, 1998, p. 599.
72. Anthony Trollope, *Australia* [1873], edited by P.D. Edwards and R.B. Joyce, Brisbane: University of Queensland Press, 1967, p. 643.
73. David Hilliard and Arnold D. Hunt, 'Religion', in Eric Richards (ed.), *The Flinders History of South Australia: Social History*, Adelaide: Wakefield Press, 1986, p. 229.
74. Ibid., pp. 204–6.
75. Ibid., p. 212.
76. David Hilliard, 'How Did Methodism Shape South Australia?', *Church Heritage*, 18(2), 2013, p. 99.
77. Garden, p. 145.
78. Williams, pp. 42–3.
79. Bowes, p. 198.

80. Ibid., p. 209.
81. Garden, p. 149.
82. Ibid., p. 69.
83. Bowes, p. 202.
84. Meinig, p. 77.
85. Eric Richards, 'The Peopling of South Australia', in Eric Richards (ed.), *The Flinders History of South Australia: Social History*, Adelaide: Wakefield Press, 1986, p. 130.
86. Ibid., pp. 131–2.
87. Cited in ibid.
88. Richards, 'The Peopling', pp. 160–1.
89. Meinig, p. 95.
90. Ibid., p. 100.
91. Eleanore Williams and Michael Williams, 'Rural South Australia in the Nineteenth Century', in Eric Richards (ed.), *The Flinders History of South Australia: Social History*, Adelaide: Wakefield Press, 1986, p. 540.
92. Trollope, p. 654.
93. Ibid., p. 651.
94. Ibid., p. 654.
95. Ibid., p. 636.
96. Ibid., pp. 638–9.
97. Ibid., p. 646.
98. W.A. Sinclair, *The Process of Economic Development in Australia*, Melbourne: Longman Cheshire, 1985, pp. 107–8.
99. J.B. Hirst, *Adelaide and the Country: Their Social and Political Relationship*, Melbourne: Melbourne University Press, 1973, pp. 216–26.
100. Jim Moss, *Sound of Trumpets: History of the Labour Movement in South Australia*, Adelaide: Wakefield Press, 1985, p. 92.
101. Ibid., p. 92; E.S. Richards, 'The Genesis of Secondary Industry in the South Australian Economy to 1876', *Australian Economic History Review*, 15(2), 1975, p. 116.
102. Gwenda Painter, *The River Trade: Wool and Steamers*, Sydney: Turton & Armstrong with Pioneer Settlement Press, 1979, pp. 12–43.
103. Ibid., pp. 77–8.
104. Ibid., pp. 89–94.
105. Bowes, pp. 84–5.
106. Richards, 'The Genesis of Secondary Industry', p. 126.
107. Meinig, p. 60.
108. Derek Whitelock, *Adelaide 1836–1976: A History of Difference*, Brisbane: University of Queensland Press, 1977, p. 164.
109. Karen Magee, 'Captain Sweet's Colonial Imagination: The Ideals of Modernity in South Australian Views Photography 1866–1886', PhD thesis, University of Adelaide, 2014, pp. 65–140.

110. Christine Finnimore, 'Art Galleries', in Wilfrid Prest, Kerrie Round and Carol Fort (eds), *The Wakefield Companion to South Australian History*, Adelaide: Wakefield Press, 2001, p. 48.
111. Pavla Miller, *Long Division: State Schooling in South Australian Society*, Adelaide: Wakefield Press, 1986, pp. 23–9.
112. Hilliard, 'How Did Methodism Shape South Australia?', p. 99.
113. Miller, p. 37.
114. Ibid., p. 57.
115. Hilliard and Hunt, p. 220.
116. Helen Jones, *Nothing Seemed Impossible: Women's Education and Social Change in South Australia 1875–1915*, Brisbane: University of Queensland Press, 1985, p. 9.
117. Ibid., p. 40.
118. Ibid., p. 65.
119. Rob Linn, *The Spirit of Knowledge: A Social History of the University of Adelaide, North Terrace Campus*, Adelaide: University of Adelaide Press, 2011, pp. 7–11.
120. Ibid., pp. 26–9.
121. Jones, pp. 86–8.
122. Ibid., pp. 89–90.
123. Ibid., pp. 181–2.
124. Denis Molyneux, *Time for Play: Recreation and Moral Issues in Colonial South Australia*, Adelaide: Wakefield Press, 2015, pp. 6–18.
125. Ibid., pp. 84–96.
126. Ibid., p. 37.
127. Ibid., pp. 53–9.
128. *Advertiser*, 28 March 1874, p. 5.
129. Molyneux, pp. 29–30.
130. *South Australian Register*, 14 August 1880, p. 6.
131. David Hilliard, 'The City of Churches', in Brian Dickey (ed.), *William Shakespeare's Adelaide: 1860–1930*, Adelaide: Association of Professional Historians Inc., 1992, p. 66.
132. Ibid., pp. 67–70.
133. Hilliard and Hunt, p. 223.
134. Jim Jose, 'Social Purity Society', in Wilfrid Prest, Kerrie Round and Carol Fort (eds), *The Wakefield Companion to South Australian History*, Adelaide: Wakefield Press, 2001, p. 493.
135. Margaret Allen, 'Women's Christian Temperance Union', in Wilfred Prest, Kerrie Round and Carol Fort (eds), *The Wakefield Companion to South Australian History*, Adelaide: Wakefield Press, 2001, pp. 587–8.
136. Susan Magarey, *Unbridling the Tongues of Women: A Biography of Catherine Helen Spence*, Adelaide: Adelaide University Press, 2010, pp. 87–8.

137. Helen Jones, 'South Australian Women and Politics', in Dean Jaensch (ed.), *The Flinders History of South Australia: Political History*, Adelaide: Wakefield Press, 1986, pp. 422–3.
138. G.L. Buxton, *South Australian Land Acts, 1869–1885*, Adelaide: Libraries Board of South Australia, 1968, pp. 78–83.
139. Moss, pp. 96–7.
140. Ibid., pp. 85–9.
141. Ibid., p. 105.
142. Ibid., pp. 134–9.
143. Garden, p. 8.
144. Meinig, pp. 78–85.
145. Ibid., p. 91.
146. Moss, p. 113.
147. Michael H. Glantz, 'Introduction', in Michael H. Glantz (ed.), *Drought Follows the Plough: Cultivating Marginal Areas*, Melbourne: Cambridge University Press, 1994, p. 3.
148. Garden, pp. 16, 237–8.
149. Williams, p. 147.
150. Ibid., pp. 148–50.
151. Ibid., pp. 11–12.
152. Ibid., pp. 279–96.
153. Ibid., pp. 228–39.
154. Ibid.
155. *South Australian Register*, 24 September 1881, p. 6; *South Australian Register*, 2 August 1882, p. 1; and *Southern Argus*, 17 August 1882, p. 4.
156. *South Australian Parliamentary Debates* (henceforth *SAPD*), 15 November 1883, p. 1612.
157. *SAPD*, 11 November 1885, pp. 1498, 1538–9.
158. Ibid., pp. 1457, 1498, 1910; *South Australian Register*, 20 December 1884, p. 1.
159. *South Australian Weekly Chronicle*, 1 January 1887, p. 19.
160. *South Australian Register*, 27 December 1887, pp. 4–5.
161. *South Australian Register*, 21 June 1887, p. 4.

Chapter 5 Making a State, 1888–1913

1. Graeme Davison, J.W. McCarty and Ailsa McLeary (eds), *Australians 1888*, Sydney: Fairfax, Syme and Weldon, 1987, pp. 1–18.
2. *Sydney Morning Herald*, 1 February 1888.
3. *Advertiser*, 26 January 1888.
4. Anthony Trollope, *Australia and New Zealand*, vol. 1, London: Chapman and Hall, 1876, p. 174.
5. Roslyn Russell and Philip Chubb, *One Destiny! The Federation Story – How Australia Became a Nation*, Melbourne: Penguin, 1998, pp. 29–32.

6. P.A. Howell, *South Australia and Federation*, Adelaide: Wakefield Press, 2002, pp. 128, 209.
7. H.J. Zwillenberg, 'Citizens to Soldiers: The Defence of South Australia 1836–1901', MA thesis, University of Adelaide, 1970, pp. 166–70.
8. Ibid., pp. 196–9.
9. Ibid., pp. 299–306.
10. Stephen Jeisman, *Colonial Gunboat: The Story of the HMCS Protector and the South Australian Naval Brigade*, Adelaide: Digital Print Australia, 2012, pp. 42–61.
11. John Hirst, *The Sentimental Nation: The Making of the Australian Commonwealth*, Melbourne: Oxford University Press, 2000, p. 46.
12. John Bannon, 'The Colonies' Paths to Federation: South Australia', in Helen Irving (ed.), *The Centenary Companion to Australian Federation*, Melbourne: Cambridge University Press, 1999, pp. 131–2.
13. Ibid., pp. 134–6.
14. Ibid., pp. 139–43.
15. Ian Turner and Leonie Sandercock, *In Union Strength: A History of Trade Unions in Australia 1788–1983*, Melbourne: Nelson, 1983, pp. 40–7.
16. Jim Moss, *Sound of Trumpets: History of the Labour Movement in South Australia*, Adelaide: Wakefield Press, 1985, pp. 145–57.
17. Ibid., pp. 159–68.
18. Ibid., p. 168.
19. L.F. Crisp, *Federation Fathers*, Melbourne: Melbourne University Press, 1990, p. 274.
20. Ibid., p. 225.
21. Margaret Glass, *Charles Cameron Kingston: Federation Father*, Melbourne: Melbourne University Press, 1997, p. 63.
22. Ibid., pp. 63–9.
23. Ibid., p. 70.
24. Ibid., p. 73.
25. Moss, p. 174.
26. Gordon D. Combe, *Responsible Government in South Australia: From Foundations to Playford*, revised edition, Adelaide: Wakefield Press, 2009, p. 125.
27. Moss, pp. 161–74.
28. Geoffrey Blainey and Geoffrey Hutton, *Gold and Paper 1858–1982: A History of the National Bank of Australasia Ltd*, Melbourne: Macmillan, 1958, pp. 84–102; Howell, p. 146.
29. W.A. Sinclair, *The Process of Economic Development in Australia*, Melbourne: Longman Cheshire, 1985, pp. 147–51.
30. Moss, pp. 173–5.
31. Bannon, pp. 143–4.
32. Cited in Crisp, p. 279.
33. Glass, p. 90.

34. Ibid., p. 10; Combe, p. 126.
35. Dean Jaensch, 'Party, Party System and Federation, 1890–1912', in Dean Jaensch (ed.), *The Flinders History of South Australia: Political History*, Adelaide: Wakefield Press, 1986, pp. 184, 194.
36. Glass, p. 140.
37. Michael Davitt, *Life and Progress in Australasia*, London: Methuen, 1898, p. 60.
38. Robin Gollan, *Radical and Working Class Politics: A Study of Eastern Australia*, Melbourne: Melbourne University Press, 1960, p. 123.
39. Moss, pp. 175–8.
40. Ibid., p. 177.
41. Davitt, p. 60.
42. Michael Williams, *The Making of the South Australian Landscape: A Study of the Historical Geography of Australia*, London: Academic Press, 1974, pp. 237–41.
43. Helen Jones, *In Her Own Name: Women in South Australian History*, Adelaide: Wakefield Press, 1986, p. 81.
44. Ibid., pp. 85–6.
45. Ibid., p. 25.
46. Ibid., pp. 85–114.
47. *Register*, 9 July 1892, cited in Jones, p. 96.
48. Helen Jones, 'South Australian Women and Politics', in Dean Jaensch (ed.), *The Flinders History of South Australia: Political History*, Adelaide: Wakefield Press, 1986, p. 431.
49. Helen Jones, *Nothing Seemed Impossible: Women's Education and Social Change in South Australia 1875–1915*, Brisbane: University of Queensland Press, 1985, pp. 141–2.
50. Jones, *In Her Own Name*, p. 103.
51. Carol Bacchi, 'The "Woman Question" in South Australia', in Eric Richards (ed.), *The Flinders History of South Australia: Social History*, Adelaide: Wakefield Press, 1986, p. 416.
52. Jones, *In Her Own Name*, p. 78.
53. Jones, 'South Australian Women and Politics', pp. 432–4.
54. Ibid., p. 433.
55. Jones, *Nothing Seemed Impossible*, pp. 181–3.
56. Mark Twain (Samuel Clemens), *Following the Equator: A Journey around the World*, New York: American Publishing Company, 1898, pp. 390, 402.
57. Ibid., pp. 402–3.
58. Ibid., p. 402.
59. Ibid., p. 406. For an account of the Commemoration banquet, see *Advertiser*, 31 December 1895, pp. 5–6.
60. Twain, p. 408.
61. Chapters were published weekly in the *South Australian Chronicle* beginning on 25 November 1893 and concluding on 31 March 1894.

62. Simpson Newland, *Paving the Way: A Romance of the Australian Bush* [1893], facsimile edition, Adelaide: Moroak Pty Ltd, 1982, preface.
63. Ibid.
64. Twain, p. 362.
65. Williams, pp. 51–3.
66. Ibid., p. 55.
67. Geoffrey Blainey, *The Rush that Never Ended: A History of Australian Mining*, 4th edn, Melbourne: Melbourne University Press, 1993, pp. 139–49.
68. Eric Eklund, *Mining Towns: Making a Living, Making a Life*, Sydney: UNSW Press, 2012, pp. 37–40.
69. Blainey, p. 149.
70. Eklund, pp. 42–6.
71. Ibid., pp. 135–46.
72. Bannon, pp. 144–5.
73. Ibid., p. 147.
74. John Bannon, *The Crucial Colony: South Australia's Role in Reviving Federation, 1891 to 1897*, Canberra: Federalism Research Centre, ANU, 1994, p. 4.
75. Ibid., pp. 1–2.
76. Ibid., p. 3.
77. Robert Foster and Amanda Nettelbeck, 'Proclamation Day and the Rise and Fall of South Australian Nationalism', in Robert Foster and Paul Sendziuk (eds), *Turning Points: Chapters in South Australian History*, Adelaide: Wakefield Press, 2012, pp. 48–51.
78. Bannon, 'The Colonies' Paths', pp. 143–4.
79. Annely Aeuckens, 'Emergence of a New Industry, 1892–1918', in Annely Aeuckens *et al.* (eds), *Vineyard of the Empire: Barossa Valley Vignerons 1842–1939*, Adelaide: Australian Industrial Publishers, 1988, pp. 148–54.
80. Bannon, 'The Colonies' Paths', p. 130.
81. Bannon, *The Crucial Colony*, p. 3.
82. John Bannon, 'Great Federal Expectations: South Australia and the Commonwealth', in *The Politics of Democracy in South Australia: A Special Conference Marking 150 Years of Democracy*, Adelaide: State Electoral Office, 2008, p. 67.
83. J.A. La Nauze, *The Making of the Australian Constitution*, Melbourne: Melbourne University Press, 1972, p. 103.
84. Combe, p. 133.
85. Crisp, p. 286.
86. A.P. Haydon, 'South Australia's First War', *Historical Studies: Australia and New Zealand*, 11(42), 1964, pp. 223–4.
87. A.P. Haydon, 'Boer War', in Wilfrid Prest, Kerrie Round and Carol Fort (eds), *The Wakefield Companion to South Australian History*, Adelaide: Wakefield Press, 2001, pp. 77–8.

88. Combe, p. 136.
89. Glass, pp. 208–23.
90. Jaensch, pp. 194–5.
91. Ibid., pp. 197–202.
92. Ibid., pp. 202–4.
93. Ibid., p. 209.
94. Ibid., p. 213.
95. R.L. Reid, 'South Australia and the First Decade of Federation', MA thesis, University of Adelaide, 1954, pp. 94–5.
96. Ibid., p. 107.
97. Ibid., p. 94.
98. Ibid., p. 128.
99. Ibid., p. 138.
100. Ibid., p. 85.
101. *Immigration Act 1872*; Alan Powell, *Far Country: A Short History of the Northern Territory*, Melbourne: Melbourne University Press, 1997, p. 105.
102. Powell, p. 90.
103. Ibid.
104. *Chinese Immigration Restriction Act 1888*; M.P. Rendell, 'The Chinese in South Australia and the Northern Territory in the Nineteenth Century', MA thesis, University of Adelaide, 1952, pp. 137–63.
105. Rendell, pp. 157–62.
106. Powell, pp. 90–5.
107. Reid, pp. 142–5.
108. Ibid., pp. 146–52.
109. Ibid., pp. 159–60.
110. Ibid., p. 175.
111. Don Garden, *Droughts, Floods & Cyclones: El Niños that Shaped Our Colonial Past*, Melbourne: Australian Scholarly Publishing, 2009, pp. 236–77.
112. *Advertiser*, 1 January 1901.
113. Howell, p. 292.
114. Ibid., p.293.
115. *Register*, 10 February 1910, p. 5.
116. *Register*, 26 January 1910, p. 7.
117. *Register*, 6 October 1911, p. 7.
118. *Advertiser*, 29 December 1913, p. 9; *Daily Herald*, 1 January 1914, p. 5.
119. *Daily Herald*, 9 January 1911, p. 3.
120. Howell, pp. 214–15.
121. P. Jones, 'The Horn Expedition's Place Among Nineteenth-Century Inland Expeditions', in S.R. Morton and D.J. Mulvaney (eds), *Exploring Central Australia: Society, the Environment and the 1894 Horn Expedition*, Sydney: Surry Beatty & Sons, 1996, pp. 19–28.

122. D.J. Mulvaney, '"A Splendid Lot of Fellows": Achievements and Consequences of the Horn Expedition', in S.R. Morton and D.J. Mulvaney (eds), *Exploring Central Australia: Society, the Environment and the 1894 Horn Expedition*, Sydney: Surry Beatty & Sons, 1996, pp. 3–12.
123. Howard Morphy, 'More Than Mere Facts: Repositioning Spencer and Gillen in the History of Anthropology', in S.R. Morton and D.J. Mulvaney (eds), *Exploring Central Australia: Society, the Environment and the 1894 Horn Expedition*, Sydney: Surry Beatty & Sons, 1996, pp. 135–48.
124. Beau Riffenburgh, *Racing with Death: Douglas Mawson – Antarctic Explorer*, London: Bloomsbury, 2009, pp. 23–105.
125. Ibid., pp. 213–70.
126. Andrew Markus, *Australian Race Relations: 1788–1993*, Sydney: Allen & Unwin, 1994, p. 111.
127. *The Bulletin*, 22 June 1901.
128. *Advertiser*, 5 August 1908.
129. Markus, pp. 124–7.
130. Robert Foster, 'Rations, Co-existence and the Colonisation of Aboriginal Labour in the South Australian Pastoral Industry, 1860–1911', *Aboriginal History*, 24, 2000, pp. 21–5.
131. Michael T. Shepherd, 'Compulsory Military Training: The South Australian Debate, 1901–1914', MA thesis, University of Adelaide, 1976, p. 24.
132. Ibid., pp. 132–3.
133. Ibid., pp. 197–201.
134. Jeffrey Grey, *A Military History of Australia*, Melbourne: Cambridge University Press, 1999, p. 79.
135. Shepherd, pp. 190–6.
136. Douglas Newton, *Hellbent: Australia's Leap into the Great War*, Melbourne: Scribe, 2014, p. 26.
137. Ibid., pp. 37–8.
138. Ibid., pp. 38–9.
139. Chris Cunneen, 'Denman, Thomas', *Australian Dictionary of Biography*, http://adb.anu.edu.au/biography/denman-thomas-5956/text10161.
140. *Advertiser*, 19 December 1913, p. 10.

Chapter 6 War and Peace, 1914–35

1. 'Patriotic Demonstration', *Advertiser*, 9 August 1914, p. 3.
2. Ernest Scott, *Australia During the War*, 7th edn, Sydney: Angus and Robertson, 1941, p. 874.
3. 'World War 1', RSL Virtual Museum, https://rslvirtualwarmemorial.org.au/explore/conflicts/2.

4. 'The Late Lance-Corporal Robin', *Adelaide Chronicle*, 19 June 1915, p. 17; R.A. Blackburn, 'Blackburn, Arthur Seaforth', *Australian Dictionary of Biography*, http://adb.anu.edu.au/biography/blackburn-arthur-seaforth-5256.
5. Letter to parents, 15 July 1916, quoted in Bill Gammage, *The Broken Years: Australian Soldiers in the Great War*, Melbourne: Penguin, 1975, p. 157.
6. Ross McMullin, 'Disaster at Fromelles', *Wartime*, 36, http://www.awm.gov.au/wartime/36/article.asp.
7. C.E.W. Bean, *The Australian Imperial Force in France 1916*, 12th edn, Brisbane: University of Queensland Press, 1941, p. 422.
8. Kirsty Harris, *More than Bombs and Bandages: Australian Army Nurses at Work in World War I*, Sydney: Big Sky Productions, 2011, pp. 239–59.
9. Alison Mackinnon, *Love and Freedom: Professional Women and the Reshaping of Personal Life*, Cambridge: Cambridge University Press, 1997, pp. 77–9, 138–9.
10. Quoted in A.G. Butler, *The Australian Army Medical Services in the War of 1914–1918, Volume III*, Canberra: Australian War Memorial, 1943, p. 528 (footnote 3).
11. 'All British', *Mail*, 8 July 1916, p. 14.
12. 'War Work Notes: What Our Women Are Doing', *Mail*, 20 July 1918, p. 7; Scott, pp. 697–738.
13. 'Honouring Motherhood', *South Australian Register*, 8 May 1915, p. 8.
14. Verity Burgmann, *Revolutionary Industrial Unionism: The Industrial Workers of the World in Australia*, Melbourne: Cambridge University Press, 1995, p. 296 (footnote 1).
15. Jim Moss, *Sound of Trumpets: History of the Labour Movement in South Australia*, Adelaide: Wakefield Press, 1985, p. 234.
16. 'Report on the Financial Effect of Federation on South Australia', *South Australian Parliamentary Papers*, no. 55, 1927, p. 10.
17. Scott, pp. 481–2.
18. Moss, pp. 246–8.
19. Ibid., p. 249.
20. 'Barrier Police Raid – 30 Men Arrested', *Express and Telegraph*, 3 September 1917, p. 3.
21. 'The War Censorship', *Advertiser*, 28 December 1914, p. 6.
22. 'Enlist! Enlist!' [leaflet], c. 1916, State Library of South Australia (henceforth SLSA), B2164528; 'Coo-ee!' [recruitment poster], c. 1916, SLSA, B2164581.
23. Letter from R.M. Orchard to South Australian men, September 1918, SLSA, B2164534.
24. 'Only the brave deserve the fair' [postcard], SLSA, B2164499.

25. Jenny Tilby Stock, 'Conscription', in Wilfrid Prest, Kerrie Round and Carol Fort (eds), *The Wakefield Companion to South Australian History*, Adelaide: Wakefield Press, 2001, p. 120.
26. Philip Payton, *Regional Australia and the Great War: 'The Boys from Old Kio'*, Exeter: University of Exeter Press, 2012, pp. 143–62.
27. Stock, p. 120.
28. Judith Jeffery, 'World War I', in Wilfrid Prest, Kerrie Round and Carol Fort (eds), *The Wakefield Companion to South Australian History*, Adelaide: Wakefield Press, 2001, p. 592.
29. Arnold D. Hunt, 'Verran, John', *Australian Dictionary of Biography*, http://adb.anu.edu.au/biography/verran-john-8917/text15669.
30. Ann Elias, '"Art Has No Country": Hans Heysen and the Consequences of the First World War', *History Australia*, 6(1), 2009, pp. 04.1–04.16.
31. 'Captain G.E. Hawkes, 77th Infantry – Court of Enquiry – Torrens Island Concentration Camp', 10 August 1925, National Archives of Australia (henceforth NAA), MP367/1, 567/3/2202 (parts 1–6).
32. Letter written by Walter Emde on behalf of the camp's internees to the American Consul-General, 17 April 1915, NAA, MP367/1, 567/3/2202 (part 5, pp. 320–4).
33. John Williams, *German Anzacs of the First World War*, Sydney: UNSW Press, 2003, pp. 103–6.
34. This relates to settlement up to 30 June 1934. See *Official Year Book of the Commonwealth of Australia, No. 28, 1935*, p. 130.
35. Pam O'Connor and Brian O'Connor, *In Two Fields: Soldier Settlement in the South East of South Australia*, Millicent, SA: S.E. Soldier Settlers Committee, 1991, p. 16.
36. R.M. Gibbs, *A History of South Australia*, Adelaide: Balara Books, 1969, p. 195.
37. Australian Bureau of Statistics, *Australian Demographic Trends 1997*, pp. 118, 130. Adelaide's population reached this level in 1927.
38. Gibbs, p. 192.
39. See Peter Donovan, *An Industrial History of South Australia*, Adelaide: University of Adelaide, 1979, p. 70; and Payton, *passim*.
40. Gibbs, p. 192. Also see Geoffrey Blainey, *The Steel Master: A Life of Essington Lewis*, Melbourne: Macmillan, 1971, pp. 41–7.
41. Bruce McFarlane and Kyoko Sheridan, 'The Minerals and Energy Sector', in Kyoko Sheridan (ed.), *The State as Developer: Public Enterprise in South Australia*, Adelaide: Wakefield Press, 1986, p. 95.
42. Jon G. Chittleborough, 'Holden Car', in Wilfrid Prest, Kerrie Round and Carol Fort (eds), *The Wakefield Companion to South Australian History*, Adelaide: Wakefield Press, 2001, p. 262.
43. *Statistical Register of South Australia, 1917–18*, 1918, p. vii.

44. Ibid., p.26.
45. Ibid.
46. R.G. MacFarlane, *Howard Florey: The Making of a Great Scientist*, Melbourne: Oxford University Press, 1979.
47. *Statistical Register of South Australia, 1926–27*, 1928, p. 22; and *Statistical Register of South Australia, 1929–30*, 1931, p. 20.
48. Jon G. Chittleborough, 'Motor Vehicles', in Wilfrid Prest, Kerrie Round and Carol Fort (eds), *The Wakefield Companion to South Australian History*, Adelaide: Wakefield Press, 2001, p. 364.
49. 'Highways and Local Government Department Fourteenth Annual Report, 1930–31', *South Australian Parliamentary Papers*, no. 37, 1931, p. 9.
50. Commonwealth of Australia, *Report of the Royal Commission on the Basic Wage*, Melbourne: AGPS, 1920, p. 58.
51. 'Report on the Financial Effect of Federation on South Australia', *South Australian Parliamentary Papers*, no. 55, 1927, p. 14.
52. Ibid., p. 15.
53. M. Thompson, 'Government and Depression in South Australia', MA thesis, Flinders University, 1972, p. 52.
54. Ray Broomhill, *Unemployed Workers: A Social History of the Great Depression in Adelaide*, Brisbane: University of Queensland Press, 1978, p. 3. Also see Moss, p. 273.
55. C.B. Schedvin, 'The Long and the Short of Depression Origins', in Robert Cooksey (ed.), *The Great Depression in Australia*, Canberra: Australian Society for the Study of Labour History, 1970, pp. 1–13.
56. *Statistical Register of South Australia, 1930–31*, 1932, p. 90.
57. Ibid., p. 89. The period is 1927–28 to 1930–31.
58. *Statistical Register of South Australia, 1931–32*, 1933, p. 93.
59. For a comprehensive discussion of unemployment data and the methodology by which this figure is derived, see Broomhill, pp. 11–19.
60. *Census Bulletin No. 12: Summary for the State of South Australia*, 1933, p. 10.
61. Broomhill, p. 12.
62. Ray Broomhill, 'Underemployment in Adelaide during the Depression', *Labour History*, 21, 1974, pp. 31–40.
63. *Census 1933*, Volume 1, Part IV, p. 423.
64. Broomhill, *Unemployed Workers*, p. 20.
65. Joan Hancock and Eric Richards, 'Holden, Henry James', *Australian Dictionary of Biography*, http://adb.anu.edu.au/biography/holden-henry-james-6704/text11571.
66. Ibid.
67. *Census 1933*, Volume 2, Part XXV, pp. 1719, 1721.
68. Broomhill, *Unemployed Workers*, pp. 8–9.
69. W.G. Waye quoted in ibid., p. 33.
70. R. Prince quoted in ibid., p. 53.

71. *Advertiser*, 3 July 1934, p. 12.
72. Steve Dyer, 'Farm Relief in South Australia during the Great Depression', *Journal of the Historical Society of South Australia*, 2, 1976, p. 64.
73. See *Statistical Register of South Australia, 1931–32*, 1933, p. 94; and *Statistical Register of South Australia, 1935–36*, 1937, p. 84.
74. Dyer, p. 65.
75. Broomhill, *Unemployed Workers*, pp. 30–40 *passim*.
76. Commonwealth Bureau of Census and Statistics, *South Australia Year Book 1966*, pp. 508, 517.
77. Dirk van Dissel, 'Alexander Hore-Ruthven', in Wilfrid Prest, Kerrie Round and Carol Fort (eds), *The Wakefield Companion to South Australian History*, Adelaide: Wakefield Press, 2001, p. 264; and Ray Broomhill, 'Hill, Lionel Laughton', *Australian Dictionary of Biography*, http://adb.anu.edu.au/biography/hill-lionel-laughton-6671/text11485.
78. See, for example, the *Debt Adjustment Act 1929* (SA), the *Farmers' Relief Act 1931* (SA) and, later, the *Farmers' Assistance Act 1933* (SA).
79. Brian Dickey, *Rations, Residence, Resources: A History of Social Welfare in South Australia since 1836*, Adelaide: Wakefield Press, 1986, p. 181; Broomhill, *Unemployed Workers*, p. 81.
80. Broomhill, *Unemployed Workers*, p. 45.
81. Dickey, p. 194.
82. Ibid., p. 182.
83. Commonwealth Bureau of Census and Statistics, *Labour Report No. 22, 1931*, 1933, p. 55.
84. Broomhill, *Unemployed Workers*, p. 7.
85. 'Ten Per Cent Reduction in Wages', *Advertiser*, 23 January 1931, p. 15.
86. Verity Burgmann, 'Industrial Workers of the World', in Wilfrid Prest, Kerrie Round and Carol Fort (eds), *The Wakefield Companion to South Australian History*, Adelaide: Wakefield Press, 2001, p. 280.
87. Broomhill, *Unemployed Workers*, p. 121.
88. Burgmann, *Revolutionary Industrial Unionism*, p. 265.
89. Wally Bourne interviewed by Annely Aeuckens and Susan Marsden, April 1978, SLSA, OH 24/18.
90. 'Iron Bars and Spiked Sticks in City Riot', *Advertiser*, 10 January 1931, p. 9.
91. Ibid.
92. Broomhill, *Unemployed Workers*, p. 167.
93. Ibid., p. 69.
94. Robert Foster, '"Endless trouble and agitation": Aboriginal Activism in the Protectionist Era', *Journal of the Historical Society of South Australia*, 28, 2000, p. 15.
95. Kevin Blackburn, 'White Agitation for an Aboriginal State in Australia (1925–29)', *Australian Journal of Politics and History*, 45(2), 1999, pp. 157–80.

96. Charles Duguid, *The Doctor and the Aborigines*, Adelaide: Rigby, 1982, p. 95.
97. 'The Wondergraph. Success of "The Jazz Singer"', *Advertiser*, 4 March 1929, p. 8.
98. 'The Jazz Singer', *Advertiser*, 18 March 1929, p. 17.
99. 'Censoring "Talkies" May Be Difficult', *Advertiser*, 9 March 1929, p. 14; 'Beaten By Progress', *Mail*, 4 January 1930, p. 3.
100. 'Wool Industry Hit Again', *Chronicle*, 11 August 1938, p. 42.
101. *Statistical Register of South Australia, 1931–32*, 1933, p. 18.
102. David Frith, *Bodyline Autopsy*, Sydney: ABC Books, 2002, pp. 242–8.
103. Ibid., pp. 255–9.

Chapter 7 Industrialisation and the Playford Legend, mid-1930s to 1965

1. Dean Jaensch, *The Government of South Australia*, Brisbane: University of Queensland Press, 1977, p. 12.
2. Hugh Stretton, 'An Intellectual Public Servant: William Wainwright, 1880–1948', *Meanjin*, 50(4), 1991, p. 575.
3. *Broken Hill Proprietary Company's Indenture Act 1937*.
4. *South Australian Parliamentary Debates* (henceforth *SAPD*), House of Assembly (HoA), 19 October 1937, pp. 1125–7.
5. Michael Stutchbury, 'State Government Industrialisation Strategies', in Kyoko Sheridan (ed.), *The State as Developer: Public Enterprise in South Australia*, Adelaide: Wakefield Press, 1986, p. 71.
6. Ibid., pp. 69–70.
7. *SAPD*, HoA, 12 November 1936, p. 2402.
8. *SAPD*, HoA, 10 November 1936, pp. 3313–14.
9. Susan Marsden, *Business, Charity and Sentiment: The South Australian Housing Trust 1936–1986*, Adelaide: Wakefield Press, 1986, p. 8.
10. See *SAPD*, HoA, 16 November 1936, pp. 2460–1.
11. These were the *Housing Improvement Act 1940* and the *Homes Act 1941*.
12. Susan Marsden, 'The South Australian Housing Trust, Elizabeth and Twentieth Century Heritage', *Journal of the Historical Society of South Australia*, 28, 2000, p. 52.
13. For further discussion of the Trust's role in country areas, see Marsden, *Business, Charity*, pp. 185–226.
14. Ibid., pp. 428–9.
15. Ibid., p. 88.
16. M.A. Jones, *Housing and Poverty in Australia*, Melbourne: Melbourne University Press, 1972, p. 16.
17. Marsden, 'The South Australian Housing Trust', p. 58.

18. Mark Peel, 'Making a Place: Women in the "Workers' City"', *Australian Historical Studies*, 26(102), 1994, p. 22. For broader commentary on the history of Elizabeth, see Mark Peel, *Good Times, Hard Times: The Past and the Future in Elizabeth*, Melbourne: Melbourne University Press, 1995.
19. Margaret Allen, 'Salisbury (S.A.) in Transition', MA thesis, University of Adelaide, 1975, p. 78.
20. Susan Marsden, 'Playford's Metropolis', in Bernard O'Neil, Judith Raftery and Kerrie Round (eds), *Playford's South Australia: Essays on the History of South Australia 1933–1968*, Adelaide: Association of Professional Historians Inc., 1996, p. 123.
21. Marsden, *Business, Charity*, pp. 298–9.
22. Amelia Redmond quoted in City of Playford, *Migrant Heritage Places in Australia: City of Playford (Elizabeth District)*, Adelaide: Australian Heritage Commission and City of Playford, 1997, pp. 100–2.
23. Ibid.
24. Geoffrey Blainey, *The Steel Master: A Life of Essington Lewis*, Melbourne: Sun Books, 1981, pp. 120–41.
25. Carol S. Fort, '"Equality of Sacrifice"? War Work in Salisbury, South Australia', in Bernard O'Neil, Judith Raftery and Kerrie Round (eds), *Playford's South Australia: Essays on the History of South Australia 1933–1968*, Adelaide: Association of Professional Historians Inc., 1996, pp. 216–7; Carol Fort, 'World War II', in Wilfrid Prest, Kerrie Round and Carol Fort (eds), *The Wakefield Companion to South Australian History*, Adelaide: Wakefield Press, 2001, p. 594.
26. Fort, 'World War II', p. 594.
27. Fort, '"Equality of Sacrifice"?', p. 215.
28. Susan Marsden, *A History of Woodville*, Adelaide: Corporation of the City of Woodville, 1977, pp. 215, 216.
29. Fort, 'World War II', p. 594.
30. Marsden, *Woodville*, p. 228.
31. Ibid., p. 231.
32. See speeches by J. Fletcher and R.S. Richards, *SAPD*, HoA, 13 October 1942, pp. 835, 847; 'Tension Over N.S.W. Strike', *Advertiser*, 17 October 1945, p. 1.
33. Stewart Cockburn assisted by John Playford, *Playford: Benevolent Despot*, Adelaide: Axiom Publishing, 1991, pp. 109–11.
34. P.A. Howell, 'Cudmore, Sir Collier Robert', *Australian Dictionary of Biography*, http://adb.anu.edu.au/biography/cudmore-sir-collier-robert-9873/text17471.
35. Bruce Muirden, 'The Electricity Trust Affair', in Dean Jaensch (ed.), *The Flinders History of South Australia: Political History*, Adelaide: Wakefield Press, 1986, p. 276.
36. Ibid., pp. 276–7.
37. Ibid., p. 280.

38. Murray McCaskill, '1950: Forging an Industrial State', in Trevor Griffin and Murray McCaskill (eds), *Atlas of South Australia*, Adelaide: SA Government Printing Division and Wakefield Press, 1986, p. 28; and Stutchbury, pp. 70–1.
39. Australian Bureau of Statistics (henceforth ABS), *Labour Report No. 58*, 1973, pp. 348–50; ABS, *Labour Statistics, Australia*, 1990, p. 116; ABS, *Labour Statistics, Australia*, 1997, p. 175.
40. John Wanna, 'The State and Industrial Relations', in Kyoko Sheridan (ed.), *The State as Developer: Public Enterprise in South Australia*, Adelaide: Wakefield Press, 1986, p. 138.
41. Ibid., p. 135. For elaboration of these and other factors, see John Wanna, 'A Paradigm of Consent: Explanations of Working Class Moderation in South Australia', *Labour History*, 53, 1987, pp. 54–72.
42. Wanna, 'A Paradigm of Consent', p. 64.
43. See T.J. Mitchell, 'J.W. Wainright [*sic*]: The Industrialisation of S.A., 1935–40', *Australian Journal of Politics and History*, 8(1), 1962, pp. 30–6 *passim*; Jim Moss, *Sound of Trumpets: History of the Labour Movement in South Australia*, Adelaide: Wakefield Press, 1985, p. 362.
44. McCaskill, '1950: Forging an Industrial State', p. 28. The information in this and the following paragraph is largely derived from this source. For subterranean clover, see David F. Smith, *Natural Gain: In the Grazing Lands of Southern Australia*, Sydney: UNSW Press, 2000, pp. 89–99.
45. Ibid.
46. Ibid.
47. Murray McCaskill, '1985: Achievement and Uncertainty', in Trevor Griffin and Murray McCaskill (eds), *Atlas of South Australia*, Adelaide: SA Government Printing Division and Wakefield Press, 1986, p. 34.
48. Cockburn, pp. 217–18.
49. Ibid., p. 218.
50. P.A. Howell, 'Playford, Politics and Parliament', in Bernard O'Neil, Judith Raftery and Kerrie Round (eds), *Playford's South Australia: Essays on the History of South Australia 1933–1968*, Adelaide: Association of Professional Historians Inc., 1996, p. 65.
51. Ibid., p. 65.
52. The biographies of Playford published in the 1980s and 1990s reflect this trend. For a recent example, see Bob Byrne, 'Adelaide, Remember When … Tom Playford Ruled South Australia?', *Advertiser*, 14 March 2014; accessible at http://www.adelaidenow.com.au/news/south-australia/adelaide-remember-when-tom-playford-ruled-south-australia/story-fni6uo1m-1226855067404.

53. Hugh Stretton and Pat Stretton, 'Wainwright, John William', *Australian Dictionary of Biography*, http://adb.anu.edu.au/biography/wainwright-john-william-8945/text15721.
54. Marsden, 'Playford's Metropolis', p. 130.
55. See Jenny Tilby Stock, 'The "Playmander": Its Origins, Operation and Effect on South Australia', in Bernard O'Neil, Judith Raftery and Kerrie Round (eds), *Playford's South Australia: Essays on the History of South Australia 1933–1968*, Adelaide: Association of Professional Historians Inc., 1996, pp. 87–9.
56. Howell, 'Playford, Politics and Parliament', p. 48.
57. Cockburn, p. 194.
58. See, for example, Cockburn, pp. 329–30; Kerrie Round, 'A Deputation for a National Trust', in Bernard O'Neil, Judith Raftery and Kerrie Round (eds), *Playford's South Australia: Essays on the History of South Australia 1933–1968*, Adelaide: Association of Professional Historians Inc., 1996, pp. 325–6.
59. See Jaensch, pp. 13–14.

Chapter 8 War and Society in the Playford Era, 1939–65

1. 'Thousands Fight State's Worst Bushfire', *Advertiser*, 11 January 1939, p. 19; Richard Evans, *Disasters that Changed Australia*, Melbourne: Victory Books, 2009, pp. 110–11.
2. 'Another War Secret', *Chronicle*, 30 August 1945, p. 26.
3. Geoffrey Bolton, *The Oxford History of Australia. Volume 5: 1942–1988*, Melbourne: Oxford University Press, 1990, pp. 7–8.
4. 'Labor Party Endorses Prime Minister's Militia Plans', *Daily Mercury*, 6 January 1943, p. 2.
5. 'Conflicts: World War Two: Women's Auxiliary Services and Land Army', State Library of South Australia, http://www.samemory.sa.gov.au/site/page.cfm?u=1006.
6. Joan Beaumont, *Australian Defence: Sources and Statistics*, Melbourne: Oxford University Press, 2001, p. 306; and Gavin Long, *Australia in the War of 1939–1945*, Series 1 (Army), Vol. VII ('The Final Campaigns'), Canberra: Australian War Memorial, 1963, p. 635.
7. Carol Fort, 'World War II', in Wilfrid Prest, Kerrie Round and Carol Fort (eds), *The Wakefield Companion to South Australian History*, Adelaide: Wakefield Press, 2001, p. 594.
8. State Library of South Australia, D 6478(L).
9. Robert Hall, 'Hughes, Timothy', *Australian Dictionary of Biography*, http://adb.anu.edu.au/biography/hughes-timothy-10567/text18767.

10. Helen Crisp, 'Women in Munitions', *Australian Quarterly*, 13(3), 1941, pp. 71–6.
11. 'Explosives Factory, Salisbury. Ministry of Munitions draft history 1940–45', cited in Carol S. Fort, '"Equality of Sacrifice"?: War Work in Salisbury, South Australia', in Bernard O'Neil, Judith Raftery and Kerrie Round (eds), *Playford's South Australia: Essays on the History of South Australia 1933–1968*, Adelaide: Association of Professional Historians Inc., 1996, p. 221.
12. 'Re Explosion on Detonator Section', 19 October 1942, in file titled 'Reports of Incidents at Salisbury Explosives Factory', National Archives of Australia (henceforth NAA), D1915, SA10875E Part 1.
13. 'Accident report, 11 June 1943', and 'Manager's report, June 1943, Tetryl Plant – Salisbury', NAA, MP959/13, 363/25C/124, cited in Fort, '"Equality of sacrifice"?', p. 219.
14. 'Munition Establishments Declaration as Protected Undertaking', 13 February 1942, NAA, B551, 452/79/37.
15. Fort, 'World War II', pp. 594–5.
16. 'Austerity Recipes', *The Australian Women's Weekly*, 17 October 1942 and 24 July 1943.
17. Paul Nursey-Bray, 'Anti-Fascism and Internment: The Case of Francesco Fantin', *Journal of the Historical Society of South Australia*, 17, 1989, pp. 88–111.
18. Christine J. Lockwood, '"We are here to round up Nazis": The Military Raid on Immanuel College and Seminary in World War Two', *Journal of the Historical Society of South Australia*, 36, 2008, pp. 75–90.
19. Ibid., p. 76.
20. Anthony Kaukas, 'Images from Loveday: Interment in South Australia, 1939–1945', *Journal of the Historical Society of South Australia*, 29, 2001, pp. 49–50, 54.
21. Bolton, p. 11.
22. *Land*, 15 September 1939, cited in Mark Peel and Christina Twomey, *A History of Australia*, Melbourne: Palgrave Macmillan, 2011, p. 200.
23. David Hilliard and Arnold D. Hunt, 'Religion', in Eric Richards (ed.), *The Flinders History of South Australia: Social History*, Adelaide: Wakefield Press, 1986, pp. 226–30; Australian Bureau of Statistics, *Census 1986 – Summary Characteristics of Persons and Dwellings South Australia*, p. 13.
24. Susan Lemar, '"Sexually Cursed, Mentally Weak and Socially Untouchable": Women and Venereal Diseases in World War Two Adelaide', *Journal of Australian Studies*, 27(79), 2003, p. 155.
25. Kay Saunders and Helen Taylor, '"To Combat the Plague": The Construction of Moral Alarm and State Intervention in Queensland during World War II', *Hecate*, 14(1), 1988, p. 13.

26. These figures are calculated from Table 1.3 in Wray Vamplew *et al.* (eds), *South Australian Historical Statistics*, Adelaide: History Project Incorporated, 1984, pp. 18–19.
27. These figures have been calculated from Commonwealth Bureau of Census and Statistics, *Census 1954, Volume IV – South Australia. Part II*, p. 152, and *Census 1961, Volume IV – South Australia. Part II*, p. 95.
28. See, for example, 'Bodgie Nuisance to be Curbed in City', *Advertiser*, 16 February 1955, p. 6.
29. Elizabeth Kwan, *Living in South Australia: A Social History. Volume 2: After 1914*, Adelaide: South Australian Government Printer, 1987, p. 132.
30. See Table 8.14 and Table 8.15 in Vamplew *et al.* (eds), pp. 223–4, 225.
31. A further premiership was won when the team played as Port/Torrens in the non-official competition that took place during the war.
32. See Table 8.8 in Vamplew *et al.* (eds), p. 212.
33. Ian W. McLean, *Why Australia Prospered: The Shifting Sources of Economic Growth*, Princeton: Princeton University Press, 2013, pp. 196–7.
34. See Table 11.13 in Vamplew *et al.* (eds), p. 309.
35. Peter Donovan, 'Motor Cars and Freeways: Measures of a South Australian Love Affair', in Bernard O'Neil, Judith Raftery and Kerrie Round (eds), *Playford's South Australia*, Adelaide: Association of Professional Historians Inc., 1996, pp. 210–11.
36. Craig Campbell, 'Developing a 1950s Imagination in Woodville Gardens', in Susan Blackburn (ed.), *Growing Up in Adelaide in the 1950s*, Sydney: Hale & Iremonger, 2012, p. 42.
37. P.A. Howell, 'Playford, Sir Thomas', *Australian Dictionary of Biography*, http://adb.anu.edu.au/biography/playford-sir-thomas-tom-15472/text26686.
38. Stewart Cockburn, 'Dumas, Sir Frederick Lloyd', *Australian Dictionary of Biography*, http://adb.anu.edu.au/biography/dumas-sir-frederick-lloyd-10058/text17741.
39. Katharine West, *Power in the Liberal Party: A Study in Australian Politics*, Melbourne: Cheshire, 1965.
40. Ken Inglis provides the most compelling examination of the case and the personalities involved. See K.S. Inglis, *The Stuart Case* [1961], 2nd edn, Melbourne: Black Inc., 2002.
41. Quoted in Stewart Cockburn assisted by John Playford, *Playford: Benevolent Despot*, Adelaide: Axiom Publishing, 1991, p. 302.
42. Cockburn, *Playford*, p. 303.
43. 'Max Stuart Finds Peace in the Lore of His Country', *Age*, 19 August 2002, p. 1; Inglis, pp. 383–4.
44. Cockburn, *Playford*, pp. 292–310.
45. *Angry Penguins*, 5, 1944, p. 5.

46. Max Harris, 'Appendix', in *Ern Malley's Poems*, Melbourne: Lansdowne Press, 1961, p. 44, cited in Clare Parker, 'Abortion, Homosexuality and the Slippery Slope: Legislating "Moral" Behaviour in South Australia', PhD thesis, University of Adelaide, 2013, pp. 47–8.
47. 'Harris Fined £5 in "Penguins" Case', *Mail*, 20 October 1944, p. 3.
48. 'S.A's "Barbaric" Law Criticised', *News*, 13 November 1944, p. 4.
49. For further examples, see Nicole Moore, *The Censor's Library*, Brisbane: University of Queensland Press, 2012.
50. 'Ban Amazes U.S. Singer', *Advertiser*, 28 March 1960, p. 3; see Parker, p. 48.
51. 'Protecting Our "Good Manners"', *Advertiser*, 29 March 1960, p. 2.
52. *Sydney Morning Herald*, 1 March 2003, 'Spectrum' supplement, pp. 4–5, cited in Parker, p. 48.
53. 'Divertissements' [letter to the editor], *Advertiser*, 30 March 1960, p. 4.
54. '"Ghoul Singer" Sets His Sights on Adelaide', *Advertiser*, 29 March 1960, p. 5.
55. Ibid.
56. 'Protecting Our "Good Manners"', *Advertiser*, 29 March 1960, p. 2.
57. Laucke, quoted in Cockburn, *Playford*, p. 333.
58. Also referred to as the *Aborigines Act 1934–1939*.
59. Judith Raftery, *Not Part of the Public: Non-Indigenous Policies and Practices and the Health of Indigenous South Australians 1836–1973*, Adelaide: Wakefield Press, 2006, p. 177.
60. Ibid., p. 181.
61. Cyril Coaby quoted in Christobel Mattingley with Ken Hampton, *Survival in Our Own Land: "Aboriginal" Experiences in South Australia" since 1836*, Adelaide: Wakefield Press, 1988, p. 51.
62. Vi Deuschle quoted in Mattingley, p. 54.
63. *South Australian Parliamentary Debates*, House of Assembly, 17 October 1962, p. 1525.
64. Peggy Brock, *Outback Ghettos: Aborigines, Institutionalisation and Survival*, Melbourne: Cambridge University Press, 1993, p. 18.
65. Mattingley, pp. 124–5.
66. See 'Gladys has battled for her people', *Advertiser*, 9 July 1981, p. 3; 'Funeral Tomorrow for "Aunty Glad"', *Advertiser*, 21 January 1988, p. 14.

Chapter 9 The Dunstan 'Decade', 1965–79

1. Clem Macintyre, 'Politics', in John Spoehr (ed.), *State of South Australia: Trends and Issues*, Adelaide: Wakefield Press, 2005, p. 121.
2. '"Doomsday" in Adelaide No Great Shake', *Advertiser*, 20 January 1976, p. 3.

3. Quoted in Susan Magarey and Kerrie Round, *Roma the First: A Biography of Dame Roma Mitchell*, Adelaide: Wakefield Press, 2007, p. 154.
4. *Don Dunstan, The First 25 Years in Parliament*, compiled by Richard Yeeles, Melbourne: Hill of Content, 1978, p. 127.
5. Andrew Parkin, 'The Dunstan Governments: A Political Synopsis', in Andrew Parkin and Allan Patience (eds), *The Dunstan Decade: Social Democracy at the State Level*, Melbourne: Longman Cheshire, 1981, pp. 4–5.
6. Macintyre, p. 121.
7. *Criminal Law Consolidation Act Amendment Act 1969*.
8. Clare Parker, 'From Immorality to Public Health: Thalidomide and the Debate for Legal Abortion in Australia', *Social History of Medicine*, 25(4), 2012, pp. 863–80.
9. For comprehensive discussion of this issue, see Clare Parker, 'Abortion, Homosexuality and the Slippery Slope: Legislating "Moral" Behaviour in South Australia', PhD thesis, University of Adelaide, 2013.
10. Robert Martin, *Responsible Government in South Australia: Playford to Rann 1957–2007*, Adelaide: Wakefield Press, 2009, p. 32.
11. This was facilitated by the *Aboriginal Affairs Act Amendment Act 1966–1967*.
12. *Maralinga-Tjarutja Land Rights Act 1984*.
13. Helen Mills, 'Equal Opportunities', in Andrew Parkin and Allan Patience (eds), *The Dunstan Decade: Social Democracy at the State Level*, Melbourne: Longman Cheshire, 1981, p. 119.
14. See John Warhurst, 'The Public Service', in Andrew Parkin and Allan Patience (eds), *The Dunstan Decade: Social Democracy at the State Level*, Melbourne: Longman Cheshire, 1981, p. 196.
15. See Sylvia Kinder, *Herstory of Adelaide Women's Liberation 1969–1974*, Adelaide: Salisbury Education Centre, 1980.
16. 'Two More Vice Men Quit', *Advertiser*, 13 July 1972, p. 3.
17. An editorial published in *The Advertiser* (1 July 1972, p. 5) amidst reports about the inquest into Dr Duncan's death was titled 'Legalise Homosexuality'.
18. *South Australian Parliamentary Debates* (henceforth *SAPD*), House of Assembly (HoA), 18 October 1972, pp. 2211 (Evans), 2213 (King), 2201 (Hopgood).
19. 'Prison No Solution, say Clerics', *Advertiser*, 17 February 1972, p. 20.
20. Men could still be charged with committing a homosexual act, but conviction could be avoided by proving that the act was consensual and conducted in private.
21. 'The Few in "the Band"', *Advertiser*, 8 April 1970, p. 1; 'Play Cuts of "No Effect"', *Advertiser*, 9 April 1970, p. 1.
22. Dawn B. Sova, *Banned Plays: Censorship Histories of 125 Stage Dramas*, New York: Facts on File, 2004, pp. 27–8.

23. 'Dunstan Backs Right to Read', *Advertiser*, 2 September 1970, p. 6.
24. 'Residents at Maslin Will Protest', *Advertiser*, 14 February 1975, p. 3.
25. 'Cricket On Sunday' [letter to the editor], *Advertiser*, 26 November 1969, p. 2.
26. 'A Warning to All Birds ...', *Advertiser*, 24 November 1969, p. 22.
27. For evidence and explanation of this decline, see David Hilliard, 'The Religious Crisis of the 1960s: The Experience of the Australian Churches', *The Journal of Religious History*, 21(2), 1997, pp. 209–27.
28. David Hilliard, 'How Did Methodism Shape South Australia?', *Church Heritage*, 18(2), 2013, p. 97.
29. Hilliard, 'Religious Crisis'.
30. See 'Table 3.4 Growth of Secondary Education, 1961–1970', in 'Report of the Minister for the Year Ended 31st of December 1970', *South Australian Parliamentary Papers*, no. 44, 1971, p. 58; *Statistical Register of South Australia, 1963–64: Part 1*, 1966, p. 15; *1964–65: Part 1*, 1967, p. 15; *1967–68: Part 1*, 1972, p. 15; *1969–70 and 1970–71: Part 1*, 1973, p. 20; *1972–73: Part 1*, 1975, p. 16.
31. 'Report of the Minister', p. 62.
32. *SAPD*, HoA, 29 June 1965, pp. 612–18 *passim*; Pavla Miller, *Long Division: State Schooling in South Australian Society*, Adelaide: Wakefield Press, 1986, pp. 290–1.
33. Bernard Hyams, 'Education', in Andrew Parkin and Allan Patience (eds), *The Dunstan Decade: Social Democracy at the State Level*, Melbourne: Longman Cheshire, 1981, p. 76.
34. Ibid., p. 75.
35. Miller, p. 308; Hyams, p. 77.
36. Hyams, p. 83.
37. Ibid., p. 81.
38. See Table 2.3 in Kevin Davis and Ian McLean, 'Economic Policy', in Andrew Parkin and Allan Patience (eds), *The Dunstan Decade: Social Democracy at the State Level*, Melbourne: Longman Cheshire, 1981, p. 27.
39. Ibid.
40. Neal Blewett and Dean Jaensch, *Playford to Dunstan: The Politics of Transition*, Melbourne: Cheshire, 1971, p. 10.
41. Rod Oxenberry, 'Community Welfare', in Andrew Parkin and Allan Patience (eds), *The Dunstan Decade: Social Democracy at the State Level*, Melbourne: Longman Cheshire, 1981, pp. 53–4.
42. Ibid.
43. Ibid., p. 59.
44. Ian Cox interviewed by Bruce Guerin, 5 July 2007, Don Dunstan Oral History Project, Flinders University Library.
45. Stewart Cockburn assisted by John Playford, *Playford: Benevolent Despot*, Adelaide: Axiom, 1991, p. 190.
46. Ibid., pp. 189–90.

47. Jo Caust, 'The Arts', in John Spoehr (ed.), *State of South Australia: Trends and Issues*, Adelaide: Wakefield Press, 2005, pp. 276–7.
48. Peter Ward, 'Arts', in Wilfrid Prest, Kerrie Round and Carol Fort (eds), *The Wakefield Companion to South Australian History*, Adelaide: Wakefield Press, 2001, p. 51.
49. Peter Ward, 'Colin Sandergrove Ballantye', in Wilfrid Prest, Kerrie Round and Carol Fort (eds), *The Wakefield Companion to South Australian History*, Adelaide: Wakefield Press, 2001, p. 65.
50. Rex Ingamells, *Conditional Culture*, Adelaide: F.W. Preece, 1938, p. 5.
51. For elaboration, see Elizabeth Salter, *Robert Helpmann*, Sydney: Angus & Robertson, 1978.
52. 'The 1980s: Prosperity If We Don't Mess It Up', *Advertiser*, 18 February 1980, p. 5.
53. Davis and McLean, pp. 46–7.
54. Table 2.8 in ibid., p. 43.
55. Davis and McLean, p. 24.
56. See Table 2.1 in ibid.
57. Davis and McLean, pp. 30–1.
58. Ibid., p. 36 and p. 49 (footnote 15).
59. John Warhurst, 'The Politics of the South Australian Economy', *Australian Quarterly*, 51(2), 1979, p. 90.
60. Bruce McFarlane and Kyoko Sheridan, 'The Minerals and Energy Sector', in Kyoko Sheridan (ed.), *The State as Developer: Public Enterprise in South Australia*, Adelaide: Wakefield Press, 1986, p. 95.
61. Australian Bureau of Statistics (henceforth ABS), *Year Book Australia, No. 58, 1972*, p. 903; and ABS, *Year Book Australia, No. 65, 1981*, p. 383.
62. Parkin, p. 16.
63. Andrew Lothian, 'Environment', in John Spoehr (ed.), *State of South Australia: Trends and Issues*, Adelaide: Wakefield Press, 2005, p. 192.
64. See Matthew Jordan, 'Procuring Industrial Pollution Control in South Australia', PhD thesis, University of Adelaide, 2001, pp. 199–239.
65. Ibid.
66. See Committee on Environment, *The Environment in South Australia*, Adelaide: Government Printer, 1972.
67. Ibid., p. 91.
68. ABS, *South Australia Year Book 1983*, p. 127.
69. Malcolm Saunders, 'Opposition to the Vietnam War in South Australia, 1965–1973', *Journal of the Historical Society of South Australia*, 10, 1982, p. 64.
70. Ibid., p. 65.
71. 'Soldiers Attack City Marchers', *Advertiser*, 9 May 1970, p. 1; 'Army Fines 16 After Attacks', *Advertiser*, 11 May 1970, p. 3.
72. Royal Commission, 'Report on the September Moratorium Demonstration', *South Australian Parliamentary Papers*, no. 76, 1971, pp. 7, 65.

73. Ibid., pp. 51–3.
74. Ibid., p. 56.
75. Ibid., p. 67; 'Police Arrest 141 in City Clash', *Advertiser*, 19 September 1970, p. 1.
76. 'New Claims of A-Test Link with Cancer', *Advertiser*, 17 April 1980, pp. 1, 11; 'The Terrible Legacy of Maralinga', *National Times*, 4–10 May 1984, p. 3.
77. Martin, p. 18.
78. Bruce Duncan, *Crusade or Conspiracy? Catholics and the Anti-Communist Struggle in Australia*, Sydney: UNSW Press, 2001, p. 356.
79. P.L. Reynolds, *The Democratic Labor Party*, Brisbane: Jacaranda Press, 1974, pp. 20, 54–5.
80. Dean Jaensch, 'Democratic Labor Party (DLP)', in Wilfrid Prest, Kerrie Round and Carol Fort (eds), *The Wakefield Companion to South Australian History*, Adelaide: Wakefield Press, 2001, p. 147.
81. Parkin, p. 6.
82. See Dean Jaensch and Joan Bullock, *Liberals in Limbo: Non-Labor Politics in South Australia, 1970–1978*, Melbourne: Drummond, 1978.
83. 'Exposed ... The Secret Police Dossiers on Demonstrators', *Australian*, 3 September 1977, p. 1.
84. 'S.A. Police Chief Dismissed', *Advertiser*, 18 January 1978, p. 1.
85. Peter N. Grabosky, *Wayward Governance: Illegality and its Control in the Public Sector*, Canberra: Australian Institute of Criminology, 1989, pp. 114–15.
86. See Salisbury's statement in *Royal Commission 1978: Report on the Dismissal of Harold Hubert Salisbury*, Adelaide: Government Printer, 1978, p. 19.
87. Grabosky, p. 123.
88. 'Thousands Rally to Salisbury', *Advertiser*, 26 January 1978, p. 1.
89. Don Dunstan, *Felicia: The Political Memoirs of Don Dunstan*, Melbourne: Macmillan, 1981, pp. 126–7.
90. See Des Ryan and Mike McEwan, *It's Grossly Improper*, Dulwich, S.A.: Wenan, 1979.

Chapter 10 Triumph of the Market, 1980–2001

1. Robert Martin, *Responsible Government in South Australia: Playford to Rann 1957–2007*, Adelaide: Wakefield Press, 2009, p. 99.
2. Ibid.
3. 'Invest in SA Boom, Tonkin Tells UK', *Advertiser*, 10 April 1980, p. 3.
4. Martin, p. 106.
5. Clem Macintyre, 'Politics', in John Spoehr (ed.), *State of South Australia: Trends and Issues*, Adelaide: Wakefield Press, 2005, p. 122.
6. 'Bannon: A New Captain Surveys a Sinking Ship', *Australian Financial Review*, 12 November 1982, p. 3.

7. Australian Bureau of Statistics (henceforth ABS), *Census 1986: Summary Characteristics of Persons and Dwellings, South Australia*, p. 29 (contains data from 1981 and 1986 Census); ABS, *1991 Census: Census Characteristics of South Australia*, p. 28.
8. Martin, pp. 112–13, 133.
9. Lionel Orchard, 'Urban Policy', in Andrew Parkin and Allan Patience (eds), *The Bannon Decade: The Politics of Restraint in South Australia*, Sydney: Allen & Unwin, 1992, p. 149.
10. Quoted in ibid.
11. D. Damania, 'Environmental Policy', in Andrew Parkin and Allan Patience (eds), *The Bannon Decade: The Politics of Restraint in South Australia*, Sydney: Allen & Unwin, 1992, pp. 163–4.
12. Cited in Manuel Castells and Peter Hall, *Technopoles of the World: The Making of Twenty-First-Century Industrial Complexes*, London: Routledge, 1994, p. 208.
13. 'The City that Never Was', *Sydney Morning Herald*, 16 August 1997, p. 40.
14. Bernard O'Neil, 'Minerals and Energy', in Andrew Parkin and Allan Patience (eds), *The Bannon Decade: The Politics of Restraint in South Australia*, Sydney: Allen & Unwin, 1992, p. 185.
15. See, for example, 'SA Uranium Plant Risks "High"', *Canberra Times*, 18 September 1989, p. 10.
16. See, for example, Allan Patience, 'The Bannon Decade: Preparation for What?', in Andrew Parkin and Allan Patience (eds), *The Bannon Decade: The Politics of Restraint in South Australia*, Sydney: Allen & Unwin, 1992, pp. 343–54.
17. Ian Radbone, 'Public-Sector Management', in Andrew Parkin and Allan Patience (eds), *The Bannon Decade: The Politics of Restraint in South Australia*, Sydney: Allen & Unwin, 1992, p. 108.
18. Deborah Jordan, 'Women's Policy', in Andrew Parkin and Allan Patience (eds), *The Bannon Decade: The Politics of Restraint in South Australia*, Sydney: Allen & Unwin, 1992, p. 309.
19. *Equal Opportunity Act 1984* and *Equal Opportunity Act Amendment Act 1990*.
20. See Vern Marshall, 'Schools', in Andrew Parkin and Allan Patience (eds), *The Bannon Decade: The Politics of Restraint in South Australia*, Sydney: Allen & Unwin, 1992, esp. pp. 210–11. For health, see Robert Kosky, 'Health Policy', in the same book, pp. 237–50.
21. South Australia (Treasury), *Financial Statement 1991–92: Financial Paper No.1*, Adelaide: Government Printer, 1991, p. 94.
22. G. McL. Scott, 'Economic Policy', in Andrew Parkin and Allan Patience (eds), *The Bannon Decade: The Politics of Restraint in South Australia*, Sydney: Allen & Unwin, 1992, p. 83.
23. See South Australia (Treasury), p. 89.
24. See McL. Scott, p. 93.

25. ETSA, 'Annual Report, 1988–89', *South Australian Parliamentary Papers*, no. 64, 1989, p. 33; ETSA, 'Annual Report, 1989–90', *South Australian Parliamentary Papers*, no. 64, 1990, p. 3.
26. McL. Scott, p. 85.
27. *South Australian Parliamentary Debates* (henceforth *SAPD*), House of Assembly (HoA), 25 November 1992, p. 1689.
28. Martin, p. 123.
29. McL. Scott, p. 88.
30. Ibid.
31. Ibid., p. 91.
32. See Ian Macfarlane, 'The Recession of 1990 and its Legacy', Boyer Lectures, http://www.abc.net.au/radionational/programs/boyerlectures/lecture-4-the-recession-of-1990-and-its-legacy/3353124#transcript.
33. *Report of the Auditor-General on an Investigation into the State Bank of South Australia*, Sections 14.2.8 and 14.2.9; http://www.audit.sa.gov.au/Publications/Other-reports/SBSA-1993/Chapter-14.
34. Martin, p. 131; Chris Kenny, *State of Denial: The Government, the Media, the Bank*, Adelaide: Wakefield Press, 1993, pp. 45, 183.
35. 'Bannon $970m Bail-Out', *Australian Financial Review*, 11 February 1991, p. 1.
36. South Australia (Treasury), p. 58.
37. *SAPD*, HoA, 13 December 1990, p. 2757.
38. Martin, p. 131.
39. Ibid., p. 132.
40. Duncan in the Foreword to Kenny, p. xii.
41. Royal Commission into the State Bank of South Australia, *First Report*, 1992, p. 259.
42. Oliver Stone [director], *Wall Street*, Twentieth Century Fox, 1987.
43. Hugo Armstrong, 'The Tricontinental Affair', in Mark Considine and Brian Costar (eds), *Trials in Power: Cain, Kirner and Victoria, 1982–1992*, Melbourne: Melbourne University Press, 1992, pp. 43–58.
44. *Dorrestijn v South Australian Planning Commission* [1984] HCA 76; (1984) 56 ALR 295.
45. Damania, pp. 168, 169.
46. ABS, *South Australia Year Book 1983*, p.494; *South Australia Year Book 1990*, p. 239.
47. R.L. Heathcote, 'Agriculture', in Andrew Parkin and Allan Patience (eds), *The Bannon Decade: The Politics of Restraint in South Australia*, Sydney: Allen & Unwin, 1992, pp. 173–4.
48. Ibid., p. 174.
49. H.P.K. Dunn, *SAPD*, Legislative Council, 18 August 1983, p. 347; W.E. Chapman, *SAPD*, HoA, 25 August 1983, p. 530. See Heathcote, p. 177.
50. Heathcote, p. 178.

51. See John Spoehr and Steven Barrett, 'Public Sector Workforce', in John Spoehr (ed.), *State of South Australia: Trends and Issues*, Adelaide: Wakefield Press, 2005, pp. 102–3.
52. *SAPD*, HoA, 23 August 1994, pp. 218–20; *SAPD*, HoA, 30 November 1994, pp. 1305–6; *SAPD*, HoA, 13 April 1994, p. 684.
53. Adrian Vicary, 'Social Welfare', in Wilfrid Prest, Kerrie Round and Carol Fort (eds), *The Wakefield Companion to South Australian History*, Adelaide: Wakefield Press, 2001, esp. pp. 497–8.
54. McL. Scott, p. 98 (footnote 7).
55. Martin, p. 135.
56. See, for example, Don Dunstan, 'The Road to Ruin', *Adelaide Review*, February 1996, p. 92.
57. Martin, p. 155.
58. '25% Official AGL Electricity Price Rise', *Advertiser*, 30 September 2002, p. 1; 'Message Horribilis', *Advertiser*, 1 October 2002, p. 1.
59. 'Privatisation: Selling Australia – The Price We Pay', *Advertiser*, 3 June 2004, p. 29, citing a study by social and economic analyst Professor John Spoehr.
60. See David McDonald, *Deaths in Custody Australia. National Police Custody Survey 1992: Preliminary Report*, Canberra: Australian Institute of Criminology, 1993, p. 3; *Indigenous Deaths in Custody 1989 to 1996: Summary Report*, https://www.humanrights.gov.au/publications/indigenous-deaths-custody-report-summary.
61. See *Royal Commission into Aboriginal Deaths in Custody*, 1987–1991, chapter 1.2, http://www.austlii.edu.au/au/other/IndigLRes/rciadic/national/vol1/9.html.
62. Ibid.; and *Indigenous Deaths in Custody 1989 to 1996*.
63. *Royal Commission into Aboriginal Deaths in Custody*, chapter 2.2.9.
64. Ibid., chapter 1.4. Also see, *Bringing Them Home: Report of the National Inquiry into the Separation of Aboriginal and Torres Strait Islander Children from Their Families*, Sydney: Human Rights and Equal Opportunity Commission, 1997, p. 13.
65. See *Bringing Them Home*, pp. 36–37.
66. Ibid., pp. 6–7.
67. Ibid., pp. 29–30, 119–30.
68. For all statistics and trends identified in this paragraph, see ABS, *Census Characteristics of South Australia 1991 – Census of Population and Housing*, pp. 17, 20; ABS, *1996 Census of Population and Housing: Selected Social and Housing Characteristics for Statistical Local Areas, South Australia*, p. 27.
69. Janet Phillips, 'Asylum Seekers and Refugees: What Are the Facts?', Parliamentary Library, *Parliament of Australia*, 2011, pp. 7–8, available at http://www.aph.gov.au/binaries/library/pubs/bn/sp/asylumfacts.pdf.

70. Table 1.2 in ABS, *Australian Historical Population Statistics*, 2014, http://www.abs.gov.au/ausstats/abs@.nsf/mf/3105.0.65.001.
71. Table 2.10 in ibid.; ABS, *1996 Census of Population and Housing: Selected Social and Housing Characteristics for Statistical Local Areas, South Australia*, p. 1; ABS, *Census of Population and Housing: Selected Social and Housing Characteristics for Statistical Local Areas, South Australia*, 2001, p. 1.
72. See Table 2.1 in ABS, *Australian Historical Population Statistics*, 2014, http://www.abs.gov.au/ausstats/abs@.nsf/mf/3105.0.65.001.
73. Graeme Hugo, 'Population', in John Spoehr (ed.), *State of South Australia: Trends and Issues*, Adelaide: Wakefield Press, 2005, pp. 32–3.

Chapter 11 Age of Anxiety, 2002–present

1. 'Y2K May Force Qantas Flights Out of the Skies', *Sydney Morning Herald*, 31 March 1999.
2. Graeme Hugo *et al.*, *Bringing Them Back Home – Factors Influencing Interstate Migration To and From South Australia*, Adelaide: University of Adelaide, 2000, pp. 110–18.
3. The Economist Intelligence Unit, *A Summary of the Liveability Ranking and Overview, August 2015*, http://www.eiu.com/Handlers/WhitepaperHandler.ashx?fi=Liveability-Ranking-Aug-2015.pdf&mode=wp&campaignid=Liveability2015.
4. Australian Bureau of Statistics (henceforth ABS), 'Patterns of Internet Access in Australia, 2006', http://www.abs.gov.au/ausstats/abs@.nsf/mf/8146.0.55.001.
5. 'Shark Attacks in Australia', *National Geographic*, http://www.australiangeographic.com.au/topics/science-environment/2015/07/shark-attacks-in-australia-a-timeline; and Royal Life Saving Society of Australia, *Royal Life Saving National Drowning Report 2015*, http://www.royallifesaving.com.au/__data/assets/pdf_file/0006/14559/RLS_NDR2015_Report_LR.pdf.
6. See, for example, 'Housing Market Worst in Europe for Falling Prices', *Irish Independent*, 6 March 2008; 'Joblessness: The Kids Are Not Alright', *Wall Street Journal*, 8 April 2010, p. A19.
7. John Spoehr and Rasika Ranasinghe, 'Employment', in John Spoehr (ed.), *State of South Australia: Turbulent Times*, Adelaide: Wakefield Press, 2013, p. 257.
8. It is estimated that in the absence of the stimulus package, Australia's economy would have contracted by 0.7% in 2009. See Australian Government, 'Budget Paper No. 1: Budget Strategy and Outlook 2010–11', Statement 2: Economic Outlook, 2010, p. 3.
9. Between December 2008 and June 2014, the value of the Australian dollar appreciated by 38% against the Euro, 40% against the US

dollar, and 24% against the British pound. See ABS, 'Export and Import Invoice Currencies, June 2014', http://www.abs.gov.au/ausstats/abs@.nsf/featurearticlesbyCatalogue/49C2F3FF2ADEF150CA257D2A00114B37?OpenDocument.

10. See ABS, *Labour Force, Australia, Detailed, Quarterly*, Time Series Workbook, Table 5.
11. Toby Hagan, 'Holden Commits $1 Billion until 2022', *Drive*, 22 March 2012, http://www.drive.com.au/motor-news/holden-commits-1-billion-until-2022-20120321-1vl34.html.
12. 'Holden's Dramatic Exit Puts Toyota at Risk', *Australian Financial Review*, 12 December 2013, p. 1.
13. 'Gold Mine: Olympic Dam Deal Delivers $350 million a Year', *Advertiser*, 13 October 2011, p. 1.
14. BHP Billiton, 'Olympic Dam Update', 22 August 2012, http://www.bhpbilliton.com/investors/news/Olympic-Dam.
15. Government of South Australia, *Economic Statement*, 2013, p. 3. Available (cached) at http://www.premier.sa.gov.au/ecostat/economic_statement_web.pdf.
16. John Spoehr, 'Turbulent Times', in John Spoehr (ed.), *State of South Australia: Turbulent Times*, Adelaide: Wakefield Press, 2013, p. 6.
17. See ABS, *Labour Force, Australia, Detailed, Quarterly*, Time Series Workbook, Table 5; ABS, *Characteristics of Australian Exporters, 2011–12*, Table 7; and ABS, *Research and Experimental Development, Businesses, Australia 2011–12*, Data Cube 'Business Expenditure on R&D'.
18. Spoehr, p. 3.
19. Jane Andrew and John Spoehr, 'Manufacturing Creativity and Innovation', in John Spoehr (ed.), *State of South Australia: Turbulent Times*, Adelaide: Wakefield Press, 2013, p. 302.
20. 'AAA Foley Gets His Credit Rating, Now Pressure is on to Loosen Strings', *Advertiser*, 29 September 2004, p. 3.
21. An $11 billion dollar loss in expected GST revenue nationally translated to a $2 billion hit to the South Australian budget. See Spoehr, p. 4.
22. '"Rack'em, Pack'em, Stack'em": Outrage Over Jail Comments', *Independent Weekly*, 9 May 2008, pp. 3, 5.
23. See Gabrielle Appleby and John M. Williams, 'Law and Order', in John Spoehr (ed.), *State of South Australia: Turbulent Times*, Adelaide: Wakefield Press, 2013, pp. 88–97.
24. 'Voters Reject Rann's Crime Boast', *Advertiser*, 6 February 2007, pp. 1, 6.
25. 'We Want Our Streets Safe Again', *Advertiser*, 17 February 2006, p. 5.
26. South Australian Police, *Annual Report 2010–2011*, pp. 19–21.
27. Appleby and Williams, p. 85.

28. ABS, *Household Income and Wealth, Australia, 2011–12*, Table 17, p. 44.
29. Ibid. Also see ABS, *Household Income and Wealth, Australia, 2013–14*, Table 15.11.
30. Martin Shanahan, 'Income and Wealth', in John Spoehr (ed.), *State of South Australia: Turbulent Times*, Adelaide: Wakefield Press, 2013, p. 230.
31. ABS, *Household Wealth and Wealth Distribution 2009–10*, pp. 12–13.
32. ABS, *Labour Force, Australia, Detailed, Quarterly*, Time Series Workbook, Table 5.
33. ABS, *Labour Force, Australia, July 2017*, p. 5.
34. See ABS, *Labour Force, Australia, December 1993*, p. 15.
35. Spoehr and Ranasinghe, p. 276.
36. ABS, *Labour Force, Australia, November 2015*, Time Series Spreadsheets, Table 23, available at http://www.abs.gov.au/AUSSTATS/abs@.nsf/DetailsPage/6202.0Nov%202015?OpenDocument.
37. ABS, *1976 Census – South Australia Population and Dwellings: Summary Tables*, p. 4; ABS, *Labour Force, Australia, July 2017*, p. 15.
38. Spoehr and Ranasinghe, p. 259
39. Ibid.
40. ABS, *Labour Force, Australia, July 2017*, p. 15; ABS, *1976 Census-- South Australia Population and Dwellings: Summary Tables*, p. 4. NB: The same definition of 'part time' has been applied to both time periods, i.e. 34 hours or less of work.
41. ABS, *Average Weekly Earnings Australia. Time Series Spreadsheets*, various years. Also see Ray Broomhill and Rhonda Sharp, 'Gender at Work and in the Home', in John Spoehr (ed.), *State of South Australia: Turbulent Times*, Adelaide: Wakefield Press, 2013, pp. 195–6.
42. Ibid.
43. See ABS, *Gender Indicators, Australia, August 2016*, Work and Family Balance, Tables 1 and 2; ABS, *Unpaid Work and the Australian Economy 1997*, pp. 6–9.
44. Broomhill and Sharp, p. 199.
45. Ibid., pp. 199–200.
46. Ibid., p. 200.
47. ABS, *2011 Census – South Australia: Time Series Profile*, Table 33.
48. Australian Institute of Health and Welfare (henceforth AIHW), *Australia's Health 2014*, Canberra: AIHW, 2014, pp. 18, 67.
49. See Table 2.10 in *Health Expenditure Database 2013–14*, AIHW, http://www.aihw.gov.au/publication-detail/?id=60129552713&tab=3.
50. Productivity Commission, *Economic Implications of an Ageing Australia*, Canberra: Productivity Commission, 2005, p. 147.
51. See the views of Richardson & Robertson (1999), Jacobzone (2003), and Seshamani & Gray (2004) summarised in ibid., p. 146.

52. For evidence of living healthier for longer, see AIHW, p. 260.
53. WRVS, *Gold Age Pensioners: Valuing the Socio-Economic Contribution of Older People in the UK*, May 2011, pp. 6–7, http://www.goldagepensioners.com/Uploads/PDF/main-report.pdf. We were alerted to this study by Kate Barnett, 'Ageing and Aged Care', in John Spoehr (ed.), *State of South Australia: Turbulent Times*, Adelaide: Wakefield Press, 2013, pp. 210–11.
54. See, for example, Weatherill quoted in 'New Thinking on Old Age', *Advertiser*, 11 November 2015.
55. Richard Percival and Simon Kelly, *Who's Going to Care? Informal Care and an Ageing Population*, 2004, pp. 30–1, available at https://www.bsl.org.au/knowledge/browse-publications/who-s-going-to-care-informal-care-and-an-ageing-population.
56. AIHW, p. 302.
57. For all these figures, see ABS, *Deaths, Australia, 2012*; ABS, *Life Tables for Aboriginal and Torres Strait Islander Australians, 2010–2012*.
58. ABS, *Australian Demographic Statistics, June 2015*, pp. 36, 38. Note: these figures derive from the 2011 Census.
59. AIHW, pp. 301–2.
60. Ibid., p. 52.
61. See https://internationaleducation.gov.au/research/International-Student-Data/Pages/InternationalStudentData2017.aspx.
62. Graeme Hugo, 'Population', in John Spoehr (ed.), *State of South Australia: Turbulent Times*, Adelaide: Wakefield Press, 2013, p. 164.
63. Department of State Development, *Invest in South Australia*, May 2015, p. 5, available at http://www.statedevelopment.sa.gov.au/upload/investinsa/publications/invest.pdf.
64. Department for Manufacturing, Innovation, Trade, Resources and Energy, 'South Australia–China Engagement Strategy' (December 2012) and 'South Australia–India Engagement Strategy' (October 2012).
65. Purnendra Jain and John Spoehr, 'South Australia's International Engagement', in John Spoehr (ed.), *State of South Australia: Turbulent Times*, Adelaide: Wakefield Press, 2013, pp. 57–8.
66. KPMG, *Demystifying Chinese Investment in Australia*, 'March 2013 Update' and 'March 2014 Update', both available from http://demystifyingchina.com.au/reports.
67. Andrew Lothian, 'Environment', in John Spoehr (ed.), *State of South Australia: Turbulent Times*, Adelaide: Wakefield Press, 2013, p. 98.
68. Ibid.
69. Department of Environment, *Australian National Greenhouse Accounts, National Inventory Report 2013, Volume 1*, Commonwealth of Australia, 2015, p. x.
70. Comparison and figure derived from data in ibid., esp. pp. 4–5, 37–40.

71. International Energy Agency, *IEA Wind Energy Annual Report 2001*, http://www.ieawind.org/annual_reports_PDF/2001/2001%20annual.pdf; 'Australian PV market since April 2001', *Australian PV Institute*, http://pvmap.apvi.org.au/analyses.
72. Australian Energy Market Operator, *South Australian Electricity Report August 2015*, http://www.aemo.com.au/Electricity/Planning/South-Australian-Advisory-Functions/~/media/Files/Electricity/Planning/Reports/SAER/2015/2015_SAER.ashx.
73. 'Interview: The Hon Mike Rann', *Public Accountant*, http://www.pubacct.org.au/features/interview-the-hon-mike-rann.
74. *South Australian Parliamentary Debates* (henceforth *SAPD*), House of Assembly (HoA) – Estimates Committee A, 19 June 2001, p. 12.
75. *SAPD*, HoA, 6 December 2006, p. 1522; *SAPD*, HoA – Estimates Committee A, 20 June 2000, p. 106.
76. *SAPD*, Legislative Council, 3 May 2004, p. 1396; *SAPD*, HoA – Estimates Committee A, 18 October 2006, p. 17.
77. Clean Energy Council, *Clean Energy Australia Report 2014*, p. 44, available at https://www.cleanenergycouncil.org.au/dam/cec/policy-and-advocacy/reports/2015/Clean-Energy-Australia-Report-2014.pdf.
78. Clean Energy Council, p. 45; Climate Council, *The Australian Renewable Energy Race: Which States Are Winning or Losing?*, 2014, p. 15, http://www.climatecouncil.org.au/uploads/ee2523dc632c9b01df11ecc6e3dd2184.pdf.
79. Ben Heard, Corey Bradshaw and Barry Brook, 'Beyond Wind: Furthering Development of Clean Energy in South Australia', *Transactions of the Royal Society of South Australia*, 139(1), 2015, pp. 66–7.
80. 'Warning of Hotter Planet as Germany Axes Nuclear Plants', *The Times* [UK], 31 May 2011, p. 15; 'A Clear and Present Danger to the Australian Economy', *Huffington Post*, 20 January 2016, http://www.huffingtonpost.com.au/chris-bowen/post_10886_b_9013388.html.
81. Nuclear Fuel Cycle Royal Commission, *Nuclear Fuel Cycle Royal Commission: Tentative Findings*, February 2016, pp. 18–20, available at http://nuclearrc.sa.gov.au/tentative-findings.
82. See 'Ions in the Fire', *Advertiser*, 23 February 2016, pp. 1, 4.
83. See, for example, 'Follow the French' [letter to the editor], *Advertiser*, 23 February 2016, p. 16.
84. Robert Martin, *Responsible Government in South Australia: Playford to Rann, 1957–2007*, Adelaide: Wakefield Press, 2009, pp. 165–6.
85. 'Uranium Plant in Fifth Spill This Year', *Australian*, 17 December 2003, p. 5.

BIBLIOGRAPHY

The following list contains the published works cited in this book. It does not include the many 'primary sources', such as archived documents, statistical reports, and newspaper articles, that we have drawn upon. The details and locations of these sources are, however, comprehensively cited in the endnotes for each chapter.

Adams, John W., *My Early Days in the Colony*, Adelaide: E.J. Walker, 1902.

Aeuckens, Annely, 'Emergence of a New Industry, 1892–1918', in Annely Aeuckens, Geoffrey Bishop, George Bell, Kate McDougall and Gordon Young (eds), *Vineyard of the Empire: Barossa Valley Vignerons 1842–1939*, Adelaide: Australian Industrial Publishers, 1988, pp. 148–54.

Allen, Margaret, 'Salisbury (S.A.) in Transition', MA thesis, University of Adelaide, 1975.

—— 'Women's Christian Temperance Union', in Wilfrid Prest, Kerrie Round and Carol Fort (eds), *The Wakefield Companion to South Australian History*, Adelaide: Wakefield Press, 2001, pp. 587–8.

Andrew, Jane, and John Spoehr, 'Manufacturing Creativity and Innovation', in John Spoehr (ed.), *State of South Australia: Turbulent Times*, Adelaide: Wakefield Press, 2013, pp. 301–12.

Angas, G.F., *Savage Life and Scenes in Australia and New Zealand*, vol. 1, London: Smith, Elder & Co., 1847.

Appleby, Gabrielle, and John M. Williams, 'Law and Order', in John Spoehr (ed.), *State of South Australia: Turbulent Times*, Adelaide: Wakefield Press, 2013, pp. 88–97.

Armstrong, Hugo, 'The Tricontinental Affair', in Mark Considine and Brian Costar (eds), *Trials in Power: Cain, Kirner and Victoria, 1982–1992*, Melbourne: Melbourne University Press, 1992, pp. 43–58.

Atkinson, Alan, and Marian Aveling (eds), *Australians 1838*, Sydney: Fairfax, Syme & Weldon Associates, 1987.

Auhl, Ian, *The Story of the 'Monster Mine': The Burra Burra Mine and its Townships 1845–1877*, Adelaide: Investigator Press, 1986.

Australian Energy Market Operator, *South Australian Electricity Report August 2015*, http://www.aemo.com.au/Electricity/Planning/South-Australian-Advisory-Functions/~/media/Files/Electricity/Planning/Reports/SAER/2015/2015_SAER.ashx.

Australian Institute of Health and Welfare, *Australia's Health 2014*, Canberra: Australian Institute of Health and Welfare, 2014.

Bacchi, Carol, 'The "Woman Question" in South Australia', in Eric Richards (ed.), *The Flinders History of South Australia: Social History*, Adelaide: Wakefield Press, 1986, pp. 403–32.

Bailey, John, *Mr Stuart's Track*, Sydney: Picador, 2010.

Baldwin, B.S., 'Letters of Samuel Davenport, chiefly to his father George Davenport, 1842–1849, Part VI: 29 April – 1 August 1846', *South Australiana*, 16(2), 1977, pp. 127–70.

—— 'Letters of Samuel Davenport, chiefly to his father George Davenport, 1842–1849, Part VIII: 6 August 1847 – 27 September 1849', *South Australiana*, 19(2), 1980, pp. 87–141.

Bannon, John, 'Great Federal Expectations: South Australia and the Commonwealth', in *The Politics of Democracy in South Australia: A Special Conference Marking 150 Years of Democracy*, Adelaide: State Electoral Office, 2008, pp. 65–72.

—— 'The Colonies' Paths to Federation: South Australia', in Helen Irving (ed.), *The Centenary Companion to Australian Federation*, Melbourne: Cambridge University Press, 1999, pp. 130–85.

—— *The Crucial Colony: South Australia's Role in Reviving Federation, 1891 to 1897*, Canberra: Federalism Research Centre, ANU, 1994.

Barnett, Kate, 'Ageing and Aged Care', in John Spoehr (ed.), *State of South Australia: Turbulent Times*, Adelaide: Wakefield Press, 2013, pp. 209–24.

Bean, C.E.W., *The Australian Imperial Force in France 1916*, 12th edn, Brisbane: University of Queensland Press, 1941.

Beaumont, Joan, *Australian Defence: Sources and Statistics*, Melbourne: Oxford University Press, 2001.

Blackburn, Kevin, 'White Agitation for an Aboriginal State in Australia (1925–29)', *Australian Journal of Politics and History*, 45(2), 1999, pp. 157–80.

Blackburn, R.A., 'Blackburn, Arthur Seaforth', *Australian Dictionary of Biography*, http://adb.anu.edu.au/biography/blackburn-arthur-seaforth-5256.

Blainey, Geoffrey, *The Rush that Never Ended: A History of Australian Mining*, 4th edn, Melbourne: Melbourne University Press, 1993.

—— *The Steel Master: A Life of Essington Lewis*, Melbourne: Sun Books, 1981.

Blainey, Geoffrey, and Geoffrey Hutton, *Gold and Paper 1858–1982: A History of the National Bank of Australasia Ltd*, Melbourne: Macmillan, 1958.

Blewett, Neal, and Dean Jaensch, *Playford to Dunstan: The Politics of Transition*, Melbourne: Cheshire, 1971.
Bolton, Geoffrey, *Land of Vision and Mirage: Western Australia since 1826*, Perth: University of Western Australia Press, 2008.
—— *The Oxford History of Australia. Volume 5: 1942–1988*, Melbourne: Oxford University Press, 1990.
Bonyhady, Tim, *Burke and Wills: From Melbourne to Myth*, Sydney: David Ell Press, 1991.
Bowes, K.R., *Land Settlement in South Australia, 1857–1890*, Adelaide: Libraries Board of South Australia, 1968.
Brock, Peggy, *Outback Ghettos: Aborigines, Institutionalisation and Survival*, Melbourne: Cambridge University Press, 1993.
Brock, Peggy and Doreen Kartinyeri, *Poonindie: The Rise and Destruction of an Aboriginal Agricultural Community*, Adelaide: Aboriginal Heritage Branch, 1989.
Broomhill, Ray, 'Hill, Lionel Laughton', *Australian Dictionary of Biography*, http://adb.anu.edu.au/biography/hill-lionel-laughton-6671/text11485.
—— 'Underemployment in Adelaide during the Depression', *Labour History*, 21, 1974, pp. 31–40.
—— *Unemployed Workers: A Social History of the Great Depression in Adelaide*, Brisbane: University of Queensland Press, 1978.
Broomhill, Ray, and Rhonda Sharp, 'Gender at Work and in the Home', in John Spoehr (ed.), *State of South Australia: Turbulent Times*, Adelaide: Wakefield Press, 2013, pp. 189–208.
Burgmann, Verity, 'Industrial Workers of the World', in Wilfrid Prest, Kerrie Round and Carol Fort (eds), *The Wakefield Companion to South Australian History*, Adelaide: Wakefield Press, 2001, p. 280.
—— *Revolutionary Industrial Unionism: The Industrial Workers of the World in Australia*, Melbourne: Cambridge University Press, 1995.
Butler, A.G., *The Australian Army Medical Services in the War of 1914–1918, Volume III*, Canberra: Australian War Memorial, 1943.
Buxton, G.L., *South Australian Land Acts, 1869–1885*, Adelaide: Libraries Board of South Australia, 1968.
Campbell, Craig, 'Developing a 1950s Imagination in Woodville Gardens', in Susan Blackburn (ed.), *Growing Up in Adelaide in the 1950s*, Sydney: Hale & Iremonger, 2012, pp. 29–51.
Campbell, Judy, *Invisible Invaders: Smallpox and Other Diseases in Aboriginal Australia 1780–1880*, Melbourne: Melbourne University Press, 2002.
Castells, Manuel, and Peter Hall, *Technopoles of the World: The Making of Twenty-First-Century Industrial Complexes*, London: Routledge, 1994.
Castles, Alex C., and Michael C. Harris, *Lawmakers and Wayward Whigs: Government and Law in South Australia 1836–1986*, Adelaide: Wakefield Press, 1987.

Caust, Jo, 'The Arts', in John Spoehr (ed.), *State of South Australia: Trends and Issues*, Adelaide: Wakefield Press, 2005, pp. 276–88.
Chittleborough, Jon G., 'Holden Car', in Wilfrid Prest, Kerrie Round and Carol Fort (eds), *The Wakefield Companion to South Australian History*, Adelaide: Wakefield Press, 2001, pp. 262–3.
—— 'Motor Vehicles', in Wilfrid Prest, Kerrie Round and Carol Fort (eds), *The Wakefield Companion to South Australian History*, Adelaide: Wakefield Press, 2001, pp. 363–5.
City of Playford, *Migrant Heritage Places in Australia: City of Playford (Elizabeth District)*, Adelaide: Australian Heritage Commission and City of Playford, 1997.
Clarke, Philip A., 'The Aboriginal Presence on Kangaroo Island, South Australia', in Jane Simpson and Luise Hercus (eds), *History in Portraits: Biographies of Nineteenth Century South Australian Aboriginal People*, Canberra: Aboriginal History Monograph 6, 1998, pp. 14–48.
—— *Where the Ancestors Walked: Australia as an Aboriginal Landscape*, Sydney: Allen & Unwin, 2003.
Clarkson, Chris, *et al.*, 'Human Occupation of Northern Australia by 65,000 Years Ago', *Nature*, 547, 20 July 2017, pp. 306–25.
Clean Energy Council, *Clean Energy Australia Report 2014*, available at https://www.cleanenergycouncil.org.au/dam/cec/policy-and-advocacy/reports/2015/Clean-Energy-Australia-Report-2014.pdf.
Climate Council, *The Australian Renewable Energy Race: Which States Are Winning or Losing?*, 2014, http://www.climatecouncil.org.au/uploads/ee2523dc632c9b01df11ecc6e3dd2184.pdf.
Clune, Frank, *Overland Telegraph: The Story of a Great Australian Achievement and the Link Between Adelaide and Port Darwin*, Sydney: Angus and Robertson, 1955.
Cockburn, Rodney, *Pastoral Pioneers of South Australia*, vol. 1, Adelaide: Publishers Limited Printers, 1925.
Cockburn, Stewart, 'Dumas, Sir Frederick Lloyd', *Australian Dictionary of Biography*, http://adb.anu.edu.au/biography/dumas-sir-frederick-lloyd-10058/text17741.
—— assisted by John Playford, *Playford: Benevolent Despot*, Adelaide: Axiom Publishing, 1991.
Combe, Gordon D., *Responsible Government in South Australia: From the Foundations to Playford*, revised edition, Adelaide: Wakefield Press, 2009.
Committee on Environment, *The Environment in South Australia*, Adelaide: Government Printer, 1972.
Crisp, Helen, 'Women in Munitions', *Australian Quarterly*, 13(3), 1941, pp. 71–6.

Crisp, L.F., *Federation Fathers*, Melbourne: Melbourne University Press, 1990.
Cross, Jack, *Great Central State: The Foundation of the Northern Territory*, Adelaide: Wakefield Press, 2011.
Cunneen, Chris, 'Denman, Thomas', *Australian Dictionary of Biography*, http://adb.anu.edu.au/biography/denman-thomas-5956/text10161.
Damania, D., 'Environmental Policy', in Andrew Parkin and Allan Patience (eds), *The Bannon Decade: The Politics of Restraint in South Australia*, Sydney: Allen & Unwin, 1992, pp. 159–71.
Davies, Mel, 'Establishing South Australia', in Pamela Stratham (ed.), *The Origins of Australia's Capital Cities*, Melbourne: Cambridge University Press, 1990.
Davis, Kevin, and Ian McLean, 'Economic Policy', in Andrew Parkin and Allan Patience (eds), *The Dunstan Decade: Social Democracy at the State Level*, Melbourne: Longman Cheshire, 1981, pp. 22–50.
Davison, Graeme, J.W. McCarty and Ailsa McLeary (eds), *Australians 1888*, Sydney: Fairfax, Syme and Weldon, 1987.
Davitt, Michael, *Life and Progress in Australasia*, London: Methuen, 1898.
Department of Environment, *Australian National Greenhouse Accounts, National Inventory Report 2013, Volume 1*, Canberra: Commonwealth of Australia, 2015.
Depasquale, Paul, *A Critical History of South Australian Literature 1836–1930*, Adelaide: Warradale Pioneers Books, 1978.
Diamond, A.I., 'Some Aspects of the History of the South Australian Company: The First Decade', MA thesis, University of Adelaide, 1955.
Dickey, Brian, *Rations, Residence, Resources: A History of Social Welfare in South Australia since 1836*, Adelaide: Wakefield Press, 1986.
Dickey, Brian, and Peter Howell (eds), *South Australia's Foundation: Select Documents*, Adelaide: Wakefield Press, 1986.
Donovan, P.F., 'South Australian Imperialism', *Flinders Journal of History and Politics*, 3, 1973, pp. 45–53.
Donovan, Peter, *An Industrial History of South Australia*, Adelaide: University of Adelaide, 1979.
—— 'Motor Cars and Freeways: Measures of a South Australian Love Affair', in Bernard O'Neil, Judith Raftery and Kerrie Round (eds), *Playford's South Australia: Essays on the History of South Australia 1933–1968*, Adelaide: Association of Professional Historians Inc., 1996, pp. 201–14.
Duguid, Charles, *The Doctor and the Aborigines*, Adelaide: Rigby, 1982.
Duncan, Beth, *Mary Thomas: Founding Mother. The Life and Times of a South Australian Pioneer*, Adelaide: Wakefield Press, 2011.
Duncan, Bruce, *Crusade or Conspiracy? Catholics and the Anti-Communist Struggle in Australia*, Sydney: UNSW Press, 2001.

Duncan, Peter, 'Foreword', in Chris Kenny, *State of Denial: The Government, the Media, the Bank*, Adelaide: Wakefield Press, 1993, pp. ix–xiii.

Dunstan, Don, *Don Dunstan, The First 25 Years in Parliament*, compiled by Richard Yeeles, Melbourne: Hill of Content, 1978.

—— *Felicia: The Political Memoirs of Don Dunstan*, Melbourne: Macmillan, 1981.

—— 'The Road to Ruin', *Adelaide Review*, February 1996, p. 92.

Dutton, Francis, *South Australia and its Mines with an Historical Sketch of the Colony* [1846], Adelaide: Austraprint Facsimile Edition, 1978.

Dutton, Geoffrey, *Founder of a City: The Life of Colonel William Light*, Melbourne: F.W. Cheshire, 1960.

Dyer, Steve, 'Farm Relief in South Australia during the Great Depression', *Journal of the Historical Society of South Australia*, 2, 1976, pp. 64–75.

Eklund, Eric, *Mining Towns: Making a Living, Making a Life*, Sydney: UNSW Press, 2012.

Elder, David (ed.), *William Light's Brief Journal and Australian Diaries*, Adelaide: Wakefield Press, 1984.

Elias, Ann, '"Art Has No Country": Hans Heysen and the Consequences of the First World War', *History Australia*, 6(1), 2009, pp. 04.1–04.16.

Ellis, R.W. 'The Aboriginal Inhabitants and their Environment', in C.R. Twidale, M.J. Tyler and B.P. Webb (eds), *Natural History of the Adelaide Region*, Adelaide: Royal Society of South Australia, 1976, pp. 113–20.

Evans, Richard, *Disasters that Changed Australia*, Melbourne: Victory Books, 2009.

Eyre, Edward, *Journals of Expeditions of Discovery into Central Australia and Overland from Adelaide to King George's Sound in the Years 1840–41*, vol. 2, London: T. and W. Boone, 1845.

Feeken, Erwin, Gerda Feeken and O.H.K. Spate, *The Discovery and Exploration of Australia*, Melbourne: Nelson, 1970.

Finnimore, Christine, 'Art Galleries', in Wilfrid Prest, Kerrie Round and Carol Fort (eds), *The Wakefield Companion to South Australian History*, Adelaide: Wakefield Press, 2001, pp. 48–50.

Finnis, H.J., 'Before the Buffalo: The Story of South Australia 1800–1836', *Pioneers' Association of South Australia*, 39, 1964, pp. 14–21.

Fischer, G.L. (ed.), 'Captain John Hindmarsh's Letters to George Fife Angas. Part II: 1837–1839', *South Australiana*, 1(2), September 1962, pp. 49–83.

Flannery, Tim, *The Future Eaters: An Ecological History of the Australasian Lands and People*, Sydney: Reed Books, 1994.

Flood, Josephine, *The Original Australians: Story of the Aboriginal People*, Sydney: Allen & Unwin, 2006.

Foley, J.C., *Droughts in Australia: Review of Records from the Earliest Years of Settlement to 1955*, Melbourne: Bureau of Meteorology, 1957.

Fornasiero, Jean, Peter Monteath and John West-Sooby, *Encountering Terra Australis: The Australian Voyages of Nicolas Baudin and Matthew Flinders*, Adelaide: Wakefield Press, 2004.

Fort, Carol, 'Election Day, 1857', in *The Politics of Democracy in South Australia: A Special Conference Marking 150 Years of Democracy*, Adelaide: State Electoral Office, 2008, pp. 19–23.

—— '"Equality of sacrifice"? War Work in Salisbury, South Australia', in Bernard O'Neil, Judith Raftery and Kerrie Round (eds), *Playford's South Australia: Essays on the History of South Australia 1933–1968*, Adelaide: Association of Professional Historians Inc., 1996, pp. 215–32.

—— 'World War II', in Wilfrid Prest, Kerrie Round and Carol Fort (eds), *The Wakefield Companion to South Australian History*, Adelaide: Wakefield Press, 2001, pp. 593–5.

Foster, Robert, '"Endless trouble and agitation": Aboriginal Activism in the Protectionist Era', *Journal of the Historical Society of South Australia*, 28, 2000, pp. 15–27.

—— 'Feasts of the Full-Moon: The Distribution of Rations to Aboriginal People in South Australia 1836–1861', *Aboriginal History*, 13(1), 1989, pp. 63–79.

—— 'Rations, Co-existence and the Colonisation of Aboriginal Labour in the South Australian Pastoral Industry, 1860–1911', *Aboriginal History*, 24, 2000, pp. 1–26.

—— 'The Aborigines Location in Adelaide: South Australia's First "Mission" to the Aborigines', *Journal of the Anthropological Association of South Australia*, 28(1), 1990, pp. 11–37.

Foster, Robert, and Amanda Nettelbeck, *Out of the Silence: The History and Memory of South Australia's Frontier Wars*, Adelaide: Wakefield Press, 2012.

—— 'Proclamation Day and the Rise and Fall of South Australian Nationalism', in Robert Foster and Paul Sendziuk (eds), *Turning Points: Chapters in South Australian History*, Adelaide: Wakefield Press, 2012, pp. 48–62.

Foster, Robert, and Tom Gara, 'Aboriginal Culture', in Eric Richards (ed.), *The Flinders History of South Australia: Social History*, Adelaide: Wakefield Press, 1986, pp. 63–95.

Foster, Robert, Rick Hosking and Amanda Nettelbeck, *Fatal Collisions: The South Australian Frontier and the Violence of Memory*, Adelaide: Wakefield Press, 2001.

Frith, David, *Bodyline Autopsy*, Sydney: ABC Books, 2002.

Gammage, Bill, 'The Adelaide District in 1836', in Robert Foster and Paul Sendziuk (eds), *Turning Points: Chapters in South Australian History*, Adelaide: Wakefield Press, 2012, pp. 7–23.

—— *The Broken Years: Australian Soldiers in the Great War*, Melbourne: Penguin, 1975.

—— *The Greatest Estate on Earth: How Aborigines Made Australia*, Sydney: Allen & Unwin, 2011.

Garden, Don, *Droughts, Floods & Cyclones: El Niños That Shaped Our Colonial Past*, Melbourne: Australian Scholarly Publishing, 2009.

Gibbs, R.M., *A History of South Australia*, Adelaide: Balara Books, 1969.

Glantz, Michael H. (ed.), *Drought Follows the Plough: Cultivating Marginal Areas*, Melbourne: Cambridge University Press, 1994.

Glass, Margaret, *Charles Cameron Kingston: Federation Father*, Melbourne: Melbourne University Press, 1997.

Gollan, Robin, *Radical and Working Class Politics: A Study of Eastern Australia*, Melbourne: Melbourne University Press, 1960.

Grabosky, Peter N., *Wayward Governance: Illegality and its Control in the Public Sector*, Canberra: Australian Institute of Criminology, 1989.

Grey, Jeffrey, *A Military History of Australia*, Melbourne: Cambridge University Press, 1999.

Griffin, Trevor, and Murray McCaskill (eds), *Atlas of South Australia*, Adelaide: Wakefield Press, 1986.

Hagan, Toby, 'Holden Commits $1 Billion until 2022', *Drive*, 22 March 2012, http://www.drive.com.au/motor-news/holden-commits-1-billion-until-2022-20120321-1vl34.html.

Haines, Robin F., *Emigration and the Labouring Poor: Australian Recruitment in Britain and Ireland, 1831–60*, New York: Macmillan, 1997.

Hall, Robert, 'Hughes, Timothy', *Australian Dictionary of Biography*, http://adb.anu.edu.au/biography/hughes-timothy-10567/text18767.

Hamilton, Reg, *Colony: Strange Origins of One of the Earliest Modern Democracies*, Adelaide: Wakefield Press, 2010.

Hancock, Joan, and Eric Richards, 'Holden, Henry James', *Australian Dictionary of Biography*, http://adb.anu.edu.au/biography/holden-henry-james-6704/text11571.

Harmstorf, Ian, and Michael Cigler, *The Germans in Australia*, Melbourne: AE Press, 1985.

Harris, Kirsty, *More than Bombs and Bandages: Australian Army Nurses at Work in World War I*, Sydney: Big Sky Productions, 2011.

Harris, R. McL., 'The "Princeland" Secession Movement in Victoria and South Australia 1861–67', *Australian Journal of Politics and History*, 17(3), 1971, pp. 365–76.

Hawker, Frankie, and Rob Linn, *Bungaree: Land, Stock and People*, Adelaide: Turnbull Fox Phillips, 1982.

Haydon, A.P., 'Boer War', in Wilfrid Prest, Kerrie Round and Carol Fort (eds), *The Wakefield Companion to South Australian History*, Adelaide: Wakefield Press, 2001, pp. 77–8.

—— 'South Australia's First War', *Historical Studies: Australia and New Zealand*, 11(42), 1964, pp. 222–33.

Heard, Ben, Corey Bradshaw and Barry Brook, 'Beyond Wind: Furthering Development of Clean Energy in South Australia', *Transactions of the Royal Society of South Australia*, 139(1), 2015, pp. 57–82.

Heathcote, R.L., 'Agriculture', in Andrew Parkin and Allan Patience (eds), *The Bannon Decade: The Politics of Restraint in South Australia*, Sydney: Allen & Unwin, 1992, pp. 172–80.

Hilliard, David, 'How Did Methodism Shape South Australia?', *Church Heritage*, 18(2), 2013, pp. 94–108.

—— 'The City of Churches', in Brian Dickey (ed.), *William Shakespeare's Adelaide: 1860–1930*, Adelaide: Association of Professional Historians Inc., 1992, pp. 61–86.

—— 'The Religious Crisis of the 1960s: The Experience of the Australian Churches', *The Journal of Religious History*, 21(2), 1997, pp. 209–27.

Hilliard, David, and Arnold D. Hunt, 'Religion', in Eric Richards (ed.), *The Flinders History of South Australia: Social History*, Adelaide: Wakefield Press, 1986, pp. 194–234.

Hirst, J.B., *Adelaide and the Country: Their Social and Political Relationship*, Melbourne: Melbourne University Press, 1973.

—— *Convict Society and its Enemies: A History of Early New South Wales*, Sydney: Allen & Unwin, 1987.

—— 'Selection', in Graeme Davison, John Hirst and Stuart Macintyre (eds), *The Oxford Companion to Australian History*, Melbourne: Oxford University Press, 1998, p. 579.

—— 'South Australia and Australia: Reflections and their Histories', in Robert Foster and Paul Sendziuk (eds), *Turning Points: Chapters in South Australian History*, Adelaide: Wakefield Press, 2012, pp. 118–30.

—— *The Sentimental Nation: The Making of the Australian Commonwealth*, Melbourne: Oxford University Press, 2000.

Hiscock, Peter, 'Creators or Destroyers? The Burning Questions of Human Impact in Ancient Aboriginal Australia', *Humanities Australia*, 5, 2014, pp. 40–52.

Hope, Penelope, *The Voyage of the Africaine: A Collection of Journals, Letters and Extracts from Contemporary Publications*, Melbourne: Heinemann, 1968.

Howell, P.A., 'Constitutional and Political Development, 1857–1890', in Dean Jaensch (ed.), *The Flinders History of South Australia: Political History*, Adelaide: Wakefield Press, 1986, pp. 95–154.

—— 'Cudmore, Sir Collier Robert', *Australian Dictionary of Biography*, http://adb.anu.edu.au/biography/cudmore-sir-collier-robert-9873/text17471.

—— 'Playford, Politics and Parliament', in Bernard O'Neil, Judith Raftery and Kerrie Round (eds), *Playford's South Australia: Essays on the History of South Australia 1933–1968*, Adelaide: Association of Professional Historians Inc., 1996, pp. 47–72.

—— 'Playford, Sir Thomas', *Australian Dictionary of Biography*, http://adb.anu.edu.au/biography/playford-sir-thomas-tom-15472/text26686.

—— *South Australia and Federation*, Adelaide: Wakefield Press, 2002.

Hugo, Graeme, 'Population', in John Spoehr (ed.), *State of South Australia: Trends and Issues*, Adelaide: Wakefield Press, 2005, pp. 20–48.

—— 'Population', in John Spoehr (ed.), *State of South Australia: Turbulent Times*, Adelaide: Wakefield Press, 2013, pp. 144–74.

Hugo, Graeme, Kevin Harris, Martin Bell, John Spoehr and Neil Coffee, *Bringing Them Back Home – Factors Influencing Interstate Migration To and From South Australia*, Adelaide: University of Adelaide, 2000.

Hunt, Arnold D., 'Verran, John', *Australian Dictionary of Biography*, http://adb.anu.edu.au/biography/verran-john-8917/text15669.

Hyams, Bernard, 'Education', in Andrew Parkin and Allan Patience (eds), *The Dunstan Decade: Social Democracy at the State Level*, Melbourne: Longman Cheshire, 1981, pp. 70–90.

Ingamells, Rex, *Conditional Culture*, Adelaide: F.W. Preece, 1938.

Inglis, K.S., *The Stuart Case*, 2nd edn, Melbourne: Black Inc., 2002.

International Energy Agency, *IEA Wind Energy Annual Report 2001*, http://www.ieawind.org/annual_reports_PDF/2001/2001%20annual.pdf.

Ioannou, Noris, *Barossa Journeys: Into a Valley of Tradition*, 2nd edn, Sydney: New Holland Publishers, 2000.

Jacques, W.R.C., 'The Impact of the Gold Rushes on South Australia 1852–1854', BA (Hons) thesis, University of Adelaide, 1963.

Jaensch, Dean, 'Democratic Labor Party (DLP)', in Wilfrid Prest, Kerrie Round and Carol Fort (eds), *The Wakefield Companion to South Australian History*, Adelaide: Wakefield Press, 2001, pp. 146–7.

—— 'Party, Party System and Federation, 1890–1912', in Dean Jaensch (ed.), *The Flinders History of South Australia: Political History*, Adelaide: Wakefield Press, 1986, pp. 178–214.

—— *The Government of South Australia*, Brisbane: University of Queensland Press, 1977.

Jaensch, Dean, and Joan Bullock, *Liberals in Limbo: Non-Labor Politics in South Australia, 1970–1978*, Melbourne: Drummond, 1978.

Jain, Purnendra, and John Spoehr, 'South Australia's International Engagement', in John Spoehr (ed.), *State of South Australia: Turbulent Times*, Adelaide: Wakefield Press, 2013, pp. 52–66.

Jeffery, Judith, 'The Small Farmers in South Australia 1836–1869: An Assessment', *Flinders Journal of History and Politics*, 11, 1985, pp. 53–60.

—— 'World War I', in Wilfrid Prest, Kerrie Round and Carol Fort (eds), *The Wakefield Companion to South Australian History*, Adelaide: Wakefield Press, 2001, pp. 592–3.

Jeisman, Stephen, *Colonial Gunboat: The Story of the HMCS Protector and the South Australian Naval Brigade*, Adelaide: Digital Print Australia, 2012.

Jenkin, Graham, *Conquest of the Ngarrindjeri: The Story of the Lower Murray Lakes Tribes*, Adelaide: Rigby, 1979.

Jones, Helen, *In Her Own Name: Women in South Australian History*, Adelaide: Wakefield Press, 1986.

—— *Nothing Seemed Impossible: Women's Education and Social Change in South Australia 1875–1915*, Brisbane: University of Queensland Press, 1985.

—— 'South Australian Women and Politics', in Dean Jaensch (ed.), *The Flinders History of South Australia: Political History*, Adelaide: Wakefield Press, 1986, pp. 414–47.

Jones, M.A., *Housing and Poverty in Australia*, Melbourne: Melbourne University Press, 1972.

Jones, P., 'The Horn Expedition's Place Among Nineteenth-Century Inland Expeditions', in S.R. Morton and D.J. Mulvaney (eds), *Exploring Central Australia: Society, the Environment and the 1894 Horn Expedition*, Sydney: Surry Beatty & Sons, 1996, pp. 19–28.

Jones, Philip, *Ochre and Rust: Artefacts and Encounters on Australian Frontiers*, Adelaide: Wakefield Press, 2007.

Jordan, Deborah, 'Women's Policy', in Andrew Parkin and Allan Patience (eds), *The Bannon Decade: The Politics of Restraint in South Australia*, Sydney: Allen & Unwin, 1992, pp. 307–15.

Jordan, Matthew, 'Procuring Industrial Pollution Control in South Australia', PhD thesis, University of Adelaide, 2001.

Jose, Jim, 'Social Purity Society', in Wilfrid Prest, Kerrie Round and Carol Fort (eds), *The Wakefield Companion to South Australian History*, Adelaide: Wakefield Press, 2001, pp. 492–3.

Kaukas, Anthony, 'Images from Loveday: Interment in South Australia, 1939–1945', *Journal of the Historical Society of South Australia*, 29, 2001, pp. 47–57.

Kenny, Chris, *State of Denial: The Government, the Media, the Bank*, Adelaide: Wakefield Press, 1993.

Kinder, Sylvia, *Herstory of Adelaide Women's Liberation 1969–1974*, Adelaide: Salisbury Education Centre, 1980.

Kosky, Robert, 'Health Policy', in Andrew Parkin and Allan Patience (eds), *The Bannon Decade: The Politics of Restraint in South Australia*, Sydney: Allen & Unwin, 1992, pp. 237–50.

Kwan, Elizabeth, *Living in South Australia: A Social History. Volume 2: After 1914*, Adelaide: South Australian Government Printer, 1987.

La Nauze, J.A., *The Making of the Australian Constitution*, Melbourne: Melbourne University Press, 1972.

Leigh, W.H., *Travels and Adventures in South Australia 1836–38* [1839], Sydney: Currawong Facsimile, 1982.

Lemar, Susan, '"Sexually Cursed, Mentally Weak and Socially Untouchable": Women and Venereal Diseases in World War Two Adelaide', *Journal of Australian Studies*, 27(79), 2003, pp. 153–64.

Linn, R., *The Spirit of Knowledge: A Social History of the University of Adelaide, North Terrace Campus*, Adelaide: University of Adelaide Press, 2011.

Lockwood, Christine, 'A Vision Frustrated: Lutheran Missionaries to the Aborigines of South Australia 1838–1853', in Peter Monteath (ed.), *Germans: Travellers, Settlers and their Descendants in South Australia*, Adelaide: Wakefield Press, 2011, pp. 17–40.

—— '"We Are Here to Round Up Nazis": The Military Raid on Immanuel College and Seminary in World War Two', *Journal of the Historical Society of South Australia*, 36, 2008, pp. 75–90.

Long, Gavin, *Australia in the War of 1939–1945*, Series 1 (Army), Vol. VII ('The Final Campaigns'), Canberra: Australian War Memorial, 1963.

Lothian, Andrew, 'Environment', in John Spoehr (ed.), *State of South Australia: Trends and Issues*, Adelaide: Wakefield Press, 2005, pp. 190–213.

—— 'Environment', in John Spoehr (ed.), *State of South Australia: Turbulent Times*, Adelaide: Wakefield Press, 2013, pp. 98–143.

Lumb, R.D., and K.W. Ryan, *The Constitution of the Commonwealth of Australia Annotated*, Sydney: Butterworths, 1974.

Macfarlane, Ian, 'The Recession of 1990 and its Legacy', Boyer Lectures, http://www.abc.net.au/radionational/programs/boyerlectures/lecture-4-the-recession-of-1990-and-its-legacy/3353124#transcript.

MacFarlane, R.G., *Howard Florey: The Making of a Great Scientist*, Melbourne: Oxford University Press, 1979.

Macintyre, Clem, 'Politics', in John Spoehr (ed.), *State of South Australia: Trends and Issues*, Adelaide: Wakefield Press, 2005, pp. 117–32.

Mackinnon, Alison, *Love and Freedom: Professional Women and the Reshaping of Personal Life*, Cambridge: Cambridge University Press, 1997.

Magarey, Susan, *Unbridling the Tongues of Women: A Biography of Catherine Helen Spence*, Adelaide: Adelaide University Press, 2010.

Magarey, Susan, and Kerrie Round, *Roma the First: A Biography of Dame Roma Mitchell*, Adelaide: Wakefield Press, 2007.

Magee, Karen, 'Captain Sweet's Colonial Imagination: The Ideals of Modernity in South Australian Views Photography 1866–1886', PhD thesis, University of Adelaide, 2014.

Main, Jim, 'Social Foundations of South Australia: Men of Capital', in Eric Richards (ed.), *The Flinders History of South Australia: Social History*, Adelaide: Wakefield Press, 1986, pp. 96–104.

—— 'The Foundation of South Australia', in Dean Jaensch (ed.), *The Flinders History of South Australia: Political History*, Adelaide: Wakefield Press, 1986, pp. 1–25.

Manwaring, Rob, *A Collaborative History of Social Innovation in South Australia*, Adelaide: Hawke Research Institute for Sustainable Societies, 2008.

Markus, Andrew, *Australian Race Relations: 1788–1993*, Sydney: Allen & Unwin, 1994.

Marsden, Susan, *A History of Woodville*, Adelaide: Corporation of the City of Woodville, 1977.

—— *Business, Charity and Sentiment: The South Australian Housing Trust 1936–1986*, Adelaide: Wakefield Press, 1986.

—— 'Playford's Metropolis', in Bernard O'Neil, Judith Raftery and Kerrie Round (eds), *Playford's South Australia: Essays on the History of South Australia 1933–1968*, Adelaide: Association of Professional Historians Inc., 1996, pp. 117–34.

—— 'South Australia', in Graeme Davison, John Hirst and Stuart Macintyre (eds), *The Oxford Companion to Australian History*, Melbourne: Oxford University Press, 1998, pp. 598–600.

—— 'The South Australian Housing Trust, Elizabeth and Twentieth Century Heritage', *Journal of the Historical Society of South Australia*, 28, 2000, pp. 49–61.

Marshall, Vern, 'Schools', in Andrew Parkin and Allan Patience (eds), *The Bannon Decade: The Politics of Restraint in South Australia*, Sydney: Allen & Unwin, 1992, pp. 219–21.

Martin, Robert, *Responsible Government in South Australia: Playford to Rann 1957–2007*, Adelaide: Wakefield Press, 2009.

Mattingley, Christobel with Ken Hampton, *Survival in Our Own Land: 'Aboriginal' Experiences in 'South Australia' since 1836*, Adelaide: Wakefield Press, 1988.

McCarthy, Therese, and Paul Sendziuk, 'Deserted Women and the Law in South Australia', *Journal of Australian Colonial History*, 20, 2018, pp. 95–114.

McCaskill, Murray, '1950: Forging an Industrial State', in Trevor Griffin and Murray McCaskill (eds), *Atlas of South Australia*, Adelaide: SA Government Printing Division and Wakefield Press, 1986, p. 28.

—— '1985: Achievement and Uncertainty', in Trevor Griffin and Murray McCaskill (eds), *Atlas of South Australia*, Adelaide: SA Government Printing Division and Wakefield Press, 1986, p. 34.

McDonald, David, *Deaths in Custody Australia. National Police Custody Survey 1992: Preliminary Report*, Canberra: Australian Institute of Criminology, 1993.

McFarlane, Bruce, and Kyoko Sheridan, 'The Minerals and Energy Sector', in Kyoko Sheridan (ed.), *The State as Developer: Public

Enterprise in South Australia, Adelaide: Wakefield Press, 1986, pp. 92–111.

McL. Scott, G., 'Economic Policy', in Andrew Parkin and Allan Patience (eds), *The Bannon Decade: The Politics of Restraint in South Australia*, Sydney: Allen & Unwin, 1992, pp. 71–100.

McLean, Ian W., *Why Australia Prospered: The Shifting Sources of Economic Growth*, Princeton: Princeton University Press, 2013.

McMullin, Ross, 'Disaster at Fromelles', *Wartime*, 36, http://www.awm.gov.au/wartime/36/article.asp.

Meinig, D.W., *On the Margins of the Good Earth: The South Australian Wheat Frontier, 1869–1884*, Adelaide: South Australian Government Printer, 1988.

Miller, Pavla, *Long Division: State Schooling in South Australian Society*, Adelaide: Wakefield Press, 1986.

Mills, Helen, 'Equal Opportunities', in Andrew Parkin and Allan Patience (eds), *The Dunstan Decade: Social Democracy at the State Level*, Melbourne: Longman Cheshire, 1981, pp. 115–26.

Mitchell, T.J., 'J.W. Wainright [*sic*]: The Industrialisation of S.A., 1935–40', *Australian Journal of Politics and History*, 8(1), 1962, pp. 27–40.

Molyneux, Denis, *Time for Play: Recreation and Moral Issues in Colonial South Australia*, Adelaide: Wakefield Press, 2015.

Monaghan, Paul, 'Structures of Aboriginal Life at the Time of Colonisation in South Australia, in Peggy Brock and Tom Gara (eds), *Colonialism and its Aftermath: A History of Aboriginal South Australia*, Adelaide: Wakefield Press, 2017, pp. 3–26.

Moore, Nicole, *The Censor's Library*, Brisbane: University of Queensland Press, 2012.

Moore, Peter, 'Torrens Title', in Wilfrid Prest, Kerrie Round and Carol Fort (eds), *The Wakefield Companion to South Australian History*, Adelaide: Wakefield Press, 2001, pp. 544–5.

Morphy, Howard, 'More Than Mere Facts: Repositioning Spencer and Gillen in the History of Anthropology', in S.R. Morton and D.J. Mulvaney (eds), *Exploring Central Australia: Society, the Environment and the 1894 Horn Expedition*, Sydney: Surry Beatty & Sons, 1996, pp. 135–48.

Moss, Jim, *Sound of Trumpets: History of the Labour Movement in South Australia*, Adelaide: Wakefield Press, 1985.

Moyal, Ann, 'Telecommunications in Australia: An Historical Perspective, 1854–1930', *Prometheus*, 1(1), 1983, pp. 23–41.

Muirden, Bruce, 'The Electricity Trust Affair', in Dean Jaensch (ed.), *The Flinders History of South Australia: Political History*, Adelaide: Wakefield Press, 1986, pp. 270–82.

Mulvaney, D.J., '"A Splendid Lot of Fellows": Achievements and Consequences of the Horn Expedition', in S.R. Morton and D.J. Mulvaney (eds),

Exploring Central Australia: Society, the Environment and the 1894 Horn Expedition, Sydney: Surry Beatty & Sons, 1996, pp. 3–12.

—— '"The Chain of Connection": The Material Evidence', in Nicolas Peterson (ed.), *Tribes and Boundaries in Australia*, Canberra: Australian Institute of Aboriginal Studies, 1976, pp. 72–94.

Munyard, Anna, 'Making a Polity: 1836–1857', in Dean Jaensch (ed.), *The Flinders History of South Australia: Political History*, Adelaide: Wakefield Press, 1986, pp.52–75.

Nance, Christopher, 'The South Australian Social Experiment 1836–71: A Study of Some of the Aspects of South Australia's Early Social Development', MA Thesis, Flinders University, 1977.

Nettelbeck, Amanda, and Robert Foster, 'Food and Governance in the Frontiers of Colonial Australia and Canada's North-West Territories', *Aboriginal History*, 36, 2012, pp. 21–42.

Newland, Simpson, *Paving the Way: A Romance of the Australian Bush* [1893], facsimile edition, Adelaide: Moroak Pty Ltd, 1982.

Newton, Douglas, *Hellbent: Australia's Leap into the Great War*, Melbourne: Scribe, 2014.

Nuclear Fuel Cycle Royal Commission, *Nuclear Fuel Cycle Royal Commission: Tentative Findings*, February 2016, available at http://nuclearrc.sa.gov.au/tentative-findings.

Nursey-Bray, Paul, 'Anti-Fascism and Internment: The Case of Francesco Fantin', *Journal of the Historical Society of South Australia*, 17, 1989, pp. 88–111.

Ó Murchadha, Ciarán, *The Great Famine: Ireland's Agony 1845–52*, London: Bloomsbury, 2013.

O'Connor, Pam, and Brian O'Connor, *In Two Fields: Soldier Settlement in the South East of South Australia*, Millicent, S.A.: S.E. Soldier Settlers Committee, 1991.

O'Neil, Bernard, 'Minerals and Energy', in Andrew Parkin and Allan Patience (eds), *The Bannon Decade: The Politics of Restraint in South Australia*, Sydney: Allen & Unwin, 1992, pp. 181–94.

Orchard, Lionel, 'Urban Policy', in Andrew Parkin and Allan Patience (eds), *The Bannon Decade: The Politics of Restraint in South Australia*, Sydney: Allen & Unwin, 1992, pp. 145–58.

Oxenberry, Rod, 'Community Welfare', in Andrew Parkin and Allan Patience (eds), *The Dunstan Decade: Social Democracy at the State Level*, Melbourne: Longman Cheshire, 1981, pp. 51–69.

Painter, Gwenda, *The River Trade: Wool and Steamers*, Sydney: Turton & Armstrong with Pioneer Settlement Press, 1979.

Parker, Clare, 'Abortion, Homosexuality and the Slippery Slope: Legislating "Moral" Behaviour in South Australia', PhD thesis, University of Adelaide, 2013.

—— 'From Immorality to Public Health: Thalidomide and the Debate for Legal Abortion in Australia', *Social History of Medicine*, 25(4), 2012, pp. 863–80.

Parkin, Andrew, 'The Dunstan Governments: A Political Synopsis', in Andrew Parkin and Allan Patience (eds), *The Dunstan Decade: Social Democracy at the State Level*, Melbourne: Longman Cheshire, 1981, pp. 1–21.

Patience, Allan, 'The Bannon Decade: Preparation for What?', in Andrew Parkin and Allan Patience (eds), *The Bannon Decade: The Politics of Restraint in South Australia*, Sydney: Allen & Unwin, 1992, pp. 343–54.

Payton, Philip, *Regional Australia and the Great War: 'The Boys from Old Kio'*, Exeter: University of Exeter Press, 2012.

Peel, Mark, 'A Place to Grow: Making a Future in Postwar South Australia', in Robert Foster and Paul Sendziuk (eds), *Turning Points: Chapters in South Australian History*, Adelaide: Wakefield Press, 2012, pp. 88–102.

—— *Good Times, Hard Times: The Past and the Future in Elizabeth*, Melbourne: Melbourne University Press, 1995.

—— 'Making a Place: Women in the "Workers' City"', *Australian Historical Studies*, 26(102), 1994, pp. 19–38.

Peel, Mark, and Christina Twomey, *A History of Australia*, Melbourne: Palgrave Macmillan, 2011.

Percival, Richard, and Simon Kelly, *Who's Going to Care? Informal Care and an Ageing Population*, 2004, available at https://www.bsl.org.au/knowledge/browse-publications/who-s-going-to-care-informal-care-and-an-ageing-population.

Phillips, Janet, 'Asylum Seekers and Refugees: What Are the Facts?', Parliamentary Library, *Parliament of Australia*, 2011, available at http://www.aph.gov.au/binaries/library/pubs/bn/sp/asylumfacts.pdf.

Pike, Douglas, *Paradise of Dissent: South Australia 1829–57*, Melbourne: Melbourne University Press, 1957.

Pikusa, Stefan, *The Adelaide House 1836 to 1901: The Evolution of Principal Dwelling Types*, Adelaide: Wakefield Press, 1986.

Pope, Alan, *One Law for All: Aboriginal People and Criminal Law in Early South Australia*, Canberra: Aboriginal Studies Press, 2011.

Powell, Alan, *Far Country: A Short History of the Northern Territory*, Melbourne: Melbourne University Press, 1997.

Price, A. Grenfell, *Founders and Pioneers of South Australia*, Adelaide: Mary Martin Books, 1978.

Productivity Commission, *Economic Implications of an Ageing Australia*, Canberra: Productivity Commission, 2005.

Radbone, Ian, 'Public-Sector Management', in Andrew Parkin and Allan Patience (eds), *The Bannon Decade: The Politics of Restraint in South Australia*, Sydney: Allen & Unwin, 1992, pp. 101–11.

Raftery, Judith, *Not Part of the Public: Non-Indigenous Policies and Practices and the Health of Indigenous South Australians 1836–1973*, Adelaide: Wakefield Press, 2006.

Reid, R.L., 'South Australia and the First Decade of Federation', MA thesis, University of Adelaide, 1954.

Rendell, M.P., 'The Chinese in South Australia and the Northern Territory in the Nineteenth Century', MA thesis, University of Adelaide, 1952.

Reynolds, Henry, *A History of Tasmania*, Melbourne: Cambridge University Press, 2012.

—— *Forgotten War*, Sydney: NewSouth Publishing, 2013.

—— *The Law of the Land*, Melbourne: Penguin, 1992.

Reynolds, P.L., *The Democratic Labor Party*, Brisbane: Jacaranda Press, 1974.

Richards, Eric, 'Migration', in Wilfrid Prest, Kerrie Round and Carol Fort (eds), *The Wakefield Companion to South Australian History*, Adelaide: Wakefield Press, 2001, pp. 352–5.

—— 'The Genesis of Secondary Industry in the South Australian Economy to 1876', *Australian Economic History Review*, 15(2), 1975, pp. 107–35.

—— 'The Peopling of South Australia', in Eric Richards (ed.), *The Flinders History of South Australia: Social History*, Adelaide: Wakefield Press, 1986, pp. 115–42.

Riffenburgh, Beau, *Racing with Death: Douglas Mawson – Antarctic Explorer*, London: Bloomsbury, 2009.

Round, Kerrie, 'A Deputation for a National Trust', in Bernard O'Neil, Judith Raftery and Kerrie Round (eds), *Playford's South Australia: Essays on the History of South Australia 1933–1968*, Adelaide: Association of Professional Historians Inc., 1996, pp. 325–6.

Russell, Roslyn, and Philip Chubb, *One Destiny! The Federation Story – How Australia Became a Nation*, Melbourne: Penguin, 1998.

Rutherford, J., *Sir George Grey: A Study in Colonial Government*, London: Cassell, 1961.

Ryan, Des, and Mike McEwan, *It's Grossly Improper*, Dulwich, S.A.: Wenan, 1979.

Salter, Elizabeth, *Robert Helpmann*, Sydney: Angus & Robertson, 1978.

Saunders, Kay, and Helen Taylor, '"To Combat the Plague": The Construction of Moral Alarm and State Intervention in Queensland during World War II', *Hecate*, 14(1), 1988, pp. 5–30.

Saunders, Malcolm, 'Opposition to the Vietnam War in South Australia, 1965–1973', *Journal of the Historical Society of South Australia*, 10, 1982, pp. 61–71.

Schedvin, C.B., 'The Long and the Short of Depression Origins', in Robert Cooksey (ed.), *The Great Depression in Australia*, Canberra: Australian Society for the Study of Labour History, 1970, pp. 1–13.

Scott, Ernest, *Australia During the War*, 7th edn, Sydney: Angus and Robertson, 1941.

Seaman, Keith, 'The South Australian Constitution Act of 1856', in Dean Jaensch (ed.), *The Flinders History of South Australia: Political History*, Adelaide: Wakefield Press, 1986.

Sendziuk, Paul, 'No Convicts Here: Reconsidering South Australia's Foundation Myth', in Robert Foster and Paul Sendziuk (eds), *Turning Points: Chapters in South Australian History*, Adelaide: Wakefield Press, 2012, pp. 33–47.

Shanahan, Martin, 'Income and Wealth', in John Spoehr (ed.), *State of South Australia: Turbulent Times*, Adelaide: Wakefield Press, 2013, pp. 225–39.

Shaw, Ian W., *On Radji Beach*, Sydney: Pan Macmillan, 2010.

Shepherd, Michael T., 'Compulsory Military Training: The South Australian Debate, 1901–1914', MA thesis, University of Adelaide, 1976.

Short, Augustus, *A Visit to Poonindie and Some Accounts of that Mission to the Aborigines of South Australia*, Adelaide: William Kyffin Thomas, 1872.

Sinclair, W.A., *The Process of Economic Development in Australia*, Melbourne: Longman Cheshire, 1985.

Smith, David F., *Natural Gain: In the Grazing Lands of Southern Australia*, Sydney: UNSW Press, 2000.

Sova, Dawn B., *Banned Plays: Censorship Histories of 125 Stage Dramas*, New York: Facts on File, 2004.

Spence, Catherine Helen, *Clara Morison*, Adelaide: Rigby Ltd, 1971.

Spoehr, John, 'Turbulent Times', in John Spoehr (ed.), *State of South Australia: Turbulent Times*, Adelaide: Wakefield Press, 2013, pp. 1–8.

Spoehr, John, and Rasika Ranasinghe, 'Employment', in John Spoehr (ed.), *State of South Australia: Turbulent Times*, Adelaide: Wakefield Press, 2013, pp. 256–79.

Spoehr, John, and Steven Barrett, 'Public Sector Workforce', in John Spoehr (ed.), *State of South Australia: Trends and Issues*, Adelaide: Wakefield Press, 2005, pp. 102–15.

Steiner, Marie, *Servant Depots in Colonial South Australia*, Adelaide: Wakefield Press, 2009.

Stevenson, T.L., 'Population Change Since 1836', in Eric Richards (ed.), *The Flinders History of South Australia: Social History*, Adelaide: Wakefield Press, 1986, pp. 171–93.

Stock, Jenny Tilby, 'Conscription', in Wilfrid Prest, Kerrie Round and Carol Fort (eds), *The Wakefield Companion to South Australian History*, Adelaide: Wakefield Press, 2001, pp. 120–1.

—— 'The "Playmander": Its Origins, Operation and Effect on South Australia', in Bernard O'Neil, Judith Raftery and Kerrie Round (eds),

Playford's South Australia: Essays on the History of South Australia 1933–1968, Adelaide: Association of Professional Historians Inc., 1996, pp. 73–90.

Stretton, Hugh, 'An Intellectual Public Servant: William Wainwright, 1880–1948', *Meanjin*, 50(4), 1991, pp. 555–78.

Stretton, Hugh, and Pat Stretton, 'Wainwright, John William', *Australian Dictionary of Biography*, http://adb.anu.edu.au/biography/wainwright-john-william-8945/text15721.

Sturt, Charles, *Two Expeditions into the Interior of South Australia* [1833], Facsimile Edition, Sydney: Doubleday, 1982.

Stutchbury, Michael, 'State Government Industrialisation Strategies', in Kyoko Sheridan (ed.), *The State as Developer: Public Enterprise in South Australia*, Adelaide: Wakefield Press, 1986, pp. 60–91.

Taylor, Peter, *An End to Silence: The Building of the Overland Telegraph Line from Adelaide to Darwin*, Sydney: Methuen, 1980.

Taylor, Rebe, *Unearthed: The Aboriginal Tasmanians of Kangaroo Island*, Adelaide: Wakefield Press, 2002.

Temple, Philip, *A Sort of Conscience: The Wakefields*, Auckland: Auckland University Press, 2002.

Thompson, M., 'Government and Depression in South Australia', MA thesis, Flinders University, 1972.

Tolmer, Alexander, *Reminiscences of an Adventurous and Chequered Career at Home and at the Antipodes* [1882], vol. II, Adelaide: State Libraries Board of South Australia facsimile, 1972.

Trollope, Anthony, *Australia* [1873], edited by P.D. Edwards and R.B. Joyce, Brisbane: University of Queensland Press, 1967.

—— *Australia and New Zealand*, vol. 1, London: Chapman and Hall, 1876.

Tunbridge, Dorothy, *The Story of the Flinders Ranges Mammals*, Sydney: Kangaroo Press, 1991.

Turner, Ian, and Leonie Sandercock, *In Union Strength: A History of Trade Unions in Australia 1788–1983*, Melbourne: Nelson, 1983.

Twain, Mark (Samuel Clemens), *Following the Equator: A Journey around the World*, New York: American Publishing Company, 1898.

Vamplew, Wray (ed.), *Australian Historical Statistics*, Sydney: Fairfax, Syme, Weldon Associates, 1987.

Vamplew, Wray, Eric Richards, Dean Jaensch and Joan Hancock (eds), *South Australian Historical Statistics*, Adelaide: History Project Incorporated, 1984.

van Dissel, Dirk, 'Alexander Hore-Ruthven', in Wilfrid Prest, Kerrie Round and Carol Fort (eds), *The Wakefield Companion to South Australian History*, Adelaide: Wakefield Press, 2001, pp. 263–4.

Vicary, Adrian, 'Social Welfare', in Wilfrid Prest, Kerrie Round and Carol Fort (eds), *The Wakefield Companion to South Australian History*, Adelaide: Wakefield Press, 2001, pp. 496–8.

Wanna, John, 'A Paradigm of Consent: Explanations of Working Class Moderation in South Australia', *Labour History*, 53, 1987, pp. 54–72.

—— 'The State and Industrial Relations', in Kyoko Sheridan (ed.), *The State as Developer: Public Enterprise in South Australia*, Adelaide: Wakefield Press, 1986, pp. 130–51.

Ward, J.M., *Colonial Self-Government: The British Experience 1759–1856*, London: Macmillan, 1976.

Ward, Peter, 'Arts', in Wilfrid Prest, Kerrie Round and Carol Fort (eds), *The Wakefield Companion to South Australian History*, Adelaide: Wakefield Press, 2001, pp. 50–2.

—— 'Colin Sandergrove Ballantye', in Wilfrid Prest, Kerrie Round and Carol Fort (eds), *The Wakefield Companion to South Australian History*, Adelaide: Wakefield Press, 2001, p. 65.

Warhurst, John, 'The Politics of the South Australian Economy', *Australian Quarterly*, 51(2), 1979, pp. 83–92.

—— 'The Public Service', in Andrew Parkin and Allan Patience (eds), *The Dunstan Decade: Social Democracy at the State Level*, Melbourne: Longman Cheshire, 1981, pp. 179–204.

West, Katharine, *Power in the Liberal Party: A Study in Australian Politics*, Melbourne: Cheshire, 1965.

Whitelock, Derek, *Adelaide 1836–1976: A History of Difference*, Brisbane: University of Queensland Press, 1977.

—— *Adelaide: A Sense of Difference*, 3rd edn, Melbourne: Australian Scholarly Publishing, 2000.

Williams, Eleanore, *A Way of Life: The Pastoral Families of the Central Hill Country of South Australia*, Adelaide: Adelaide University Union Press, 1980.

Williams, Eleanore, and Michael Williams, 'Rural South Australia in the Nineteenth Century', in Eric Richards (ed.), *The Flinders History of South Australia: Social History*, Adelaide: Wakefield Press, 1986, pp. 513–49.

Williams, John, *German Anzacs of the First World War*, Sydney: UNSW Press, 2003.

—— 'The Making of the South Australian Constitution: Fear, Optimism and Reform', in *The Politics of Democracy in South Australia: A Special Conference Marking 150 Years of Democracy*, Adelaide: State Electoral Office, 2008, pp. 12–18.

Williams, Michael, *The Making of the South Australian Landscape: A Study of the Historical Geography of Australia*, London: Academic Press, 1974.

Woodburn, Susan, 'The Irish in New South Wales, Victoria and South Australia, 1788–1880', MA thesis, University of Adelaide, 1979.

Woollacott, Angela, *Settler Society in the Australian Colonies: Self-Government and Imperial Culture*, Oxford: Oxford University Press, 2015.

WRVS, *Gold Age Pensioners: Valuing the Socio-Economic Contribution of Older People in the UK*, May 2011, http://www.goldagepensioners.com/Uploads/PDF/main-report.pdf.

Zwillenberg, H.J., 'Citizens to Soldiers: The Defence of South Australia 1836–1901', MA thesis, University of Adelaide, 1970.

INDEX

Entries in bold indicate figures.

Printed in the United States
By Bookmasters